Which? kind
of
GARDEN

Which? kind of GARDEN

Published by Consumers' Association
and Hodder & Stoughton

Editor:
Lizzie Boyd

Art Editor:
Pat Gilliland

Design Assistants:
Suzanne Stevenson
Mike Strickland

Illustrations:
Chris Forsey
Charlotte Styles

Picture Research:
Anne-Marie Ehrlich
Elizabeth Ogilvie
Mari Zipes

Contributors:
Gillian Beckett
Kenneth A. Beckett
John Brookes
Michael W. Charlton
Mary Everitt
John Farmer
Basil Fox
J.R. Hare, M.V.O., N.D.H.
A.G.I. Hellyer, M.B.E., F.L.S.,
V.M.H., A.H.R.H.S.
John Negus, Dip.Hort. (Wisley)
Peter Russell, Dip.Hort. (Wisley)
Alan Titchmarsh
Robin Williams

Which? kind of Garden is
published in Great Britain by
Consumers' Association
14 Buckingham Street
London WC2N 6DS
and **Hodder & Stoughton Ltd**
47 Bedford Square
London WC1B 3DP

First edition, second printing

© Consumers' Association 1983

Typeset by
Brown Knight & Truscott Ltd, Tonbridge, Kent
Colour separations by
DS Colour International Ltd, London N1
Printed and bound in Belgium by
Casterman SA, Tournai
All rights reserved.
No part of this book may be reproduced,
in any manner whatsoever, without prior
permission from the publisher.

ISBN 0 340 25935 3

CONTENTS

FOREWORD

A garden, like a home, is indisputably a private matter, and unsolicited advice is seldom accepted with gratitude. A home, though, differs from a garden in its greater scope for alteration and extension, whereas all gardeners, novices and veterans alike, are faced with certain unalterable facts unrelated to their plot's size and shape: little can be done about the climate and its effects and, while regular cultivation of the soil can improve its structure and texture, no amount of loving care can alter the underlying rock strata or convert acid to alkaline soil. Successful and rewarding gardening, whether of tender exotics or mundane vegetables, is based firmly on the ability to accept such limitations and to seize the opportunities that every garden offers.

The opportunities are numerous even if they do not reveal themselves instantly. The smallest garden has its mood, changing with the seasons and with its age, yet with an inner personality the gardener must seek to express, in the plants and in the inanimate objects with which it is decorated.

For a thousand years and more, gardening has been an enduring passion in Britain, progressing from the walled monastery garden through romantic Elizabethan parterres and knot gardens to grand landscaped parks on one hand and scratchy cottage plots on the other. The movement from country to city led to the development of town and suburban gardens; more recently, limitations on space have encouraged would-be gardeners, like architects, to expand upwards, with balcony and roof-top gardens. Fashions have come and gone, styles have appeared and disappeared, but certain traits have endured, usually because they express a harmonious relationship with their surroundings.

Modern principles of garden design are freer and more fluid than those by which the great landscape designers of former days worked. Often this freedom, and the wealth of plants available, has resulted in gardens containing numerous unrelated features — a tiny rose arbour near the cabbage patch, a sundial on a tiny lawn, a chestnut tree in a mean front garden.

Taste is a personal matter, and it is not the aim of this book to lay down rules on what should and should not be grown, which materials should be used for patios and fences or what shape and size a pool or rock garden should take. Rather, it aims to give inspiration and to encourage the reader to assess his or her garden's potential, and to recognise the type of design that suits both garden and gardener best. There are certain broad categories from which to choose a predominant style: the country garden, for example, typified by sweeping drives skirting velvety lawns, dense shrubberies, formal rose beds and long, broad herbaceous borders spilling over with colours; or the cottage garden, fragrant with hollyhocks, sweet peas and roses twining over whitewashed wall. But within such themes there is ample scope for variation by the gardener. Mention of a suburban garden need no longer conjure up views of dusty hedges and standard roses.

Every gardener cherishes a dream of creating his own particular kind of garden. The specialists who have contributed to this book have drawn on many years of experience and experiment; they have outlined the difficulties and pitfalls that nature imposes and sketched the design possibilities which can transform a piece of ground into a remarkable garden. Ultimately, the kind of garden that emerges will be a combination of common sense, personal taste and imagination.

INHERITING A GARDEN

New or old, a rubble heap
or an overgrown wilderness,
few gardens meet
with their new owners' approval

INHERITING A GARDEN 1

CREATING A NEW GARDEN

The builders have finished the new house and have departed. Surveying the hills and hollows, deep excavations, compacted soil and piles of rubbish, your main feelings will probably be a mixture of dread and excitement at the thought of turning this chaotic terrain into a garden.

It can be difficult trying to sight through or round obstructions of various kinds. Line and vista become obscured if the land is broken up with objects such as old sheds, overgrown, dead or dying trees, shrubs or general undergrowth.

However, a systematic approach will soon reduce the problem to one of manageable proportions. Begin by clearing the land of all rubbish and debris left by the builders, burning what is possible and despatching the remainder to the local council rubbish tip. Remember that decent bricks or moulded stone blocks may come in useful in later construction work, while rubble, if it can be conveniently collected and stored, is excellent in the foundation for paths and paved areas.

Once the arena is completely clear, garden development can begin at almost any time. At the outset draw up a coordinated plan based on a simple survey.

Over and above the purely practical considerations, the first object is to decide which kind of garden scheme will give the land the best chance to express itself. Ideally, the end result should look as if it belongs, with scale and freedom of movement, both physically and visually, rather than as a fixed idea firmly imposed on the land.

State of the land

Just possibly the land will be in a workable state, with the subsoil left below, where it belongs, and the topsoil above. Sometimes they will have been reversed or inextricably mixed. Before garden-making can begin, the land should be restored to a reasonable profile, with subsoil and topsoil in their proper positions to a proportionate extent. To be dogmatic about this could pose impossible problems, and cultivation, with organic matter, will in time build up fertility.

Fresh topsoil is a possibility in unhelpful circumstances, but it is not always easy to obtain, quality can be uncertain and expense is likely to be considerable. Profitable results can be achieved by annual inclusion of garden compost, leaf-mould or well-rotted animal manures if available. Any of these will increase soil fertility, and peat and sharp sand will improve the soil structure.

Drainage problems

Where rainwater remains within surface soil for a considerable time, attention must be given to drainage before anything else. Poor drainage may be due to geological or mechanical reasons, the former causing the greatest problems. On a fresh site, impeded drainage is more often than not caused by soil compacted into an impervious pan by builders' machinery and lorries.

Thorough tilling, either by hand or by a rotary cultivator, will usually break up a hard pan and allow water to drain through properly. Remember also that heavy clay soils drain slowly, especially in winter, and here the structure can be made more permeable by the inclusion of sharp sand and peat or strawy manure, and by rough digging so as to expose the clods to frost which will break them down.

However, if poor drainage is caused by geological factors, the problem becomes more serious. The natural water table (see page 28) may be high, especially at the base of a slope, and during rainy periods it may rise and flood an otherwise well-drained topsoil. Where waterlogging is persistent over a small area, due to a high

A neglected garden may hide unseen treasures in the wilderness. The overgrown perennials must be lifted, discarded if past their prime or divided and replanted in new beds and borders. Judicious pruning will often bring new life to old shrubs.

water table, artificial drainage is of no use, and such land will have to be lived with. Luckily it is possible to make a virtue of necessity by growing moisture-loving plants and shrubs, quite considerable in number.

Sometimes though, poor drainage over the entire garden area is caused by a hard subsoil over the underlying rock strata. In this case artificial drainage may be required to lead away the excess water in the soil. Temporary grooves cut across heavy

*A **virgin plot** (top) crying out for attention. The levelled site is ready for deep tilling — the first step towards its transition into a garden. Below, a shallow, starved topsoil is in drastic need of both thorough cultivation and plenty of organic manures.*

clay can be useful in channelling away excess rainwater during winter, but they look unsightly, need frequent clearing and constitute a potential danger for young children. Where artificial drainage is a necessity one kind of system consists of covered drain pipes leading to one or several soakaways or deep holes.

Installing a drainage system is both expensive and hard work, and it may well be worthwhile to call in a professional. Depending on soil type, 30cm wide trenches are dug to a maximum depth of 1.2 metres. Unglazed clay tiles or perforated PVC reinforced pipes are laid in the bottom of the trenches, commonly constructed in a herring-bone pattern, with side drains emptying into the wider main drain which is connected to the soakaway. This should be about 1.5 metres across and deep and filled almost to the top with brick rubble covered with a concrete slab. Before filling in the trenches with the excavated soil, protect the pipes with a covering of small stones or clinkers beneath a layer of inverted turf.

Preparation of the land

In due course the site will be cleared, reasonably drained and ready for its transition into a garden. The first step towards this is thorough cultivation, by digging or rotovation.

Heavily weed-infested land may need repeat rotary cultivation; leave the chopped off weeds on the surface to dry before burning them.

Ideally you should complete the cultivation of the whole site before turning to the more interesting gardening aspects. The initial preparation of the site is important for there will rarely be another chance for thorough cultivation; any time of year, weather permitting, is suitable, but avoid digging heavy clay soils when they are wet.

During the preparation of the land, other considerations must be taken into account, such as aspect, the lie and nature of the land, and size

INHERITING A GARDEN 2

and shape of the area. A tendency to wetness or dryness of the soil will also come into the reckoning and may determine later plant selections.

The degree of soil acidity or alkalinity also has a bearing on planting, and this is a good time to conduct a soil test (see page 24). Depending on the results, favourite plantings may have to be foregone or steps taken to redress the balance.

Lie of the land

Once the cleared site has been dug over, it becomes easier to establish the overall plane so that lawn and border levels end up in the right relationship to each other.

Despite a certain pre-occupation with flatness, especially where lawns are concerned, the level plane is by no means a pre-requisite for a successful garden. A gently sloping site can be eased into flowing and practical contours and appears tailor-made for a naturalised garden, with winding paths traversing the slope.

On the other hand, steeply sloping sites are likely to impose a special discipline on garden planning. Rather than attempt a major earth-moving operation, the introduction of retaining walls offers a simple solution, with flights of steps linking a series of level surfaces and terraces for lawns and planting areas.

Garden planning

By tradition and convention much garden design follows the straight and narrow. Stylised gardens of formal outline undoubtedly have their place, but in the average small garden marked formality can introduce a static result. Gardens hemmed in by straight boundaries need release with help from casual lines. Straightness emphasises the dominance of their basic outline. Flowing curves soften the ugliness of awkwardly-shaped gardens and release others from the box created by sharply-jutting fences.

A steeply sloping front garden designed as a series of terraces, newly planted with shrubs, perennials and bedding plants. Below, an island bed in a large lawn.

Front gardens are the commonest victims of regimented planning. Ubiquitous, they are hemmed-in by boundaries and crucified by straight or absurdly-angled paths, offering the most difficult passage imaginable to the front doors they were intended to serve.

The box appearance is further highlighted by plantings, often out of scale, that follow the straight lines and fussy details at the expense of flow and simplicity. Smooth and economical curves are the most effective, and while the larger back garden offers more scope for such designs, the bold sweep of a path from front gate to door can be very telling.

A garden plan based on curved, flowing lines helps to soften or lose essential sheds and service areas and also makes garden maintenance easier: lawn-mowing becomes a more fluent activity than when having to deal with sharp corners.

Any specimen trees or shrubs, remaining after the initial clearance, can be effectively blended into the new design by using curves in the planning of lawns, beds and borders. Here shrubs and trees can provide fine focal points, and if they stand perhaps in a somewhat uncompromising, straight row, the curved line can come to the rescue again: the lawn line might be allowed to travel between the trunks, thereby contriving to leave some of the trees in the lawn and others in the border.

Curves make it easier to design gardens of more awkward outline. The dominance of a tapering triangle is reduced by a curving lawn shape, and the sectioned off corner becomes a likely choice for kitchen garden or utility areas.

By abandoning convention and letting the garden express its full potentials, the vegetable plot, for instance, may occupy one side of the garden, as opposed to the end, though compost heaps and bonfire areas are best sited where they will remain unobtrusive. Greenhouses need to be within easy reach of water and ideally electricity and where they will receive good light.

The actual siting of any permanent features are naturally governed by garden size; on average a vegetable plot measuring 6 metres by 12 metres is adequate for most families, with the remaining space given to ornamental and utility sections.

Fruit growing requires more room, but by growing cane fruits, red and white currants and trained forms of apples, pears, plums and cherries against fences and walls, space is utilised to its maximum. Fruit trees can be grown as lawn specimens.

Planning to scale

Before you decide on any type of design, you are advised to measure and draw up a scaled plan of the garden—on squared graph paper each square might represent 1 square metre. On the plan draw in the house, including windows and doors facing the garden, mark the compass points and the prevailing wind direction. Mark also any permanent fixtures, such as an oil tank or coal shed and a neighbour's tree, a factory chimney on the horizon or an open view, any of which you may wish to obscure or integrate in your own scheme for visual pleasure.

Once you have drawn up your scale plan, begin to pencil in your design ideas. Mark tentatively sites for patio, retaining walls on a sloping site, areas for sheds, compost and bonfire heaps, greenhouses and frames. Connecting the various points to the house with any necessary service paths requires thought and finesse.

Thereafter you can sketch in areas for lawns, borders and beds, rock garden and pool, and kitchen garden. Try to follow simple and flowing design lines that merge easily and naturally.

Having arrived at your final scheme, mark out the design in the garden, using short wooden pegs, pushed in at approximately 1 metre intervals. Move the pegs until you achieve pleasing lines, and remember to plot island beds in proportion to the lawn, with space for mowing.

When the lawn has been pegged out, borders reveal themselves instantly; in curved designs they will consist of peaks and recesses which can be made deeper or shallower according to the type of plants envisaged. Large peaks permit group plantings which then become focal points of their own. A particularly good effect is achieved if the border—or path—leaves the line of vision behind a peak.

Circular lawns and curving borders create an aura of space and mystery in a small *garden. Gently flowing lines also distract the eye from the rigidity of a town garden.*

15

INHERITING A GARDEN 3

Plantings are a matter of individual taste, combined with soil and aspect, but before you decide on any major planting scheme, consider the seasonal aspect, the visual effect of sun, especially in winter, from the garden as well as from the house. For maximum year-round impact, include in your planting schemes shrubs and trees which, outside the flowering season, are attractive for their foliage texture or colour, berries, bark or naked outline.

Where to start
Usually the boundaries of a new house and garden will be demarcated with some kind of fencing. If not, make this a priority job and check the house deeds and local by-laws.

In exposed places, walls and solid fencing offer good if short-distance shelter. For the most effective windbreak, however, a hedge makes the best shelter and can be planted within chain-link fencing. The fast-growing conifer x *Cupressocyparis leylandii* is particularly suitable; planted slightly less than 1 metre apart it will soon form a thick hedge which can be maintained at almost any height from 1 metre upwards.

Paved areas
The actual sequence of garden construction may differ according to means and circumstances, but if a patio is contemplated, it pays to have this constructed first. It virtually becomes the garden launching platform from where it is easy to relate general garden levels and design.

A patio also forms the link between house and garden, and the construction material should complement both. As for shape, repeat the general garden line, curved or straight. Make the patio as large as possible, bearing scale and proportion in mind. If steps are needed to descend from the patio, they are often best recessed into the patio rather than jutting out beyond.

Paths with a purpose: Crazy paving (top) winds like a stone bed through rocky outcrops with alpines and conifers. In the centre, stepping stones of sawn logs echo the woodland setting, and below a brick path epitomises the cottage garden.

Paths need careful consideration, and only where necessary should one be included to link the service areas with the house. If at all possible, avoid the domineering grey concrete path and settle for materials which will harmonise with the surroundings. Give path and lawn-line a unity. On large expanses of grass, stepping-stones sunk just below the surface are effective as meandering paths. Mark out the area for a path, but leave construction of it until the finished lawn level has been established to avoid leaving it at an obtrusively high level. It should be about 25 mm below the lawn level to facilitate mowing.

Sterner stonework, such as the building of boundary and retaining walls, extensive laying of general paving, construction of major steps and patios—and large-scale rock gardens, is possibly best left to professional landscape gardeners, although likely to hold no qualms for the skilled amateur. A variety of paving materials, styles and patterns can be used provided they are kept unobtrusive and in neutral tones.

At an early stage, lay foundations for the greenhouse and the service area where shed, compost and refuse bins, bonfire plot, etc. are to be erected. Also have a convenient outside tap installed; this, as well as large-scale, underground irrigation systems, needs permission from the local water authority and installation by a qualified engineer. Outside lighting—for a greenhouse, shed or general garden illumination—also requires professional help.

Patio made, paths, lawns, borders and other planting areas marked out, the garden framework is established, and full-scale planting can begin. Specimen trees and other focal plantings may be put in first, but if general plantings have been worked out and plotted on the design plan, they can be put in their precise positions as and when required.

Raised terrace beds make the most of limited space. Designed chiefly for foliage plants, the different levels give emphasis to contrasting colours, textures and shapes.

Lawns, sown or turfed

After the initial cultivation of the ground, render the lawn area smooth and firm, in readiness for sowing or turfing. Firm it by rolling or treading and rake the surface soil loose and free of stones.

Spring and late summer are the best times for sowing a lawn, autumn through winter for turfing (See also page 164).

Trees and shrubs

Taking prevailing conditions of soil and climate into consideration, certain factors govern the choice of trees and shrubs. Consider the available space, not only for young specimens, but also their height and spread after 10-20 years, and ponder how well companion plantings will associate in stature, character and performance. Certain trees, notably poplars on heavy clay soil, should be planted well away from buildings as the roots may penetrate the foundations.

Make maximum use of all possible sites, including walls, fences, arches, banks and so on, and choose specimens that will give the garden interest throughout the four seasons.

Conifers and evergreens in general give gardens year-round strength. Deciduous trees and shrubs have their own obvious merits, not least in their wide range of outline. Lawn specimens are particularly effective underplanted with spring bulbs.

At planting time work bone-meal into the holes and excavated soil to give trees and shrubs a good start. Make the holes a little larger than imagined so that the plants can be installed with maximum ease and minimum cramping of the roots. Stakes should be driven in first, facing the direction of the prevailing wind. Fill in with soil up to the original soil mark on the trunk and secure each tree to its stake with an adjustable plastic tie or sacking and soft string.

Beds and borders

Perennial borders also call for thoughtful planting, in order to ex- tend the display as long as possible. There is a vast choice of plants to meet most conditions, and where the garden may not have room for a herbaceous border, many perennials associate well with shrubs.

Free-standing or island beds are often dominated by annuals and bedding plants, but they can also be occupied by perennials which flower in succession from early summer into autumn.

Rock and water

Pools and rock gardens, separately or in combination, feature in many garden schemes. Both need open, sunny positions, away from overhanging trees, and both should appear natural in the design.

A large-scale rock garden can often be the perfect solution to the problem of sloping land, with outcrops of rock strata preventing erosion. Weathered boulders are set at intervals deep in the bank, at a slight backward tilt to allow rainwater to run back, and the crevices provide ideal planting pockets. In small gardens, where large rocks would be out of scale, a scree garden is a better proposition. This could perhaps be described as a low-profile rock garden, with pieces of rock spilt out across a deepish mixture of stone chippings (two parts) and loam and peat (one part each). For best effect, a scree garden should be on a gentle slope.

Pools associate well with rock gardens. Concrete pools are extremely durable, but pools made with heavy duty plastic liners or in rigid, pre-formed plastic shells are inexpensive and easy to install.

RESTYLING AN OLD GARDEN

Taking over an established garden will often present an easier situation than a totally new garden, for there is something to see, to add to or take away from, in terms of layout and plant contents.

INHERITING A GARDEN 4

On occasions, it is a good idea to leave a mature, well-established garden alone for a full year, in order to assess its year-round plant content and to gauge potentials. However, if this is not possible, garden alterations can go ahead, with basics receiving first attention.

Overgrown shrubs and trees

Begin by taking careful stock of the garden and determine how much debris and dilapidation needs to be cleared away and burnt. Amongst the plantings which it may seem worthwhile to retain, there will probably be some whose useful life is clearly finished and others which are overgrown. The proper seasonal time for pruning should be observed.

Caution should be applied to cutting back overgrown shrubs and ideally extended over a couple of seasons rather than ruthlessly hacking away. Many poor specimens can be coaxed into agreeable form, given time. Assessing and reclaiming trees needs particularly careful consideration, for good shape is important; it is easy to spoil the framework of a tree, and regrowth tends to be slow.

During work amongst trees and shrubs, with saw and secateurs, it should be easy enough to decide if any specimens are past reclamation and need to come right out. Shrubs are the least difficult to grub out. Equipped with a good spade, fork and stocking mattock, the job need not be over-difficult. Cut away a few of the lower branches, in order to clear a working space round the base. Rhythmical work with the mattock alone will remove many shrubs, while on larger or more deeply-rooted ones, the major roots may first have to be exposed.

A more careful approach is needed with trees. The secret lies in leaving as much top on the tree as possible and in having clearance for the tree as it sinks to the ground so that, as the tree begins to topple, its own weight will

Rock and water beneath a spreading juniper break a grassy slope. Planting is informal yet arresting as a focal point among competing specimen shrub and tree groups.

help to bring it down. It is a great mistake to cut a tree off short; with nothing to get hold of, it becomes an appalling job to grub the deep roots out. Root-rotting agents are useful, but slow-acting.

First remove as much of the top as seems prudent, leaving a fair section of trunk, with or without a sawn-off branch or two. Next, make a wide excavation round the base of the tree to achieve working space, and work the soil from the roots so that they become exposed. Now the roots can be cut through, the tree lowered and, with the top used as a lever, rolled out of the hole. Deep taproots may have to be cut across.

As the tree rests in a half-down position, the remaining branches can be cut off. Clear and burn the debris progressively; a power saw will reduce stout trunks to useful logs. Unwanted shrubs and trees out of the way and general rubbish disposed of, a better assessment of the garden becomes possible.

The removal of large trees requires the attention of professional tree surgeons, and it is advisable to check with the local council that no preservation order applies.

Repairs and renewals

With more freedom to move, any necessary repair of fences becomes an easier proposition, as does demolition and removal of unwanted sheds or other auxiliary structures. Crumbling fence-posts should be replaced, or they can be rescued temporarily with pre-cast concrete spurs, obtainable from builders' merchants. They are sunk to the appropriate level and bolted to the faulty posts. Although less likely, wall repairs may be necessary and will require professional help.

Removing a concrete path calls for a methodical approach: start at one end and work along, dispersing and disposing of the debris during the process. If a concrete path is prised up at one end with a pick-axe or mattock, it will start to break there, perhaps with the aid of a sledge-hammer. It may be necessary or advantageous to start at a point away from the end of the path; begin by breaking the edge of the section, 'chewing' a way across the path in order to open up a working space.

Hopefully, any existing greenhouse will be in a good position and reasonable condition. Otherwise resite it or erect a new one at an early stage, having first decided on the new garden style to be adopted.

Redesigning the garden

After the main clearances, work out a plan of the intended new garden.

A simple survey will facilitate the process. With a piece of paper attached to a clipboard, draw a freehand outline of the garden, taking in house and patio lines. Use the same approach when redesigning individual sections of large gardens.

Elementary as it may sound, always face the portion of outline being sketched. This becomes particularly relevant when taking in jutting outlines of houses, patios or outbuildings. The outline complete, jot down individual measurements.

Trees and shrubs to be retained are plotted in by measuring along boundaries to adjacent points, then in to each specimen. Other permanent objects are marked on the drawing in the same way, including manholes, rubbish areas, oil tanks and other service structures. All gas, electricity and water pipes must be located, particularly in front gardens, before any work commences.

Make a fair copy of the drawing, using a convenient scale. Mark also the compass points, essential in selecting the right plants for the right place, in terms of sun, shade or visual aspect. When everything has been plotted in, the new design can begin to emerge. It may include all the required features or show up the necessity for resiting others.

A scale plan makes it possible to conceive new schemes with the help of pencil and paper, without the confusion of surrounding objects of any kind. Pegging out of the new design can go ahead from the plan.

Pegs are particularly useful when altering an old garden, because existing beds and borders can be marked through to show the new line of lawns, beds and borders. Use white-painted pegs which show up better amongst existing plantings.

Extension of a patio can offer the opportunity of improving a dull one. Flagstones can be added in broken outline to ease a severely straight edge, or they can be broken for crazy-paving and laid to form an additional apron of softer, more casual outline.

Lawn extensions

It is not always easy to unite existing lawn areas with proposed extensions as levels may vary if parts of beds or borders are to be converted. It may pay to rotovate those parts of the existing lawn which fall within the new, so that the complete area can be prepared for turf or seed.

Rejuvenating an existing lawn, as it stands, may need patching with new turf, or re-seeding. Fork over and clear trouble spots. If re-turfing, prick the soil out just sufficiently to accommodate the new turf. Leave this slightly high to avoid the risk of sinking. It will settle and press down within a short time. When cutting out the area to be patched, make the edges straight and lift them slightly; in this way old and new turf edges will then become firmly welded as they are pressed down together.

For re-seeding, prepare the soil as above. It may be necessary to add or remove extra soil to bring the level up to that of the surrounding lawn, before seed is sown and raked in. (See also page 164).

Beds and borders

Herbaceous plants may have grown too large and ungainly. In autumn or spring lift such plants and split them up; replant the best divisions and discard the rest. Overgrown bulb clumps can be split and replanted after flowering or in autumn.

If the wait to achieve specimens of adequate size can be accepted, many deciduous shrubs will strike easily from hardwood cuttings, inserted outside in late summer and early autumn; a sandy cold frame is useful for striking softwood cuttings.

Borders with poor soils and neglected vegetable plots may be brought into condition through thorough digging and inclusion of garden compost or other organic matter. Existing kitchen gardens will probably have had their annual share of a general fertiliser in the course of normal cropping. Digging-in of weeds and certain vegetable debris, in addition to rotted compost or animal manure during the dormant season, will steadily improve soil texture and structure.

The basic principles of garden design apply to any garden, anywhere and at any time. Their object is to give a piece of land a chance to express itself to advantage. Every situation, considered on its own merits and handled accordingly, offers its own clues on how to succeed, governed always by soil and climate.

Plant selection

Soil, if acutely acid or alkaline for example, will exert limitations on the selection of plants. Rhododendrons are well-known for disliking lime; so do summer-flowering heathers and certain other ericaceous plants. While there is a wide tolerance among the majority of plants, trees and shrubs, and while certain chemical and organic elements can redress soil imbalances, it pays to choose plants which thrive in given situations.

Climatic factors also have a bearing on plant selection and positioning. Dampness and dryness, stemming from the normal or expected weather pattern in a given area, exert their own obvious influence. Prevailing winds may determine the best sites for plants needing shelter.

ANALYSIS
OF A
GARDEN

The potential of any garden
is affected by the unchanging factors
of soil type, climatic variations
and man-made fixtures

SOIL 1

Soil—the thin surface layer of the earth—is a complex body whose properties are dependent on the interaction of various physical, chemical and biological processes acting on the parent material. The climate and relief of the area in which soil forms are other important factors, as well as the age of the soil and the effects of cultivation. Essentially soil is formed by mineral and organic decomposition, and while it is the result of decay, it is also the medium of growth, teeming with life.

Soil has four major constituents: mineral matter, organic material, water and air. Mineral matter is derived from the breakdown of the underlying parental material, which may be solid rock or unconsolidated material such as sand or gravel. This inorganic material forms the bulk of most soils, although peaty soils may have a larger organic content.

Organic matter consists of decaying plant and animal debris and also contains living organisms such as worms, insects and bacteria. Soil water contains organic and inorganic substances in solution. Water and air occupy the pore spaces between the particles; unlike the atmosphere, soil air is highly saturated.

Inorganic content of soil

The underlying parental material strongly influences the type of soil being formed. A sandstone bedrock will inevitably lead to a sandy soil which is light and highly porous, while clay produces a very heavy and impervious soil.

The inorganic matter is not always derived from one rock type. The transportation of material by physical processes may lead to a mixture of various types of inorganic material, and under certain circumstances the soil may be virtually independent of the underlying parent rock. However, in Britain where many soils are relatively 'young', the parent material is important.

Physical and chemical processes disintegrate and decompose the rock material into particles which vary in size from large stones and gravel to silt and clay. The most common materials which result from disintegration of rock and form the bulk of a soil include silica (quartz), various silicates and oxides.

Many metallic elements are also present, including aluminium, iron, potassium, calcium, sodium and magnesium, with small amounts or trace elements of iodine, manganese and boron, all of which are important for the growth and development of plants. Non-metallic elements, such as nitrogen, phosphorous and sulphur are also essential; they are derived partly from rock and partly from organic material.

These minerals, together with those that result from organic decomposition, form the plant nutrients of natural soils. A plant absorbs nutrients, in soluble form, through the membranes of the root hairs. Thus the necessary elements must not merely be present in the soil, but must be there in an easily

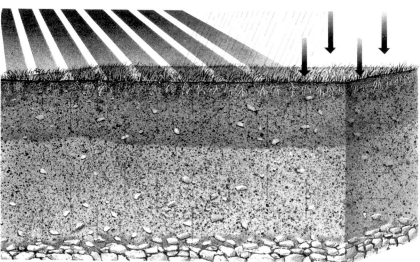

Soil inputs and outputs. The combined effects of rainfall, solar energy and atmospheric gases react on animal and decaying vegetable matter. Chemicals, such as calcium, potassium and ammonia are released into the soil, and minerals and metallic elements are provided by the parent rock. Soil fauna mix the materials, some of which are dissolved and washed out in the groundwater.

Soil balance is achieved through negative clay and/or humus colloids attracting loosely held, positive nutrient ions. The plant roots release hydrogen ions while taking up the nutrients – calcium, ammonia, potassium and magnesium.

Clay/humus colloids are essential soil components. Without them, the nutrient ions are washed out of the soil by groundwater. This leads to increasing acidity as iron and aluminium compounds are deposited further down.

assimilated form. For this purpose, the finest particles, clay grade material, is a crucial soil content.

Clay is composed of minute particles of complex aluminium silicate compounds. These small, but important particles are known as colloids which impart certain physical and chemical properties to a soil, including cohesiveness and the ability to take up water.

The colloids also provide a medium in which chemical processes can take place. Each tiny clay particle is negatively charged, while plant nutrients such as potassium, calcium and nitrogen are positively charged. Through a complex chemical exchange, the nutrients are taken from the clay particles into the fine plant roots. Without a clay content in the soil, nutrients can easily be washed out; a certain amount of organic matter, clay or similar particles is therefore necessary for a soil to be fertile.

Organic content of soil

At an early stage in the natural formation a soil consists entirely of mineral particles; later it becomes colonized by bacteria, lichens and mosses. The decay of such organisms leads to the accumulation of humus. Higher-order plants, such as ferns and grasses, can now become established, and eventually trees and shrubs can take hold.

As the humus content builds up, plant roots work further down whilst burrowing animals bring inorganic material up, and the growing mass becomes porous, allowing the passage of air. It also becomes sponge-like and therefore water-retentive.

The organic content of a soil consists of plants, parts of plants, and animals which die and remain in the earth. Fungi and bacteria cause the disintegration and decomposition of organic material into water, carbon dioxide, organic acids and various soluble salts.

Nodules on the roots of leguminous plants assimilate gaseous nitrogen and convert it into protein, which is broken down by other bacteria into ammonia and nitrates. Thus the organic content of the soil is broken down into various plant nutrients which largely take the form of a complex brown substance called humus.

Humus is colloidal with similar properties to clay particles and is

SOIL 2

twice as effective as clay with regard to its chemical exchange capacity; it is therefore a very significant soil component. Humus may be present in a soil as a mobile fluid or as a jelly coating the mineral grains; it may be predominantly acid or alkaline.

Soil humus not only provides nutrients such as nitrogen, phosphorous, calcium and potassium, it also physically improves soil texture. Humus in a sandy soil aids water retention, whereas in a clay soil it increases aeration. Not all humus has the same value; raw humus is markedly acid and deficient in calcium. Nitrogen compounds are also missing, and decomposition is greatly slowed down.

Acidity and alkalinity
The term pH is used to express the acidity or alkalinity of a soil and describes the concentration of hydrogen ions held in the soil compared with the proportion of hydroxyl ions. Hydrogen ions are provided by soil acids, and where they occur in high concentration the soil is acid, while a low proportion indicates alkaline conditions.

Neutral soils—where hydrogen and hydroxyl ions are present in equal proportions—have a pH of 7, acid soils a pH of less than 7 and alkaline soils a pH above 7.

Acids in a soil can react with plant nutrients to form salts which are washed away, leading to the soil becoming more and more acid and eventually less fertile. The removal of nutrients can be checked by certain soil constituents, such as clay and additional humus.

Rainwater, which is a weak solution of carbonic acid, is one of the main causes of a soil becoming acid. The removal of chemical bases from a soil by percolating rainwater is called leaching, a process especially noticeable in areas with high rainfall or where the soil is light and has a high sand content.

Apart from rainwater, other factors may lead to an acid soil, such as raw, slowly decomposing humus, or the composition of the parent rock. Acidity in a soil hinders the rate of absorption by plant roots and also affects the bacterial activity in decomposition.

The tolerance of plants to acidity varies enormously. Some heathland plants, such as ling, flourish in acid soil, and a number of others, such as azaleas and rhododendrons, will not grow in any other.

However, most cultivated plants, and in particular members of the brassica family, suffer if the soil becomes too acid. A pH value of 6—6.5 (slightly acid) is usually desirable; excess acids in a soil are neutralized by applications of lime. This also encourages bacterial activity and can improve the physical texture of heavy soils.

Soil chemistry
In certain soil types, particularly glacial-drift soil, alkalinity can be reduced or eliminated. Trials in Essex have shown that applications of flowers of sulphur reduced pH readings of 6.7 and 7.0 to 5.4 and 5.0 respectively, at a depth of 15cm.

Flowers of sulphur, incorporated into the soil at the rate of 100g. per square metre, was followed by annual top dressings of 40g. per square metre until the required pH was reached. In this manner it becomes possible to cultivate calcifuge plants, notably rhododendrons, without serious side effects in a formerly alkaline soil.

Soil testing
Acidity of garden soil can be easily assessed. There are a number of inexpensive soil testing kits, and the pH of the soil can be worked out rapidly. Soil samples should be taken from more than one place in a garden as slight soil variations may occur, although this is unlikely where

Acid soil supports plants which are naturally lime-hating. The cross-leaved heath, Erica tetralix, *flourishes in peat.*

cultivation has been carried out for a long time.

The pH value reflects the balance between the acidity and basic contents of the soil, and the readings do not necessarily give an indication of the quantity of the bases. For such information a more detailed test must be carried out, at an approved soil testing laboratory.

Soil texture
The texture of a soil is determined by the size of the individual particles, and these affect the soil properties in several different ways. Drainage in particular is affected by particle size as is the quality of adhesiveness.

Particles larger than 2mm in size are classed as stones or gravel and do not form part of the soil although

they may be present to a greater or lesser extent. Soils are composed of particles less than 2mm, and the individual particles can be classified as follows:

> 2 – 0.2mm: coarse sand
> 0.2 – 0.02mm: fine sand
> 0.02 – 0.002mm: silt
> 0.002mm: clay

For practical purposes three main groupings can be distinguished by observation and feel:

Sandy soil: individual particles can be seen and the soil feels strongly gritty between the fingers.

Silty soil: particles cannot be seen, and the soil feels only slightly gritty.

Clay soil: particles cannot be seen, and the soil feels smooth.

Broadly speaking most soils are made up of combinations of the three main groupings. A sandy soil, for example, may be made up of 80% sand grade material and 20% of silt and clay. Soils are therefore arranged in textural groups which indicate the *main* soil type:

Sand: 80% sand, 20% silt or clay
Loamy sand: 50 – 80% sand, 50 – 20% silt or clay
Loam: 50% sand, 50% silt and clay
Silty loam: 30 – 50% sand, 30 – 50% silt, little clay
Clay loam: 30 – 50% sand, 30 – 50% clay, little silt
Clay: 50% clay, 50% silt or sand

Simple tests can ascertain a soil type: a sandy soil will run between the fingers even when wet, and loamy sand has a slight plasticity when wet. Loam forms into threads when moist, and silty loam is quite plastic, with a recognizable spongy effect. Clay loam is sticky when moistened, but the sand content can still be detected; damp clay can be rolled into threads and easily moulded.

Soil types
Sandy soils have a high content of quartz grains. These grains tend to form an inert skeleton which is unable to hold moisture. This means that sandy soils drain freely and have

Crumb structure forms the ideal garden soil. The individual particles are granular and smooth, cemented together with clay or humus, but retaining porosity. Meadow soils have a typical crumb structure, granular even when moist.

Platy structures are common in fine-textured soils. As they are slow-draining, they become compressed and air is excluded. Such soils need liberal amounts of bulky manure to open up the pore spaces; artificial drainage may also be advisable.

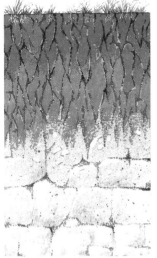

Prismatic structure occurs in soils which are poorly drained or waterlogged. The crumb particles swell into columnar clods, and the soil becomes heavy and cold. Rough autumn digging and exposure to frost help to break down the clods.

Blocky structures are chiefly found in heavy clay soils. Drainage may appear satisfactory, but the soil breaks into angular, solid clods; germination is greatly impeded. Ridging and a winter frost will help to improve poor structures.

SOIL 3

considerable air spaces between the grains leading to plant nutrients being washed out; such soils need constant manuring and fertilisers.

In periods of drought, sandy soils quickly dry out, and shallow-rooted plants will die. On the other hand, the excellent aeration causes these soils to warm up quickly in spring, and as long as plant nutrients and water are in good supply, early vegetables can be successfully grown. However, sandy soils also cool down quickly at night and are susceptible to temperature changes in spring.

Loam and clay

Loam soils are the ideal for cultivation. As they are made up of particles ranging from sand grade to clay grade they have many advantages: ability to retain some water and hold plant nutrients; they are well-drained and aerated and easy to work, with less soil temperature fluctuations.

Clay soils have a large proportion of minute particles of silica, aluminium and various oxides and hydroxides. The particles do not allow adequate drainage, and while clay soils can hold considerable amounts of water, they contain very little air.

Due to the poor drainage clay soils can easily become waterlogged, but in periods of drought the surface may dry out into a concrete-hard cracked mass. The lack of soil air means that clay soils warm up slowly in spring, and cool down slowly in autumn.

Despite these drawbacks clay soils do contain a high proportion of nutrients and with suitable cultivation such soils can produce high yields. Ridge digging in autumn exposes as much of the clay surface as possible to winter frost which breaks it down into a crumb-like structure. The addition of lime causes the clay particles to collect around particles of lime and again form a crumb-like structure. Incorporation of humus also improves the soil.

Stone and gravel

In stony soils the rock particles are larger than 2mm in diameter. Various names are applied to stones according to size and shape; well rounded stones are called pebbles while angular ones are known as gravel. The stones usually originate from the shattered parent rock, but in some instances they are introduced by natural transportation methods such as a river depositing gravels.

Stones impart particular qualities to a soil which may be regarded as advantageous or otherwise. Stony soils are generally free-draining and can usually be worked early in the season. However, they also dry out very rapidly, and added humus and fertilisers are necessary; irrigation may be needed in dry periods.

Larger surface stones should be removed from any cultivated land, but as anyone with a stony soil will know, this is a never-ending task as more stones progressively work their way up to the surface. This curious tendency takes place particularly in winter when the soil is wet.

In freezing conditions stones cool down more rapidly than the soil, and ice forms beneath them. As the ice grows it pushes the stones upwards to the surface but they are quickly replaced in the soil by others working their way up from the parent rock. It is pointless to remove stones from the soil, and the gardener must content himself with removing those already on the surface.

Soil air and oxidation

A certain amount of vital air is contained between soil particles, except under waterlogged conditions when air space is taken up by water. Soil air differs from atmospheric air in that it is usually completely saturated with water and contains less oxygen and more carbon dioxide.

An oxygen content is necessary in order to maintain organic life in the soil; it also effects chemical changes, especially oxidation. The breakdown of organic materials releases important sources of nitrogen, and oxidation converts nitrogen into a form easily absorbed by plants.

Most soil bacteria, which break down organic materials, need oxygen to flourish, and a lack of soil air slows down or prevents their activity. Earthworms also need air to live, and while the presence of worm casts are unwelcome on a lawn, worms are important to soil processing. They are responsible for carrying organic material down into the soil and also for further aeration.

Soil colour

As an indication of the composition of a soil, colour may or may not be of significance. Be careful in drawing any inferences on fertility from soil colour; black or dark brown colour is often associated with fertility and yet this is often not the case.

Very dark soil colouration is mainly due to the humus content, and yet in a soil with well distributed humus it can make up less than 10 per cent of the soil components while still giving a dark colour. Conversely, a peaty soil, which is dark in colour and may have a high organic content, can still be infertile.

On the other hand soil colour can be a useful indicator of other factors. A light grey colour indicates leaching, while a blueish colour signifies waterlogging. All dark soils warm up quickly in spring.

Soil water and drainage

Much of the water in a soil is held as a thin film round the particles, although after heavy rain or in waterlogged conditions water can also fill up the air spaces. Soil water is subject to movement, drawn upwards by evaporation and by plants and known as capillary water, or pulled down by the force of gravity through the soil. This is known as gravitational water and can remove

Boulder clay is one of the easier soils to manage. It is a glacial soil type and occurs north of a line between London and the Bristol Channel. Boulder clay is found particularly in East Anglia; although slightly heavy, it is usually productive.

various essential chemicals from the upper soil levels.

Excessive downward movement of soil water leads to leaching, and the soil may become acid. On the other hand excessive capillary action can lead to the development of highly saline soils, although this is very unlikely in Britain where precipitation is relatively high compared with the evaporation rate.

In a cool damp climate water tends to move predominantly downwards, resulting, in addition to leaching, in the formation of a hardpan. The material being leached from the soil may collect to form a thin hard layer that eventually impedes the drainage—and root penetration—and causes waterlogging. The downward movement of water consequently affects a soil's suitability for cultivation.

Drainage capacity

Natural drainage depends on several factors, including the degree of slope, the amount and distribution of precipitation, the permeability or porosity of the parent rock, the amount of vegetation cover, and the water-holding capacity of the soil. In terms of drainage a soil can be placed in one of four categories.

1. Excessive drainage = the soil dries out rapidly.
2. Satisfactory drainage = surplus water drains away.
3. Poor drainage = heavy rain does not drain away in a reasonable amount of time.
4. Impeded drainage = the soil is nearly always waterlogged.

The most common causes of plant failure occur where drainage is extreme, either excessive or poor/impeded. In the case of poor and impeded drainage, stagnant water builds up and excludes air. Bacteriological activity is reduced and decomposition poor, leading to a build-up of toxic gases.

27

SOIL 4

Artificial drainage

Under conditions of poor drainage plant growth is poor, and many cultivated plants will die unless drainage is improved. The simplest and least expensive method is to dig deep trenches into which excess water can soak horizontally.

Drainage trenches can be hazardous in the garden and are best filled with coarse gravel through which water can pass. At a more expensive level drain-pipes can be installed. Improvement to the drainage may not be noticeable for two or three years, depending on the seriousness of the problem, but gradually plant life should flourish again.

Excessive drainage is equally problematical and can be dealt with in various ways. On thin sandy and chalky soils the addition of marl and humus will improve water retention. If the surface of the soil is maintained as a fine crumbly tilth, drying out and cracking can be prevented, especially on clay soils. A covering mulch and as much vegetation cover as possible also helps.

As water drains away from the bottom, the soil dries out from the top, and in extreme cases or during droughts, the only solution is deep irrigation. A garden hose with a sprinkler attachment is the most suitable; it requires a licence from the appropriate Water Authority.

The water table

Water is chiefly derived from precipitation, the most important being rain and to a lesser extent snow. It is distributed in various ways. A certain amount remains on the surface and flows down slopes to form streams.

Another portion of rainwater is evaporated, while the remainder is absorbed by the ground. Groundwater may infiltrate downwards into the bedrock or flow superficially through the soil and subsoil, eventually running into streams.

Leached soil is typical of most heathland areas where vegetation is determined by the underlying material and its drainage capacity. The profile above shows a shallow, acid, ashy-grey soil layer above sandstone; it supports mainly bracken.

Infiltration capacity

The rate at which water passes into the soil is known as the infiltration capacity which is measured in mm/hour. If water falls to the ground at a greater rate than the infiltration capacity the excess will remain on the surface forming puddles or running downslope.

Initial infiltration is largely controlled by capillary attraction, but as more water enters the soil layers and the spaces between the particles fill up, capillary attraction decreases, and the water is pulled further down by gravity.

The rate of infiltration is largely subject to how much water is already in the soil, which in turn reflects drainage capacities and the amount of precipitation during the preceding period. Sandy soils have infiltration rates up to 200 mm/hour, while clays can transmit less than 5 mm/hour. Vegetation also has an effect in that plant roots create passageways along which water can pass. Plant cover can also break the impact of heavy raindrops which could compact the surface, thus cutting down the infiltration rate.

Waterlogging

At depth the soil becomes more compact and the downward movement of water slows down; the presence of hardpans inhibits further downward movement. In flat low-lying areas soil water can accumulate to such an extent as to cause waterlogging. However, in most localities even a gentle slope of the land means that water is diverted to flow laterally through the soil.

A certain amount of water passes beneath the soil into the underlying rock. A rock's capacity to transmit water varies according to its porosity and permeability. Coarse-grained sandstones and limestones have a very high permeability whereas clays and other fine-grained rocks have the lowest permeabilities. Eventually percolating water reaches a zone which is completely saturated.

The upper surface of the saturation level is known as the water table. The level of the water table varies, being higher at times of heavy precipitation. Generally, the level is below the level of the soil except in low-lying or badly drained areas where waterlogging occurs.

Soil structure

While the texture of a soil is determined by the sizes of the particles present, the structure describes the manner in which the particles are joined together. Clay and humus particles help to bind sand and silt grains together into larger units, and structures are controlled by pressure from wetting and the adhesive qualities.

The composition of a soil affects aeration, porosity and general workability; it may be granular with a crumb-like structure or have a platy, prismatic or blocky structure.

The ideal structure is the crumb structure which appears to be most suitable for plant life. Soils which do not have this favourable structure can be altered: on light sandy soils the addition of humus aids the formation of a crumb structure, and on heavy clay soils exposure to frost, and liming, can achieve similar beneficial results.

Soil profiles

Between the ground surface and the underlying bedrock a soil may show different vertical development at different levels, represented by colours, textures, content and structures.

Some soils are remarkably uniform throughout, but most show definite layers or horizons which can be recognised in profile. There may be a clear cut boundary from one horizon to another, but in most cases there is a gradual change. Every main soil type has a distinctive profile although there are variations.

In Britain, soil profiles often have three main horizons. The uppermost layer, known as the A horizon, extends down for about 0.5 metre; water constantly passes through this horizon removing material downwards into the B horizon. Below this is the C horizon which consists of weathered parent material grading down to parent rock.

Profiles such as these develop only in areas undisturbed by man. Where land has been cultivated, a deep layer of soil suitable for plant growth is produced, and often the A and B horizons will have been intermingled by repeated deep ploughing or double digging.

Changes in drainage, addition of fertilisers and growth of plants not only affect surface soil layers, but also those at depth. A cultivated soil therefore can have a completely different profile from a natural soil in the vicinity.

Soil classifications

Soils are a complex mixture of organic and inorganic materials, water, air and plant nutrients. The soil type produced in any area is the product of several soil-forming factors including parental rock, type and amount of organic material, the climate, the relief of the area and to a certain extent the length of time that the soil has been forming. The infinite variations amongst these factors lead to soil occurring in a wide variety of forms.

The Soil Survey of Great Britain (1974) classifies British soils into six groups: brown earths, podsols, gleys, organic soils, calcareous soils and undifferentiated alluviums. Within these groups subdivisions into soil series can be made. Most libraries stock copies of the Soil Survey and the characteristic details of local soil series can easily be obtained.

Brown earths are formed on free-draining sites. They are traditionally

SOIL 5

Brown earth soil provides some of Britain's best arable land (top). It has a good crumb or blocky structure and is rich in organic matter. Although well-drained, leaching is not excessive; salts such as calcium and magnesium are most rapidly washed out.

Podsols form where water moves easily through the soil, removing in the process minerals from the upper layers. In extreme cases a hardpan forms, and the topsoil becomes acid and infertile. Gorse and silver birches thrive (left).

Meadow soil is typical of river valleys where drainage is poor on flat, low-lying land (left). *The topsoil is usually dark brown, rich in humus and ideal for grassing, but beneath is a sticky, grey-green gley horizon where the soil is waterlogged.*

rich in organic material derived from leaf decay. These soils have been cultivated for centuries and provide Britain's best agricultural land.

Podsols occur where leaching is unusually strong. This leaves the upper horizon acid and rich in silica, with the lower horizon conversely rich in colloids and bases. There is often a hardpan; waterlogging can occur and peat can accumulate. Applications of fertilisers and humus are necessary before crops will flourish.

Gleys occur in waterlogged sites, and a podsol can develop into a gley. Waterlogging results in lack of oxygen and a reduction in bacterial action. Organic decomposition is retarded, and partly decayed material forms peat. Gley soils are common in river valleys and other low-lying areas; they are often called meadow soils, and texturally they consist of mud and silt.

Organic soils form in poorly drained localities where waterlogging is a dominant feature. In these situations, water-tolerant plants such as reeds, sedges and certain mosses flourish. Similar conditions to those in gley soils can be seen; considerable thicknesses of peat accumulate, and the bottom layers become compressed although still fibrous.

Bog and fen peat

Peat itself is not a soil, but a type of soil-forming material. There are two main types of peat formation in Britain, bog peat and fen peat. Bog peat forms in wet conditions in high moorlands. The underlying rock in high areas tends to be hard, and it supplies very few chemical bases to the soil. The humic acids produced by the partial decay of vegetation are not neutralised, and thus a very acid form of peat is produced.

Bog peat areas are only suitable for

SOIL 6

cultivation after draining, and the addition of sand or silt and liming.

Fen peat forms in low-lying boglands where the water is rich in calcareous material or other alkaline salts. This water neutralises the humic acids formed by vegetation decay, and a milder peat results. When drained, fen peat provides a rich soil as in the Fens.

Chalky soils

Calcareous soils are formed on limestone, a fairly common rock type in Britain. There are three main limestone outcrops: the Carboniferous Limestone of the Pennines, Northern England and South Wales; the Iurassic Limestone that runs as a series of scarps from Dorset, through the Cotswolds and northwards to South Yorkshire; and the Chalk Downlands of south-east England.

Limestone is essentially calcium carbonate which can be dissolved by rainwater. A soil will only form on limestone that contains impurities such as clay and silica. As the limestone is dissolved by rain, the impurities may be left on the surface to form a soil. It is usually thin, dry and loamy with a subsoil of broken limestone fragments. Frequent irrigation is necessary for the successful cultivation of such soils which are quick-draining.

Undifferentiated alluvial soils are young soils with no clear profile. There are many variations of these soils, including mountain soils, river alluviums, marine soils, glacial soils and wind-blown soils.

On mountainous slopes any soil-forming material is usually moved downslope. Soils only form where the slope is stable or in the valleys. Frost shatters the rocks, and the soils

have a high proportion of rock fragments; they will only support a sparse vegetation of coarse grasses and bilberries. The heavy rainfall causes a high rate of leaching, down to the foot of the slopes.

River and sea soils

River alluviums consist of clay, silt and sand deposited in sheets by running water. They are fine-textured and provided that they can be drained, they make excellent soils. Marine soils are composed of material of

Moorland soil in the Scottish Highlands is unsuitable for cultivation. The climatic conditions are severe, rainfall is high, and *the thin peaty soil overlies hard rock. Coarse grass provides grazing, but the vegetation is dominated by heathers.*

Calcareous soil occurs over limestone outcrops. The topsoil is dry and friable, with a thin, brown-black humus layer grading into limestone or chalk fragments. Drought-resistant vegetation (left) includes fescue grasses, hawthorn and dogwood.

marine origin. They accumulate in coastal areas and vary in content from clay to silt and sand.

In low-lying wet areas peat may develop on top, but where drained they can form a useful growing medium as long as salt is removed. The removal of sea salt, which is mainly sodium chloride, can be achieved by adding gypsum (calcium sulphate). The two substances react to form calcium chloride which can be easily washed out by natural processes.

Glacial and dust soils

Glacial soils vary extremely, according to the glacial material underneath them. This may take the form of sand, clay or gravel, and a wide range of soils have developed on them. Wind-blown soils are comparatively rare in Britain, except for East Anglia and parts of Cambridgeshire. They form in areas where the wind deposits a fine dust as a soil layer. Known as brick-earths, they are fine-textured and porous and make excellent soils.

Soil improvements

Whatever the soil type, improvement and maintenance of it will produce better results in terms of plant growth. The ideal garden soil is one of loamy texture, satisfactory drainage, sufficient plant nutrients and humus, as well as sufficient lime to counteract acidity if necessary. The nearer the soil comes to this ideal, the fewer improvements are necessary, and the work involved will be a matter of maintenance.

The first step is to put a name to your soil. Visit your local library to check your area with the National Soil Survey. From the available information the major soil classifications can be ascertained, e.g. podsol, brown earth, gley, etc. The next step is to test the soil to analyse the type and texture, check the acidity, drainage characteristics, and—for those who wish to be truly thorough—examine the soil profile by digging a deep hole. You can now decide which improvements, if any, are necessary.

SOIL 7

Excessive drainage is as serious a problem as poor or impeded drainage and should be dealt with before anything else. Improvements to drainage will not necessarily show instant results in terms of better plant growth, but the long-term benefits will be encouraging.

Soil dressings are useful for two purposes, firstly by improving texture and secondly by adding plant nutrients. There are three major forms of soil dressings: lime, humus-makers and fertilisers. The addition of such materials serves either to make up for deficiencies in poor soils or as replacements for plant nutrients.

In natural soil, food losses are replaced by decaying plant matter and possibly by addition from the underlying parent material, but in cultivated soil the main input has to come from the gardener.

Liming

The addition of lime serves several purposes. It provides calcium which is an important nutrient for the growth of root tips and shoots. Vegetables, flowers and fruit particularly need a good supply of calcium. Percolating water steadily removes lime as well as other elements, and this in turn leads to increasing soil acidity in which many plants cannot flourish.

Addition of lime counteracts acidity and is also useful in breaking up heavy clay soil (flocculation). Several types are available, including ground limestone, chalk, quicklime and hydrated lime. The most common and useful variety is ground chalk which is fine-textured and concentrated and less quickly leached out of the soil than hydrated lime. Spread the lime evenly over the soil surface after digging. Never add any other type of soil dressing at the same time and do not add lime until at least 3 months after digging in humus-making material.

Once a lime-dressing has been applied, allow 4-6 weeks for rain to wash it into the soil before using other dressings or sowing seeds. Do not add more than the recommended amount of lime as excessive doses cause the humus content to break down very rapidly.

Adding humus

A good humus content in the soil is vital as a means of holding nutrients in a form which can be used by plants. The humus content of a soil can be increased and maintained by the addition of humus-making materials, of which there are two basic types.

Raw humus is organic materials which have not been decayed by the action of bacteria. Examples include grass clippings and the very acid 'mor' peat. Addition of raw humus-making material is useful in that bacterial activity in the soil is stimulated, and textural improvements occur. On the other hand the rapid increase in bacterial activity uses up soil nitrogen which is needed by growing plants.

Matured humus is organic materials well decayed by bacterial action. Examples include fen peats, rotted manure, garden compost etc. Mature humus is slower-acting than raw humus, and it preserves the soil nitrogen because the material is already decomposed. Raw humus can be transformed into mature humus by composting.

Compost heaps

Garden compost is a readily available form of humus-making material. A compost heap can be made from a range of organic materials, including grass clippings, peat, deciduous leaves, soft weeds, kitchen refuse (potato peelings, tea leaves etc.), newspapers, straw and bracken. Such waste material is decayed and turned into compost by bacteria, provided air and moisture

are available. Properly made compost is an ideal humus.

Most gardens have room for one compost heap, which may be free-standing or enclosed in a wooden or wire-netting bin or in a ready-made compost-maker, made from polyethylene and sold under various brand names. Where space allows, a series of three compost bins can be erected, one with decayed material ready for use, one in the process of decaying and one for raw material as it becomes available.

Give the compost heap a base layer of coarse material—straw or broken-up cabbage stumps—and tread firmly without compressing the layer too much; next add a layer, similarly about 20cm deep, of soft materials such as grass clippings, kitchen waste or soft weeds, followed by a thinner layer of soil. Add water if the materials are dry. Do not use diseased or chemically treated ingredients, and avoid woody plants and twigs; the latter can be burnt and the ashes mixed with soft weeds.

Compost activators

Bacteria in the compost heap need nitrogen and lime in order to flourish. These can be supplied in the form of sulphate of ammonia and carbonate of lime lightly sprinkled over alternate layers, or by a proprietary compost activator. On no account should lime and sulphate of ammonia come into contact with each other. When the heap has reached a convenient height, top it with a 10cm layer of soil and cover with a plastic sheet to keep out rain if the heap is in the open.

As the materials in the heap begin to decompose, heat will be generated; this is the critical stage in compost-making as both excessive moisture and dryness will kill off bacterial activity. As heat builds up in the heap, the materials will shrink, especially in the centre of the heap. Turn the outer materials, which may be composting more slowly, to the centre.

A properly-made compost heap should have decayed in about 6 months, considerably less in warm summers, and be dark brown to black, with a sweet, warm aroma. It is now ready for use and is ideal for soil improvements or for mulching.

Organic manures
Manure is an equally good source of humus provided that it is properly rotted. Fresh manure not only has an unpleasant smell, but also contains many harmful acids. Stable manure and general farm manure are good additions to all types of soil. Poultry manure, high in nitrogen, is less suitable as a humus-maker but can be added to compost heaps.

Mulches and top dressing
Mature humus is widely used as a mulch or dressing of the soil surface around plants. The purpose of a mulch is to keep the soil moist and to smother weeds. A certain amount of humus and plant nutrients is also washed down into the soil.

A mulch is particularly useful in areas with low rainfall in summer. Such locations include the eastern part of Britain, which is comparatively dry in summer, and sites close to buildings and walls where normal rainfalls do not reach. Gardens with excessive or very freely draining soils also benefit from mulching.

Several organic materials are suitable as a mulch, including compost, peat, grass cuttings, spent hops and mushroom compost, and farmyard manure. Before a mulch is applied the soil must be thoroughly moist because a deep mulch can prevent rain from entering the soil. The best time to apply a mulch is in late spring when danger of frost is over, and the soil has warmed up, but before the surface soil dries out.

Organic and inorganic fertilisers
Plants need a steady amount of nutrients during the growing season, and the majority of nutrients is taken from the soil via the roots. The supply of nutrients in the soil comes from three sources— weathered parent material, humus, and, in the case of cultivated soils, added fertilisers. When a soil is cultivated plant foods are taken up at a faster rate than that at which they are naturally replaced, and additions of nutrients must be made to keep the soil fertile.

Some plant nutrients are more important than others. Large quantities of nitrogen, potash and phosphates are used for healthy growth, and these materials are therefore removed from the soil at a rapid rate.

Nitrogen promotes the growth of leaves, potash is used to form flowers and fruit, and phosphate is used for root development. Calcium and magnesium are used in smaller quantities, calcium for flower and fruit production, and magnesium also for fruit formation. Minute amounts of trace elements are also necessary for plant health and include iron, boron, sulphur, manganese, copper, zinc and molybdenum.

Straight and compound feeds
Fertilisers are used to redress the balance of plant foods in the soil, and may be organic or inorganic in origin. Straight fertilisers contain just one of the three major plant nutrients. They are provided in controlled amounts through either slow or quick-acting fertilisers.

The major types of nitrogen fertilisers include bone-meal—which also contains phosphates—dried blood and sulphate of ammonia. The latter two are quick-acting fertilisers and rapidly release nitrogen into the soil in a form that can be used by plants immediately. They are best applied as a top dressing round plants.

Bone-meal, on the other hand, is a slow-acting fertiliser, best applied as a base dressing to the soil at the time of planting trees, shrubs and roses. Slow-acting fertilisers release a steady supply of plant food over a long period.

Compound fertilisers contain several plant foods, in particular all three of the major nutrients, with the amount of each balanced to meet the needs of a particular plant group. The packages in which compound fertilisers are marketed are usually numbered to indicate the amount of each plant nutrient, for example 6:9:6. This means that there is 6 per cent nitrogen, 9 per cent phosphate and 6 per cent potash available.

Some compound fertilisers are available in forms intended for specific purposes, such as lawn or rose fertilisers, while others, such as Growmore, are for general use.

Most fertilisers, whether of organic or inorganic origin, are sold in solid form, as powders or granules. They are applied to the soil, as a top or base dressing, following the manufacturers' recommendations.

Liquid and foliar fertilisers
Many fertilisers are also available in liquid form; they are easy to apply, after dilution in water, but should never be given to dry soils.

Foliar fertiliser sprays must be diluted. They are useful for giving a quick tonic to plants of poor performance and as an adjunct to slow-acting fertilisers applied as a base dressing. Foliar feeds are generally inorganic, but they can also be had as organic sprays, with those derived from seaweed being useful in supplying trace elements.

MANURES

MANURES AND FERTILISERS

	Quick or slow-acting	Organic or inorganic	Nitrogen %N	Phosphate %P	Potash %K
MANURES					
Bark (pulverised)	S	O	trace	trace	trace
Farmyard manure	Q	O	0.6	0.3	0.5
Garden compost	Q	O	2-2.5	0.5-1	0.5-2
Hop manure	Q	O	3-4	1-2	2
Hops (spent)	S	O	0.5-0.6	1-2	trace
Leaf-mould	S	O	trace	trace	trace
Mushroom compost (spent)	Q	O	2-3	1-2	1-2
Peat	S	O	trace	trace	trace
Poultry manure (dried)	Q	O	4-6	3-5	2-3
Seaweed	S	O	0.5	0.1	1
Shoddy	S	O	3-15	—	—
FERTILISERS					
Basic slag	S	I	1	8-22	—
Blood (dried)	Q	O	7-14	1-2	1
Bone-flour (steamed)	S	O	1	27-28	—
Bone-meal	S	O	3-5	20-25	—
Fish-meal	Q	O	8-10	5-10	1-2
Growmore	Q	I	7	7	7
Hoof and horn-meal (fine)	Q	O	12-14	1-3	—
Hoof and horn-meal (coarse)	S	O	12-14	1-3	—
John Innes base fertiliser	Q	I	5.1	7.2	9.7
Nitrate of potash	Q	I	12-14	—	44-46
Nitrate of soda	Q	I	16	—	—
Nitro-chalk	Q	I	15.5	—	—
Soot (weathered)	Q	O	3-6	—	—
Sulphate of ammonia	Q	I	20-21	—	—
Sulphate of potash	Q	I	—	—	48
Superphosphate of lime	S	I	—	18.5	—
Triple superphosphate	S	I	—	47.0	—
Urea	Q	O	46	—	—

dressing q. metre	Top dressing per sq. metre	In water, 5ml. spoons per litre	When to apply
—	5kg	—	In spring as a 5cm mulch round shrubs, herbaceous plants, fruit trees and bushes.
-7kg	5-7kg	—	Work into soil during autumn digging or use as mulch in spring.
5kg	5kg	—	Work into soil during autumn digging or use as mulch in spring.
00g	—	—	Work into soil in spring.
5kg	—	—	Work into soil between autumn and spring.
.5kg	2.5kg	—	Work into soil during autumn digging or use as mulch in spring.
5-5kg	—	—	Work into soil during autumn digging.
5kg	5kg	—	Work into soil during autumn digging or use as mulch in spring.
00g	100g	—	Work into soil before sowing or planting, or use as top dressing in spring and summer.
5kg	—	—	Work into soil during autumn digging.
00g	—	—	Work into soil during autumn, winter or spring cultivation.
-200g	—	—	Apply to soil in autumn and winter. Most effective on acid soils.
—	25-50g	½	Apply in spring and summer to growing plants.
-100g	—	—	Apply to soil round roots of trees and shrubs at planting time.
-100g	—	—	Apply to soil round roots of trees and shrubs at planting time.
-100g	—	—	Work into soil during spring cultivation.
-100g	—	—	Work into soil during spring cultivation.
-100g	—	—	Work into soil during spring cultivation.
-100g	—	—	Work into soil during spring cultivation.
-100g	—	—	For use in John Innes composts; may be used instead of Growmore.
—	up to 25g	½	Apply to soil round plants in spring and summer; use as liquid feed for pot plants in summer.
—	up to 25g	½	Apply to young crops or pot plants in growing season.
25g	25g	—	Apply before sowing or planting, or to young crops. Useful on acid soils.
50g	50-100g	—	Apply round growing plants or work into soil before sowing or planting.
-50g	25g	½-1	Apply before sowing or planting; during growing season as a top dressing or liquid feed. Good for lawns.
to 25g	—	½-1	Apply before sowing or planting; use as liquid feed for fruiting and flowering plants.
-50g	—	½-1	Work into soil before sowing or planting; use as liquid feed.
-20g	—	½	As superphosphate, but three times as strong; use in dilute amounts.
—	up to 25g	Few drops	During summer, as liquid feed or mixed with sand as top dressing.

CLIMATE 1

Weather expresses the combination of temperature, humidity, light, sunshine, rainfall, wind and evaporation, experienced at one place in one moment of time. It varies from minute to minute, day to day and year to year. It also varies with height, or in the case of soil, with depth as well as horizontally from place to place.

Official weather records are taken at a large number of observing stations, under internationally agreed conditions, in an attempt to define the scale of variation. For the layman, these records must be regarded as reference values, not as precise weather indications. Weather is a sample of the climate, and the latter a compendium of weather.

Climate is the summary of weather, its variability expressed in a concise, but useful form. In its simplest form it gives the long-term averages of a single weather factor at a specific site. Anyone who wishes to know more than the average will need a knowledge of the combinations of weather factors.

For a gardener it is useful to know the rainfall climate and the probabilities of water being added to his soil, but it is far more helpful to know the transpiration climate.

Weather in the garden

The weather determines whether a plant will live or die; it dictates how it will develop, when it will produce leaves, flowers, fruits or seeds and whether such seed will be pollinated. The weather also influences the final yield.

For maximum yield or best growth a plant needs optimum weather conditions at each stage of its development, but as these rarely all occur, it is up to the gardener to

Summers in Britain do include perfect days. In hot sun, the cool colours and shady trees in a typical English garden compensate for months of drying winds and heavy rain.

select those plants best suited to his garden climate. He should also be able to modify that climate to minimise adverse weather effects.

A plant has two basic requirements: energy from the sun, which also helps to provide suitable temperatures—and moisture from the soil—which also supplies essential nutrients.

The gardener can do nothing about the sunshine, but he can often do a great deal about soil moisture. An understanding of the plant-weather relationship can nudge the garden climate towards more suitable growing conditions.

Length of day

This is the one regular feature of growing conditions and acts as a kind of calendar for plants, telling them the time of year, and as a kind of switch control in their growth programme. Some plants react to long days, others to short days (or long nights), while yet others are indifferent to light duration.

Unless a gardener attempts to control his growing climate by the use of artificial shading or additional lighting in a greenhouse or growth cabinet, he must take natural daylight requirements into account when planning his sowing.

Sunshine

The earth loses heat to outer space every minute of day and night by long-wave radiation, and the planet only keeps warm enough for life by receiving short-wave radiation from the sun. Expressed simply, the sun heats the surface of the land, and to

Climatic extremes are rare in the British Isles. In late summer, grapes ripen to perfection on sunny, sheltered walls (top). Months later, seeds experience a period of low temperatures, vernalisation, before they react to higher temperature.

White hoar frost lends a crispness to the winter garden. The majority of our garden

a lesser extent, the sea, and the surface heat warms the air above it. The energy of the sun's radiation supplies the heat necessary for leaf transpiration and energy for photosynthesis. Transpiration brings about a movement of moisture from roots to leaves; it also carries a supply of plant nutrients and acts like a one-way blood stream. If plants cannot transpire, they may die or at least grow poorly.

Green matter cannot be formed unless energy is available. The proportion of solar energy used to create green matter (photosynthesis) is numerically very small, but without it nothing would grow.

Temperature

For the sake of simplicity and convenience, the warmth requirements of a plant are generally stated in terms of temperature. However, temperature is *not* energy, merely an indicator of the level reached by a balance of energy gain and energy loss. If energy gain increases, temperature rises; if heat is being lost, temperature will fall.

Nevertheless temperature has a more subtle effect on plant growth, and like day length, temperature acts as an off-on switch. Most British garden plants make little growth if the temperature of the air or soil, or both, falls below 6°C.

Above the minimum temperature level, the speed of plant development is triggered off by temperature (phenological development). In the analogy of a car, temperature is the brake, gearbox and throttle, but heat energy is the petrol.

plants are dormant and suffer no ill effects from seasonal frost and snow.

The British Isles may be regarded as being on the cool side, and yet the gardens rank among the best in the world. Generally, the efforts of a gardener must be directed towards increasing the temperature of the soil and the air around his plants.

Frost

The most obvious example of temperature influence in the garden is frost, ranging from a dusting of white hoar frost over the lawn in autumn and spring, to a prolonged severe spell when the top spit of the soil becomes frozen.

Plants vary in their reaction to temperatures below freezing point, but they have one thing in common: if the liquid in their cells freezes and the cells burst, that part of the plant, at least, will die. Plants have

39

CLIMATE 2

different susceptibilities to frost depending on their stage of development; low temperatures during winter dormancy may be endured, but a similar temperature occurring after spring growth has begun can be fatal.

Night minimum temperatures vary appreciably with small changes in height above ground, the lower heights being the colder. Frost incidence can also vary within the confines of a small garden, so that frost damage can be highly local in incidence and intensity.

Wind

The effect of wind in the garden is often underestimated. Its strength is obvious when it causes structural damage, but less violent winds can have far-reaching results. Wind stirs up the air and tends to keep surface temperatures lower than they would be in still air. In spring soil temperatures will be lowest on a windy site. On the other hand, wind can be beneficial on a cold cloudless night, because it will help to prevent ground frost.

Wind also appears to affect plants in a more direct manner in windy areas. The taller shrubs and trees become deformed, and even at a lower level plants grow less successfully, possibly because the wind causes them to half-close their stomata. Wind increases with height above ground level, and unless there is adequate shelter, plants will confine their growth to the lower layers.

Most gardens in Britain gain by carefully planned shelter, but a price must be paid in form of the shade created by shelter belts. Shade, except for plants which have specially adapted to low light conditions, is not generally desirable in cool temperate climates.

Humidity

Although temperatures and radiation may be said to walk hand in hand, temperature and humidity play a kind of see-saw. When air temperature rises, the relative humidity goes down; when the temperature falls, relative humidity rises, and will continue to rise with further fall of temperature until it reaches 100 per cent or saturation point.

Further cooling results in condensation, and the result is dew or fog. The amount of water vapour held by the air at saturation limit will depend on the temperature; warm air holds more moisture than cold air.

The humidity of the air influences the rate of transfer of water by evaporation from the soil and by transpiration from a plant. If the air is saturated the transfer process stops because the air can hold no more moisture. A more important result of high humidity is the favourable conditions it offers for the spread of plant diseases.

Very low air humidity puts a stress on plants; the lowest humidities are found indoors in a cold winter, when they can fall to 30 per cent and below, conditions which are only likely to be reached outdoors on a very hot summer afternoon.

Soil temperature and moisture

Only part of a plant is above ground. The essential roots are in the soil, and soil temperature and moisture conditions are therefore important growth factors. Seed germination is also controlled by soil climate and condition.

As in the air, there is a diurnal fluctuation of temperature in the soil, and the day-night change is greatest at the soil surface. The soil temperature is all-important in spring, with the start of growth. The depth at which seeds are sown is important because soil temperatures decrease appreciably with depth in the daytime.

Heavy soils in spring warm up more slowly than light soils, but they also cool down more slowly; in addition a dry soil will alter its temperature, up or down, more rapidly than a moist soil.

Ideal moisture conditions are essential for successful gardening. The amount of moisture in the soil

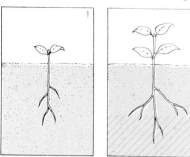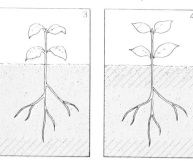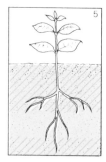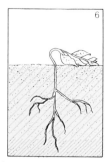

Soil moisture is essential for plant growth. At capacity, a young plant progresses steadily (1), but as the soil dries out from the top, the roots seek wider in search of liquid and nutrients (2). When the moisture

content decreases further, top growth begins to wilt (3). Water applied in insufficient amounts, by irrigation or rainfall, merely moistens the surface soil and does not penetrate to the roots (4). The addition of

more water, to near soil capacity, results in almost instant recovery (5), but if saturation point is reached and the soil becomes waterlogged and deprived of oxygen, recovery is followed by rapid death (6).

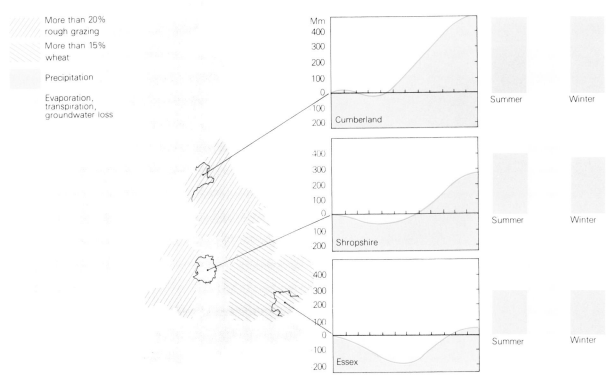

Mm
400
300
200
100
0
100
200

Cumberland

Summer   Winter

400
300
200
100
0
100
200

Shropshire

Summer   Winter

400
300
200
100
0
100
200

Essex

Summer   Winter

The agricultural pattern of the country can indicate soil moisture balance. Mainly rough grazing implies extensive areas with high rainfalls and/or poor soil, chiefly in upland regions. A wheat belt denotes high soil moisture deficiency in summer. On a regional level, Cumberland has wet soil for most of the year, while Essex is the exact opposite, with dry soil in summer and the resulting need for irrigation. Shropshire lies between the two, with the moisture balance almost even during the growing season.

depends on three factors: the soil itself, the input of rainfall, and the output of water by evaporation and by transpiration.

For a plant to grow at all, there must be moisture within range of its roots, and for it to grow well, this moisture must be easily available. Soils dry out from the top. A plant first uses the moisture in the top layer, then extracts moisture from successively lower layers. Replenishment, by rain or irrigation, takes place in a similar fashion, the top layer of soil first becoming wet.

When all the soil layers become moist, holding as much water as they can against the pull of gravity, the soil is said to be at 'field capacity'. Unless the drainage is quick and efficient more water will cause waterlogging which excludes necessary oxygen; few plants will tolerate such conditions for long. Soil at capacity is good for plant growth; soil below capacity will sustain growth, but as moisture is used up, wilting occurs.

Evaporation and transpiration

A soil loses water by evaporation from its surface, the rate being determined by the heat of the sun, by wind, temperature and air humidity. The rate is greatest in June and July and lowest in winter when it is insignificant.

Evaporation first occurs in the surface soil layer, but once dry this acts as a partial seal to water movement. Thereafter the evaporation rate decreases rapidly, and the amount of water a fallow soil can lose during a prolonged dry spell is limited. However, if the dry top crust is broken up, as by deep hoe-

ing, evaporation will resume and extract further moisture from the soil.

A plant loses water by transpiration through the leaf stomata, and the weather influences are identical to those which affect soil evaporation. The nature of the plant, and its stage of development and health, also affects the rate of transpiration loss. The plant responds to the surrounding weather by keeping its leaves from overheating.

A plant which is not transpiring freely may be able to bring in protective mechanisms which can prevent its death, but it cannot thrive.

Plant pests and diseases

The incidence and intensity of all garden pests and diseases depend on the past and present weather. Each pest or disease has its own critical and favourable conditions, and the

CLIMATE 3

progress of attack, unless checked by timely action, is inevitable and can be devastating.

Just as whole civilizations have been wiped out or radically affected by the onset of human disease, so the food supply of the present world is greatly restricted by pests and disease. These secondary effects of weather are of the greatest importance to mankind; in a garden they may be exasperating, but largely controllable; on a global scale, they may yet be the crucial factor in determining the maximum population the earth can support.

The seasons
Conventionally, the four seasons are divided into triplets of months: March, April and May as spring, June, July and August as summer, September, October and November as autumn, and December, January and February as winter.

Mark Twain maintained that in England all four seasons can occur on the same day! For the gardener, seasons based on the calendar are too rigid a model, and as far as he is concerned spring starts when plants begin to grow, and autumn ends when they cease growing.

This seasonal pattern may be more logical than one based on calendar dates, but it is not easy to ascertain the exact day when growth begins. A British spring tends to have one or more false starts, with warm spells in the early part of the year followed by a return to wintry weather.

The start of growth as expressed in terms of meteorological measurements is equally difficult. Possibly the best representation is a soil temperature of 6°C at a depth of 30cm under short grass. Using this criterion, weather records can then be examined to establish a 'date of spring'.

The long-term (30 year) averages for a site such as Oxford show the date to be in the fourth week of March, but in any one year that starting date can be up to one month early or late. There can be an even greater variation in the length of the growing season; the average is close to 250 days, but only in about half the years will the season lie within 15-20 days of the average, and in a decade it may be up to 35 days longer or shorter.

The average length of a growing season can be safely used in comparison between one garden and another, but is a poor guide to the weather of any individual year. If one part of England—and Wales—enjoys an early spring, it is more than likely that other areas are equally early.

Southern Ireland. Frosts are rare compared with England, rainfall is adequate, and the temperature range is reasonable, especially in the winter. Sunshine is generally deficient, being highest in the south-east. Grey skies predominate and may be responsible for discouraging potential gardeners. High humidity can encourage plant diseases.

North-west England and North Wales. Slow southward improvement begins to affect garden climates. Wind speeds are less, though north-westerly gales may persist. Summers are rarely hot, but the growing season is long; late frosts occur inland. In lowland areas, summer rainfall is near the optimum, and here are successful market-gardening areas. In the hills rain is excessive.

South-west England and South Wales. The earliest springs and latest autumns occur here. There is a long growing period with less frost risk than anywhere else, especially on the coast. Rainfall is higher than in the east, and summer temperatures are slightly lower. The garden climate is good, except for strong winds and salt damage.

South-west Scotland and Northern Ireland. The growing period is long; near the coast the average frost-free period can be some 225 days. Summers are generally cool, with cloudy skies. Rainfall averages are high enough for wet years to be problematic. Some of the best strawberries and potatoes come from Auchincruive on the Ayrshire coast.

Channel Islands. The sunniest and warmest part in the British Isles, with a 365-day growing season. The main disadvantage is lack of summer rainfall; with water supplies stretched to the utmost by the influx of summer visitors, watering can cause problems. Winter gales are common, but summer winds are usually less violent.

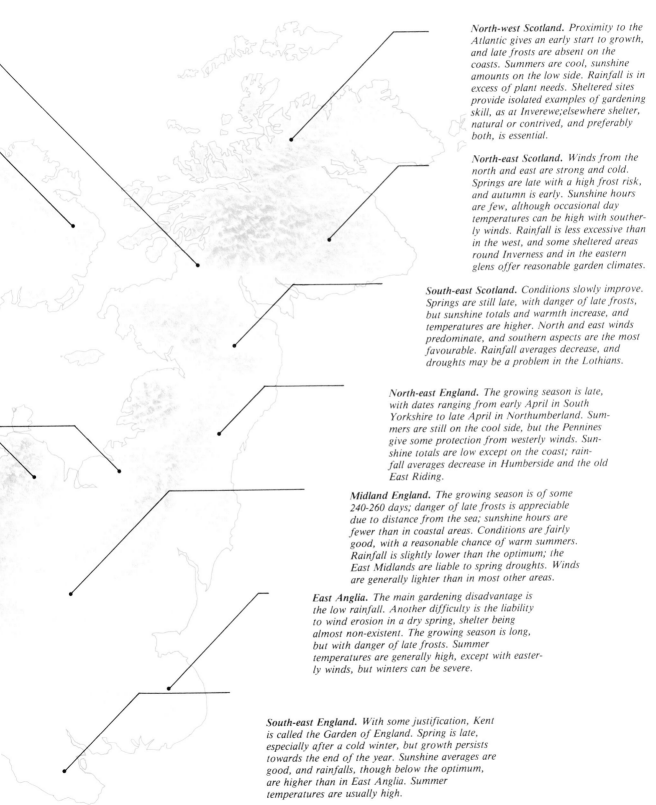

North-west Scotland. Proximity to the Atlantic gives an early start to growth, and late frosts are absent on the coasts. Summers are cool, sunshine amounts on the low side. Rainfall is in excess of plant needs. Sheltered sites provide isolated examples of gardening skill, as at Inverewe; elsewhere shelter, natural or contrived, and preferably both, is essential.

North-east Scotland. Winds from the north and east are strong and cold. Springs are late with a high frost risk, and autumn is early. Sunshine hours are few, although occasional day temperatures can be high with southerly winds. Rainfall is less excessive than in the west, and some sheltered areas round Inverness and in the eastern glens offer reasonable garden climates.

South-east Scotland. Conditions slowly improve. Springs are still late, with danger of late frosts, but sunshine totals and warmth increase, and temperatures are higher. North and east winds predominate, and southern aspects are the most favourable. Rainfall averages decrease, and droughts may be a problem in the Lothians.

North-east England. The growing season is late, with dates ranging from early April in South Yorkshire to late April in Northumberland. Summers are still on the cool side, but the Pennines give some protection from westerly winds. Sunshine totals are low except on the coast; rainfall averages decrease in Humberside and the old East Riding.

Midland England. The growing season is of some 240-260 days; danger of late frosts is appreciable due to distance from the sea; sunshine hours are fewer than in coastal areas. Conditions are fairly good, with a reasonable chance of warm summers. Rainfall is slightly lower than the optimum; the East Midlands are liable to spring droughts. Winds are generally lighter than in most other areas.

East Anglia. The main gardening disadvantage is the low rainfall. Another difficulty is the liability to wind erosion in a dry spring, shelter being almost non-existent. The growing season is long, but with danger of late frosts. Summer temperatures are generally high, except with easterly winds, but winters can be severe.

South-east England. With some justification, Kent is called the Garden of England. Spring is late, especially after a cold winter, but growth persists towards the end of the year. Sunshine averages are good, and rainfalls, though below the optimum, are higher than in East Anglia. Summer temperatures are usually high.

CLIMATE 4

If spring is late one year, the differences between regions tend to become smaller.

Within the growing season, frost can check, or terminate, the growth of plants. The average length of the frost-free period might be thought a better guide, but frost is usually localised, and plants are variable in their response.

Variations about average dates of last spring and first autumn frost are also greater than those about start and end of growth. Frost risks can never be ignored, but each site must be treated on its merits.

The seasonal pattern

Spring comes first to the Scillies and the coasts of Cornwall and Kerry. Early or mid-February is a typical average date, but in mild years these areas may be said to have had no winter at all. Spring progresses slowly eastwards and northwards along the coastal strip, until by mid-March it has generally reached all the coasts between the Isle of Wight and Anglesey, and between Wexford and Clare.

During the next fortnight, on average, spring arrives in all inland districts of southern England and Ireland, followed by a rapid advance northwards into lowland areas up to the Scottish border, leaping across the southern uplands into the Scottish lowlands. The west coast of Scotland is earlier than the east, and spring is always latest on the hills. With a mid-April average date of spring in an upland garden, the start of the growing season in May is not uncommon.

Summer behaves in a different fashion. The highest summer temperatures are those in the Home Counties, and summer may be said to begin in the lower Thames Valley or the Weald of Kent and spread north and west through June. North of the Trent summers are inevitably cooler than farther south.

Autumn approaches from the north-west, coming first to the Scottish hills and spreading southwards towards central southern England, before branching into the latest autumn areas of south-eastern and south-western England.

Winter also comes from the north, spreading southwards until it covers the whole country, except perhaps the extreme south-west, with all coastal strips, especially those in the west, fighting a rearguard action. However, the most severe winters are those with a south-east wind in January or February when Kent can be far colder than the Hebrides.

Rainfall and sunshine

While temperature patterns are much the same every year, the yearly rainfall patterns are far more complex. On average the lowest annual totals are in lowland Essex (about 500mm), and the highest in the west and north (1-2,000mm and more on the hills), but in any one month the rainfall can be as much as twice the average, and in dry spells less than a tenth of the average.

In wetter areas, the average rainfall is heavier in winter than in summer, but again there are large year to year variations.

Except for summers with predominating easterly winds, when western areas receive an unexpected bonus, the sunshine pattern is relatively constant. The sunniest areas are on the south coast, particularly the Isle of Wight and the Channel Islands.

All coastal areas have more sun than inland areas, and sunshine totals decrease with the distance from the south coast, the distance from the nearest coast, and with height above sea level.

The general climate

The British Isles do not experience extreme weather conditions, and disasters are on a relatively small scale compared with many other locations. Our extreme temperatures are almost modest, the strongest winds are rarely of hurricane or typhoon force, and droughts cannot be compared with those of Africa or India.

Most floods are on a small short-lived scale; the main flood threat comes from a triple coincidence of maximum river outflow caused by high rainfall, a high spring tide and an on-shore gale. The low-lying east coast of England and the Thames Estuary are the areas most liable to such a sea invasion.

The climate of England could be said to be the result of a three-way stretch. First there is the north-south influence, with nothing but cold seas to separate northern Scotland from the Arctic Circle, and with the south-west coasts of England and Ireland claiming, sometimes with justification, a Mediterranean climate.

Next is the west-east contrast, with the Atlantic Ocean exercising a moderating influence to the west, and the proximity of a large land mass to the east offering the possibility of increased winter cold or summer heat. Finally there is the upland-lowland difference, for the effect of hills and mountains can be appreciable.

Traditionally the prevailing wind direction is westerly, but in recent decades the dominance of the westerly wind has diminished, resulting in a higher frequency of northerly or southerly winds.

Local climates

The term 'local climate' refers to areas from a large garden to a small parish. Under certain topographical conditions, the local climate will vary appreciably over relatively small distances. Such changes occur with changes in height above sea level, with distances from a coast or

Gardens on lee sides can enjoy good summers. As rising moist air cools on the wind side of the hill range, clouds and rain form. Descending on the lee side, the air warms up and disperses clouds. The climate here is sunnier, warmer and drier.

the side of a large lake, and in the vicinity of large towns.

The effect of height

As height of ground above sea level increases, so average air and soil temperatures decrease; so do sunshine hours, transpiration and evaporation. Averages of humidity, rainfall and wind, on the other hand, increase with height.

On balance, general climatic conditions become less favourable for successful gardening the more height rises above sea level. However, there may be some small compensation in the correspondingly smaller danger of late spring frosts.

The average rate of decrease of mean air temperature in Britain is 0.6°C for every 100 metres, and the decrease of the 30cm soil temperature is 0.3°C per 100m in winter and 0.9°C in summer. These changes may not seem large in themselves, but the net effect on the growing season is appreciable, with spring arriving later and the start of autumn coming earlier.

In Scotland, Northern Ireland and over much of England, the growing season decreases by some 15-20 days per 100m; in Wales, south and south-east England by 25 days per 100m. In the south-west of England and in southern Ireland the growing season can be shortened by as much as 30-35 days per 100m.

The loss in growing time occurs about half in spring and half in autumn. As an example, there is a 7-10 day delay in the start of spring from a garden in the Thames Valley to one in the nearby Chilterns, only some 50km distant.

Aspect is equally important. A south-facing slope can advance spring by some 10 days, and a corresponding extension in autumn. A north-facing slope can be 10 days late, but this is not always a disadvantage, and fruit blossom can be delayed beyond the time when late-spring frost damage is likely.

The decrease in sunshine with height due to increased cloud is relatively small; as a result transpiration changes but slowly, and the decrease does not become significant until heights of 300 metres are reached. The wind increase, on the other hand, is far more important, being about 1½ mph for every 100m; shelter is vital in upland gardens.

The rate of average rainfall increase with height is greatest in the wettest areas, least in the drier eastern side of England. This increase, except in the wetter part of the west and north, is generally helpful, for despite the reputation of being a wet country, our gardens could do with extra soil moisture during the summer.

The general increase of relative humidity with height cannot be ignored. Although fogs are more likely in the valleys, high humidity persists for longer over upland sites.

The lee effect

Nearby hills, especially a range running across the prevailing wind, can have important effects. The climate on the weather or up-wind side is quite different from that on the lee or down-wind side. On the weather side there is more wind, cloud and rain and a higher relative humidity. On the lee side there can be pronounced shelter, with higher temperatures, lower humidity, more sunshine and less wind and rain.

Areas affected in this way do not extend over large distances downwind from the hill, but result in favourable pockets of local climate.

Valley climates

On a sunny, windless day, a valley is the warmest site, but on a calm cloudless night the situation is drastically altered. The ground surface cools rapidly, thus reducing the temperature of the air above it. This cooler air becomes heavy and slips downwards to collect in the valley bottom. The pooling of cold air results in frost hollows or frost plains, where the lowest night temperatures are much less than those on the hillsides.

Although a valley garden enjoys higher daytime temperatures, it is

CLIMATE 5

liable to a greater frost risk. Winds can be similarly disadvantageous: a garden may have some protection from winds blowing across the hills on either side, but if it is blowing up or down the valley, the strength may be increased.

Coastal climates

Climatic changes occur rapidly over small distances in the vicinity of the coast. The linear extent of this effect depends on the nature of the coast and is greatest on a flat coast and on one with prevailing onshore winds. The nature of the sea, deep ocean or shallow estuary, is also important.

The sea has a moderating effect on temperature because water heats up and cools down less rapidly than land. The larger and deeper the sea, the greater the tendency to oppose temperature change. The Atlantic has more coastal effect than the Irish Sea, which in turn is more effective than the southern North Sea and the English Channel.

A coastal strip is cooler in summer than an inland site, and this effect can spread inland by sea breezes on a summer afternoon. In contrast, the coastal strip is milder than inland in winter, to the extent that the coasts of the south-west can be almost frost-free.

There is also increased sunshine, and the sunniest places in England are those on the south coast, especially the Isle of Wight. Moving inland from the coast, sunshine average amounts decrease.

The greatest disadvantage of coastal climates is the frequency and strength of gales. Strong onshore winds carry airborne salt particles which, when deposited on plants, damage the tissues. Shelter is essential in a coastal garden.

Lakes and rivers

A large stretch of inland water has a similar effect to that of the sea, but on a reduced scale. Frost reduction, in particular, is much less because lakes are found in the valley bottoms where cold air collects on frosty nights. Winds may be increased and summer temperatures reduced.

However, there is the possibility of a high watertable near lakes and large rivers which minimises drought. Although flooding can be a danger, most garden plants recover from a short period of waterlogging.

Town and city climates

A few decades ago, any garden in or near a large industrial town had to endure a certainty of high pollution levels, in the air and in the soil. With the introduction of the Clean Air Acts, pollution has been greatly reduced, to the benefit of gardens and gardeners alike.

Ironically, the reduction in the amounts of airborne sulphur has led to an increase of plant disease such as black-spot on roses.

Lead pollution from car exhausts is on the increase. Soils and plants in close proximity to a busy road can be shown to contain an unacceptable high lead content. As lead is a cumulative poison it is unwise to eat food crops from a garden close to busy traffic, unless it has been thoroughly washed.

A thick hedge between a kitchen garden and the road can do much to reduce the pollution risk, but proper distance from the source is the better safeguard.

Frost pockets occur when cold air flows down a slope and collects in the valley at the bottom on still, cloudless nights. In the normal course of events cold air would drift over the house shown, but the construction of a wall at the bottom of the garden has resulted in a frost pocket forming.

Pollution apart, the major effect of a large built-up area is the phenomena known as a heat-island. Roads and buildings soak up the heat of the day and that generated by people and traffic; the heat is released back into the air at night, reducing the risk of low night temperatures.

Gardens within large towns also experience less wind, but walls and high buildings create large zones of shade. Walled corners of town gardens can act as sun-traps if they are facing in the right direction, with the walls reflecting the incoming solar heat.

On balance, the advantages of a town site are outweighed by the disadvantages, but once the climatic limitations are understood, very rewarding results can be achieved.

Microclimates

A microclimate expresses the weather conditions in soil and air immediately surrounding a plant and its roots. There are numerous, slightly different microclimates in any garden, each plant having its own. The only place where any degree of uniformity is likely occurs away from the edges of a lawn.

The average precipitation, measured at a nearby observation site, will only be a general guide to the garden rainfall. It will be similar to that experienced in the centre of an open garden, but much less near boundary walls and hedges, trees and the house itself.

A flower bed adjoining the house on its south-west side will probably receive about three quarters of the rain falling in the open; a bed on the north-east side even less, about a third or a quarter of the 'official' rain. Walls and hedges have similar, less extensive, rain-shadow effects.

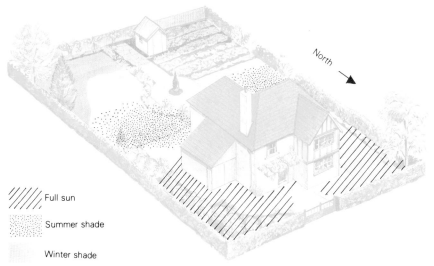

///// Full sun

Summer shade

Winter shade

Shade intensity will depend on the position of house and garden. In a north-facing site, nearly all parts of the garden will receive shade for part of the day. In addition, beds adjoining the east side of the house will be dry, those on the west side will be moist.

In summer overhanging trees prevent light rain from reaching the soil, although in heavy showers they will continue dripping water for some time after the shower has gone. The rainfall intercepted by trees either evaporates back into the air or flows slowly down the branches and trunk (the stemfall).

The house itself intercepts a great deal of rain on walls and roofs, much of which is lost down drains, unless the gardener is sensible enough to collect it in water butts.

Apart from rain-shadow, light-shadow (shade) from the rays of the sun will affect the microclimate. A shaded or semi-shaded bed will have lower soil temperatures by day, but

will probably lose less soil moisture by evaporation and transpiration.

Heat gains and losses
At night a bed in the open garden will be losing heat to almost a full hemisphere of sky, but a bed adjoining a house or hedge will emit heat to a smaller open space, with less risk of night ground frost.

The nature of the ground surface and the ground cover affect the microclimate in the critical upper soil and lower air layers.

The greatest change in garden microclimates occurs with the introduction of low plant cover, such as glass or plastic cloches and frames. A cold greenhouse is a larger version of such cover, and a heated greenhouse opens up a whole new gardening world.

Tempering the garden climate
Few people are able to select the most favourable climate in Britain for their garden. Once a new residence is chosen, it is up to the gardener to make the best of the site's possibilities.

The problem must be tackled

from the beginning, with new garden planning or alteration of the existing plan. Most important is due consideration to the effects of shelter. As this will chiefly be a permanent feature, it must be considered at the early planning stage. Answers must be found to questions such as whether existing shelter is sufficient or too much — whether a hedge should be planted or removed, or whether a wall would be a help or a hindrance.

Assess the site by listing advantages and disadvantages of shelter.

Advantages:
1. Less wind in the garden; less risk of wind damage to plants and structures, including glass cover.
2. Higher day temperatures, especially in the soil.
3. Less heat loss to frames, greenhouses and the house itself.
4. Diversion of down-slope flow of cold night air.
5. Reflection of solar radiation, especially from walls and fences.
6. In a hedge, improved habitats for beneficial predators, such as birds and insects.
7. Decoration and privacy.
8. Absorption of sound, a significant factor near busy roads.

Disadvantages:
1. Shade, depending on height and orientation.
2. Lower night temperatures.
3. Risk of frost pockets.
4. Depletion of soil moisture and nutrients by a hedge, especially if it has a long horizontal root range.
5. Harbouring of pests and over-wintering diseases.
6. Loss of space.
7. Cost of maintenance.

Screens and shelter-belts
There are three main types of shelter: the large tree shelter-belt, the living hedge, and the inanimate wall or fence. Glass or plastic cover, including greenhouses and frames, is also a form of shelter.

CLIMATE 6

Few gardens are large enough to need or to allow the space for a high-tree shelter-belt. Even so, some upland houses and gardens may be so exposed that such shelter becomes mandatory for successful gardening, and also for reducing the heat loss from the house, which increases with the square of the wind speed.

Almost all upland farmhouses have thick shelter-belts, often composed of sycamore or hawthorn trees. Valley residences may need extra protection from winds which blow up or down the valley with increased strength.

Permeable and non-permeable wind barriers

Hedges, walls and fences might be thought to have equal shelter value, with the advantage that walls and fences do not have to be trimmed several times a year and do not compete for soil moisture and nutrients. However, the choice is less simple, because the best shelter is a filter and not an abrupt halt.

There is a great deal of difference in the air flow after it has passed through the filter of a hedge or has passed over the solid obstacle of a stone wall. Downwind from a hedge, the decreased wind influence extends over a distance determined by the height of the hedge, not the strength of the wind.

Wind strength decreases to about a quarter of its original force over a distance of 10 times the hedge height; it then increases slowly and, most important of all, smoothly, until it reaches its full speed again some 30 hedge heights downwind.

A wall or solid fence cuts down the wind to almost nothing immediately in its lee, but thereafter it causes turbulence and downdraughts which reach their maximum some five to seven heights of the barrier downwind. While a wall gives good protection to plants

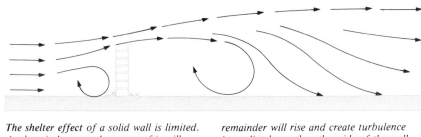

The shelter effect of a solid wall is limited. As the wind approaches, part of it will spend itself against the obstacle, but the remainder will rise and create turbulence immediately on the other side of the wall before continuing its undisturbed flow.

A thick permeable hedge filters part of the uninterrupted flow of wind and deflects the remainder. This decreases in strength over a distance equal of up to 30 times the height of the hedge before picking up speed again. The drawback is soil depletion.

Mulches are beneficial if they are correctly applied. A winter mulch may protect the roots and crowns from excessive rain and frost, but it also prevents the soil from warming up in spring. A summer mulch should always be applied to warm, damp

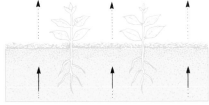

soil as a conservation medium. In open ground heat is lost from the soil by radiation and replaced by conduction. Insulated with an organic mulch, the upward flow of heat is halted while the mulch is colder than the open soil.

close to it, it can create worse conditions than before for plants a short distance away. Therefore walled gardens are always designed with a restricted width.

Stone walls may be a contribution to the landscape and a help to the garden climate in exposed areas, such as the Cotswolds and the Pennines, but in lowland districts hedges play a more favourable role in garden design.

A south-facing wall, however, has several virtues: although the adjoining bed may be on the dry side and need careful watering, the addi-

tional heat reflected by the wall is ideal for maturing fruit.

Semi-permeable or non-solid fences, even trellis, provide useful shelter, but on a lesser scale as they reduce the wind less effectively than a thick hedge. They are useful as temporary protection for young hedge plants.

Wind directions

The orientation of the hedge or fence is usually determined by the garden boundaries. The strongest winds in Britain come from the west or south-west, though in some areas north-west winds can be a serious hazard. North or east winds are always cold, but the heaviest snowfalls in southern Britain generally occur with a south-east wind which may lead to deep drifting behind a wall or hedge.

Snow does not necessarily represent a danger to plants provided that it does not break stems and branches. Most plants are more comfortable under a snow cover than exposed to hard bare frost.

An east-west hedge offers the least shade, and a north-south hedge throws long shadows at sunrise and sunset with low altitude sun.

The winter sun rises in the southeast and sets in the south-west; in summer it rises in the north-east and sets in the north-west — unless you live in the north of Scotland where it never seems to go to bed at all in midsummer and might as well not be there at all in midwinter for all the good it does to a garden.

The height and direction of a hedge, fence or wall controls the length of shadows cast and the duration of shade.

Intercropping

A degree of shelter can be provided in the vegetable garden by intercropping. Cultivation in strips of tall-growing crops, such as runner beans or Jerusalem artichokes, offer reasonable protection to lower crops on either side.

This idea can be extended to flower beds, by planting the edges with plants taller than those in the centre. The edge of the bed away from the house is a convenient site for tall plants, giving a backdrop and a modicum of shelter. The old custom of surrounding a flower bed with a low box or lavender hedge has much to recommend it.

Air drainage

For a garden on a slope, make sure that the windbreak or hedge design will not form a frost pocket. Where possible, prevent cold air from higher ground from invading the garden by ensuring that the boundary at the highest part of the garden is dense and high.

The lower boundary should be as open as possible to allow cold air to drain away. A hillside garden has less frost risk than one in a valley, but this advantage is lost if the shelter results in collecting or preventing the onward flow of cold night air.

Soil climate improvements

Much of a garden microclimate depends on the physical conditions at the soil surface. Digging loosens the soil structure and thereby incorporates a greater proportion of air space in the soil.

Air is a poor conductor of heat, so less warmth can move upwards from the lower soil layers to counteract night surface cooling. Recently dug ground will therefore have a lower night minimum surface temperature. If the surface is left rough, frost will penetrate the soil and help to break up the clods and produce a better crumb structure on heavy clay soils.

Manuring and ridging

Rotted compost or farmyard manure incorporated in the soil may have a slight adverse effect on its temperature regime. However, the beneficial effects more than balance this, in moisture-retention capacity and improved fertility.

The advantages of ridging the soil, in an east-west or a north-south direction, are controversial. In most circumstances it is doubtful if there is much to be gained by the extra effort, though in some situations ridging can improve drainage.

A south-facing bank has higher soil temperatures in spring and summer, and can be the ideal site for low glass cloches or frames.

Hoeing

Devotees of the hoe claim for it so many virtues that it might appear to be used almost as an act of devotion to the Goddess of Fertility. However, hoeing is not all unmitigated gain; principally it removes weeds which rob garden plants of soil moisture and nutrients, but the soil disturbance leads to side effects.

A disturbed soil contains more air and is therefore more liable to frost. Loosening the capped or panned soil is a plus factor for the penetration of light rain and for the gaseous exchange at soil surface. The exchange improves the soil-air supply and therefore encourages microbiological activity, one of the means of releasing nitrogen for plants. The minus factor is greater moisture loss by direct evaporation, significant if the hoeing is deep.

Mulching

This is a valuable gardening aid if done properly, at the right season. Organic mulches are efficient at restricting loss of soil moisture, but there is little to be gained by putting down the mulch after the soil has dried out.

A mulch has several other consequences. It will prevent light rainfall from reaching the soil at all, but will at the same time lessen the impact of heavy rain, and so prevent capping of the soil.

A mulch also suppresses weed growth and it keeps the soil cool, which is important in high summer, but has an adverse effect in spring, and for autumn sowing.

Never allow a mulch to remain over the ground in late winter and spring, unless you are trying to prevent frost penetration to the plant roots. The major disadvantage of a winter mulch is that though it prevents soil from freezing it may encourage low night temperatures in the air immediately above it.

CLIMATE 7

Frost protection

Cold air temperatures may be brought in winter or early spring by winds between north and south-east direction.

In late winter, the east or southeast winds can be the coldest of all, coming over a short sea track from a cold continent and bringing the sub-zero temperatures which are a feature of our most severe February weather. Under such conditions Kent can be colder than anywhere else in Britain.

Little can be done about such winter frosts, except to rely on existing shelter to mitigate the worst wind penetration; snow cover acts as insulation and can do much to stop the soil from freezing.

Most spring and autumn frosts are made locally. At night the soil receives some heat from the lower layers, but by radiation loses large amounts to the sky. A thick low cloud cover will reflect the heat and reduce the fall in temperature.

The wind also offers some frost protection. It mixes the cooling surface air with warmer air above, spreading it over a greater volume of air and thus reducing the drop of any one layer. On still nights, the cooling of surface air on a hillside will occasion a downslope flow known as a katabatic wind, the curse of the valley frosts.

The coldest garden surface on a frosty night will be in the centre of a lawn. The open soil surface will be slightly warmer, and the soil adjoining the house or close to a wall or hedge will be the least cold. Minimum temperatures above a mulch will be even colder than those over grass.

Ground frosts are more frequent than air frosts because the lowest layer of air cools first, but a white frost over the lawn and on rooftops in the early morning does not necessarily imply that plants in the garden have been damaged.

Late spring frost

The type of weather which brings late spring frosts is easier to describe than to foresee. In most cases the afternoon wind would be coming from a northerly or easterly direction; few frosts occur when the general wind direction is between west and south.

The air would be dry, with a lower than usual relative humidity — moist air cooling is more likely to produce fog which acts as a protective blanket against further rapid surface cooling. Freezing fogs are a winter phenomenon.

The wind would be light or fall to calm soon after dusk, and the skies would be clear of clouds. If all these events take place at the same time, a rapid surface cooling will follow.

Plant foliage should be either dry or supplied with water throughout the night. Constant light water sprinkling over valuable crops is a successful commercial anti-frost practice, but probably beyond the scope of most amateur gardeners.

Watering in the morning after frost is sometimes recommended. If the frost was light, and especially if the morning is sunny, watering of plants helps to warm them. It also reduces the risk of a breakdown in the water status if the leaves are receiving too little water from the roots to cope with evaporation by sunshine. *But*, if the frost has been severe enough to rupture the plant cells, no amount of watering can restore them.

Soil as heat conductor

The soil influences the frost risk, which is less on clay than on sandy soil and worst with a dried-out peaty soil. Clay is often described as a cold soil, but its smaller particles and higher water content make it a better heat conductor and a slower cooler than soils with larger air spaces.

The distance upwind from the sea is also important; the longer the land track of the air, the lower the dawn temperature will be after a frosty night.

To make the most of the upward heat conduction, the soil must be kept compact, and digging or hoeing should be avoided. It should be kept free from weeds and be as moist as possible. It is no coincidence that late frosts are more frequent and more severe in dry than in wet springs.

Glass and plastic cover

Steps taken to restrict soil heat from moving upwards to the open sky involve some kind of man-made cover. The most usual form of plant cover is a glass or plastic cloche or frame; of the two, glass is probably the most successful. Plastic has many garden uses, but some forms are ineffective at reducing outgoing longwave radiation.

For valuable plants it may well be worthwhile to supply additional heat at night. The most effective method is by undersoil heating from special electric cables. This need not be expensive, but it does involve a semi-permanent installation and should ideally be combined with glass or plastic overhead cover.

Glass admits incoming solar radiation and yet reflects back the outgoing earth radiation of heat. A translucent and thin cover also loses heat by conduction; night cooling is therefore delayed but not stopped completely.

The major effect of plant cover is to eliminate wind so that daytime heat is not lost. If the glass is clean or the plastic in good condition, it admits almost all the incoming heat and warms first the soil and then the air above. The warmer soil is available at night to offset the unavoidable heat loss.

The cover must be clean, receive the maximum sunshine by day and be subject to the least possible wind.

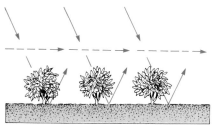

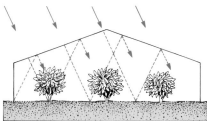

Open-ended cloches (far left) *provide some winter protection and are suitable for autumn sown crops, choice alpines and early spring bulbs. In open ground* (left) *wind cools the soil which also loses heat by radiation; glass or plastic covers keep the wind and rain out and the heat in. A young shrub* (above) *is insulated against severe winter weather with a screen of chicken wire and bracken, with a polythene cap for cold nights.*

It will not give protection against all frosts, but it can extend the growing season by two to four weeks. It will also stop rainfall to some of the soil; in the early stages this may not be important, but later in the season water must be given to soil and plants under cover when necessary.

Watering

The one part of a microclimate which the gardener can control is soil moisture. If necessary, he can install an efficient drainage system and break up lower impermeable soil layers. More importantly, he can add water to the soil, at the right time and in the right amounts.

The amount of available water depends on the moisture-holding capacity of the soil and the extent of the plant roots.

If soil moisture within range of the roots is exhausted, the plant will wilt, temporarily at first, followed by permanent wilting and possible death if the soil moisture deficit is not made up.

Input and output

Correct watering aims at keeping the soil moisture supply between the two limits of too much and too little. It is important to know how much water goes into the soil and how much goes out.

It is relatively easy to measure the input of water in the soil. A rain-gauge, or preferably two or three at various parts of the garden, will record the natural rainfall. Inexpensive plastic gauges are adequate for garden use.

Calculating the output of moisture from the soil is more difficult. Monthly averages of potential transpiration can be estimated for any garden site, but in any one year the loss in a month can be up or down by a quarter of the average, and daily variations are four times as great. Luckily the soil has natural moisture reserves which can range from 20-30mm for young and shallow-rooted plants, to four or five times this amount for mature shrubs and trees.

For practical purposes, we can assume for southern England and Wales that 25mm of water, or 20 litres per square metre, is lost in every 15 days during April and September, every 10 days in May and August, and every 7 days in June and July.

The corresponding figures for northern Scotland are probably 20, 15 and 10 days, with intermediate areas somewhere in between.

Working on this assumption, it is merely necessary to read from the raingauge how much rain falls short of the output in the appropriate period. For maximum growth, the total shortage — and no more — should be replaced; for prevention of drought, half the shortfall may be sufficient.

Water should never be given in small amounts which will only moisten the surface soil, and most of the moisture will evaporate. About 4.5 litres (1 gal.) per square metre is a sensible minimum, equivalent to about 6mm of rain.

51

THE BASIC ELEMENTS 1

Many successful gardens simply evolve, sometimes by luck and sometimes by the sure touch of an instinctive gardener. Such miracles are generally the exceptions, and most good gardens are based on initial planning. What constitutes a successful garden may be adjudged a matter of opinion, and success comes in many forms. Even so, coordinated yet varied interest is likely to be at the core of any garden for it to provide constant pleasure. Emphasis can lay in a number of qualities, including pleasing design, seasonal plant content, harmoniously introduced features or the successful exploitation of existing contours, views and other natural influences.

Before the first tentative attempts at creating a garden can be made, a thorough and detailed analysis of the site can help in avoiding costly mistakes. A number of factors will always influence a garden's potentials, factors against which it is useless to struggle. Little can be done about climatic conditions, and not much more about existing soil type even if precautions can be taken and improvements made.

Obstacles are not limited to natural elements, they also exist where man has exercised constraint. The shape and size of a garden, the lie and aspect of the land, the proximity of buildings, existing or yet to come, outside views and overhead cables are all factors which the gardener must accept and adapt to. Boundaries and manhole covers cannot be moved, and bylaws imposed by local authorities may determine the type and height of fences and walls.

Frameworks and foundations
Most gardens consist of terrace, lawn, borders and beds in a range of styles, and here and there major features such as pools, rock and scree gardens. The most satisfactory sequence of garden-making events is the construction of the terrace, followed by lawn, borders and beds after thorough cultivation.

Established gardens can sometimes be more difficult than starting with a completely open option. There may be sections or aspects to retain, others to eliminate or adapt. Without being unnecessarily destructive, some boldness is often an advantage in redeveloping an established garden.

The large garden in a rural setting, perhaps with mature, well-grown trees and shrubs within its boundaries and beyond, often appears agreeably to have come about without a great deal of studied development. Gardens of more restricted size, particularly in urban areas, need much more thoughtful handling to avoid becoming the kind of uninteresting garden which can be seen almost everywhere. Personal circumstances and a lack of interest in gardening frequently result in arbitrary treatment of the garden area, with automatic straight lines, meaningless curves, poor scale and haphazard plantings.

There may be compelling reasons for preventing the garden from realising its full potentials, such as the need for extra lawn space or more hardstanding for utility purposes. Acutely labour-saving layouts may also impose restrictions in terms of line and planting. The smaller the garden, the more important planning becomes.

The basic framework of a garden is largely formed by the association of beds, borders and other planting areas pleasingly related to main features such as mature trees, large specimen shrubs or marked peculiarities in the lie of the land.

Boundaries exert their own influence, especially where demarcated with walls or fences. A warm wall, with a south or south-western aspect, can take on enough impor-

Mature trees and tall clipped hedges are the backdrop for the famous white border created by Vita Sackville-West at Sissinghurst Castle in Kent (far left). In a smaller garden, a scaled-down version will have similar visual impact.

The tiny garden richly furnished with perennials, flowering shrubs and luxuriant wall climbers (top) is in sharp contrast to the formal parterre (below) consisting entirely of clipped bay trees and low box hedges, reminiscent of 18th-century garden design.

THE BASIC ELEMENTS 2

tance to allow it to determine the general layout. Clothed with climbers or sheltering choice shrubs and exotic bulbs of doubtful hardiness, other plantings may take second place. Boundary hedges, depending on their type, height and colour, are other influential components of a garden's framework. They will have considerable bearing on what can be effectively planted within them, by way of appearance as well as by cultural possibilities.

Terraces and steps
The best beginning to a garden is a well-scaled patio or terrace, with easy access and movement. The rest of the garden framework can be related to it in coordinated fashion.

Soft, preferably neutral colours are the most suitable for patio stonework, especially if the terrace must by necessity be on the small side. Patios are relatively expensive to install but of infinite value to the garden and the house if well designed and well constructed. In after years they will need little if any maintenance.

A shallow flight of steps built into a terrace to give easy access to a lower garden level will not make much difference in terms of constructional expense. Where considerable difference in levels exists, a retaining wall will probably be the best answer, and costs of materials and labour will rise in proportion. Steps of any significance built at other points in the garden, will also be fairly expensive.

The garden will in due course take on its own intimacy, created by selected plantings. Ideally, these should be chosen so as to span the four seasons of the year and at the same time complement each other in colour, stature and outline. It is rarely possible to complete a planting scheme from the outset, but time spent in thinking out the positions of borders, beds and focal

points is well used.

Although desirable, a perfect planting plan is hardly feasible from the beginning; unforeseen factors may crop up, and many people find their own pleasure in creating a garden in stages. A greenhouse, for example, acquired after some years, will have to be fitted into the existing layout. The place for this and other service areas, such as compost heap and bonfire, should preferably be decided upon at the planning stage so that they can be sited most conveniently and unobtrusively.

Rock and water
In the majority of cases, plants and planting areas will give a garden its final definition. On occasions they may have to take second place or be governed by such features as lakes and streams, natural or manmade. A successful garden layout should be deliberately aimed at integrating a natural water feature rather than attaching a design to it. The same mental attitude should prevail when a pool is installed; in scale it should be in proportion to the rest of the garden, and in visual terms it should appear as a natural part of the design, not an uncomfortable afterthought.

A rock garden, on its own or in association with a water feature, requires just as much careful siting before it blends into the rhythm of the layout. If a rock garden cannot be positioned and created in the early stages, it is still worthwhile to allow space for it in the design. Bear in mind that it is not essential to think in absolute terms in planning a garden's basic elements. What is important is a sense of realism with regard to the time, energy and enthusiasm which will be needed for garden upkeep. If the layout results in a garden that remains manageable as the years progress, pleasure and success will go hand in hand.

The construction of rock gardens,

concrete pools, waterfalls and the installation of fountains entails a major financial outlay. Size obviously has a bearing on the costs, but even so professional help will generally be necessary. Remember that for a rock garden to realise its full promise and give year-round pleasure, it needs a great deal of care, and this may well be the deciding factor on its size; a raised bed may be a better choice.

Beds and border
Smooth, firm curves help to produce a garden of charm and simplicity. Curving lines work well over extensive areas, but are particularly effective in releasing smaller ones from their inherent rigidity. Strictly formal gardens will be created by those with a penchant for them and who do not object to the meticulous care that the upkeep of such gardens demands.

Gardens given a smooth pattern in the first place can be developed in progressive stages, as inclination, enthusiasm and ability allow. It is always easier to add to a simple layout than trying to simplify a too complicated design. Within a lawn curve created at an early stage, the introduction of an island bed, a pool or a low-profile rock garden will appear as a natural development of the garden. However, it is important that all late features should blend in outline with nearby borders or paths so as to form an easy unity.

Positions in lawns, within border-framed curves, often make ideal places for trees and large-growing shrubs which instantly take on specimen status; leave sufficient room to allow passage between them and the adjacent border. Such focal points affirm the design framework in the immediate vicinity by bringing out the full merit of the surrounding curves. Other focal points can be sited at distant

A rock-garden pool edged with moisture-loving marginals creates the perfect illusion of a mountain landscape. The formal pool (far left) serves to emphasise the curving lines of house, borders and paths, complemented by lush mounds of hostas.

corners, including diagonals, to draw attention to outside views.

Island beds may, incidentally, help to make a virtue out of necessity: a couple of handsome trees, in an existing or prospective lawn, may make mowing difficult, but an island bed linked with the surrounding border can take in the trees, eliminate mowing and add strength to the overall design — quite apart from offering an opportunity for underplanting.

Rose beds

Rose gardens of any size involve quite heavy initial expense — and work. There is more to tending a rose garden than the obligatory annual pruning; weeding, feeding and, inevitably, spraying against pests and diseases are equally important. As a major feature, a rose garden must be considered in terms of the time and maintenance involved in caring for it. In addition, the period of non-display is comparatively long, and for those reasons an over-population of roses in otherwise bare beds in a small garden is perhaps not the wisest of ploys.

Investing in plants

Stocking a garden of any size with new plants can call for considerable expenditure even when done in phases. However, many shrubs and trees will last a lifetime; bulbs and herbaceous plants generally live for several years. In any case, propagation is often a simple matter of division to create new plants from old. Many rock garden plants survive for indefinite periods though the less robust may call for replacement from time to time.

Considering the constant interest and pleasure to be derived from permanent and semi-permanent plantings, and the character they give to a garden, the initial outlay is generally a sound investment.

Bedding plants have their place, but theirs is almost entirely a supporting role. Large bedding schemes have two disadvantages: firstly the annual expense of replacement plants for spring and summer, and secondly the relatively long wait between planting and floral display, particularly with spring bedding.

The rigid approach to bedding schemes can result in a static layout; beds devoted entirely to temporary plants often leave a garden short of its potentials and cause twice-yearly expense and cultivation of the beds, a chore which might not have been fully realised at the outset.

Tiny gardens are sometimes given over to seasonal bedding on the basis that there is room for nothing else. With the wide range of plant material, of infinite variety, stature, growth habit and capacity to succeed in inhospitable circumstances, there is no reason why permanent planting should not dominate, in containers, troughs, window boxes and as wall covering.

Kitchen gardens

Keen growers of vegetables and fruit will give preference to the site and design of a kitchen garden. The layout of the decorative garden will then depend on available space after the utility areas have been apportioned. It may always be possible to grow fan-trained fruit trees and bushes against walls and fences, and an apple tree growing in the lawn is an attractive sight, especially with an underplanting of spring bulbs.

55

WHICH KIND OF GARDEN?

From country landscapes to humble
cottage plots and diminutive town gardens,
perspective, harmony and charm
depict the ideal garden

COUNTRY GARDENS 1

The English country garden is famous throughout the world, with a long pedigree going back at least 300 years. In the 17th century gardens burst out of the protective walls of castle and monastery; they became status symbols as places for recreation and for the cultivation of an ever increasing variety of plants. In the 18th century the shackles of formality were thrown off, nature was embraced as a guide, and gardens became picturesque and romantic under the direction and influence of Lancelot ('Capability') Brown and Humphry Repton.

During the following century gardening techniques developed rapidly, in line with the great influx of new species discovered by plant explorers and the equally numerous hybrids raised by breeders at home and abroad. But the country garden, as we know it today, was chiefly influenced by the so called Arts-and-Crafts movement of the last quarter of the 19th century. Many architects, artists and designers, led by William Morris and John Ruskin, revolted against the growing mechanisation of the Industrial Revolution and re-discovered the virtues of traditional styles and craftmanship. For the next generation or more many country houses were built in what came to be known as the vernacular style, and gardens were made to suit them. This style also suited gardeners so well that, when the architecture went out of fashion, garden-making barely changed. Such alterations as were made mainly adapted the style to the wider resources of later years.

The Arts-and-Crafts movement decreed that good design must relate to local conditions, including the geology and climate, and to its landscape and traditions. These elements probably vary more widely in Britain than in any other area of comparable size, because of the great range of geological formations, the variations in climate and the diverse origin of people. It is therefore not surprising that gardens which reflect these differences will themselves be very different.

Garden architecture

It is possible to trace basic features that are common to all 19th-century country gardens though they may be present in different proportions and be applied in many original manners. Anyone purchasing a fairly large country house built in the first 30 years of this century is likely to acquire with it a garden which becomes progressively less formal in design and planting the further one moves away from the house. Around the building itself there is likely to be at least one terrace or paved area, so that the house appears firmly based on a level platform. Beyond the paved area there is almost certainly a lawn, probably quite extensive and possibly originally intended for croquet; round this there will be beds for ornamental plants. If the situation is favourable some parts of the garden may visually extend outwards, framed by trees and shrubs to allow the beauty of the surrounding countryside to be appreciated.

This broad scheme is by no means invariable. Many highly successful English country gardens are entirely enclosed and inward-looking, such vistas as they possess being confined within the garden and terminated by thick belts of trees and shrubs. If they have a particular terminal feature, this will be contrived within the garden, perhaps an elegant summerhouse, a striking statue or a specimen tree chosen for its distinctive shape or colour.

Levens Hall in Westmorland is an outstanding example of Elizabethan architecture and garden design. Landscaped in the 17th century, the gardens feature self-contained beds punctuated with topiary specimens of box, yew and holly.

COUNTRY GARDENS 2

One school of country garden-making centres round this idea of enclosure and derives more from 17th than 18th century traditions. Two of the most remarkable examples are found at Hidcote Manor near Chipping Campden in Gloucestershire, and at Sissinghurst Castle in Kent. In both almost the entire garden consists of linked enclosures, each different in shape, size and planting.

This kind of garden-making owes much of its design to architecture and its planting to interior decoration, the various garden divisions being rather like rooms without ceilings, with plants and ornaments comparable to the furnishings. In both examples are informal areas which conform to the pictorial principles of 18th century garden-making, but they are subsidiary to the enclosures and intended to contrast with them.

At Hidcote Manor there is a 'wilderness', or wild garden, in which a profusion of plants grows in a seemingly artless manner. At Sissinghurst Castle is an old orchard in which the fruit trees are no longer expected to produce useful crops, but are maintained as a link between the garden and the surrounding countryside, largely devoted to fruit growing; they also serve as natural supports for vigorous climbing roses. In spring the orchard is thickly carpeted with naturalised daffodils and, as the grass cannot be cut until midsummer, many wild flowers also grow and flower.

The same idea is used on a smaller scale and in a more consciously contrived manner in another garden, created early in the 20th century and now a favourite with the garden-visiting public. This is Great Dixter at Northiam, East Sussex, which represents the design ideas of Sir Edwin Lutyens, a leading exponent of the vernacular style of architecture, and the planting ideals of Ger-

Sissinghurst Castle. Modelled on Elizabethan design, separate enclosures radiate from a rondel of clipped yew.

Sir Edward Lutyens (1869-1944) often included ornate stonework, balustrades and narrow water rills in his designs.

trude Jekyll, the Victorian amateur painter and interior decorator. In middle life she took up garden-planning professionally, often in collaboration with Lutyens. At Great Dixter, Lutyens worked on an original half-timbered, ancient building, enlarging and adapting it to suit the needs of a fairly large and well-to-do family. Nathaniel Lloyd, who commissioned the work, thoroughly approved of Miss Jekyll's ideas about the association of plants, carefully organised so that their colours and shapes created pleasing and harmonious compositions. There is no record that Miss Jekyll prepared planting plans for Great Dixter, as she did for many other Lutyens houses, but she offered much acceptable advice.

The unique features of Great Dixter are several small wild areas, used close to the house as well as in more outlying places. The approach to the house is through a tiny rectangular meadow with fritillarias and other flowering bulbs in spring. Another area behind the house separates a small courtyard garden from a larger enclosure with massive topiary specimens of clipped yew.

Wild gardening as seen at Great Dixter has not had many followers, but another form of 'natural' design, the woodland garden, has attracted numerous devotees (see page 84). An adaptation of the woodland garden, tailored to fit effortlessly into more sophisticated surroundings, is the garden glade. This is based on a natural woodland

glade, but tidied up and provided with a rich surround of mainly exotic plants. The turf is likely to be close mown, with few if any naturalised bulbs except, perhaps, around the edge. The plants are grown in borders, and the lawn verges are often as neatly trimmed as round the main flower borders, but a few groups of silver birch may be scattered here and there to fortify the impression that the glade might well have been a natural feature.

Ornamental water has been important in many aspects of English garden-making, especially during the 18th and early 19th century landscape period when a lake of some kind in the middle distance was almost obligatory. That aspect of garden-making is rarely attemp-

ted today, partly because of the expense involved, and partly because sufficient land is seldom available to make it feasible. Instead water is used formally, as in 17th century gardens, in neat stone-edged basins, narrow rills or other largely architectural ways; alternatively it may be given a more natural effect in association with rock and bog gardens. Swimming pools have to be accommodated in many modern gardens, and if they are not entirely enclosed for privacy or sited inside buildings, they are often made the main water feature of the garden (see also page 146), and positioned in the vicinity of the house.

A different aspect relates to water in association with a rock garden as these features are meant to imitate

nature and often look awkward and contrived if sited too close to buildings. Informal water features of this kind can be planted freely, with aquatics in the water and with sub-aquatics and moisture-loving plants in shallow margins and the damp soil by pools and streams.

Terraces, paving and courtyards

A level well-paved area round the house is desirable for several reasons: it affords easy access to and from the rest of the garden and provides a sitting area during fine weather however wet the surrounding soil may be. Visually it links the house with the garden and, if the land slopes downwards, a terrace gives an appearance of solidity and overcomes the impression that the

COUNTRY GARDENS 3

house is about to slip downhill. It also provides a principal viewpoint for the garden and any attractive features outside it.

Terracing figures prominently in many country gardens, and although rising construction costs have all but eliminated former elaborate designs, a terrace need be no less effective. Good proportions and materials suited to the size and character of the house are the most important considerations. Terraces or paved areas too narrow for the size of building they adjoin or too small for leisure activities will always appear unsatisfactory. If it proves too expensive to pave the whole area, it is possible to cut costs by using gravel in some parts, or by inserting panels of grass or soil filled with neat, low-growing plants.

Local materials are nearly always preferable. It is precisely because so many old houses are constructed from local stone or brick that they blend with the countryside. The variety of local material has also contributed to variety of style, for each has its special qualities and limitations which stimulate yet impose discipline on the imagination of builder and garden-maker alike.

Unfortunately local stone or brick is now often too scarce or expensive to be practical. Many gardeners turn to concrete or artificial stone as the most readily available alternatives, and there is no reason why either should not be satisfactory if chosen and handled with discretion. There are almost as many ways of making artificial stone as there are geological formations from which to obtain the raw material. Reconstituted granite blocks, for example, can make a good substitute for quarried granite and may be the perfect building or paving material for gardens in granite regions. On the other hand, if the local rock is sandstone or limestone, artificial blocks and slabs made by grinding

Natural stone, mellowed by time, forms an imperceptible link between house and garden. Large urns emphasise the gently curving design of terrace and balustrade.

and binding these materials are more likely to be suitable.

Even concrete can be prepared and finished in many different ways. The aggregate can be made to suit local conditions and can be given greater importance by brushing the half-dry concrete so that surface cement is removed and the aggregate exposed. Various ornamental finishes can also be applied by raking or scoring, and concrete can be permanently coloured by mixing colourant with the dry materials before they are wetted and turned. However, colouring must be used with extra care in country gardens where the aim is usually a natural rather than an aggressively sophisticated effect.

Paved surfaces need not be entirely of one material, and in practice it is often preferable to mix two or three. Smooth slabs are the most pleasant to walk on in all weathers, but gravel can make a useful contrast, especially loose gritty gravel which gives a different surface texture. Cobbles set in cement look picturesque and, as they are uncomfortable to walk on, can be used to deter garden users from treading where they are not wanted.

Bricks are dangerously slippery in wet weather unless kept free of green scum and moss. However, they are highly decorative, can be obtained in several colours and laid in many patterns, including herringbone and concentric circles. All these possibilities should be considered when determining what type of paving is most appropriate to the country setting.

Steps are of great importance, visually from the way light and shade play on them and from the dominance their design and extent

can assert. Their practical purposes are self-evident. The best source of inspiration comes from the work of such masters as Sir Edwin Lutyens, who favoured elaborate ornamentation and finishes, and Percy Cane, who was more severe and restrained in style. The staircases of both often curve or turn at right angles, and the steps themselves are sometimes straight-edged, sometimes bow-fronted or concave.

Retaining walls
Terraces must be retained by walls, and these provide opportunities for architectural invention. For walls, as for paving, local stone or brick is most satisfactory. Garden walls can be built with or without mortar, the latter being known as 'dry walls'. Their principal merit, apart from the fact that they are cheaper to construct than solid stone walls, is that plants can be grown in them. This suits country gardens well, and it is not uncommon to find a dry wall one of their most attractive features,

Functional steps (opposite) can become unifying design elements between two different levels. A curving staircase flows smoothly into circular paving round an imaginatively sited pool. The stone steps effectively diminish the drop from house to lawn and visually rank second to the expanse of water. On a gentle slope, semicircular steps lead effortlessly from the sitting area to the garden beyond; the brick-built wall and floor contrast well with the wide stone steps.

especially in spring and early summer when arabis, alyssum, aubretia and dianthus are in flower.

A dry wall more than one metre high requires a good deal of skill in construction as it must be able to withstand considerable outward pressure from the soil, particularly after heavy rain and frost. Success depends partly on using blocks of adequate size, especially in the lower part of the wall, bonding them well so that each successive row grips the row immediately below, and partly in giving the whole wall a slight backward slope, or batter, so that it actually lies against the soil, holding this back with its own weight.

Most garden designers would prefer to work on a site that slopes downward from the house as this gives the greatest scope for organising and framing extensive views and for creating a feeling of spaciousness. But an upward slope may give greater prominence to terrace walls, especially if they are built dry and are well planted or used for climbing plants and trained shrubs. Whether it is better to exploit this possibility to the full, making the garden rise in a series of giant and clearly defined steps, or to soften the effect with screening plants so that only parts of the whole can be seen from any one viewpoint, is a matter of personal taste, also influenced by the character of the site and of the building.

Lawns
In country gardens lawns are often made from indigenous or wild grasses, and there is a good deal in favour of this. It saves time and money, and the grasses will certainly be of a nature to suit the soil and the climate. There will, of course, be the problem of weeds and coarse grasses, but some of these will automatically disappear after a period of close mowing, and others can be killed with selective lawn

COUNTRY GARDENS 4

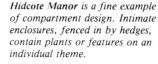

Green lawns, closely mown, weave like broad ribbons between island beds; from the house the grassy carpet appears to stretch indefinitely.

Hidcote Manor is a fine example of compartment design. Intimate enclosures, fenced in by hedges, contain plants or features on an individual theme.

weedkillers, such as 2,4-D, MCPA and mecoprop. It is worth bearing in mind that much of the mown grass in the great traditional English gardens was produced over generations solely by mowing, without the aid of herbicides or fertilisers.

However, there will be many occasions when the use of native grass is impracticable or undesirable. The alternatives are seeding or turfing, and though the latter can be excellent for a fairly small area, expense usually restricts the choice to seed for larger lawns. Broadly speaking there are two possibilities: to attempt smooth, close-mown lawns from fine-leaved grasses, such as fescues and bent grasses (*Festuca* and *Agrostis* species) or to opt for longer, slightly rougher but probably more constantly green lawns made from broad-leaved kinds, such as rye grasses and meadow grasses (*Lolium* and *Poa* species).

Often the best answer is to make a lawn of fine grasses immediately adjacent to the paved area or terrace round the house, and beyond this let any further lawns be of coarser grasses. This will have two advantages. The fine-grass lawn can be close-mown and used for games requiring a true playing surface, while the outlying lawns can be left longer for colour and texture contrast.

In spring and summer a fine-grass lawn may need to be cut three times a week, preferably with a cylinder-type lawn mower, whereas a coarser lawn will only need a once-weekly cutting, preferably with a rotary machine. An extension of the idea is to underplant the outer areas with spring-flowering bulbs, mainly daffodils which thrive well under such conditions. The grass should not be mown at all until about mid-June, when the bulb leaves will be dying down and weeds in the grass will not yet have ripened their seeds.

Hedges and topiary

In town gardens the main purpose of hedges is to demarcate the plot and keep out intruders. In country gardens, hedges are chiefly used to separate one part of the garden from another, perhaps to screen the vegetable and fruit area or to make the rose garden into a self-contained unit. Such hedges need not always be particularly strong or impenetrable, and it may be possible to grant them freedom to flower and fruit as well.

The scope for hedge selection and treatment is therefore wider in country than in town gardens. Privet no longer monopolises that function and is rarely used, its place being taken by more interesting or attractive shrubs, such as various forms of yew and holly, beech, hornbeam, cherry plum, cherry and Portugal laurels, aucubas, fuchsias, escallonias, tamarisk, shrub roses, various cypresses and thujas. For small hedges, box, lavender and rosemary are favourites.

It is necessary to consider soil and climate as well as the purpose for which the hedge is required. Hornbeam has much the same appearance as beech and can be trimmed in the same way to form a thin, yet tall and rigid hedge or screen. It is better than beech on heavy damp soil. Yew is unsurpassed for dark green colour and makes an ideal background for white or light-coloured statues, ornaments or garden furniture. There are also several golden-leaved varieties.

Holly is almost as dark as yew, grows more rapidly and is available in variegated forms, some white, others golden. Fuchsias, escallonias and rosemary are not fully hardy, but are excellent near the sea and will flower even after trimming, provided this is done at the right time. Lavender hedges are usually allowed to flower freely and can be beautiful features where the purpose of the interior hedge is to emphasise a boundary rather than to create an obstacle.

Shrub-clipping can be used for another purpose, quite unrelated to hedge formation, and may become a kind of adornment. The ancient art of training and cutting shrubs into artificial, ornamental shapes is known as topiary, and the most suitable shrubs are those that branch freely and have small leaves. Yew and box in both green and golden-leaved forms are favourites for this kind of living sculpture.

Topiary specimens often play key roles in country gardens, especially in the more formal areas round the house, in rose gardens or other places where beds or paths are arranged in a regular pattern. In these

Slopes and curves. A steeply sloping site has been transformed into a level lawn against a dramatic backdrop of grass-clad terraces; from the top, a statue by Henry Moore surveys this example of garden sculpture. In contrast, the formal lines of a curving path are softened by a loose hedge of foliage and flowering shrubs and trees.

COUNTRY GARDENS 5

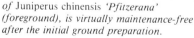

A garden glade features often in large country gardens. The mixture of evergreen and deciduous trees, above arching sprays of Juniperus chinensis *'Pfitzerana' (foreground), is virtually maintenance-free after the initial ground preparation.*

circumstances well-formed evergreen cones, balls or mushrooms can convert a flat pattern into a three dimensional composition and can also act as eye catchers to draw attention to special features. Identical shapes repeated at set intervals on each side of a straight path can increase its importance and exaggerate its length. This is the principle of the tree avenue greatly reduced in scale.

Topiary specimens can also be used to ornament hedges, a famous example being the hounds that top the dense yew hedge surrounding one of the formal gardens at Knightsbridge Court near Tiverton, Devon. Peacocks, bears or other fanciful shapes can be seen decorating many a cottage garden hedge. It is cheaper to fashion ornaments from living material than to purchase them ready-made in bronze, stone or plastic.

Deciduous and evergreen trees

Trees play three quite distinct roles in country gardens. Where the garden is exposed to gales, they may be used as windbreaks, in which case they are likely to be evergreen trees planted closely along those sides from which most damage can be expected. Secondly, trees may form a woodland or coppice shelter for other plants. For this purpose there may be a few well-scattered conifers, probably mainly pines, but most of the trees will be deciduous which do not spread many of their roots near the surface where they would dry and impoverish the soil. Silver birch is notorious in this respect, but so attractive in bark and growth that it is usually admitted in restricted numbers. Beech, elm and poplar should be avoided, but oak and alder are ideal as their roots plunge steeply, leaving the surface soil free for other vegetation.

Thirdly, choice, exotic trees are given individual attention so that they can be seen and admired in isolation. Specimen trees have long been a feature of English country gardens, and it is particularly with these that limitations are imposed by soil and climate. There are similar limitations for plants grown

Autumn colours. The brilliant Japanese maple, Acer palmatum, *is suitable for the smaller garden, unlike* Nyssa sylvatica *whose leaves turn bright scarlet in late autumn.*

Avenue planting belongs to grandiose gardens of former times. On a more realistic scale, pleached lime trees can create a leafy canopy. Wisteria and laburnum can also be used.

in borders, but here the choice of material is much wider, and if one thing fails, a dozen more will suggest themselves as replacements. The soil in a border can also be manipulated and altered to suit the plants in a way that would be impossible for a tree which in time may extend its roots over an area of up to 300 square metres.

Specimen trees must be chosen to suit the planting position as well as the decorative purpose they are intended to fulfil. For chalky soils and exposed places, the whitebeams (*Sorbus aria* and cultivars) and some of the maples (*Acer* species) are excellent. Hornbeam and beech both favour chalk, and there are fine ornamental varieties of each. The

thorns (*Crataegus*) are all good and will stand any amount of exposure, but the mulberry and the Judas tree, though liking lime, need warmth and shelter.

On acid soils, some of the birches can be considered; most have an astonishingly wide tolerance of soils as long as these are reasonably well-drained. The Spanish chestnut makes a noble tree and readily accepts acid conditions; the same is true of the false acacia (*Robinia*), the honey locust (*Gleditsia*), the sweet gum (*Liquidambar styraciflua*), the handsome, fast-growing tree of heaven (*Ailanthus altissima*), the rowan (*Sorbus aucuparia*) and all its varieties. If the situation is sheltered as well as

acid, a tree rhododendron or large magnolia might be the answer, or the scarlet-flowered embothrium or richly autumn-coloured stewartia.

For wet places alders are excellent, as well as the willows. The rare but easily-grown, large pterocarya is outstanding, with long trails of green flowers followed by winged fruit.

Specimen trees
From the outset it is necessary to determine the function of a specimen tree. Is it primarily required for foliage effect or will it be expected to produce showy flowers and, maybe, fruit? Truly spectacular flowering trees are not numerous although there is plenty

COUNTRY GARDENS 6

of variety in the *Prunus* and *Malus* families, the former including the ornamental cherries, plums, almonds and peaches, the latter the different crab apples. The dense-flowered Japanese cherries can seem a little too sophisticated for a country garden, except in the immediate vicinity of the house; another reason for keeping these close to habitation is that birds are less liable to strip the flower buds where there is movement and traffic. Also handsome in flower are the horse chestnuts, not only the well-known types of *Aesculus hippocastanum*, but also the later-flowering *A. indica*.

Coloured foliage can often be more important than flowers, and excellent colour is to be found among the maples. *Acer platanoides* 'Crimson King' has about the richest beetroot-red leaves of any tree, while *A. pseudoplatanus* 'Brilliantissimum' glows with pink and yellow in May and June; it then lapses into a rather dull green and grows so slowly that it is useless for quick results. The yellow-leaved *Gleditsia triacanthos* 'Sunburst' can be rather slow in starting, but thereafter grows well, and *Robinia pseudoacacia* 'Frisia', another yellow-leaved tree, usually grows well from the outset. For a really large, yellow-leaved specimen there is nothing to surpass the golden poplar, *Populus* x *serotina* 'Aurea'.

Gold is also to be found in plenty among the conifers, and the gold is evergreen which makes it particularly valuable. Numerous conifers are also available in narrowly columnar or conical forms which can be used to make effective focal points. Erect forms among deciduous trees can be used in a similar way; the distinctive shape of the Lombardy poplar is familiar, but it is not a good garden tree because of its thirsty, far-reaching roots, many of them just beneath the surface. Far better is the columnar form of the common

Japanese maples are equally at home in stately and suburban gardens. Their foliage is as outstanding in formal settings as in woodland areas where leaves unfold over forget-me-nots and young ferns (top).

Shrub borders and beds are invaluable in country-garden designs. They can break up a large lawn, form a boundary to the ornamental garden or draw the view to a distant apple orchard.

Winter beauty. Flowers and leaves are not the only attributes of garden-worthy trees. Many willows — Salix alba 'Chermesina' and S. daphnoides — brighten the scene with orange or violet shoots.

Specimen trees like this Cercidiphyllum japonicum *need careful siting. Sun and shelter bring out the deep golden, pink and scarlet colours of autumn, echoed in the low-growing fothergilla below.*

beech, known as the Dawyck beech, now available in purple-leaved as well as green-leaved forms, and the so-called cypress oak, an erect, or fastigiate, cultivar of the common oak. The form of maidenhair tree, *Gingko biloba*, grown in Britain is also narrowly erect, and there is a columnar form of the tulip tree.

In complete contrast to the upright trees are the weeping or pendulous varieties. The natural habit of the common silver birch is for its slender stems to droop, and this is exaggerated in such cultivars as 'Tristis' and 'Young's Weeping'. The beautiful golden weeping willow (*Salix* x *chrysocoma*) is popular, but so fast-growing that it can become a nuisance if not given ample space. It should not be confused with the common weeping willow, *S. babylonica,* which is much too coarse and large for general garden planting. Other fine examples are the weeping beeches, green and copper-leaved, the weep-

ing ash and the weeping elm. *Pyrus salicifolia* 'Pendula', the ornamental pear, is a beautiful, small weeping tree, with narrow, silvery-grey leaves; there is also a weeping form of the mulberry.

In the 17th-century garden, trees were mainly planted in avenues, and the fashion was revived in the 19th century as a means of adding dignity to the approaches to a house or the vistas from it. Straight lines become more important and appear longer when emphasised by trees of similar size and character, repeated at regular intervals. In modern times garden-makers have been more concerned with cosiness and privacy than with self-advertisement and conspicuous display; avenue planting has declined but is still a valid instrument of design, and we have excellent material which was not formerly available. Who, one may wonder, will plant a fine avenue of *Nothofagus obliqua,* a southern beech that grows much faster than

our native beech, or of the Castlewellan form of x *Cupressocyparis leylandii* which could make a 20 metre high golden avenue in a mere 20 years?

Shrubberies and specimen shrubs

Shrubs frequently form the foundation planting of mixed borders, but in large country gardens they can be used for other purposes. Many are sufficiently attractive in form and foliage to be planted as single specimens and allowed to develop their characteristics without competition. All the coloured and cut-leaved forms of the Japanese maples, *Acer palmatum* and *A. japonicum*, are ideal for planting in this way though they dislike alkaline soils. Others that can stand on their own are the various forms of cotinus, some cotoneasters and viburnums, particularly *Viburnum plicatum* var. *tomentosum,* and evergreens such as *Pieris japonica* and several bushy conifers.

COUNTRY GARDENS 7

Informal borders of low, dense and evergreen shrubs can, in secluded settings, follow the boundary lines; they need a minimum of pruning or trimming.

The shrubbery, or wilderness, once the principal home for all garden shrubs, has lost much of its popularity, but is not without its uses. In the form of island beds, separated by winding grass paths, shrubs can be used to break up large spaces, suggesting a maze and exaggerating the size of the actual area they occupy.

Shrubs, on their own or in collaboration with trees, can be used to shape and enclose vistas. Since many naturally grow in woodlands and forests, they can also be used as cover under trees, particularly in woodland gardens (page 84).

Like trees, shrubs vary enormously in their hardiness, their tolerance of wind, hot sun or shade, and in preference for soils of a particular character. Also like trees they can be divided into groups with particular

A semi-wild shrub border of low azaleas is lifted to the vertical as the eye travels from the blaze of spring colour to fastigiate and purple-leaved Japanese cherries.*

Mixed borders of shrubs and perennials have today replaced herbaceous borders. Silver and grey-leaved shrubs contrast well amid all-green foliage.

decorative functions. Evergreens remain with little change throughout the year, except when they are in flower or fruit. They can be used with other shrubs to mould the shape of the garden, and in autumn when the leaves fall from the deciduous kinds, the evergreens emerge from the ruck to create new forms and patterns of their own.

The British Isles is pitifully short of truly native evergreens, and when new types began to arrive from abroad, they were seized on eagerly and often planted to excess. Treated in this way evergreens tend to lose their individuality and become boring. It is the happy mixture of evergreen and deciduous kinds that produces the most exciting results and can create gardens that are in constantly changing moods from January to December.

Very few shrubs have an extended flowering season, and some of the most spectacular in flower are among the dullest in leaf or habit. It is therefore unwise to select shrubs solely on the merit of their flowers, and it is probably best to choose first those that are admirable in foliage or form, before adding sufficient good flowering or fruit-bearing shrubs.

Shrubs with coloured leaves, evergreen or deciduous, can be enormously valuable in keeping the garden cheerful. There are golden-leaved varieties, greys, silvers, creamy-whites, the variegations usually appearing as central splashes or marginal colouring, purples, coppers and bronzes. There are shrubs which grow upright, and others that branch horizontally, spray out gracefully like fountains or sprawl along the ground. There are types with large leaves, and others with very small foliage, some with leaves composed of numerous separate leaflets, arranged along a central stalk like a feather, called pinnate, or radiating from a common point like fingers, and called palmate.

There are also a few shrubs with stiff, sword-like leaves like the rosette-forming, spine-tipped yuccas and the shuttlecock phormiums. These are so alien to our own flora that they create an unmistakably exotic atmosphere in the garden. In the right setting they can be highly effective, but badly placed they become a disaster. Bear in mind that our rather soft climate has produced a native vegetation correspondingly soft in outline. Spiky plants tend to come from hotter, more arid places, and in gardens they should be used in settings intended to create some such illusion. This is why they can seem right in a sunny seaside garden, or on a terrace beside a swimming pool, but will appear out of character in settings that are intended to look natural.

Climbers and wall shrubs

It is in scale rather than in manner that the use of climbers in country gardens differs from that in town gardens. In both, climbers perform functions comparable to those of drapes in interior decoration. They can be spread over walls, wrapped around pillars or tripods and used to convert open pergolas into covered walks. This can be done more lavishly in the country so that climbers that are too rampant to be comfortable companions in town gardens may be welcome in the country garden.

Very vigorous roses, such as 'Kiftsgate' and *Rosa longicuspis,* may be sent scrambling into tall trees; the climbing hydrangea can be used to clothe tall tree trunks, and *Clematis montana* can be permitted to grow and flower with the vigour of which it is capable when there is no necessity to curb it.

In small gardens it would be foolish to admit *Vitis coignetiae* or *Actinidia chinensis*, both of which could reach a height of 9 or 10 metres in a couple of years, covering themselves and everything else with large heart-shaped leaves. The vitis, really a Chinese vine, colours vividly in autumn, and actinidia clothes its twining stems with dense, plush-crimson hairs.

A pergola must be a rather puny affair in a town garden if there is room for it at all. In a country garden it can become a major feature, used much as a cloister might have been, with stone or brick piers to match the masonry of the house, and ample beams to carry with ease the weight of climbers growing over them. However, climbers need not be thought of as always ascending. The natural habit of many is to sprawl on the ground or scramble into scrub. Rambler roses are of this kind and make excellent ground cover, especially for sunny banks. In shady places ivies

COUNTRY GARDENS 8

Wall shrubs are of various kinds. Some, like wisterias, need walls as supports for their twining stems. Others, such as the evergreen, blue-flowered ceanothus and violet-purple abutilons are half-hardy and need the shelter of sunny walls.

make good ground cover, though they must be watched as they will climb up and attach themselves to any solid support that they meet.

Walls can be reserved for the more tender climbers, such as aristolochia, campsis and passiflora, and they are also useful for those hardy shrubs, such as pyracantha, ceanothus and chaenomeles (Japanese quince) which do not actually climb, but can readily be pruned and trained to cover walls.

True climbers support themselves in various ways. Some, such as the ivies and some of the Virginia creepers (*Parthenocissus*), produce aerial roots or little adhesive pads which cling to any firm surface. Others, such as the honeysuckles and wisterias, are twiners which need fairly robust supports to lash around, and yet others, clematis and vines among them, hold on with coiling tendrils. In the wild these twist round twigs or small stems, but in gardens tendril climbers are often grown on trelliswork or strained wires. However, there is no reason why the natural system should not be considered: clematis, for example, can be grown on columnar conifers used as supports or lying on close carpets of heather.

Roses, brambles and other well-armed plants use their thorns to hang on once they have pushed their sturdy stems upwards through the branches of shrubs or trees. In small gardens the stems must be tied to suitable supports, but in country gardens the more informal and natural approach may be possible and can save both time and labour.

Rose gardens

Roses have been first and firm favourites with both town and country gardeners ever since, late in Queen Victoria's reign, some of the finest flowered of them were induced to keep on flowering more or less continuously from June to October.

It could be said that roses thrive better in town than in country gardens; in the latter the air is so clean that it does nothing to deter the mildew and black spot diseases that can sometimes ravage them. However, careful selection and regular spraying can level the score, for there are many roses naturally resistant to disease, and there are improved systemic fungicides, such

Rose gardens in traditional designs feature prominently in country gardens. Some of the finest are found in Scotland; at

Tyninghame near Dunbar, a free-standing arbour swathed with heavily scented roses frames a romantic Victorian gazebo.

Polesden Lacey near Dorking, owned by the National Trust, is renowned for its roses. Pergolas span flagstones and lavender paths.

as benomyl and triforine, that can keep rose diseases at bay for weeks at a time.

Country gardens do have one outstanding advantage. They are usually large enough to enable roses to be grown in a variety of ways: shrubby kinds as individual specimens, as informal hedges or as partners in mixed borders; bedding varieties in beds, or possibly in gardens devoted to them. Some of the most vigorous climbers, such as the magnificent *Rosa longicuspis* and the even more rampant *R. filipes* 'Kiftsgate', will scramble to the top of quite tall trees, from where they cascade in swathes of richly scented flowers.

The rose garden proper is one of the most traditional country-garden features, rarely differing greatly in conception though there may be variation in extent and in detail. It is nearly always regular and balanced, probably centering round a sundial,

ornament or water basin. There will be numerous beds, all neatly shaped and clean-edged and each probably occupied by one variety of rose only. These will be the free-flowering bedding types, either Hybrid Teas, now called Large-flowered, or Floribundas, now called Cluster-flowered. Both types are bred to be of short or medium height, carrying nearly all their flowers on top. When numerous roses of the same variety are planted 45-60cm apart, they make, at the peaks of their flowering periods, sheets of colour. The cluster-flowered roses are even better at this than the large-flowered varieties, but the latter score in shapeliness as well as in greater flower size and remain the favourite type despite much competition.

Quite likely the beds will be surrounded by rose-covered pillars or a rustic screen of climbing roses. Some gardeners may prefer an informal hedge of shrub roses or wild

species, or there may be room for borders of old-fashioned roses. The old Damask, Cabbage, Gallica, Moss, Alba and China roses are back in fashion after generations of neglect. They are better suited to country than town gardens as most require ample space, and few flower for more than two or three weeks each summer, after which they are not particularly attractive. In a large garden, colour and interest are not necessary everywhere all the time – indeed if it were possible it would become overpowering and a bore.

Much argument and discussion takes place on the question of whether rose gardens should have other companions. As far as bedding roses are concerned they are probably best on their own; planted closely to create a solid display, there will be no room for anything else. In addition such beds need considerable attention; detailed pruning in February or March, mulching

COUNTRY GARDENS 9

and feeding in spring, spraying from mid-April until September, deadheading for much of the summer, and removal of suckers whenever they appear. Such activities do not give companion plants much chance. However, it is possible to edge the beds neatly with box or lavender or to grow early pansies and pinks which associate with bedding roses better than most.

Flower borders

The two things that most impress overseas visitors to British gardens are our lawns and our flower borders. Climate has played a large part in the success of both, for in Britain there is an absence of those extremes of heat and cold and long periods of drought which so greatly restrict the growth of grass and the selection of plants.

True herbaceous borders are more often written or spoken about than seen. They were largely the product of a movement led a century ago by William Robinson who was keenly interested in the herbaceous flora of the Northern Hemisphere and liked the idea of devoting some sections of the garden entirely to it. However, at precisely the time that Robinson was promoting the herbaceous border, an equally influential Victorian-Edwardian gardener, Gertrude Jekyll, was making and writing about borders of a far more traditional English kind. These were mixed borders of herbaceous perennials, shrubs, roses, bedding plants and annuals in which each item was chosen not for its botanical character, but for its contribution to a carefully orchestrated whole.

Miss Jekyll delighted in the cottage gardens of Surrey, where she lived, and undoubtedly gained some of her inspiration from them. While the typical cottage garden is a more or less haphazard assemblage of plants which happen to be available

and is effective because of its very artlessness, every plant in Miss Jekyll's carefully planned borders was chosen with a purpose and discarded if it failed to fulfil it .

It was the mixed border that won the affection of most British gardeners, and today it has become the floral mainstay of almost every country garden. Typically it surrounds or flanks the lawn where it can be seen from many of the principal rooms of the house and can be studied in detail. The essence of such borders is that they give great pleasure, in whole and in part.

A well-planned mixed border will have a carefully considered colour scheme. It will also contain well-chosen and strategically placed foliage plants to set off the flowers to perfection when they are there and to maintain the beauty of the border when the flowers have faded. Some plants will be chosen solely for the display they make as group plantings, while others are fascinating as individuals. This is why, time and again, one is drawn to a mixed border to study the detail, discover unfamiliar plants or renew acquaintances with old friends.

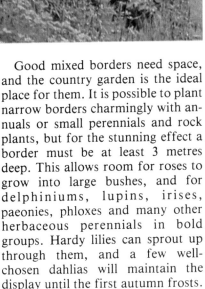

Herbaceous borders on the grand scale are impressive in early summer. Often the backdrop is a massed display of blue or white delphiniums whose towering spires provide a good foil for golden heliopsis and lilac-pink 'Claridge Druce' geraniums.

Mixed shrub borders in late summer glow with the warm orange-brown colours of rudbeckias and floribunda roses. The colour impact is muted with airy panicles of golden-yellow solidagos and loose spikes of Salvia x superba.

Good mixed borders need space, and the country garden is the ideal place for them. It is possible to plant narrow borders charmingly with annuals or small perennials and rock plants, but for the stunning effect a border must be at least 3 metres deep. This allows room for roses to grow into large bushes, and for delphiniums, lupins, irises, paeonies, phloxes and many other herbaceous perennials in bold groups. Hardy lilies can sprout up through them, and a few well-chosen dahlias will maintain the display until the first autumn frosts.

There will be some shrubs, too, probably sweet-scented viburnums and gay forsythias for the spring, with early spiraeas to be followed by deutzias, philadelphus, potentillas and weigelas, and hypericums, berberis and cotoneasters for berries in autumn. There will certainly be grey and silver-leaved shrubs as a foil to all the colour.

At the back of the border there will most likely be pillars or tripods for climbing roses and clematis, possibly with sweet peas scrambling lightly over them. Annuals will be sown each spring to fill any gaps

that have been left for them or that have occurred through winter losses. Bedding plants, such as begonias, heliotropes, marguerites and pelargoniums, all valuable for their long flowering season, also have a role to play. It is the ideal manner of flower-growing, for it imposes no rules or limitations on fancy or favour other than those dictated by personal taste.

Herbaceous borders must be remade every third or fourth year because by then many of the plants will be growing too large and threatening to exhaust themselves.

COUNTRY GARDENS 10

In order to restore their vigour, they must be lifted and divided, and the border itself should be dug over and manured. In mixed borders only certain plants need to be treated in this way, and rarely all at one time. The work of renewal is therefore more or less constant, but it makes little impact on the appearance of the planting and imposes no sudden strain on the gardener's time.

Rock gardens and dry walls

Rock gardens and water are often complementary features, the rock garden backing or partly encircling a pool into which a stream may cascade over the rocks. Such features were very common in gardens made during the first half of this century, but have become less popular as mounting costs of construction and labour made rock gardens expensive to build and maintain. With existing rock gardens it can be maintenance that proves the greatest obstacle to their retention, for in the complex pockets and crevices of a rock garden there are few opportunities for labour-saving shortcuts. Hoeing, forking and applications of herbicides are difficult, and most weeds must be removed by hand.

Once a rock garden becomes badly infested with deep-rooted or stoloniferous weeds, which wend their way between and under the rocks, there is usually nothing for it but to pull the whole construction to pieces and rebuild after thorough cleaning of the soil. Alternatively, remove all valuable plants and give a blanket treatment with a powerful herbicide, such as paraquat or glyphosate. Two or three treatments at intervals of a month may be required before all the weeds are destroyed, and only then will it be safe to replant the rock garden.

Nevertheless a well-made rock garden can be an extremely picturesque feature. Some of the finest rock

Rough quarry stones extend from a house terrace to form a natural rock garden planted with red helianthemums, hummocks of white saxifrages and clumps of ornamental grasses. A covering of chippings simulate alpine conditions.

gardens were constructed in the years between the two World Wars, and some remain in good condition, while others are derelict or have been completely destroyed. It would be sad if they all disappeared, and owners with rock gardens of fine quality should be encouraged to maintain them wherever possible.

One way of preserving a rock garden is to alter the character of the planting by replacing most herbaceous plants, especially those that creep or trail widely, with small shrubs. With these it is easier to get at weeds with herbicides applied through sprinkler-bars or small sprays directly on to the weeds growing beneath the branches.

When new rock gardens are made in country surroundings, they are usually simpler in construction. Local stone, if available, should be used and, as already explained, this is aesthetically as well as economically advantageous. It is also probable that large blocks will be used to create a few bold but simple outcrops, set in cultivated soil with no awkward fingers of turf

Drystone walls come alive in late spring with cascading sheets of pure white Iberis sempervirens, *golden* Alyssum saxatile, *rich reddish-purple aubrietas and bright yellow, trailing cytisus.*

Rock terraces wind from a steep slope to a lower lawn level skirting a deep pool of water lilies. *A carpet of white* Cerastium tomentosum *spreads beneath a deep blue ceanothus.*

running into the rock work and requiring to be cut with shears. The planting, too, will be kept simple, with shrubby plants predominating.

There are excellent examples of this kind of rock garden in the Northern Horticultural Society's demonstration garden at Harlow Car, Harrogate. At the Scottish National Trust's training college at Threave, Castle Douglas, there are also good examples of scree gardening, another practical way of introducing an element of mountain scenery to the garden.

Rock gardens have rarely been the most satisfactory homes for true alpine plants, many of which are small, easily overrun and quickly devoured by slugs, snails or mice. Far better are unmortared terrace walls and raised beds retained by similar dry walls. Many alpine plants survive in the vertical or nearly vertical faces of these walls, finding in them the quick drainage they

need round their collars, combined with an ample supply of food and moisture in the large volume of soil behind the walls.

With raised beds it is possible to empty and refill a whole bed comparatively easily, and if this is done every six or seven years there will be little likelihood of perennial weeds becoming firmly established. Raised beds can often be used as divisions between one part of the garden and another or as interesting decoration on terraces or paved areas around the house. In such situations raised beds, because of their obvious artificiality, look right while supposedly 'natural' rock gardens often appear out of place.

Water features

Water can add many qualities to a garden: movement, sound, reflections, sparkle and the possibility of cultivating a whole range of aquatic and sub-aquatic plants that would

not otherwise be possible. The traditional English landscape garden, from which the country garden is in part descended, nearly always made use of still or slow-moving water in the middle distance, and in this context it was always the mirror element, the sheet of silver presented to the sky, that was paramount.

In modern gardens, with their greater emphasis on interesting and varied planting, water will usually be more densely surrounded and often partially covered with plants, water lilies prominent among them; reflections will be a bonus rather than the main objective.

The strongly romantic bias of many country gardens may also find expression in a stream, for the most part flowing slowly so that plants can grow beside it without risk of being washed away, yet also in places cascading to create the splash and spume of water in rapid motion. Sometimes great ingenuity is

COUNTRY GARDENS 11

shown in tapping springs or diverting brooks so that natural water is made available for these purposes, but when this is impossible similar effects may be produced by recycling water from a pool with the aid of an electrically operated, submerged pump.

In large country gardens both stream and pool should ideally appear to be natural features adapted to garden requirements, but more formal alternatives may in some circumstances prove desirable. Many architect-designed gardens have canals in place of streams, and formal basins instead of casual pools. Sir Edwin Lutyens was particularly fond of what he called a rill, a canal reduced to a mere 30cm or less in width, broken along its length by 'tanks' which were rectangular water basins, large enough to contain clumps of water irises, small rushes, reed maces and other shallow water plants. Such rills and tanks could be used appropriately in the elaborate terraces with which Lutyens often surrounded his buildings. Notable examples have been restored at Hestercombe near Taunton, a famous Lutyens-Jekyll garden now owned by the Somerset (Avon) County Council.

In modern gardens obviously artificial water is usually required for recreational purposes, and the swimming pool has become a desirable amenity as well as a status symbol. Because the water must be kept limpidly clear and clean, and because the surround must be firm and smooth so that bare feet are not bruised, swimming pools can be awkward features to assimilate in a unified garden design. Two most favoured solutions are to conceal the pool within an enclosure of its own, which may contain or be partly screened by a changing room or loggia, or to site the pool near the house where it can be associated with other architectural features.

Marginals (top) *such as mimulus and primulas thrive in boggy ground and light shade at the edge of pools. Other marginal acquatics, such as water irises,* Calla palustris, *the spreading reedmace and marsh marigolds do better in full sun.*

Bog bean (Menyanthes trifoliata) *is a rare occupant in pools. Strangely so, for its versatile growth habit allows it to proliferate in water, scramble over pool edges and root in moist ground. The creeping stems bear white flower spikes.*

Occasionally one encounters a swimming pool that flouts all conventions and is considered primarily as part of the garden design. One of the most successful is the huge, circular pool, retained by rough hewn sandstone blocks, which Sir Winston Churchill built for himself on the valley side at Chartwell. Another is the much smaller stone basin which almost fills one of the rectangular enclosures in the intricate garden made in the early years of this century at Hidcote Manor, Gloucestershire.

Vegetable and fruit gardens

In country gardens it is usually possible to set aside one part for fruit and vegetables, and if the garden is an old one it is quite likely that the whole area will be walled. The enclosed kitchen garden was one of the glories of 18th and 19th century garden-making and often had its own staff controlled by a professional foreman. The walls would be used mainly for fruit trees: Morello cherries, currants and maybe blackberries on those facing north; apricots, peaches and nectarines on those facing south; pears, plums and the choicest apples on the others. Some of the sunny walls would be further protected with glazed fruit cases or lean-to greenhouses at least one of which would be sufficiently lofty and wide to accommodate grape vines of the dessert varieties.

Many such gardens have now passed into public ownership, but where they do remain under private control they can present their owners with serious problems. Skilled staff is rarely available today to maintain such gardens, and it is hopeless to attempt to run a large walled kitchen garden with inadequate labour. Some owners have been tempted to solve the problem by becoming commercial, but unless there are special circumstances

Walled kitchen gardens on a large scale are uncommon. Apple and pear cordons are trained against the walls, with early vegetables ripening under tall cloches.

which guarantee a market for the fruit and vegetable crops this can be a disappointing experience.

The commercial markets are dominated by large-scale producers and have little time for small operators. To the already considerable difficulties of producing crops of adequate quality are added those of packing and marketing them satisfactorily. A few enthusiastic amateurs succeed and find this a fascinating and modestly profitable addition to their hobby. Far more fail and soon search for other methods of using large walled kitchen gardens.

The most satisfactory solution is to plan most of it ornamentally, to create a lawn and flower beds, maybe primarily for roses, and to use the walls for climbing plants and

shrubs that will benefit from the protection. No more fruit and vegetables need be grown than are necessary to meet the requirements of the household, and the greenhouses or fruit cases can be pulled down or operated without heat for plants, such as camellias and the more tender rhododendrons, which can be grown quite satisfactorily in this way.

A vinery might be retained for its original purpose, but confined to comparatively hardy varieties such as 'Black Hamburgh' or 'Buckland Sweetwater', or used for peaches and nectarines which do not monopolise a greenhouse quite as much as vines. This also leaves it free for raising early seedlings, growing pot plants and protecting semi-tender plants in winter.

COUNTRY GARDENS 12

Mellow walls surround a former kitchen garden, now a mixture of food and ornamental plants. A pink, scented 'Albertine' rose clothes the wall, and Iceland poppies separate rows of vegetables.

If no such problems exist, the country vegetable and fruit garden can be integrated with the ornamental garden in a balanced manner. As there will be periods each year when it will almost certainly look dishevelled, it may well be decided to screen it, at least in part, with hedges or fruit trees trained on espaliers, a satisfactory method of combining profitability with amenity.

An old practice, somewhat out of fashion now, but with much to commend it, is to have at least one path running through the kitchen garden, flanked by trained fruit trees and flower borders and with an open vista throughout its length. Flower

By Tudor times, herb gardens were planted as much for scent as for culinary purposes.

Then as now, sweetly fragrant roses, santolinas and Alchemilla mollis *were favourites.*

Trimmed box hedges in a geometric pattern separate beds of aromatic herbs. In the centre is a huge terracotta urn.

Potager beds in the French manner confine vegetables to neat beds. One plot is surrounded by strawberry plants.

and fruit trees will adequately screen the vegetables, and vistas along the central path will be wholly decorative. This method is still much practised in Scotland where garden fashions change more slowly and good ideas, though old, are not readily discarded.

Yet another alternative has an even more ancient pedigree dating back to Stuart times. This is to divide the vegetable plot into a number of separate beds arranged in a regular pattern which can be emphasised by trim hedgings of box, lavender, thyme or hyssop.

Vegetables are grown in orderly rows within the beds, one perhaps devoted entirely to salads, another to brassicas, a third to onions, shallots and leeks. This makes annual crop rotation both easy and obvious, and the pattern of beds

preserves a feeling of good order even when crops are being harvested with the inevitable disorder.

The French have generally managed these matters better, and the French potager is justly renowned for its excellent design and good appearance. Herbs mingle with vegetables and are frequently grown at the edges of beds where they can be readily gathered fresh as required; trained fruit trees enclose the garden or divide it into sections.

When fruit and vegetables are associated there must be a clear demarcation line between them. Most vegetables are annual crops, sown or planted, grown for a few months and then harvested and cleared away after which the ground they have occupied must usually be deeply cultivated. Fruits by contrast, are permanent occupants of

the site, and they fill the soil for some distance with their roots, many of them just below the surface. Deep cultivation close to them can do much harm. The surface must be kept free of weeds by hoeing, hand weeding or appropriate herbicides, not by forking.

This applies as much to old walled kitchen gardens as to more open modern vegetable plots, and one of the most common mistakes made with the former is to dig the borders at the foot of the walls each winter. This destroys most of the feeding roots of the fruit trees, and as a result they grow badly and crop hardly at all. Soil for at least 2 metres around or in front of fruit trees should be surface cultivated only, with mulching used to maintain fertility, porosity and a good clean appearance.

COUNTRY GARDENS 13

PLANTS FOR COUNTRY GARDENS

§ = evergreen † = deciduous

TREES AND SHRUBS FOR ACID SOILS

Trees

Ailanthus altissima †
Gingko biloba †
Halesia †
Liquidambar styraciflua †
Liriodendron tulipifera †
Magnolia †§ (*M.x soulangiana* (†) and *M. grandiflora* (§) tolerate some lime)
Nothofagus †
Nyssa sylvatica †
Quercus coccinea †
Q. palustris †
Q. rubra †
Stewartia †
Styrax †
Tsuga heterophylla §

Shrubs

Azalea † §
Calluna vulgaris §
Camellia §
Crinodendron §
Desfontainea spinosa §
Erica § (*E. carnea, E. x darleyensis, E. purpurascens* (*E. mediterranea*) and *E. terminalis* are lime-tolerant)
Eucryphia §†
Fothergilla major †
Gaultheria §
Hamamelis †
Kalmia angustifolia §
K. latifolia §
Leptospermum §
Leucothoe fontanesiana §
Magnolia stellata †
Pernettya mucronata §
Pieris §
Rhododendron §
Skimmia reevesiana §
Ulex europaeus †
Vaccinium † §
Zenobia pulverulenta †

TREES AND SHRUBS FOR ALKALINE SOILS

Trees

Acer campestre †
Aesculus hippocastanum †
Carpinus betulus †
Cedrus atlantica §
Chamaecyparis lawsoniana §
Crataegus laviegata †

C. monogyna †
Fagus sylvatica †
Fraxinus excelsior †
Juniperus §
Picea omorika §
Pinus nigra §
Pyrus salicifolia †
Sorbus aria †
Taxus baccata §
Thuja occidentalis §
T. plicata §
Tilia †

Shrubs

Abelia †
Berberis † §
Buddleia †
Buxus sempervirens §
Cotoneaster † §
Deutzia †
Euonymus † §
Forsythia †
Hibiscus syriacus †
Hypericum † §
Juniperus §
Ligustrum § †
Lonicera † §
Philadelphus †
Prunus laurocerasus §
Rhamnus †
Ribes †
Spiraea †
Syringa †
Taxus baccata §
Yucca §

HERBACEOUS PLANTS FOR ALKALINE AND NEUTRAL SOILS

On acid soils, below pH 5.5, add hydrated lime or ground chalk at 1 kg to 5 square metres before planting and repeat every three years.

Achillea
Allium
Alyssum saxatile
Anemone
Arabis
Aster
Aubrieta
Campanula
Centaurea
Centranthus
Chrysanthemum maximum
Convallaria
Coreopsis
Crocus

Delphinium
Dianthus
Doronicum
Eremurus
Erysimum
Filipendula vulgaris
Gaillardia
Geranium
Geum
Helenium
Helianthemum
Helleborus
Hyacinthus
Iberis
Iris
Narcissus
Paeonia
Papaver
Penstemon
Phlox
Polygonatum
Polygonum
Potentilla
Pyrethrum
Rudbeckia
Salvia x *superba*
Sanguisorba
Scabiosa
Sedum
Sidalcea
Solidago
Stachys olympica (S. lanata)
Thalictrum
Tulipa
Verbascum
Viola

PLANTS FOR WET SOILS

Trees

Alnus †
Metasequoia glyptostroboides †
Populus †
Quercus palustris †
Salix †
Taxodium †

Shrubs

Arundinaria §
Bambusa §
Cornus alba and cultivars †
C. stolonifera and cultivars †
Phyllostachys §
Salix †
Sambucus †
Sorbaria †

Herbaceous perennials

Aruncus dioicus
Arundo donax
Astilbe
Caltha palustris
C. polypetala
Filipendula palmata
F. purpurea
F. rubra
F. ulmaria
Gunnera manicata
G. tinctoria
Iris kaempferi
I. laevigata
I. ochroleuca
I. pseudacorus
I. spuria
Ligularia
Lysimachia
Miscanthus
Peltiphyllum peltatum
Polygonum campanulatum
P. cuspidatum
Primula beesiana
P. bulleyana
P. denticulata
P. florindae
P. helodoxa
P. 'Inverewe'
P. 'Insriach'
P. japonica
P. pulverulenta
P. sikkimensis
Rheum palmatum
Rodgersia
Trollius
Typha
Veratrum album
V. viride
Zantedeschia aethiopica

SHRUBS FOR SHADY SITES

Azalea † §
Aucuba japonica §
Buxus sempervirens §
Camellia §
Elaeagnus † §
Euonymus fortunei §
E. japonicus §
Hypericum calycinum §
Ilex §
Mahonia aquifolium §
M. repens §
Phillyrea §
Prunus laurocerasus §
P. lusitanicus §
Rhododendron §

es alpinum †
us † §
cococca §
nmia §
phoricarpos †
urnum davidii §
ca §

**LDEN OR VARIEGATED
EES AND SHRUBS**
es
r japonicum 'Aureum' †
negundo 'Auratum' †
seudo-platanus
Brilliantissimum' †
o. 'Leopoldii' †
alpa bignonioides
Aurea' †
maecyparis lawsoniana
Lanei' §
l. 'Lutea' §
l. 'Stewartii' §
l. 'Winston Churchill' §
nus controversa
Variegata' †
ressus macrocarpa
Donard Gold' §
n. 'Goldcrest' §
n. 'Lutea' §
ditsia triacanthos
Sunburst' †
x altaclarensis 'Golden
ing' §
quifolium
Argenteomarginata' §
. 'Madame Briot' §
odendron tulipifera
Aureomarginatum' †
ulus x candicans
Aurora' †
Serotina Aurea' †
inia pseudoacacia
Frisia' †
ja plicata 'Zebrina' §
us glabra 'Lutescens' †

ubs
lia elata 'Variegata' †
uba japonica
Crotonifolia' §
beris thunbergii 'Aurea' †
ldleia davidii 'Harlequin' †
us sempervirens 'Aureo
endula' §
. 'Elegantissima' §
maecyparis pisifera
urea' §
o. 'Filifera Aurea' §
nus alba 'Elegantissima' †
. 'Spaethii' †
lternifolia 'Argentea' †

Elaeagnus pungens
  'Maculata' §
Euonymus fortunei 'Silver
  Queen' §
E. japonicus 'Aureopicta' §
Fuchsia magellanica
  'Variegata' †
F. m. 'Versicolor' †
Griselinia littoralis
  'Variegata' §
Hebe x andersonii
  'Variegata' §
H. x franciscana 'Variegata' §
Hypericum x moserianum
  'Tricolor' †
Ligustrum ovalifolium
  'Aureum' § †
Lonicera nitida 'Baggeson's
  Gold' §
Philadelphus coronarius
  'Aureus' †
Phormium tenax
  'Variegatum' §
Pieris japonica 'Variegata' §
Pittosporum tenuifolium
  'Silver Queen' §
Prunus lusitanica 'Variegata' §
Ribes sanguineum
  'Brocklebankii' †
Sambucus nigra 'Aurea' †
S. racemosa 'Plumosa
  Aurea' †
Viburnum tinus
  'Variegatum' §
Vinca major 'Variegata' §
V. minor 'Variegata' †
Weigela florida 'Variegata' †

**AUTUMN COLOUR:
TREES AND SHRUBS (all †)**
Trees
Acer japonicum
A. nikoense
A. palmatum
A. platanoides
A. saccharinum
Amelanchier
Cercidiphyllum japonicum
Crataegus x prunifolia
Liquidambar styraciflua
Metasequoia glyp-
  tostroboides
Nyssa
Parrotia persica
Prunus sargentii
Quercus coccinea
Q. palustris
Q. rubra
Sorbus discolor
S. 'Joseph Rock'
S. sargentiana

Stewartia pseudocamellia
Taxodium distichum
Ulmus procera

Shrubs
Aronia
Azalea (Ghent Hybrids)
Berberis thunbergii
Callicarpa
Cotinus
Disanthus cercidifolius
Enkianthus campanulatus
Euonymus alatus
Fothergilla major
Hydrangea quercifolia
Rhododendron luteum
Rhus
Rosa nitida
R. virginiana
Sorbaria aitchisonii
Viburnum opulus

**FRUIT AND BERRY
SHRUBS**
Berberis †
Callicarpa †
Cotoneaster † §
Euonymus latifolius †
E. hamiltonianus yedoensis †
Hippophae rhamnoides †
Ilex §
Leycesteria formosa †
Pernettya mucronata §
Pyracantha §
Rosa moyesii †
R. setipoda †
R. villosa †
Ruscus aculeatus §
Sambucus †
Skimmia japonica §
S. reevesiana §
Stransvaesia davidiana §
Symphoricarpos albus
  laevigatus †
S. orbiculatus †
Viburnum betulifolium †
V. opulus †

**COLUMNAR OR NAR-
ROWLY CONICAL TREES**
Calocedrus decurrens §
Carpinus betulus 'Fastigiata' †
Chamaecyparis lawsoniana
  'Allumii' §
C.l. 'Columnaris' §
C.l. 'Elwoodii' §
C.l. 'Erecta' §
C.l. 'Kilmacurragh' §
C.l. 'Stardust' §

Crataegus monogyna
  'Stricta' †
x Cupressocyparis leylandii §
x C.l. 'Castlewellan' §
Cupressus glabra
  'Pyramidalis' §
C. sempervirens §
Fagus sylvatica 'Dawyck' †
F.s. 'Dawyck Purple' †
Gingko biloba 'Fastigiata' †
Juniperus communis
  'Hibernica' §
J. virginiana 'Skyrocket' §
Liriodendron tulipifera
  'Fastigiatum' †
Malus tschonoskii †
Morus alba 'Fastigiata' †
Populus alba 'Pyramidalis' †
P. nigra 'Italica' †
Prunus 'Amanogawa' †
Quercus robur 'Fastigiata' †
Q.r. 'Fastigiata Purpurea' †
Robinia pseudoacacia
  'Pyramidalis' †
Sorbus aucuparia
  'Fastigiata' †
S. scopulina †
Taxodium distichum var.
  nutans †
Taxus baccata 'Fastigiata' §
T. b. 'Standishii' §

**PENDULOUS OR
WEEPING TREES**
Betula pendula 'Dalecarlica' †
B. p. 'Tristis' †
B. p. 'Youngii' †
Cedrus deodara §
Chamaecyparis lawsoniana
  'Intertexta' §
C. nootkatensis 'Pendula' §
Fagus sylvatica 'Pendula' †
F. s. 'Purpurea Pendula' †
Fraxinus excelsior 'Pendula' †
Ilex aquifolium 'Argenteo-
  marginata Pendula' §
I.a. 'Pendula' §
Juniperus recurva §
J. r. 'Coxii' §
Morus alba 'Pendula' †
Larix x pendula †
Picea breweriana §
Prunus subhirtella 'Pendula
  Rosea' †
P. 'Cheal's Weeping Cherry' †
Pyrus salicifolia 'Pendula' †
Salix x chrysocoma †
Tilia petiolaris †
Tsuga canadensis
  'Pendula' †
Ulmus glabra 'Pendula' †

WOODLAND & WILD GARDENS 1

A woodland garden, densely underplanted with symphytums, brunneras and native ferns. They thrive in moist soil and the dappled shade of deciduous trees.

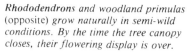

Rhododendrons and woodland primulas (opposite) *grow naturally in semi-wild conditions. By the time the tree canopy closes, their flowering display is over.*

Woodland and wild gardening are not entirely synonymous terms, for although woodland gardens are forms of wild gardening, it is possible to make a wild garden without any trees.

Woodland gardening received its greatest boost in Britain when the magnificent Asiatic rhododendrons began to arrive in quantity during the second half of the 19th century. They had a range of colour and form previously beyond imagination, and at the peak of their flowering season they created a display unmatched by any other flowering shrubs. Azaleas, which botanists had decided were correctly

rhododendrons with certain special characteristics of their own, added to the multiplicity of types, and plant breeders soon found that many of the new species could be crossed to produce a seemingly limitless range of new hybrids.

The lime-hating rhododendrons
Rhododendrons became a cult; nurseries devoted much of their space to them, and amateur gardeners vied with one another in creating ever larger and more magnificent collections. However, many of the newly introduced rhododendrons were forest plants, growing best in the dappled shade of

forest glades or where the trees thinned out as they climbed the mountain sides. With a little thinning and clearing the woodlands and coppices of Britain could provide ideal conditions for them, and soon large landowners were extending plantings far out into the estates where formerly only game had lived.

Rhododendrons and azaleas have one considerable limitation: nearly all, no matter their origin, will die in limy soil unless this is regularly fed with iron and manganese sequestrols or chelates. These plants are lime-haters and suitable only for acid soils. It is in those parts of Britain where the soil is acid, pH 6.5 or

84

also thrives in woodland, and although the common form is a rather sombre plant, the golden-leaved cultivars are cheerful.

One essential factor for all woodland gardens is that the trees must not be planted so closely that they exclude all sun. In heavy shade the range of plants that can be grown beneath the trees is limited; it will depend on the type of trees and the extent to which they rob the surface soil of food and moisture. There is seldom much ground vegetation in beech or pine woods, but a few pine trees mingled with broad-leaved trees, particularly oaks, alders and maples, make an ideal combination of evergreen and deciduous cover.

Design and style

Woodland gardens are of all kinds, from those almost completely undesigned and in which shrubs and other plants have been established where space permitted, to carefully considered landscapes with variation in planting density and attractive vistas through glades and along paths and rides. In size they may vary from large-scale plantings to tiny coppices turned to useful decorative account, or even rough corners of a large garden in which a few well chosen trees simulate woodland conditions .

Grassy glades are an essential feature of most woodland gardens. They strive to look natural and may fit in logically as the terminal features of a design which starts with architectural terraces or paved areas round a house and proceeds by way of smooth lawn and flower borders to a glade enclosed by trees and shrubs. The glade may emerge directly from the lawn and provide one of the main vistas from the house, or it may be concealed by island beds and discovered as a surprise at a sudden widening of one of the winding grass paths.

less, that woodland gardens have been most popular. There is plenty of such soil, even in woodland overlying limestone, since decaying leaves slowly build up a cap of acid soil sufficient for the needs of comparatively shallow-rooting shrubs.

Good woodland gardens can, of course, be made where the surface soil is alkaline, but rhododendrons and azaleas must then be excluded, and their place taken by shrubs and herbaceous plants that tolerate or enjoy chalk and lime. The best types for a mass display comparable to that made by rhododendrons are hydrangeas in their numerous species and garden varieties. Others include aucubas - green, variegated and berry-bearing; cotoneasters, cherry laurels (*Prunus laurocerasus*) in numerous interesting cultivars, elaeagnus - green, grey and golden - and hypericums, including the carpet-forming *H.calycinum*.

Also recommended are the honeysuckles (*Lonicera*), both shrubby and climbing; mahonias; phyllyreas, photinias; *Rubus* species; ruscus; sarcococcas; skimmias - male and female plants both for good flowers and abundant scarlet berries; spiraeas, some of which are thicket-forming, and symphoricarpos, the white or pink-fruited "snowberries". Native yew

There are all manner of variations on this theme, from the neat glade in which the grass edges are trimmed as cleanly as those round the flower beds, to the more casual effect of naturalised shrubs with the grass disappearing beneath them.

Water can be used more dramatically in woodland than in open landscape gardens. The sudden glint of silver seen through trees emerges as a mirror reflecting not only sky but also the encircling trees. Water, however, is not essential, and there are many effective woodland gardens without it.

Woodland trees and shrubs

One of the pitfalls with woodland gardening is that trees are slow-growing and change greatly in scale as they mature. Young trees may give insufficient cover, and old trees cast too heavy shade over the ground. Glades and paths inevitably become smaller and narrower as the trees grow in on them.

After the first few years, it is probable that annual thinning of the trees will be required, followed in time by progressive felling of trees to keep vistas open and allow adequate light to reach growing plants. By taking these matters into account from the beginning, it will be possible to arrange new planting so that the less valuable trees will eventually be removed, leaving the rare and exotic specimens.

Protected wild plants, from left, top row: Dianthus gratianopolitanus *(pink);* Saxifraga cernua; S. cespitosa; Diapensia lapponica; Cicerbita alpina *(sow thistle);* Veronica spicata *(speedwell);* Lloydia serotina *(Snowdon lily). Centre row:* Minuartia stricta *(sandwort);* Phyllodoce caerulea *(blue heath);* Gentiana nivalis *above* G. verna; Woodsia alpina; W. ilvensis; Trichomanes speciosum *(Killarney fern). Bottom row:* Orchis militaris *(military orchid);* Cephalanthera rubra *(helleborine);* Orchis simia *(monkey orchid);* Epipogium aphyllum *(ghost orchid);* Cypripedium calceolus *(lady's slipper orchid);* Daphne mezereum; Gladiolus illyricus.

Carpeting bluebells or wild hyacinths (Endymion non-scriptus) *and snow-white drifts of star-like ramsons (*Allium ursinum*) flower profusely in late spring, hiding the forest floor.*

Apart from thinning and occasional felling, the maintenance of a woodland garden is low. Since the aim is to simulate a natural appearance, a high degree of grooming is undesirable, and many weeds will in any case be suppressed by the cover of trees and shrubs. Brambles and elders are likely to be the most unpleasant intruders; they should be grubbed out early.

Rhododendrons and azaleas can provide flower colour from January until July, with the main display in May and early June. Most woodland gardeners will seek to extend the season with earlier and later-flowering plants. Two genera that rival rhododendrons in display and equally enjoy woodland conditions are camellias, which can be in flower from October until May, with their peak in March and April, and hydrangeas. The latter are at their best in July and August, but continue into autumn; the faded flower heads remain attractive.

There are also trees with outstanding autumn colours, especially among maples, scarlet oaks, liquidambars, nyssas, some species of sorbus, stewartia, parrotia, amelanchier and cercidiphyllum. Certain undercover shrubs can supplement these rich colours, especially the common yellow azaleas and the Ghent hybrids. Vacciniums, fothergillas, hamamelis and deciduous euonymus, which also berry well, are other hardy shrubs which will keep a woodland garden colourful until the last leaves have fallen in November. (See also Plants for Country Gardens, pp. 82–83).

Herbaceous ground covers

Woodland underplanting need not be confined to shrubs. Some herbaceous plants and bulbs grow well in shady conditions. Bluebells are an obvious choice, and the wild garlic (*Allium ursinum*) makes a showy if rather smelly companion. Winter aconites and snowdrops are among the earliest flowers, and the wild English snowdrop in all its forms thrives in the shade of trees. Daffodils are better in more open situations beneath deciduous trees; in heavy shade in spring they will produce plenty of leaves but few flowers.

Several summer-flowering lilies grow well in woodland, *Lilium martagon* and *L. pyrenaicum* to the extent of naturalising themselves in

87

fertile, moisture-retentive soil. Lilies-of-the-valley make ever widening carpets of broad, milky-green leaves interspersed in late spring with their graceful, sweet-scented flowers. Solomon's seal (*Polygonatum*) and smilacina both have handsome foliage and flowers.

Wood anemones make delightful ground cover, and in addition to the white-flowered *Anemone nemorosa* there is a cultivar, 'Robinsoniana', with pale lavender-blue flowers. Another good carpeting plant is *Claytonia sibirica*, with small pointed leaves and sprays of tiny pink flowers; it is native to North America, but has naturalised itself in many British woodlands.

Some hellebores grow well beneath trees, especially *Helleborus foetidus* and *H. viridis*, both with clusters of apple-green flowers, and *H. orientalis*, the Lenten rose, in white or shades of purple or pink, often flushed or speckled with a contrasting colour.

Violets, including purple-leaved *Viola labradorica*, enjoy woodland conditions, and so do hardy cyclamens, such as *Cyclamen neapolitanum* and *C. coum*. The dog's-tooth violet, *Erythronium dens-canis*, thrives and also related species, such as *E. revolutum* and *E. tuolumnense*.

The North American wood lilies, the popular name for trilliums, are natural subjects; they range from pure white *Trillium grandiflorum* to the deep maroon *T. sessile*.

Meconopsis, members of the poppy family, also enjoy open shade on the edge of woodlands. The small Welsh poppy, *Meconopsis cambrica*, with yellow or orange flowers, will seed itself freely and require no care once established. The magnificent Himalayan species, such as blue-flowered *M. betonicifolia* and *M. grandis*, purple, pink or rose *M. napaulensis* and yellow *M. integrifolia* and *M. regia*,

require more attention. They are short-lived perennials or even biennials, and must be renewed frequently from seed.

Moist and shady clearings

Flourishing naturally in woodland conditions are most of the hardy ferns since they are nearly all shade lovers. Among the most beautiful are the ostrich-plume fern, *Matteuccia struthiopteris*, most effective planted in drifts; and the soft-shield fern, *Polysticum setiferum*, available with crested, plumed or finely divided fronds.

The hard-shield fern, *Polysticum aculeatum*, makes handsome shuttlecocks of strongly upstanding fronds. The royal fern, *Osmunda regalis*, a large and handsome plant, favours deep moist soil. Also suitable are the male fern, *Dryopteris filix-mas*, one of the commonest and sturdiest native species, and the lady fern, *Athyrium filix-femina*.

In very damp soil the Asiatic primulas, also called candelabra primroses, should be tried, for under such conditions they often naturalise themselves and spread by self-sown seedlings. There are outstanding colours among them: crimson and magenta in *Primula japonica* and *P. pulverulenta,* numerous pink shades in the Bartley Hybrids, buttercup-yellow in *P. helodoxa* and *P. florindae,* orange in *P. bulleyana,* and coppery-red in the hybrids 'Inverewe' 'Inverleith' and 'Insriach'.

All the astilbes thrive in wet soil, and so do the rodgersias, with large leaves and spiraea-like clusters of small white or pink flowers. For sheer sculptural beauty there is *Gunnera manicata,* whose huge, umbrella-like leaves are large enough for a man to shelter beneath. On a smaller scale there are several good forms of *Rheum palmatum,* the ornamental rhubarb.

Dry shade

A greater problem is posed by dry shade, and few ornamental plants will thrive in this. The Alexandrian laurel, *Danae racemosa*, and butcher's broom, *Ruscus aculeatus*, are two exceptions. Both are small evergreen shrubs, the former with orange, and the latter with bright red berries in autumn.

Iris foetidissima is a herbaceous perennial that will grow in dry and very shady sites, and though its pale purple flowers are not particularly attractive, they are followed by seed pods that split open to reveal vivid orange seeds.

The native wood spurge, *Euphorbia amygdaloides*, will grow in dry shade, and so will the more handsome *E. robbiae* and the semi-shrubby *E. characias wulfenii*. Ivies, in their great variety of leaf shapes,

Woodland glades, with tulips and other spring flowers naturalised in rough grass, extend the manicured garden via shrubs and wide-spaced trees to the countryside.

Wild gardens quickly become overgrown; trees and shrubs need occasional thinning out to prevent rampant growers from swamping the herbaceous undercover.

sizes and variegations, cope effortlessly with dry shade, and so does the yellow-flowered rose of Sharon, *Hypericum calycinum*. The latter also tolerates limy soil.

Wild gardens

Woodland gardens are one form of wild gardening, but trees are not obligatory. Alpine meadow gardens are another example; these take their character from high mountain valleys in which herbaceous plants and bulbs of many kinds grow in short grass. The simplest expression of this is seen in the popular practice of naturalising narcissi in grass. It means delaying mowing until June so that the bulbs can fatten up for flowering the following spring, but some areas of rough cut grass can contrast effectively with other areas of close-mown lawn.

Other bulbs and tubers can be naturalised in a similar way. Colchicums, which superficially resemble crocuses and flower in the autumn, do well in grass, and crocuses themselves can also be naturalised provided the grass does not grow too strongly. The best place for crocuses—and snowdrops —is usually round a fairly large tree. In damp ground, the unusual and beautiful *Fritillaria meleagris* and its cultivars do well.

Certain herbaceous plants will grow quite happily in grass, including the early-flowering, yellow daisy, *Doronicum pardalianches*, and the creeping bellflower, *Campanula rapunculoides*. Taller campanulas, such as *C. trachelium*, *C. latifolia* and *C. lactiflora*, can also be grown semi-wild if given a little attention to ensure that they do not

become overgrown. The same is true of foxgloves, which will succeed in the open or in shade, and of the great mullein, *Verbascum thapsus*, which needs sun and good drainage.

Several of these are common native plants well worth a place in the wild garden, and there are many others which will appeal. Several can be obtained from the wild (as long as you get permission from the land's owner or occupier), but it is generally better to start a wild garden with seedlings than with established plants, particularly as seed is so freely produced and easily gathered, and the seedlings are easier to establish.

Some British wild plants are protected by law and must not be dug up or disturbed under any circumstances. However, it is sometimes possible to purchase seed from specialist nurseries.

COTTAGE GARDENS 1

A romantic view (opposite) of a Victorian cottage garden. The tranquil scene depicts well-loved favourites, such as wallflowers, tulips, pansies, bellis and forget-me-nots.

Low massed borders edge the approach to a modern cottage garden. Beyond the old gate and sentinels of roses, typical cottage-garden flowers fill the herbaceous border.

Cottage gardening is unique in that it owes its origins and designs to no single architect or school of gardening. The flower-and-vegetable-filled plots surrounding the artisans' cottages arose out of necessity rather than from a desire to create an artistically pleasing picture.

The traditional cottage garden as we think of it today was in its prime from the middle of the 19th century until the first quarter of this century. During that period food-crop cultivation was an essential skill for farm workers with small pay packets. Flower gardening gave some light relief as well as providing scented foliage herbs for linen cupboards, strewing and for stockpots, and flowers for the church, the family grave and the parlour.

Cottage gardens seem to have been most common in the warmer counties of the south and west. They proliferated in Surrey, Sussex, Somerset, Gloucestershire, Wiltshire, Devon and Cornwall, but the Victorian horticultural designer, William Robinson, noted that in Scotland and the northern counties "we do not see the same charming little gardens".

Traditional cottage gardens

There is no precise definition of a cottage garden, but it typically describes a small patch of ground at the front or back surrounding a tiny house. The ground is closely packed with a mixture of vegetables, fruit bushes, perhaps a fruit tree or two set in a patch of rough-cut grass, and massed flowers.

Little thought appears to have been given to design in the cottage garden, but the general effect would nevertheless be tidy in its informality. The plants would be positioned either where it was convenient to push them in at the time, or where the gardener thought they would "look nice".

There was often some attempt at a formal edging to the large beds which flanked the inevitable mud, brick or cinder path; clipped box or lavender were the most favoured. The plants, which today are called cottage-garden flowers, would include hollyhocks, pinks, wallflowers, sweet Williams, marigolds, stocks, snow-in-summer, sunflowers, roses, herbs, snowdrops, paeonies, crown imperials, tulips, lilies and many more.

The overall impression would be of a profusion of flowering plants, bright without being brash. The cottagers did not avoid using brilliant-flowered plants, but they had the sense to plant plenty of foliage plants which absorb the harsher tones, thus diminishing the sometimes crude effect that is commonly achieved in regimented beds of closely packed lobelias, alyssums, salvias and French marigolds.

For all their ignorance of — and indifference to — the finer points of garden design, the cottagers had an inherent talent for producing a pleasing overall effect in their gardens. It is probable that the cottage-garden style influenced Victorian pioneers of "natural gardening" such as William Robinson and Gertrude Jekyll.

Soil and aspect

Many of the cottagers worked as labourers on the farms or in some other occupation connected with the land. They knew the wisdom of not taking out of the soil more than they put into it; with quantities of manure and garden compost at their disposal, they maintained the fertility of their soils with organic nourishment every year.

COTTAGE GARDENS 2

With few pesticides at their disposal the cottagers appreciated the true value of crop rotation as a means of keeping vegetables healthy and the land in good heart. They would concoct their own insect sprays from plant leaves and other materials to keep down greenfly and other common pests.

Today there is a large selection of reliable and *selective* pesticides available, but plants, especially food plants, still benefit from crop rotation, and all soils from adequate supplies of organic matter.

Equally vital to the well-being of the massed plants in cottage gardens was and is shelter. Most of the gardens were in the milder counties, but even then they would be protected from damaging winds by walls, fences or hedges.

Cottage gardening today

Today the appearance of many gardens surrounding picturesque thatched cottages may well be disappointing. A square of grass, surrounded by narrow borders supporting a few rose bushes and dahlias, has supplanted the former massed, but orderly floral display. In many cases the affluent society has meant the destruction of the old cottage garden which was cultivated for necessity as much as for pleasure. Yet it is still possible to find what is considered to be a typical cottage garden, with climbers round the door, sweet-scented roses, an apple tree, gooseberry bushes, a beehive, and rows of runner beans and cabbages.

Many of the ornamental plants may be modern equivalents of their predecessors, but there are few rules in cottage gardening, and all flowers with a certain rustic charm can be made to look at home. Modern cottage gardens can be as versatile, more productive and just as picturesque as they were a hundred years ago.

Red and yellow honeysuckles, heady with fragrance, hide an old cottage wall and clamber over a rustic screen (opposite).

Garden paths run straight to the cottage door embellished with roses. Gravel keeps prostrate hummocks clear of mud.

It is comparatively easy to create a cottage-garden effect by cramming masses of suitable flowers into wide borders, but a more authentic atmosphere is achieved where the garden is laid out in a similar fashion to cottage gardens of old. Traditional cottage gardening demands considerable labour. With no clear rows for hoeing, weeding must be done by hand, and in the absence of herbaceous borders, most flowers are of the bedding types. Throughout the season, the garden needs constant care.

Paths, beds and edging
Garden paths were usually simple and direct, running straight from the front gate to the door of the house, and between 60 and 90cm wide. Traditionally they were made of flagstones, crazy or regular paving, flattened earth, rolled cinders or hoggin.

Paths can still be made from these materials, and also from gravel without spoiling the rustic effect. As there are no rigid design lines for cottage gardens, there is no need for slavishly following the straight and narrow path. A gently curved path may fit more easily into a garden scheme as well as minimising the appearance of a squared plot.

As much space as possible was left on either side of the path to allow sweet-scented herbs, vegetables, flowers and fruit bushes to be cultivated *en masse* in fertile beds of soil. There would be rows of carrots, cabbages, lettuces and other vegetables among currant and gooseberry bushes, clumps of

COTTAGE GARDENS 3

The earthy colour of a beaten path is picked up with red saxifrages, old-fashioned pinks and golden alyssums.

Climbing roses are ideal for turning this Victorian gazebo into a shady bower. Honeysuckle is equally suitable.

rhubarb and runner beans up tripods of hazel poles. Herbaceous perennials and annuals would be grown in the spaces between crop plants, in borders surrounding them and often in parallel rows if they were raised strictly for cutting.

Stepping stones or simple gaps in the plantings would allow access, but occasionally a large bed would be subdivided into smaller plots by narrow paths running across it at right angles to each other.

The rows of vegetables were so broken up by the haphazard grouping of flowering plants that they were seldom noticed from a distance; fruit bushes would add to the informality.

Odd areas would be reserved entirely for flowers; bulbs would be planted among herbaceous perennials and either left to come up year after year or lifted and replaced by hardy annuals sown in the bare patches in spring. If the garden stretched round the house, a plot at the back might be used for vegetables and fruits, and the front garden devoted to flowers — a pattern still frequently seen today.

Shrubs occupied less space than they do in modern gardens, but rosemary, myrtle and other sweetly-scented bushes were favourites, especially for planting by gates and doors where their perfume could be appreciated on arrival and depar-

Hollyhocks and cottage gardens go together. Today, these popular biennials come as singles or doubles, and as giants as well as dwarfs.

Bright red geraniums (Pelargonium) flame like beacons against the green grape vine on a cottage wall. In spring the pots are filled with golden daffodils, tulips and wallflowers.

ture. Fragrance was of great importance to the cottage gardener, and plants were chosen for their scent as much as for their colour. Many of the original cottage-garden flowers were dug up from woods and hedgerows and planted in odd corners to flourish and improve through thoughtful cultivation.

Although not obsessed with formality, the cottagers liked their plots to be prim and tidy, and some form of permanent edging to the beds was a regular feature. Low borders of sweet lavender and close-clipped box hedges were popular, as too were clumps of pinks with their hummocks of grey foliage and scented blooms.

If plants were not used as edging, their place would often be taken by bricks laid on edge, decorated ridge tiles as used on house roofs, large stones and even seashells brought back from visits to the coast. The shells often decorated the window-sills of the house too.

Lawns and trees

The close-mown lawn with its parallel stripes did not feature in the cottage garden. The nearest the cottager came to creating such a sward was a patch of rough grass below a gnarled apple tree, maybe with a swing slung from a sturdy branch for the children. The grass would be cut with a sickle, a scythe or a pair

of shears, unless the gardener was fortunate enough to possess a goat.

But the grassed part of the cottage garden would be as small as possible; it was non-productive and therefore less worthwhile than flower and vegetable beds. Today we prefer to be more generous with the lawn area; mowers make it easier to maintain and allow us a suitable space for leisure and lounging activities.

The old cottage garden was unlikely to have more than one or two trees, for in its confined space the shade cast by the leaf canopy made the cultivation of vegetables and flowers difficult. Apples were popular, for they provided sweet

95

COTTAGE GARDENS 4

blossom and fruit as well as shelter. Many varieties of apple still available would be grown in cottage gardens in the 19th century. 'Ribston Pippin' (dessert), 'Flower of Kent' (culinary), 'Tom Putt' (dessert or culinary), 'Orleans Reinette' (dessert) and 'Devonshire Quarrenden' (dessert) are all worth trying for the quality of their fruit and their neat growing habit if grafted on to a dwarfing root-stock.

Beehives or skeps would be placed close to the apple tree, where the bees could enjoy the flower nectar; a better crop of apples would result from thorough pollination.

Clothing the walls

The brick or stone walls of the cottage were invariably embellished with climbing plants which merged naturally with other parts of the garden. Surprisingly few gardeners today make use of the vertical plane, in spite of the fact that the same, but improved climbers are widely available.

Honeysuckle, with its fragrant, spidery flowers of pink and yellow, produces a heady scent to drift in through open windows on still evenings. Climbing and rambling roses have been bred to flower repeatedly through the summer, and such varieties can effectively replace the older types that enjoyed a rich, but brief flowering season.

Winter jasmine gives dainty colour throughout the dull months of the year; it was frequently trained over porches together with honeysuckle, not only for decoration, but also as a means of keeping out draughts.

Sweet peas were popular, and especially the everlasting pea, a perennial relative of the annual sweet pea and today not grown half as frequently as it deserves to be. In winter it dies down to a root-stock like other herbaceous perennials, to bloom again year after year.

Old-world charm is perpetuated in this peaceful garden setting. The wall hangings of dark green Parthenocissus tricuspidata *are softened with pale pink climbing roses. Clipped yew cones stand guard over pale blue and white* Campanula persicifolia.

Climbing plants were not confined to the house walls. Roses were trained up rustic poles positioned in borders among herbaceous plants, or they tumbled from arches built over gateways and paths.

Walls and hedges

If walls surrounded the cottage or separated it from the public highway, they were built of local stone, roughly mortared together or built dry. From the niches left by mortar or soil would sprout a fount of billowing flowers — wallflowers and pink and white valerians in spring — and trailing campanulas, saponarias, sedums and scented thyme in summer.

Wallflowers were so named because they grow well in walls, and their flowers smell that much sweeter for the warmth radiated by the stonework. Deep reds, yellows and oranges would be planted in a haphazard mixture wherever there was room for a handful of soil to be pushed in with the roots. Thereafter they were left to themselves, to re-emerge every year; the wallflower is a perennial and seeds itself reasonably well.

A small cottage garden, packed with bright annuals and perennials, is retained with a dry-stone wall. Here grow pink Armeria maritima, *white sandwort* (Arenaria) *among the blue-green foliage of alpine pinks and tiers of* Cotoneaster microphylla.

Ivy was less decorative, but it did provide evergreen colour and welcome insulation during the cold winter months.

Wisteria is a delightful scrambler and will quickly make its way round any small house or cottage, drooping its scented chains of lilac or white pea-flowers from almost naked branches in May. Like other climbers, except self-clingers like ivy, it should be provided with strong support such as stout wooden trelliswork or horizontal wires attached to the wall with vine eyes or masonry nails.

Fruit trees always feature in cottage gardens. The self-fertile, reliable 'Victoria' plum has lost little of its popularity since its introduction in the mid 19th century.

97

COTTAGE GARDENS 5

In summer, the native ivy-leaved toadflax (*Cymbalaria*), carpeting campanulas and arabis, together with the rampant grey-leaved and white-flowered snow-in-summmert *(Cerastium tomentosum)*, would foam freely from the top of the wall, and antirrhinums would take over from the wallflowers.

Where walls did not exist, the boundary would usually be marked with a hedge, cheaper to create than a wooden picket-fence which might well have been chosen were funds more readily available. Box was a popular hedging plant, and that ubiquitous standby, the privet, began to appear more frequently in the early 20th century. *Lonicera nitida* is a small-leaved evergreen that made its first appearance in 1901; it has subsequently become popular with those gardeners skilled with the shears, the topiarists.

Earlier carvings in foliage had been practised on box and yew, and were originally the prerogative of formal landscaped country gardens.

On a smaller scale privet and lonicera were to fall victims to the shears. Many cottagers confined themselves to simple dome or cake-stand shapes, but others created peacocks, Welsh harps, exotic animals and other elaborate adornments and fantasies.

Today the art of topiary is undergoing a revival, notwithstanding the likes of William Robinson who opined that "a gardener with shears in his hand is generally doing fool's work".

PLANTS FOR COTTAGE GARDENS
(† = deciduous; § = evergreen; ‡ = perennial/annual)

The letters after each plant indicate its suitability for particular situations. An absence of letters indicates that it will perform well in ordinary soils and under average conditions.

A = suitable for acid soil
L = suitable for chalky or limy soil
D = suitable for dry soil
M = suitable for moist soil
S = suitable for sheltered and mild areas
E = suitable for exposed areas
* = suitable for shady positions

TREES
Fruit
APPLES
(c = culinary; d = dessert)
Beauty of Bath (d)
Charles Ross (d) L,E
Devonshire Quarrenden (d)
Ellison's Orange (d) E
Flower of Kent (c)
Howgate Wonder (c)
James Grieve (d)
Lord Lambourne (d)
Orleans Reinette (d)
Rev. W. Wilks (c)
Ribston Pippin(d)
Tom Putt (d)
PEARS
Conference
Doyenné du Comice
Williams' Bon Chrétien
DAMSONS
Merryweather L
Prune Damson L
GAGES
Early Transparent L

Old Greengage
PLUMS
Czar L
Marjorie's Seedling L
Victoria L

Corylus avellana (cobnut) L
C. maxima (filbert) L
Cydonia oblonga (quince) L,M
Morus nigra (mulberry) S
Ornamental (deciduous)
Crataegus laevigata 'Paul's Double Scarlet' L,D,M,E
Laburnum x *watereri* 'Vossii' M,E
Malus floribunda L,M,S
Sambucus nigra A,L,D,M,E

CLIMBERS AND WALL PLANTS
Fruit
Morello cherry L,S
Fig 'Brown Turkey' L,S
PEACHES
Duke of York L,S
Peregrine L,S
Ornamental
Abutilon vitifolium § A,L,D,M,S
Chaenomeles speciosa † L,M,E*
C. x *superba* † L,M,E*
Clematis † L,M
Cobaea scandens ‡ A,M,S
Eccremocarpus scaber § D,S
Forsythia suspensa † A,L,D,M,E*
Hedera helix § A,L,D,M,E*
Humulus lupulus † M,S
Ipomoea violacea ‡ M,S
Jasminum nudiflorum † A,L,D,M,E*

J. officinale † A,S
Lathyrus latifolius ‡ M
L. odoratus ‡ M
Lonicera japonica 'Aureoreticulata' § A,L,D,E
L. periclymenum † A,L,D,E
Parthenocissus quinquefolia † A,D,M,E*
P. tricuspidata 'Veitchii' † A,D,M,E*
Rosa (climbing and rambling) † A,L,D,M
Solanum crispum 'Glasnevin' †§ A,D,S
Thunbergia alata ‡ M,S
Tropaeolum majus ‡ D,M,E
T. peregrinum ‡ D,M
Wisteria sinensis † A,L,D,M

SHRUBS
Fruiting
BLACK CURRANTS
Baldwin M
Boskoop Giant M,S
Westwick Choice M
GOOSEBERRIES
Golden Drop M
Lancashire Lad M
Whitesmith M
RED CURRANTS
Fay's Prolific M
Laxton's No. 1 M,S
Red Lake M
Ornamental
Artemisia abrotanum † D
A. absinthium † D
Ballota pseudodictamnus † D,S
Buddleia davidii † L,D
Buxus sempervirens 'Suffruticosa' § L*

Cistus § A,L,D,S
Daphne mezereum † L,M
Euonymus japonicus 'Aureus' § L
Forsythia spectabilis † L,D,M
Fuchsia magellanica † L
Helianthemum § A,L,D
Kerria japonica 'Pleniflora' † A,D,E
Laurus nobilis § L
Lavandula § D
Lavatera olbia † D,E,S
Mahonia aquifolium § L,D,M,E*
Phlomis fruticosa § D,S,E
Potentilla † M
Prunus spinosa † M,E
Ribes sanguineum † M
Rosmarinus officinalis § L
Ruscus aculeatus § D*
Salvia officinalis § D
Sarcococca confusa § L*
Senecio greyi § L,D
Spiraea x *arguta* † M,E
Syringa vulgaris † L
Viburnum opulus 'Sterile' † A,L,M,E
V. tinus § D,M*
Vinca § L,D,M,E*

SHRUB ROSES
Belle de Crécy
Blanc Double de Coubert
Boule de Neige
Cardinal de Richelieu
Chapeau de Napoleon
Fantin Latour
Frau Dagmar Hastrup
Königin von Dänemarck
Mme Isaac Pereire
Mme Pierre Oger

Traditional cottage-garden plants

It would be an interesting historical exercise to use only those plants which were available to the cottage gardener during the 19th and early 20th centuries. However, the result might be less rewarding than a garden where modern, cottage-like plants have been admitted. For this reason the plant lists which follow have been broadened to include species and cultivars which were not available to the former cottagers. See also pp. 182-233.

Shrub roses look more at home in the cottage garden than do hybrid teas and floribundas, and there is a vast selection of often highly scented types.

Although elaborate urns and containers were beyond the means of the average cottager, large terracotta flower pots were not. They were positioned on doorsteps and pathways and filled with tulips, daffodils, pot marigolds and other annuals, as well as the favourite geraniums or pelargoniums.

Small shrubs, especially herbs such as rosemary, sage and bay, can look most effective in large pots, as can agapanthus and lilies. All can be moved around at will for a change of scene and placed under frost-free cover in autumn. The houseleek, that succulent rosette-former more correctly known as *Sempervivum,* will creep over the edges of pots filled with well-drained compost, and will even establish itself in a wedge of clay soil moulded to roof tiles, the top of a wall, porch or gatepost.

Nevada
Rosa damascena 'Versicolor'
R. gallica 'Versicolor'
R. rubrifolia
Tuscany Superb
Vanity *
William Lobb

HERBACEOUS PERENNIALS
Achillea filipendulina 'Gold Plate' L,M
A. 'Moonshine' L,M
Aconitum napellus L,M*
Ajuga reptans M,E*
Alchemilla mollis M*
Alyssum saxatile D,E
Anemone x *hybrida* L,D,M,E*
Aquilegia L
Arabis caucasica D,E
Armeria maritima D,E
Aster novi-belgii L,D,M,E
Aubrieta deltoidea L,D,E
Campanula glomerata *
C. lactiflora *
C. persicifolia L*
C. pyramidalis L*
Centaurea dealbata L
Centranthus ruber L,D,E
Cerastium tomentosum L,D,E
Chrysanthemum coccineum L,M
C. (early flowering vars.) L,M
C. maximum L,M,E
Cymbalaria muralis D,E
Delphinium L,M
Dianthus L,E
Dicentra spectabilis M*
Digitalis purpurea L,M*
Doronicum plantagineum L*
Echinops ritro L,D,M
Eryngium planum L,D
Euphorbia characias *
E. polychroma *

Gaillardia aristata L,D
Geranium L,D,M*
Geum rivale M*
Gypsophila paniculata L,D
Helenium autumnale L,D,M
Helleborus *
Hemerocallis M*
Hesperis matronalis L,M
Heuchera sanguinea L*
Iberis sempervirens L,E
Iris germanica L,D,E
Kniphofia uvaria L,D,M
Lupinus Russell strains L
Lychnis chalcedonica L,S
L. coronaria D
Lysimachia nummularia M*
L. punctata M*
Monarda didyma M
Nepeta x *faassenii* L,D
Oenothera D
Paeonia L
Papaver orientale L,D
Penstemon barbatus L
Phlox paniculata L,M
Physalis alkekengi franchetii L*
Polemonium caeruleum *
Polygonatum x *hybridum* M*
Primula auricula vars. *
P. denticulata *
P. juliae M
P. veris L
P. vulgaris L*
Pulmonaria M*
Rudbeckia L
Saxifraga umbrosa *
Scabiosa caucasica L
Sedum spectabile L,D
Sempervivum D
Sidalcea M
Solidago L,D,E
Stachys olympica D
Symphytum grandiflorum *
Verbascum L,D
Viola L,M*

BULBS, CORMS AND TUBERS
Allium albopilosum L
A. giganteum L*
A. oreophilum L*
Alstroemeria D,S
Anemone blanda L
A. coronaria L,E
A. nemorosa L,E*
Arum italicum 'Pictum' M,E*
Chionodoxa luciliae L
Colchicum L
Convallaria majalis L,D,E*
Crocosmia masonorum L
Crocus L*
Eranthis hyemalis E*
Erythronium dens-canis L,M*
Fritillaria imperialis L
F. meleagris L,M*
Galanthus nivalis E*
Galtonia candicans S
Hyacinthus L
Iris reticulata L
Leucojum aestivum M*
L. autumnale *
L. vernum M*
Lilium auratum
L. candidum L
L. tigrinum L*
Muscari armeniacum L
Narcissus L
Nerine bowdenii D,S
Schizostylis coccinea S
Scilla sibirica E
Tulipa L

ANNUALS AND BIENNIALS
Agrostemma 'Milas'
Amaranthus caudatus
Antirrhinum
Bartonia aurea (syn. *Mentzelia lindleyi*)
Bellis perennis

Calendula
Calliopsis
Campanula medium *
Centaurea cyanus
C. moschata
Cheiranthus cheiri
Chrysanthemum carinatum
Clarkia elegans
Cleome spinosa
Delphinium ajacis
Dianthus barbatus
Echium
Eschscholzia
Godetia
Gypsophila elegans
Helianthus annuus
Helipterum manglesii
Iberis umbellata
Lavatera trimestris
Limnanthes douglasii
Limonium sinuatum
Linaria
Linum
Lobularia maritima
Lunaria annua
Malcolmia maritima
Matthiola bicornis
M. incana
Mimulus
Moluccella laevis
Myosotis alpestris *
Nemesia
Nemophila menziesii
Nicotiana alata
Nigella damascena
Phacelia campanularia
Phlox drummondii
Reseda odorata
Rudbeckia
Salvia horminum
Scabiosa
Tropaeolum majus
Verbena
Viola

SEA & RIVERSIDE GARDENS 1

Seaside gardens

Gardening by the sea is a challenge, a constant battle with the elements. The gentle breeze only too often becomes a howling gale, carrying with it a salty and sticky spray which scorches foliage in its path. The most crippling damage is usually confined to a few hundred metres from the shore, but under extreme conditions the danger zone can extend as much as 20 kilometres inland. In addition to the salt deposit, abrasive sand particles damage and often kill plant tissues.

When planning and planting a seaside garden, the sensible approach is to guard against the ever present threat from the sea and to take balmy days as an unexpected blessing. Above anything else it is essential to erect some type of shelter on the seaward side, a windscreen or hedge which can filter and slow down the force of the wind.

Once protection is achieved, coastal gardens have several advantages over inland sites; one is the fact that the sea is more reluctant than land to give up its warmth at night, and coastal temperatures are therefore likely to be several degrees higher than inland. This means fewer and less severe frosts and the possibility of growing tender plants.

Barriers and windbreaks

Few plants can withstand exposure to strong sea gales and those which do are often so blackened, twisted and contorted as to be of little ornament. Such physical damage is not dissimilar to that caused by rains borne along by high winds, but the ultimate harm of sea spray is much greater. The salt solution in an open wound may result in the death of vital tissues.

Exposure to prevailing winds can prove devastating. In some areas, particularly the north and east of Scotland, and north-east England, conditions on the coast are likely to be so difficult that gardening in the accepted sense is not possible.

Even in better favoured areas, such as parts of Cornwall and south England, or the south and west of Wales and western Scotland, affected by the Gulf Stream, salt-spray damage can still be severe. It is particularly damaging on young growth in a dry spring; several kilometres away from the sea, oak and beech trees may become almost defoliated by the combined effects of windborne salt spray, bright sunshine and a late, dry spring.

Damage by wind-borne sand is less common, but does occur where dunes are present and where the normal tides do not cover all of sandy beaches at high tide. Particles of sand picked up by strong winds are the most abrasive form of wind-damage; fortunately they are rarely carried to a great height, and shelter devices are generally effective.

Seaside gardening begins with the provision of shelter. A barrier, such as a hill, woodland, buildings, even a depression in the ground will act as a primary filter to the first fury of the wind. It will remove any danger from sand which drops at the first obstruction. Spray, unfortunately, is not held back as easily as sand.

Walls and fences

A common reaction to the problem of wind is to construct a wall for shelter. However, this is only effective for a distance equalling about twice the height of the wall. Immediately beyond that the wind, thwarted and diverted upwards by the barrier, swoops down in a series of swirls and eddies of such turbulence as to cause worse damage than the original gale.

The most satisfactory shelter is provided by a semi-permeable barrier which can filter the wind and reduce its force. A barrier, half solid and half space, is near the theoretical optimum degree of permeability — 48 per cent. It may be constructed from a framework supporting wooden slats, 25 millimetres wide, with an equal space between each. The effect of such a fence is to cut down the force of the wind by 80 per cent for a distance of up to four times the height of the barrier. From here there will be a gradual increase in wind velocity up to a distance of 30 or 40 times the barrier height. At this point another fence would be necessary.

Other artificial barriers which have proved successful include framework fencing with large branches of evergreens, such as pine or gorse, tied firmly to it, or chestnut paling, specially made with spaces equivalent to the width of the upright stakes.

Natural windbreaks

The best kind of windbreak is a hedge or, preferably, a less formal grouping of trees and large shrubs. Although evergreens provide the most effective screen they can look very dreary after a long winter, and the fresh green of deciduous foliage is welcome in the spring. A mixture of evergreen and deciduous trees is recommended.

It is essential that a newly planted windbreak is given every opportunity to grow away and establish itself quickly. Good preparation is as important as the choice of the right materials. Young sturdy and well-rooted plants should be selected, small enough to prevent their tops from being rocked in the wind before the roots are well anchored.

Close planting is advisable to allow the young plants to grow in together and protect each other in

A clifftop garden lies calmly behind a dense shelter-belt of deciduous and evergreen trees and shrubs. The grey and silver, ground-cover plants, including woolly lamb's ear (Stachys olympica), cerastiums and Senecio greyi, are largely salt-resistant.

SEA & RIVERSIDE GARDENS 2

Cornish seaside gardens typically feature solid windbreaks of wall barriers and salt-resistant foliage plants. The garden beyond is sufficiently sheltered to allow many otherwise tender trees, shrubs and herbaceous perennials to flourish.

On the south coast of Devon, golden and green conifers successfully screen a series of island beds. Senecio bicolor, French marigolds and white begonias, with splashes of salmon-pink pelargoniums, sparkle in the bright light.

the early stages. Later some thinning out must be done, but the final stand of a windbreak planting should be closer than for similar plants in a more sheltered situation.

Staking will often be necessary in the early years, and it is advisable to erect some kind of fence to protect the plants until established. A wattle hurdle fence is suitable, but a post and wire fence with brushwood tied on the windward side is better as this will filter the wind.

Before doing any planting, have a good look at nearby gardens in similar situations and note what is doing well there. There is no need to slavishly repeat obvious choices and designs, but on-the-spot reconnaissance gives a fair idea of what is likely to flourish.

North coasts
In these colder coastal regions, the choice of windbreak plants is limited and relies heavily on a few native deciduous trees and shrubs, with some imported evergreens, mainly conifers. The common sycamore (*Acer pseudo-platanus*) is not dense enough to provide an effective windbreak on its own, but is useful for mixing with other trees. The ash (*Fraxinus*) is similarly very hardy and useful with evergreens.

One of the toughest of our native plants is the hawthorn (*Crataegus monogyna*). This will withstand almost any wind force; under bad

Most of the pines, although conical in growth for their first 20 or 30 years, eventually develop into flat-headed trees on tall trunks. Even so, because of their early habit of growth, they are ideally suited for windbreak planting. *Pinus mugo*, the mountain pine from Central Europe, is a large shrub which retains its bushy habit throughout its long life.

The beach pine, *Pinus contorta*, from western North America grows particularly well on sandy, gravelly soils and has been used to stabilise sand dunes. Yet another possibility is the Austrian Pine, *Pinus nigra* ssp. *nigra*. This eventually forms a large tree and, unlike most other pines, will grow on chalky soils. The evergreen oak, *Quercus ilex*, is a handsome coastal tree nearly everywhere in the British Isles. It is difficult to establish unless planted very small, but it eventually forms a majestic, round-headed tree.

East and south coasts
The choice of the right plants, for windbreak and general planting alike, is a major key to successful seaside gardening. It pays from the outset to determine the soil type, to become acquainted with it and improve or maintain its qualities.

Along the south and east coasts, soils are widely variable. There are silty clays in Essex, but Hampshire has light sands which play satisfactory hosts to the pines which are such a characteristic feature of the Bournemouth district. Large areas of the east and south coast, from Dover to Brighton, are alkaline. No places, these, for gardeners who dream of growing rhododendrons or camellias; for them there are the acid soils of Devon and Cornwall.

The southern and eastern coasts have their fair share of climatic variability, and there is considerable difference between a garden in the north-east and one in the south-east.

There is an oft-repeated view that the east coast is bleak, cold, wind-swept and drought-prone, but this is a complete fallacy. True, it does have its share of wind, but success is there once shelter is created. It may be drier than the west coast, but that is not necessarily a disadvantage; on the credit side frost is less damaging. With a little experiment and attention to shelter, the east coast may yield excellent results.

The southern coast as far as Dorset is dry and has the best light of any of our coasts, but is not outstandingly warm. Kent is a snowy county, and winter temperatures as low as -10°C are not unusual in some parts.

The character of the southern coast changes as soon as the hills of Devon appear. From Sidmouth onwards the climate is conditioned by the warm water of the Gulf Stream and by warm rain-bearing winds from the west. In these conditions of warmth and moisture the heavily indented coast gives sheltered valleys on mainly acid soils. Here the rhododendrons and magnolias, the azaleas and camellias find some of their finest expressions.

Along the warm south and east coasts the choice of plants for wind-breaks can be considerably extended and includes many of the junipers.

Among the more interesting pines is the Bournemouth or maritime pine, *Pinus pinaster*, from the Mediterranean region. Also outstanding are the stone or umbrella pine, *P. pinea*, from the Mediterranean, too, and *P. radiata*, the Monterey pine from California.

Along the south coast the fast-growing *Cupressus macrocarpa* is extremely useful. It may sometimes be scorched by salt spray, but quickly recovers. For a formal hedge, or as a nurse tree for slower-growing plants, the quickest growing of the cypresses, x *Cupressocyparis leylandii*, is recommended.

seaside conditions it rarely grows higher than about 2.5 metres, but develops an extremely dense head. The sea buckthorn, *Hippophae rhamnoides*, is a true coastal plant. It grows 2-3 metres high and will succeed in loose sandy soil right down to the high water mark. *Ribes alpinum*, one of the ornamental currants, is another tough shrub for northern and eastern coasts. It forms a dense head and makes an excellent hedge up to 2 metres high.

SEA & RIVERSIDE GARDENS 3

West coasts

Most of the west coast is open to the south-westerlies off the Atlantic. The effect of these winds is manifold, with damage caused by direct physical violence, the abrasive effect of wind-blown sand, and in all cases the deposition of salt.

The west differs from other coasts in having higher rainfalls, especially in such places as the west coast of Scotland. It is fortunate that rain often follows a gale and clears the leaves of salt; without it severe damage can be caused to plants at a critical stage of growth. The beech, for example, produces its annual extension growth in one flush and if injured in May before the shoots have firmed up, the damage lasts throughout the season.

West-coast rainfall produces lush growth; plants grow larger and continue to grow late in the season, aided by the effect of the Gulf Stream and evening warmth from the setting sun. One drawback of lush growth is that it is susceptible to unexpected happenings, a salt gale in the middle of the growing season or a severe frost in early winter when growth is still active.

Along the largely rugged coastline are numerous sheltered spots in coves and river estuaries. In these favoured sites an enormous range of exotic plants can be grown, though it is more likely that gardeners will be faced with an exposed site.

There is a variety of climatic conditions and soil in the west, from the almost tropical Isles of Scilly and the early, but exposed areas of Cornwall, to the Bristol Channel with areas of heavy clay. There is another "early" area in Pembroke, but, conditions become comparatively cool and harsh on the Irish Sea coast of north England.

West Scotland, with its broken coastline and strong Gulf Stream influence, has milder conditions, and where shelter has been achieved the

The Abbey Gardens at Tresco, on tne Isles of Scilly, are justly famous. In the almost tropical climate, a wealth of exotic plants tumble over rocky outcrops. The contorted branches of a monkey puzzle, Araucaria araucana, *create a dramatic backcloth.*

high rainfall allows exotics such as the large-leaved Himalayan rhododendrons to excel.

Western exposure means that shelters must be on the south-west side of the plantings, and in order to gain shelter, late afternoon and evening sun may well be lost. Consider the siting and dimension of the windbreak to avoid shading.

Where exposure is not too serious, there is a wide choice of good shrubs. The windbreak may be predominantly ornamental, and *Berberis* x *stenophylla, Escallonia* 'Langleyensis' and *Fuchsia magellanica* are suitable.

Good use can be made of native trees and shrubs, but the list is short, and some, such as the elder, scorch easily and owe their success to rapid regrowth.

Our native willows hybridise freely, and many species and cultivars are both attractive and highly salt-resistant. In addition, they tolerate a wide range of soil types. For evergreen tree shelter we must again look to the exotics. Among the pines, choose types with a low branching habit, such as the Austrian pine (*Pinus nigra nigra*) as opposed to Corsican pine (*P. nigra maritima*), and beach pine (*P. contorta*) as opposed to lodgepole pine (*P. contorta latifolia*).

Some of the most useful plants for western exposure come from New Zealand, such as the hebes and griselinias, and from the southerly part of South America, such as *Berberis darwinii* and *Embothrium coccineum*. From the Pacific coast of North America come the Monterey pines and cypresses.

Several plants from the Mediterranean regions also do well, including a number with good silver foliage, such as several of the ornamental pears (*Pyrus* species). Most of these trees owe their usefulness to thick waxy or hairy coverings of the leaves, and a number of them have a high toleration to atmospheric pollution.

The shrubby evergreen olearias truly excel on the west coast. The well-known *Olearia* x *haastii* is very hardy and highly adaptable, delighting in summer with its sweet-scented, freely-borne daisy clusters. Olearias in general like moisture; some of the less hardy species, such as the showy-flowered *O. semidentata*, often survive many winters only to perish during a summer drought. They thrive so well on the west coast that they often seed themselves and produce interesting and useful foliage forms.

Many other plants of the daisy family provide good ground cover with silver foliage effects, such as the santolinas and helichrysums, or a good flowering show such as gazanias and osteospermiums.

Other noteworthy groups include

the cotoneasters. *Cotoneaster microphyllus* is a tough and successful plant, doing well along the whole coast and helping to bind the soil on steep slopes. Together with *C. horizontalis* and *C. simonsii* it has seeded far and wide.

Planting a seaside garden

For the purpose of selecting suitable plants for the coasts, seaside gardens can be considered in three separate zones. The outer zone is the first line of defence and the most exposed. Here the choice is for trees and shrubs which, while surviving in these unpromising surroundings, will provide shelter throughout the year. Once they are growing strongly, they should be cut back and encouraged to break from the base.

The middle zone should be composed of trees since height is crucial to the area sheltered. However, this is only practicable if the garden has at least 10 metres available for a shelter-belt. Two rows of trees should be planted and allowed to grow freely; they will inevitably be sheared off by the wind.

Sometimes old plantings have grown too thin at the base to be effective, but the following twining shrubs can be planted for repairs: *Elaeagnus* x *ebbingei*, *Lycium chinense*, *Muehlenbeckia complexa* and *Polygonum baldschuanicum*.

The outer and middle zones provide shelter for the inner zone which constitutes the ornamental garden.

It is frequently advised to plant in late autumn before the soil temperature drops, but consider to what you are condemning the plants if you practise this beside the sea — in all probability six months of intermittent gales! Many evergreens will die before spring by dessication. Evergreen plantings are in any case always best done in late April, with container-grown plants.

Use autumn and winter months to prepare the planting areas. Dig out a

hole large enough to take the rootball of the eventual tree. Break up the excavated soil with a fork and add an equal quantity of moist shredded peat and a handful of an organic fertiliser such as a mixture of coarse bone-meal and hoof and horn meal. Replace this in the hole and mark the centre with a cane.

When planting time comes round in March/April, dig out the mixture, remoisten if necessary and proceed with planting as usual. Firm well so that a shallow saucer is left round the plant. Water thoroughly and as soon as this has soaked in, rake dry soil round the plant to preserve a dry mulch. This can be augmented with rotted manure or garden compost. Plants treated in this way will be better prepared for a prolonged dry spell — though regular watering will still be necessary — and should immediately start into sturdy growth.

A good case can be made for lavish planting by the sea. No single plant can hope to compete with the wind, and it is sound sense to plant closely in threes or fives or multiples of these. The plants will quickly interlock and form one dense bush, helpful in smothering weeds.

Natural seaside plants

Nature has provided a number of devices to help plants survive in difficult places. Many have adapted to be resistant to wind and spray.

Close examination of the grey leaf of a plant such as lamb's ear, *Stachys olympica*, will reveal that the greyness is caused by a covering of fine hairs which can be rubbed off to show the green leaf below. These hairs protect the working parts of the leaf from storm and spray. Senecios generally have this device, and some of them, such as *Senecio monroi*, also form a thick felt on the undersides of the leaves. This makes it one of the toughest and most windworthy species.

SEA & RIVERSIDE GARDENS 4

Dianthus and similar plants appear grey from a waxy coating like the bloom on a grape. This gives protection similar to hairs. Other plants, such as escallonias, exude a sticky mucilage on their foliage which seems to serve a similar purpose. Not all escallonias have this feature, but *E.macrantha* and *E.rubra* are among the best.

Other devices which enable plants to withstand bad weather include dispensing with leaves in the normal form and transferring food manufacturing duties to the green shoots. Gorse is a good example of this as are tamarisk and *Spartium junceum*, the Spanish broom.

Some plants develop a specially tough epidermis or outer layer of cells, as in *Euonymus japonicus* and the evergreen oak, *Quercus ilex*, and that supremely good plant of the seashore, *Hippophae rhamnoides*, the sea buckthorn.

The shrubby hebes use two devices. Not only do they have a double epidermis, but they also arrange their young leaves in opposite pairs round each growing point, like hands folded in prayer. Many otherwise tough trees fail to make progress because the leading bud has been killed. It is this which causes the charasteric shorn-off appearance of many exposed trees.

Alpines and annuals
In general, all herbaceous plants, properly sheltered, perform better in seaside gardens than anywhere else. This is due to the warmer, more constant temperatures and the intensity of light.

One outstanding feature of seaside gardening is the wealth of alpine and other dwarf plants which thrive in seemingly inhospitable surroundings. Their survival is due to the mechanics of wind force which create a shallow area of low pressure immediately above the ground and in the crevices of rock work.

Provided that soil pockets are well-drained and fertile so as to create an easy root run with a steady food supply, a number of dwarf plants do exceptionally well by the sea. Among the most popular are the sea pink, *Armeria maritima*, with carpets of pink, red or white flowers in summer, and aubretia in several colours. There are the neat clusters of *Dianthus deltoides*, the maiden pink, and the Cheddar pink, *D. gratianopolitanus*. The prostrate mats of *Helichrysum bellidioides* have tiny daisy flowers, but purple-flowered *Verbena rigida* is taller, up to 30cm, and as tough as they come.

Hardy and half-hardy annual plants give vivid, month-long colour in similar situations. Among the best are trailing ivy-leaved geraniums, and the brilliantly coloured gazanias, the latter putting on a vivid and continuous display throughout the summer, even in such unlikely places as the Isle of Man.

The annual Livingstone daisy (*Mesembryanthemum criniflorum* syn. *Dorotheanthus bellidiformis*) is of the same ilk. Nowhere in the British Isles does it show off its multi-coloured, shiny flowers as brightly as by the sea.

Riverside gardens
Gardeners of river sites face problems of a different nature to those of seaside gardens. Salt spray, even along large tidal rivers, is unlikely to cause serious trouble except at estuaries, and the need for shelter is therefore no greater than in any other exposed situation inland.

Soil erosion and flooding are the major obstacles to overcome. Tidal rivers, particularly those which, like the Thames, carry considerable traffic, can suffer serious erosion of the banks. Tidal action, combined with the normal flow and wash caused by river craft, eats into the natural earth banks, gouging out hollows and undercutting the banks.

Under such conditions, any garden running down to a river should be provided with a sound protective barrier of concrete, heavy masonry or solid timber camp-shedding. The latter is probably the easiest and cheapest of the available methods; to be effective it must be properly constructed and the heavy timbers mechanically driven in well below river-bottom level. The timbers should fit closely together and be held together with strong metal straps.

The top of the barrier should be high enough to keep water out of the riverside garden in normal circumstances, including high tides; the soil in the garden beyond can

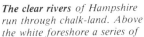
The clear rivers of Hampshire
run through chalk-land. Above
the white foreshore a series of
terraces contains low-growing
shrubs, including Japanese
azaleas and native heathers.

Dartmouth, *high above the
river Dart, enjoys a near
Mediterranean climate. Palms*
*thrive, and many shrubs, like
the hydrangeas above, remain
in bloom into late autumn.*

therefore be at the same level as the
top of the barrier. Only under exceptional circumstances will the soil
be seriously contaminated by the
partly salt river water. However,
most riverside gardens have a pronounced downward slope; if the
area is liable to frequent flooding,
terracing of the garden will give added protection and interest.

Before any work is done on reinforcement of river banks, it is
necessary to establish the boundary
lines of the land. Water authorities
are responsible for laying down
regulations governing the rivers they

control; they should be consulted in
any dispute about riverside boundaries. Applications for mooring
rights should also be made to the
water authority; the right to moor a
boat is by no means automatic.

A riverside garden, once protected from soil erosion and
flooding, can then be designed and
planted according to personal taste,
always bearing in mind climate factors and soil type. Where space is
ample, a weeping willow or two
(Salix babylonica) can be planted
near the river, but at least 3 metres
away from the barrier.

Flooding and erosion

Flooding is always a hazard on rural
riverside property, particularly on
sluggish rivers running through flat
country. Erosion also occurs where
the water is deep and the banks unprotected. Trees or large shrubs can
be helpful in both situations; the
shrubby willows are the best.

In country areas, farmers cut
strong branches from the goat or
pussy willow in winter. The pieces,
as long and thick as broom handles,
are pushed into the banks on bends
where erosion seems likely; in a
couple of years these "cuttings"

SEA & RIVERSIDE GARDENS 5

establish themselves as clumps of flourishing young willows.

These vigorous, shrubby willows are not particularly attractive garden plants, but they are invaluable as quick-growing waterside shrubs. While they cannot stop water overflowing the banks, they prevent erosion and will filter out debris carried downstream and make cleaning up afterwards easier. The alders (*Alnus* species) also do well as riverside trees.

Moist riverlands
Large riverside gardens frequently have low-lying areas near the water's edge which are more or less perpetually moist. These patches often have deep, silty soils which, after cleaning up and weeding out, make excellent planting sites for a wide range of moisture-loving plants. The same conditions occur where a stream runs through the garden, with low areas on either side. Here astilbes, primulas and many water-loving irises will grow to perfection.

Marshy areas on river and stream banks are inclined to flood at times. It is necessary therefore to confine them by raising the level of the surrounding ground with informal terracing. For the most natural effect, use rough irregular rocks, peat blocks or lengths of tree trunks.

It is also important to have access to the plants, and broad, flat stepping stones or logs can be put down and firmly positioned. They should be long enough to be deeply embedded and wide enough to give a good foothold.

Water reflections
One of the most attractive aspects of waterside gardening is the reflection of plants in the water. Unfortunately, occupants of the opposite river bank derive the most pleasure. Still

---

PLANTS FOR SEASIDE GARDENS
N = north coasts; E = east; S = south; W = west coasts

WINDBREAKS, DECIDUOUS
Acer pseudo-platanus N/E/S/W
Crataegus N/E/S/W
Fraxinus excelsior N/E/S/W
Genista S/W
Hippophae rhamnoides N/E/S/W
Lycium chinense N/S
Populus alba N/E/S
P. 'Serotina' N/E/S
Prunus spinosa N/E/S/W
Pyrus W
Ribes alpinum N/E/W
Rosa rugosa E/S/W
Salix alba E/S/W
S. *caprea* N/E/S/W
Sambucus nigra S/W
Sorbus intermedia N/E/S/W
Spartium junceum S/W
Tamarix S/W

WINDBREAKS, EVERGREEN
Atriplex halimus (semi – evergreen) S/W
Berberis darwinii E/S/W
B. x *stenophylla* E/S/W
Bupleurum fruticosum S/W
Cotoneaster microphyllus S/W
C. *simonsii* (semi – evergreen) E/S/W
x *Cupressocyparis leylandii* S/W
Cupressus macrocarpa S/W

Escallonia 'Langleyensis' E/W
E. *macrantha* S/W
Euonymus japonicus S/W
Griselinia littoralis S/W
Hebe S/W
Ilex aquifolium E/S/W
Juniperus communis 'Hornibrookii' S/W
J.c. 'Montana' N/E/S/W
J. *horizontalis* E/S/W
J. *procumbens* W
Ligustrum ovalifolium (semi - evergreen) E/S/W
Olearia x *haastii* E/S/W
O. *semidentata* W
Pinus contorta N/E/S/W
P. *mugo* N/E/S
P. *nigra* ssp. *nigra* N/E/S/W
P. *pinaster* S/W
P. *radiata* S/W
Quercus ilex N/E/S/W
Rhamnus alaternus S/parts W
Rhododendron ponticum S
Santolina chamaecyparissus S/W
Ulex europaeus E/S/W

SEASIDE TREES AND SHRUBS, DECIDUOUS
Acer davidii E/S
A. *griseum* E/S
Amelanchier lamarckii S
Arbutus unedo S/W
Artemisia arborescens S/W
Betula pendula 'Darlecarlica' S
Betula pendula 'Tristis' S

B. *p.*'Youngii' S
Buddleia davidii E/S/W
Ceanothus 'Gloire de Versailles' S
Cotoneaster divaricatus N/E/S/W
C. *frigidus* N/E/S/W
C. *horizontalis* N/E/S/W
Cytisus battandieri S/W
C. x *beanii* E/S/W
C. *kewensis* E/S/W
C. *multiflorus* E/S/W
C. *nigricans* S/W
Elaeagnus umbellata W
Fuchsia magellanica cultivars S/W
Genista hispanica S/W
G. *tinctoria* 'Plena' S/W
Hydrangea macrophylla cultivars S/W
Laburnum alpinum N/E/S/W
Lavatera olbia N/S/w
Leycesteria formosa N/E/S
Potentilla cultivars W
Prunus spinosa 'Purpurea' N/E/S/W
Pyrus salicifolia 'Pendula' N/E/S/W
Solanum crispum (climber) S
Sorbus intermedia N/E/S/W
S. *vilmorinii* N/E/S
Spiraea albiflora W
S. x *bumalda* 'Anthony Waterer' N/E/S/W
S. *japonica* 'Alpina' N/E/S

SEASIDE TREES AND SHRUBS, EVERGREEN
Berberis verruculosa N/E/S/W
Calluna vulgaris cultivars N/E/S/W
Camellia S
Carpenteria californica S/W
Ceanothus 'Delight' S/W
C. *impressus* S
Chamaerops humilis S/parts W
Cistus x *cyprius* S
C. *laurifolius* S/W
C. *palinhae* S/parts W
C. x *purpureus* S/W
C. 'Silver Pink' S
Convolvulus cneorum S/W
Cordyline australis S/parts W
Cotoneaster conspicuus 'Decoru E/S/W
C. 'Cornubia' E/S/W
C. 'Exburiensis' E/S/W
Crinodendron hookerianum S/V
Drimys winteri S/W
Elaeagnus x *ebbengei* S/W
E. *pungens* 'Maculata' S/W
Embothrium coccineum W
Erica arborea 'Alpina' S
E. *carnea* cultivars N/E/S/W
E. *cinerea* 'C.D. Eason' N/E/S/W
E.c. 'Eden Valley' N/E/S/W
E. x *darleyensis* N/E/S/W
E. *lusitanica* parts W
E. *vagans* cultivars N/E/S/W
Escallonia 'Iveyi' S/W
E. 'Langleyensis' S/W

or sluggishly-moving water reflects an exact image; in quickly flowing water the reflection is influenced by the changing pattern of light and shade on the surface.

Natural stands of reeds and rushes and aquatic plants of similar growth habit are a feature of lakesides rather than river banks, but they will often be found in shallow, slow-moving water.

Native water plants, with firmly anchored root systems, can be established fairly easily in shallow water overlying mud. Plant them in wire containers with mesh sides and base, such as the specially con-structed baskets for water lilies, and fill them with fibrous turf.

Waterside plants can be dug from large clumps along the river; bul-rush or reedmace is one of the most handsome; also recommended is the yellow flag or common water iris. These and other shallow-water plants are invasive and must be con-tained with annual cutting-out.

Water pollution

In clean, shallow water, watercress can easily be grown. However, in-dustrial pollution is becoming an in-creasing problem on rivers and streams. Although the law requires that water discharged into a river should be free of harmful matters, pollution from industrial and household waste is rampant. The ef-fect on fish life in some rivers has reached catastrophic proportions.

The careless or thoughtless river-side gardener can also be guilty of pollution to a lesser, but still impor-tant extent by washing out spraying equipment or throwing unused in-secticide sprays or weedkiller into the water. The amount of active in-gredient may be quite small, but before it disperses to a relatively harmless concentration, it may well harm wild life.

PLANTS FOR RIVERSIDE GARDENS

† = deciduous; § = evergreen

rubra S/W
nymus fortunei N/E/S/W
aponicus N/E/S/W
rya elliptica S
be 'Carl Teschner' S
x franciscana 'Blue Cem' S/W
'Great Orme' S/W
'Midsummer Beauty' S/W
pinguifolia 'Pagei' S/W
ichrysum plicatum W
splendidum S/W
altaclarensis E/S/W
cquifolium E/S/W
rus nobilis S/parts W
andula spica E/S/W
natia ferruginea S/W
inus arboreus S/W
aria 'Waikariensis' W
llyrea latifolia S/W
omis chrysophylla W
fruticosa S
rmium tenax S/W
osporum crassifolium S/parts W

alphii S/parts W
enuifolium S/W
obira S/parts W
acantha atalantoides E/S/W
coccinea 'Lalandei' N/E/S/W
rogersiana 'Flava' N/E/S/W
ododendron (hardy) N/E parts
/W
marinus officinalis S/parts W
ecio greyi S/W
nonroi S/W
nmia japonica E/S/W
hora macrocarpa W

Viburnum tinus E/S/W
Yucca filamentosa S/parts W

SEASIDE PERENNIALS
Catananche caerulea
Cortaderia selloana
Dierama pulcherrimum
Echinops ritro
Eryngium
Euphorbia characias
Kniphofia hybrids
Lavatera trimestris
Sedum spectabile
S. telephium 'Atropurpureum'
Stachys olympica
x *Venidio-arctotis* 'Grandis'

DWARF AND ALPINE PLANTS
Alyssum saxatile
Arabis
Armeria
Aubrieta
Campanula carpatica
Cerastium
Dianthus
Globularia cordifolia
Helianthemum nummularium
Iberis sempervivum
Limonium bellidifolium
L. bonduellii (annual)
Phlox subulata
Polygonum affine
Rhodiola rosea
Sedum
Sempervivum
Silene acaulis

WATERSIDE TREES AND SHRUBS
Alnus †
Amelanchier canadensis †
Cornus alba †
C. stolonifera †
Malus floribunda †
Metasequoia *glyptostroboides* †
Populus †
Prunus padus †
Rhododendron ponticum §
R. catawbiense §
Salix †
Sorbaria aitchisonii †
S. arborea †
Spiraea x *billiardii* †
S. x *vanhouttei* †
Symphoricarpos †
Taxodium distichum †
Viburnum opulus †

BAMBOOS, RUSHES, GRASSES AND FERNS
W = shallow water;
M = moist soil
Acorus calamus 'Variegata' W
Arundinaria murielae M
A. variegata M
Athyrium filix-femina M
Butomus umbellatus W
Cyperus longus W
Matteuccia struthiopteris M
Miscanthus sacchariflorus M
Osmunda regalis M
Sagittaria sagittifolia W
Typha latifolia W

WATERSIDE PERENNIALS
Aruncus dioicus M
Calla palustris M
Caltha palustris W
Filipendula kamtschatica M
F. ulmaria M
Gunnera manicata M
Hemerocallis M
Hosta M
Iris kaempferi M
I. laevigata W
I. pseudacorus W
I. sibirica M
Lysimachia clethroides M
L. nummularia M
L. punctata M
Mimulus luteus W
M. ringens W
Myosotis palustris W
Pontederia cordata W
Primula beeasiana M
P. bulleyana M
P. florindae M
P. japonica M
P. pulverulenta M
Ranunculus aconitifolius M
R. flore-pleno M
Rodgersia pinnata M
Trollius M

SUBURBAN GARDENS 1

A traditional suburban garden incorporates a winding path bordered with roses and shrubs on one side, a lawn on the other. A heather bed softens the formal outline.

The blanket word suburban covers a multitude of locations. The gardens may be in small closes, their areas nearer to town-garden scale, or they may be of considerable size in the so-called stockbroker belts which accompany most conurbations. Either way, bureaucracy has seen to it that what you do with your own property is not entirely a personal matter. You will probably need planning permission to put in a new access or to build in the garden.

The Water Board will want to know about swimming pools, and the Tree Preservation Officer about trees you wish to cut down. However, officialdom usually works to everyone's benefit. While a tree might be casting heavy shade in your garden, it is also providing pleasure for dozens of others, and while your new shed may be screened from your living-room windows, it may be blocking the light from those of your neighbour's.

The vernacular style

If you live in a close or street conceived as a whole, the boundaries and approach to the house should conform. The vernacular, or appropriate, style is usually related to older buildings but is as applicable to current styles. Its dictum is the use of local building materials, stone as in Scotland and the North, in the South brick, perhaps with stained timber, and tiled roofs as opposed to slate. The boundary technique in the surrounding area may be stone walls or a certain type of fence.

Plants also have a certain style; some trees are definitely rural, like the oak and the ash, while others are suburban in character, such as the Japanese cherries, the Leyland cypress (x *Cupressocyparis leylandii*) and the eucalyptus. This style is partly related to the scale of the plant and partly to its origin, whether indigenous or introduced.

The climate of a region will also dictate the kind of planting that can be envisaged.

House and garden compatibility

There is a close relationship between an area, its buildings and its native growth. In the past, building materials were dependent on the underlying rock; this might be a particular type of stone, or clay which, when mixed with straw, could be used in house construction.

Again dictated by availability, roofing materials might be of clay or slate, wooden shingles, stone or reed or corn-straw thatch. The siting and form of the buildings were influenced by the prevailing wind, with the roof pitched to throw off heavy rain or snowfalls. The farmer, too, used local materials for his boundary demarcations—stone or wood which could be cleft and worked to traditional patterns.

In the 20th century, less sensitive developers have produced universal surburban dwellings which blanket large areas of the countryside to such an extent that the indigenous identity has been lost. In recent decades, architects have begun to design houses so as to re-introduce the vernacular style and create unity with the surroundings.

The householder, too, has a responsiblity, in the selection of materials for and construction of his garden. The character of the area should ideally be married to the style and materials of the home and extended to the garden. The more obvious transgressions of the rule are stone walls in a brick locality, or a closed frontage in an open-plan development. For the boundaries, use materials sympathetic to the

A modern suburban garden is designed for leisure. Paved lounging areas and gravel surfaces occupy former grass spaces. The raised beds of mainly foliage plants mean less arduous work. Pots of annuals can be moved around with the seasons.

SUBURBAN GARDENS 2

house, and where the two adjoin try to pick up an architectural point. For instance, if stained wood is used on an elevational panel, construct fence and pergola in stained wood as well.

Forms and functions

You may dislike gardening and have little interest in horticulture, but within the garden there will have to be space for parking the car and room for the children to play; the dustbins and oil tank must be housed, with clear access to both. These are the main functional purposes of a modern garden, in use the whole year. In conjunction with ornamental features all aspects of the garden must be brought together in such a way that the end result presents a visual entity.

In designing a suburban garden, the layout should express its functions; once these have been thought out, plants and plantings are plotted in for they hold the conception together, blot out the eye-sores and give visual attraction. However, plants grow fast and quickly achieve, then overtake, the original purpose if left to their own devices. The same process happens to a garden plan, for it, too, has a life pattern, according to the use to which it is put.

A garden's growth cycle

A young married couple moving into their first house will probably have little money to spare in laying out a garden, but they can plan it for later development. The design should include basic functions.

Just as important, at this stage, may be space for a pram, grass for toddlers to play on and room for a clothes-line. As the children become more active, they will need a sandpit or paddling pool, a swing, Wendy house or rabbit hutches. In addition, standing space may have to be found for a boat or caravan.

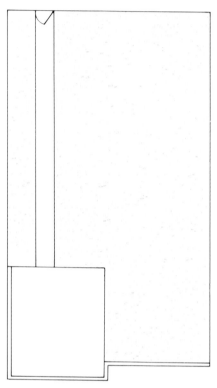

A garden's growth: In infancy a new garden may consist merely of a paved area and a path, with rear access to the plot.

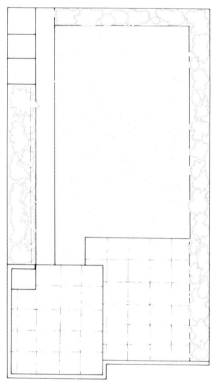

The terrace has been extended, a lawn seeded and shrubs grow on the boundary line. Service areas are demarcated.

Teenagers may want their own garden area and a place to store bicycles, canoes and camping gear. In large suburban gardens, they will demand and usually be denied an area for football practice, but a wicket and cricket stumps should be possible. Sophisticated youngsters will plead for a swimming pool or a barbecue.

Somewhere among the children's activities, parents will want a place in which to relax, either by pottering, mowing the grass and cultivating flowers and vegetables, or by seeking out a peaceful corner in which to sunbathe. Often the various functions centre round a terrace, the outdoor living room.

When the children leave home, another stage of a garden's life comes to an end. This is often the time when a couple become deeply

involved with the garden, horticulturally speaking, and start on an ambitious garden scheme. Some caution is advisable if you are not to regret, in late middle age, the work involved in constant garden maintenance.

On retirement a couple may move away because the garden, if not the house as well, has become too strenuous to look after. Anticipated at an earlier stage, it would have been possible to adapt at least the garden to a lower upkeep.

Plans and patterns

Having established the functions and growth potentials of the garden, you can begin to plan it. At this stage evaluate the existing elements and those you wish to add. Consider where to site a log pile and reach it with the minimum of discomfort on

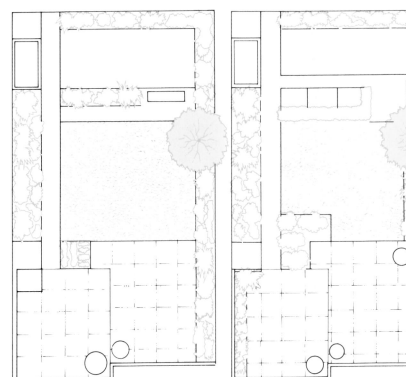
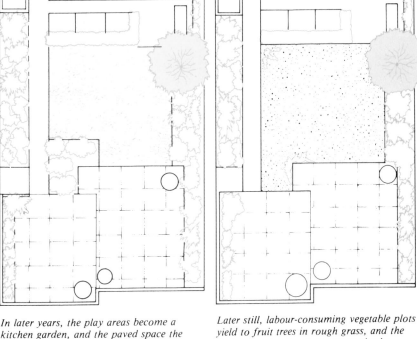

With the advent of children, part of the lawn has been converted into a play area at the bottom, separated with a paved area.

In later years, the play areas become a kitchen garden, and the paved space the foundation for frames and compost heaps.

Later still, labour-consuming vegetable plots yield to fruit trees in rough grass, and the herbaceous border gives way to shrubs.

a cold winter evening, and whether it is logical to locate vegetables, herbs and rubbish area at the point farthest from the kitchen (we always do). Determine from the outset where the dustbin will stand and remember that unsightly as an oil tank is, frequent access is necessary, with a clear run from the tanker.

Take stock of what exists already; on a new plot there may be nothing but builder's rubble, but your neighbour might have planted a willow which in a remarkably short time will be huge and inevitably dominate your garden.

On the other hand, there may be a view to the distant countryside or a fine church spire; these can be used as focal points in your design which will therefore tend to run visually out of the site. With nothing of note outside or on a site surrounded by eye-sores, the design must turn inwards, and the focal points be provided in the garden itself.

Visual effects

On a scaled plan of the garden, with the house, its windows and doors also plotted, mark all these considerations, as well as compass points, prevailing wind directions and shadows cast by buildings and walls. Next, join up the service areas with surfacing, connected to the house via a pedestrian route. Straight or curving paths may seem logical, but this linear approach can be too regimented, and a more fluid design evolves if you think in terms of surfacing rather than paths.

Imagine the garden as a patchwork quilt, with interconnecting masses kept simple and uncomplicated. Eventually they will become areas of paving, plantings or lawns, and all are easier to create and maintain if simple in outline. By working with regular shapes you can also relate to the shape of the plot and the geometry of the house, usually set square upon it. The shape of the site may suggest a square pattern or one at an angle of 45 degrees to the house, or you might design a patchwork of circles. In this case, let the radii from the centre of any circle lead back to the square pattern so as to relate to the boundary or the house.

As the basic pattern becomes apparent, the garden area can be considered as a whole. Changes in levels, which might already exist, should follow the overall pattern; site retaining walls, steps and banks so that they strengthen not weaken the ultimate layout.

113

SUBURBAN GARDENS 3

Background and specimen plants

Plants can now be plotted in on the pattern. It is the plantings and the spaces between them which transform a two-dimensional plan into a three-dimensional working design of masses and voids. If planting depths are too narrow and too low and the lawn a wide, open space, the design will appear unbalanced in its framework of the boundary fence.

Within the patchwork decide first on tall plantings which will screen or shelter the garden, and determine any possible interior divisions of the site. Background plantings provide a skeleton for the design and counteract the rigidity of the boundary lines. Secondly, within this green skeleton plan areas of lower, more interesting decorative plant material.

The remaining voids in the pattern are then broken down into areas for grass, terrace, gravel or paving, water, kitchen garden, etc. Site each area as practically as possible, taking into account sun, shade and use.

The relative merits of specific plants have little importance in the cohesive basic layout; initially they merely make up the mass, albeit influenced by the plant material.

However, there will be certain key plants—a specimen tree or an outstanding shrub group—round which the design should evolve. Too many specimen subjects tend to make the conception unrestful; fastigiate conifers, for example, are of strong, upright shape and often of emphatic colours which immediately draw the eye. They should therefore be positioned carefully and sparingly in the layout.

Too many instances of vertical emphasis introduce a staccato rhythm in a design which would otherwise flow.

Visual theories

With a well thought-out ground and planting pattern it is quite possible to create an inner garden totally different in concept to the outside boundary. This can be a shape within a shape as long as the intervening ground between the two is well planted.

The ground pattern, by taking the eye to a particular feature, can also lead away from an unpleasant one. It can make a long and narrow site appear wider by loping from side to side, or by introducing false prospectives—an old ploy which can make a linear garden seem shorter or longer.

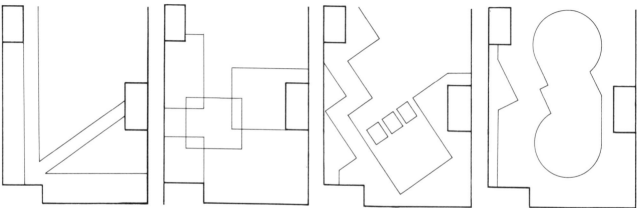

Design approaches. Traditional layouts like the one above bear no relationship to an overall pattern between house and garden.

Within the same space, a logical patchwork unites the different elements. Alternatively, set the square pattern at an angle to the

house or introduce a series of linked circles or arc segments whose radii all follow the basically square layout.

Garden designs vary from the strictly formal (left), *with a clipped hedge and narrow specimen trees, through low-maintenance foliage borders* (top) *to mixed borders and island beds busily planted with perennials, annuals and shrubs.*

Pegging the plan

Use string, pegs and canes to lay out in the garden the pattern evolved on paper. Starting from the house and generally working at an angle of 90 degrees from it, use canes to mark out the design. Replace these with pegs and join them up with white string so that you can see the pattern clearly from the house. Look at it from an upstairs room and from the living room to check that it works; mark any alterations on the paper pattern.

Live with the pegged-out pattern for a while before actually creating it. Check the pattern, too, from the other end of the garden looking back towards the house and, for a front garden, from across the street.

If you are pegging out a drive or parking space, and if the surface is hard enough, try the car on it to make sure there is enough room in which to turn in, reverse and move out comfortably.

At this stage of pegging out the design, the virtue of circles becomes obvious. Circles produce a simple, but bold geometric pattern instead of a weak, free-shaped design. String and a central peg can be used like a giant compass to mark out the arc of each circle.

Front gardens

The design theories already described will also work for small enclosed front gardens, but with a different approach. Often a front garden layout becomes a scaled-down version of the larger rear garden and is squeezed between an entrance path and a drive.

Larger suburban garden frontages tend to aspire to grandeur with a sweeping drive, too great for the size of the house and mean front-door detail; the latter is sometimes upgraded with columns and a porch approach and then becomes too grand for the house.

SUBURBAN GARDENS 4

In general, the front-garden area is small and better designed as one overall pattern. It is one of the trickiest aspects of garden design, made more difficult with the scale problem that arises from the necessary areas for car parking and for access.

However, the initial approach should be similar to that of the rear garden, plotting on graph paper the position of house and garage and any other permanent features. Thereafter indicate the ideal position for other elements and the run of the drive. On many sites this is easy, with a straight line down one side connecting the garage with the road, and an offshoot path to the front door.

A sweeping drive and, where space allows, parking space in front of the house is more difficult to design. The parking area and sweep should ideally be kept in proportion to the site; the central island technique needs a grand house behind it to be impressive! The alternative of the in and out-drive leaves an odd piece in the middle. You may consider this area as parking space for visitors, but you will have to live with a large area of surfacing for the rest of the time.

Space may also be needed in the front for a boat or caravan; ideally this space should be tucked out of the way and screened so as not to obstruct the visual approach to the house, for yourself and for your neighbours.

The remainder of the site, after the drive has been added, will always be out of scale, and the best technique is to keep the design and details strong and simple. Forget about small squares of grass and beds of colour and concentrate on bold and evergreen plantings which will look good throughout the year and need little attention.

Boundary fences and hedges

Many new properties are already provided with some kind of boundary demarcation, usually little more than a chain-link or simple post-and-rail fencing. This gives no

Natural stone and concrete slabs complement a shallow stream. Clumps of grasses add to the semi-wild atmosphere.

privacy or screen and allows dogs and children to roam. Sooner or later the developer's fence will collapse, and it becomes imperative to erect a new one; if at all possible it is a good idea to settle for a good stout boundary from the outset.

Fencing need not be all of the same type, especially if the site is irregular in shape, and this can reduce the cost considerably. Where there is an outward view, chain-link fencing is perfectly acceptable and will look unobtrusive when covered with green or black plastic. Use timber verticals to support it as they are more sympathetic to a garden than concrete uprights and easier to cover with climbing plants.

Various types of timber posts and horizontal rail fencing are visually more attractive—and more costly. The two or three-rail types blend well with surrounding countryside. Hurdles, mainly of willow, are more

Focal points and arresting views rarely occur naturally in built-up areas. The two diagrams above illustrate gardens where the view from inside is halted abruptly by the boundary. On the left, the vista is forced away from the end of the garden and towards a handsome willow next door. The planting scheme, which is concentrated along the left, apart from a massed group near the willow, helps to direct the eye to

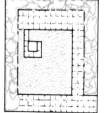

the right. In the second example of a garden with no outside view (above), the pattern is made to turn in on itself and become dominated by a feature within the garden. This can be a piece of sculpture, an ornamental seat, a sundial or bird bath, a small pool complete with fountain or an architectural foliage shrub. The eye is directed to this focal point by the paving running towards it.

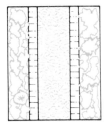

Outside views beyond the garden permit wider perspectives, and clever planning of the layout can create the illusion of gardens stretching indefinitely. Where a landscape of open fields adjoins the garden (above), planting should preferably be confined to two straight or gently curving borders at the sides so that the eye can travel effortlessly the length of the garden and beyond. A view of softly rolling hills can be treated to

the same illusion, with nothing to impede the view over the far boundary. It is also possible to bring the 'feel' of country into the garden itself by repeating the outside view in a series of curving patterns with strategically placed focal points. Deciduous and evergreen plantings of trees and shrubs will obscure the straight lines while the grassy expanse in the centre of the garden seems to merge into the rolling hills.

117

SUBURBAN GARDENS 5

rural in character; they make good short-term screens, comparatively cheap but easily damaged.

Picket fences, which can be either stained or painted, are more suitable for front gardens and convey a cottage atmosphere. Close-boarded fencing can be bought in ready-made panels, with the timber running horizontally or vertically, or the panels may be woven; feather-boarded panels have overlapping verticals and are probably the strongest type.

Wood preservatives

Panel fencing is also available with louvred timbers, horizontal or vertical. One of the virtues of timber fencing is that it can be erected without specialist help. However, there are certain basic rules to be followed so as to prolong the life of the fence: all timbers must be treated with a preservative, preferably before they are put up, and either thoroughly soaked or pressure-treated. The type of timber can vary from the cheapest softwood through cedar to oak, the most expensive, but by far the longest lasting.

Fence posts, sunk in the ground, need correct handling for if one of them should rock, the whole fence will collapse. Set the posts, after treating them with preservative, in concrete or in a metal shoe for further protection. An alternative method is to bolt the fence uprights to concrete posts set in the ground although this looks less attractive.

The panels between the posts should not touch the ground and are better set on a run of brickwork to protect them from damp soil. If this is not practical, leave a gap and fill in with chicken-wire, or set softwood panels on gravel board. A further safeguard is a coping to areas where the graining is exposed.

Instead of staining the timbers, you can paint them, but the fence

will then need a regular yearly coat on both sides to keep it looking fresh. Plants growing on this type of fence are troublesome as they will have to be let down and retied after painting.

Fencing which resembles horizontal bar-type timber but made of plastic is suitable for short sections and in most urban and suburban situations. Other materials, which can be used on timber frames, include rush and reed panels. They have a comparatively short life span, but look well for internal divisions; their life can be extended by lining them with fine-gauge wire-netting, to deter the birds.

Large bamboo canes also make handsome, loose fences; hold them together with strong wires and block both ends of each cane with corks or composition material to prevent damp in the canes.

Screen blocks

Concrete in various forms makes good boundaries. A concrete-block wall, laid on a concrete footing, can be most attractive, either painted or with the natural aggregate exposed. Finish the wall with a coping of bricks, concrete or stone slabs.

Some inexpensive blocks resemble stone and over short runs look well provided that they are used in areas

Fence types. On the far left, timber palings give a warm background to a foliage group, and the cut-out circle shows a brick wall in false perspective. In the centre, a wooden trellis supports a Rhododendron cinnabarinum *above a low planting of azaleas and pieris. The pierced wall of precast concrete blocks* (above) *lends an airy grace to a border of delphiniums, orange lilies and white antirrhimums.*

of natural stone and provided that the types match. Open-work screenblocks are in the main too demanding visually if used to a large extent as the eye is drawn to the boundary, and the garden appears smaller than it probably is.

Brick and stone walling are superior and provide the ultimate in privacy, but they are extremely expensive, in materials as well as in construction. It may be possible to use brick or natural stone adjacent to the house, where the style is suitable, with timber fencing for the rest of the boundary. While there is nothing inherently difficult in building a brick wall, it is an art to

SUBURBAN GARDENS 6

*Interior divisions given different treatment.
The retaining stone walls on the far right,
displaying a rustic charm of dense
plantings, are in stark contrast to the
flowing rhythm of a shallow flight of steps.
Planting pockets for bedding annuals relieve
the grey concrete slabs, pick up the green
lawn and widen the overall perspective.*

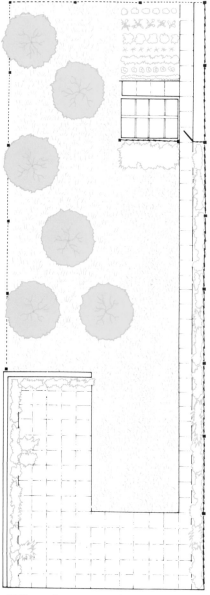

*Different fence types make up a boundary.
On the left a brick wall extends from the
house round the sitting area. The timber
fence opposite is backed by a border and a
path to the carport. Chain-link fencing is
used for the remaining boundary.*

achieve a satisfactory result on both
sides, and the work must usually be
undertaken by a contractor.

A problem arises with a boundary
fence on sloping ground. You can
let the fence follow the natural fall
of the ground, with the rails parallel
to the incline or, on steeper slopes,
the fence can be stepped in sections.
The latter then becomes a feature on
its own, sharply punctuated in the
rhythm of its flow. Before erecting
any major structure, particularly in
brick or stone, check with the Local
Authority that there are no bylaws
regarding heights, and that your
construction will not inhibit sight-
lines for traffic.

Hedges and screens

The symmetry of a meticulously cut
hedge cannot fail to appeal, but in
spite of power-driven hedge cutters
it would be foolish to pretend that a
hedge does not involve work. Where
the criteria for a good garden is its
visual attraction, a formal hedge
which needs frequent clipping must
be disregarded. Far better to plant a
loose, informal hedge or to rely on
mass plantings of reliable evergreen
material to provide screening.

Practical reasons apart, a neat
surrounding hedge visually restricts
the garden and poses the problem of
who looks after the other side. Too
often a gardener opts for quick

screening; the hedge is planted too close together and rarely watered or fed. The result is that the weaker plants die, leaving a sparse and straggly hedge. For the same reason fast-growing species, such as the ubiquitous x *Cupressocyparis leylandii*, are often chosen; they do not miraculously stop growing when the desired hedge height is reached.

A corollary to the manner of the boundary line is the internal partitions within the garden, and its changes of level. Divisions should continue the boundary style; they can become focal points within the garden and allow the use of other and cheaper materials beyond them.

Sometimes internal divisions can act in reverse and by framing a distant view can attract the eye.

Retaining walls

Changes of level should where possible utilise the same materials and patterns as on the boundary. However, retaining walls usually require more solid construction and drainage facilities than fences.

A low retaining wall of about 1 metre is not difficult to construct, in stone, brick, granite sett or concrete block. It should be laid on a concrete base, with a damp-proof layer of bitumen felt, tile or engineering brick, with bitumen paint up the rear of the wall. Good drainage is particularly important if the wall is built against heavy clay soil.

Retaining walls which need to be taller than 1 metre are probably better constructed by a stone mason; reinforcement and sharp drainage are essential to prevent such walls from cracking under soil pressure.

Certain timber walls of hardwood, logs or railway sleepers can be suitable in rustic locations, but their life-span, logs especially, is limited. Obviously, the more massive the construction, the harder the timber must be, and the more thoroughly should it be treated with a wood preservative.

SUBURBAN GARDENS 7

Broad steps link a small flagstone terrace with different garden levels. Planting pockets contain clumps of pink thyme and white-flowered geraniums.

Paved sitting areas harmonise well with the gravelled drive and forecourt. Evergreen foliage shrubs follow the gentle curve and maintain interest throughout the year.

Manhole covers

The problem of inspection chambers and manholes can to some extent be overcome by paving not quite up to the manhole and planting something tough nearby which will tolerate the odd disturbance.

Alternatively, infill an area round the manhole with gravel and continue this over the metal cover. It is also possible, and more expensive, to use an inverted manhole cover in which the paving is laid to continue the pattern. The cover can then be lifted up for inspection purposes.

A tub placed on the cover works fairly well on a terrace, but looks misplaced in the middle of a lawn.

Hard surfacing

Once the garden is fenced you can begin to realise the patchwork plan. The terrace and paved areas will usually come first.

Ideally a material which echoes that of the house would be used, but concrete paving usually wins on the economic score. However, you can introduce small areas of brick or stone to complement plant pockets.

Regulations state that paving must be 15cm below the level of the damp-proof course on the house. To achieve a running level with the inside of the house, leave a 15cm gap between house and paving and bridge it with a strip of hardwood.

Lay the paving with falls away from the house so that it will drain quickly after heavy rain. Drainage should be into surrounding beds or, if none exist, into a gulley. In most gardens, paving can be bedded in a dry mix of sand and cement, over a consolidated base.

Use the same dry mixture to brush between the joints after laying the paving; when nearly dry, rub the

changes. The cheapest slabs are usually open-textured and crumbly, breaking easily and difficult to cut.

Smaller concrete slabs in the form of interlocking tiles are available; they have a brick-like texture and look attractive when laid. Because of their shape, end slabs are necessary to finish off the pattern on the square. Rectangular slabs can be laid like bricks.

Concrete can be laid *in situ*, poured into a grid of wood, brick or paving. An area should not be larger than 3-4 metres square or it will need reinforcement to prevent cracking. When nearly set, spray the concrete with water, and brush to expose the aggregate.

BUILDING BRICKS. Old bricks have an uneven finish and give a soft mellow effect. Ask advice from a builder's merchant on the type of brick you propose using for paving. Unless they are hard they will deteriorate through damp. Hard bricks and the harder engineering bricks can be laid flat; provided that they are made without "frogs" or dimples, they will go further. Softer bricks have hard sides and should therefore be laid on edge.

BRICK PAVERS. These are readily available and a better choice than building bricks, being hard and thin. Lay all bricks on a sand-cement mix, over a base of consolidated rubble or ashes. Rub back the jointing to show off each brick.

GRANITE SETTS. These can be laid in the same way as bricks and can also be used for retaining walls. They are more often found in the North and the Midlands. Grey in colour they mix well with stone.

COBBLES. Often confused with setts, cobbles are egg-shaped stones and used in small areas to deter rather than invite users. Laid on end, in a dry mix, they are useful as a change in texture and pattern. They are obtainable in various sizes from garden centres.

mixture back until each element is defined. Avoid the messy business of pouring liquid grout or wet cement between the joints. The smaller the type of paving—bricks, setts, tiles or cobbles—the stronger the mix should be. The slabs will need edging to prevent them from breaking away with usage or frost.

Curbs should not be necessary to keep soil away from paving. If soil does spill over, there is too much of it, and the level should be reduced from the subsoil.

Before deciding who will construct the garden and how much it

will cost, consider the various materials available:

YORK STONE. Formerly used for street paving, this gives a mellow effect to older properties and town gardens. Old York stone is becoming increasingly expensive and rare. It can be laid directly on sand, being heavy and uneven.

CONCRETE. This is the most used medium for paving in any situation. It comes in the form of slabs, in differing sizes, shapes, qualities and colours. Try to match it to the colour and texture of the house and wet a slab to see how the colour

SUBURBAN GARDENS 8

Cobbles can be laid loose to create a Japanese or beach effect, or they can be laid in a pattern up the centre of a drive, to act as an oil sump for parked cars.

PEBBLES. Similar to cobbles, pebbles come from the beach. They make good small-scale surfacing for seaside gardens.

GRAVEL. Quarried gravel chippings are inexpensive and make attractive surfaces; river-washed pebbles or shingle look well with old brick. Gravel is chiefly used for paths and drives or as an alternative to grass.

TILES. Few tiles, particularly the glazed ones, are frost-proof, and they are therefore unsuitable for garden use. However, tougher quarry tiles can be used in sheltered places which are not subjected to heavy or constant traffic. Because of their finished surface, tiles become slippery after rain and frost.

WOOD. This seldom makes a successful surfacing as it becomes slimy during winter wet. Salt can reduce the slippery effect, and the wood can be cleaned with a wire brush. Wood chips are sometimes used for paths and in kitchen gardens.

Grass surfaces

Once areas of hard surface are sketched in on the layout, the remainder of the garden will consist of planting and open spaces: masses and voids.

Treatment of open spaces is limited to grass for a soft finish and gravel for a harder surface, softened with plants. Water is another alternative although the extent of its use is restricted. In a small garden it is possible to fill the centre with a water canal and position a wide border on either side.

Grass is still the most popular choice, providing a soft, attractive and useful carpet throughout the year. It is also an inexpensive surface, especially when seeded. The one drawback to a newly seeded lawn is that it should not be walked on during its first season.

A turfed lawn gives instant use and effect, but is more expensive. The ease with which grass grows in Britain often leads to misuse. For instance, it is impractical to create small areas of grass or odd-shaped lawns, both of which are difficult to mow. In towns and in shaded situations, grass quickly becomes wet and muddy. Before deciding on the grassed areas, make sure they can be easily mown.

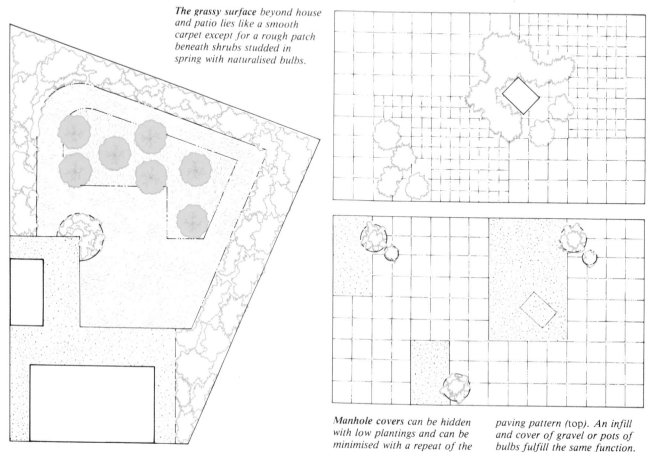

The grassy surface beyond house and patio lies like a smooth carpet except for a rough patch beneath shrubs studded in spring with naturalised bulbs.

Manhole covers can be hidden with low plantings and can be minimised with a repeat of the paving pattern (top). An infill and cover of gravel or pots of bulbs fulfill the same function.

Mowing strips

Lawn maintenance can be made easier by edging the planted spaces abutting the grass with a paving or mowing strip. This permits low perennials and sprawling shrubs to creep on and over the edging without being damaged every time the grass is mown.

For similar reasons lay a strip along the base of a wall. All mowing strips should be at least 25mm below the grass levels.

A mowing strip also avoids the necessity of edging the lawn which would otherwise shrink in size as the beds increase.

Gravel surfaces

Apart from its use as ground cover in courtyards and forecourts, gravel can substitute, on a limited scale, for a lawn. The comparatively small extra cost of gravel as opposed to seed or turf is compensated for by less maintenance.

Various types of gravel and shingle are available, and the best is rounded, washed gravel dredged from a pit or riverbed. Gravel chippings are offcuts from parent rock; they are sharp, not being water-worn, a fact which merits consideration with children about.

Construct brick or concrete curbs as part of the overall pattern and spread the gravel thinly and evenly; roll it into a layer of fine hardcore or hoggin—a mixture of clay and brick dust— over a level base. Unless you want to plant in the gravel, lay a polythene sheet over the base, under the hoggin, to restrict weed growth. Pockets can be left without sheeting for growing a few selected plants.

It is essential that the gravel layer is not too deep—maximum 75mm —or it becomes difficult to walk on. Gravel is not really suitable for gardens with children, but can be ideal for a front or small, low-maintenance rear garden.

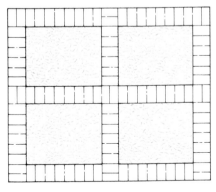

*Mowing strips of broad flagstones (*top*) contain island beds in grass and reduce the need for edge trimming. They also prevent damage by the mower to low-growing, sprawling shrubs in a mixed border (*above*). Concrete poured in* situ *can look attractive in a grid of precast concrete slabs (*left*).*

SUBURBAN GARDENS 9

Mellow stonework, in drystone walls and steps, holds together a red and orange flower display against foliage shading from silver to purple (opposite).

A small weeping cherry (above) *makes a good focal point on the edge of a herbaceous border. It contrasts well with the blue-green cedar.*

Planting design

The fact that plant selection is not considered until after the garden is laid out does not denigrate the importance of this design aspect. For many keen amateurs, plants are the reason for a garden in the first place, but as it has to serve many other functions as well, these have been considered first.

Once the garden is completed, it becomes increasingly difficult to resite plants, and early mistakes must be lived with. Although individual plants need not be selected in the early stages, it is important that consideration be given to the conditions required by particular plant types, such as shade, wind-exposure, north-facing walls, etc. Only by bearing these factors in mind can the most suitable planting positions be chosen.

The smaller the garden, the more difficult it is to work in all the demands that might be made on it; where early planning and planting mistakes were made, later attempts to rectify them often lead to the deficiencies being highlighted and compounded.

For the same reason, the plants which are eventually selected must work all the year round and should preferably have more appeal than a limited period of flowering. A plant seen in full bloom at a garden centre is frequently bought on impulse, but if the whole garden is built up of random selections, it is not surprising that it lacks an entity.

By choosing plants in a correct se-quence and to an overall planting design, impulse buys can be incor-porated into the layout. There will still be room for an outstanding specimen plant, but it will be seen against a suitable background and therefore show to better advantage.

If the background also provides shelter, screens an unsightly view, bears flowers and later berries, so much the better.

Trees and shrubs

A planting concept seeks to use plants, whatever their scale, first for a reason within the layout, secondly for their individual merits—outline, shape and character, whether this is evergreen or deciduous. The form and density of the leaves will also affect the outline.

At this stage you must consider the size of the chosen plant and how quickly it will grow to its ultimate, both upwards and outwards. This factor especially will determine where a plant can be positioned, for while the hard design into which the planting will be introduced is static, plants themselves are not.

Many plants grow remarkably quickly, and the gardener should project his thinking and take into account the kind of bulky masses his young plants will have reached in five years' time, and another five after that.

Mature gardens

In a new garden, ten years may seem a long time, but just as the first ten years of a child's life flew by, when seen in retrospect, so does the life of a garden and its plants. And in the same manner, the growing years are of immense interest. A young, healthy plant will grow far better than an expensive, half-grown one; the larger the plant on purchase, the greater the disturbance to its growth cycle, unless it is container-grown.

Colour must be taken into con-sideration—colour in flower, leaf,

127

SUBURBAN GARDENS 10

A kitchen garden, partly screened with fruit espaliers, is separated into neat square beds which makes annual crop rotation easy.

Orange marigolds (or calendulas) add decorative touches to the divisions; the parsley edging may help deter onion fly.

ample, trees may damage the house foundations due to excessive shrinkage of the clay caused by the trees' water needs.

Suitable trees include forms of mountain ash (*Sorbus aucuparia*), whitebeam (*Sorbus aria*), flowering cherries (*Prunus* sp.), crab apples (*Malus* sp.) and catalpas. Weeping willows grow too large, and hopefully the suburban phase of the monkey puzzle (*Araucaria araucana*) has exhausted itself.

Certain trees, like birch, can be planted; they have a distinct wild feel and usually look better in groups. Although growing well, they are not truly in keeping with town gardens. The concept of plants being "in keeping" or not is difficult and usually personal, but since the suburban garden is a transitional state between town and country sites, most plants do not look out of character. It is in town gardens that care must be taken.

Background planting
Having selected your specimen trees, block out areas of skeleton or background planting. Use bold evergreen groups, interspersed with tall flowering shrubs, to screen, shelter or divide. Plant groups of two or three of a kind on the smallest scale, seven or eight in larger gardens.

Most cotoneasters and pyracanthas are ideal for group planting, followed by the viburnums, evergreen as well as deciduous, and *Hippophae rhamnoides* (sea buckthorn) with its spiky, silvery-grey foliage. Portuguese laurels (*Prunus lusitanica*) are magnificent as background though slow to start, and yew (*Taxus* sp.) is excellent for large gardens.

Viburnum tinus flowers at a welcome time, in early spring; it is a slow-growing evergreen and can be interplanted with buddleia for quick colour effect. Lilacs, philadelphus,

stem and berry so that subjects can be grouped to blend or contrast and to provide year-round interest in the garden.

One of the pleasures of a maturing garden is that, within limits, groupings can be altered to perfect them; indeed, as plants mature at different ages, some must be cut out and others added. This calls for the skills of a flower arranger, on a massive scale but held together in the framework.

Plant selection
The basic design may well have focused on an existing tree or shrub group or centered round a tree in the garden next door. Or you might wish to plant your own focal point, with a favourite type of tree. Ideally it should be a tree of character which, when mature, will remain within the scale of the garden.

Few forest trees are suitable for the average suburban garden, still less for towns. Too large a tree will throw a large area into shadow and may cause problems with falling leaves. Consider, too, the root-run of the tree and its proposed proximity to the house structure. The nature of the soil plays an important role in this respect; on heavy clay, for ex-

forsythia and azaleas are among the best deciduous background shrubs.

Through the skeleton planting can be interplanted trees of secondary interest and the odd conifer as punctuation marks.

Specimen and border shrubs
Next select the medium-sized shrubs which can be used on their own, in a shrub border or mixed with smaller shrubs, herbaceous perennials and bulbs. Avoid setting specimen shrubs in grass; they are difficult to work around and appear disruptive in the design. Mahonias, berberis, *Choisya ternata*, rhus, hydrangeas, shrub roses and senecios are some of the more obvious choices in the medium range.

Lower in stature are some of the cotoneasters and junipers, as well as certain herbs like rosemary, the shrubby thymes, rue, and grey and golden sage. You can also incorporate floribunda and bedding roses (not Hybrid tea roses), certain perennials and biennials. By growing these through shrubs, they need less staking, and if they do it will be less visible.

Plant bold groups of lilies through the shrubs, for scent and a magnificent summer show; drifts of tulips are pleasing, too, but narcissi look better naturalised in grass. Include also other bulbs, notably eremurus, the stately crown imperials (*Fritillaria imperialis*), Solomon's seal (*Polygonatum*) and lily-of-the-valley (*Convallaria*) for its fragrance.

Sculptural shapes
Several shrubby and herbaceous plants have exceptional sculptural beauty. They include among others

Herbs in a raised garden all benefit from full sun, shelter and sharp drainage. The individual beds are confined with heavy planking which prevents rampant growers such as mint and tarragon from swamping their less vigorous neighbours.

SUBURBAN GARDENS 11

A shady wall heavily draped with climbers. The gold-green leaves of the evergreen ivy, Hedera helix *'Goldheart' provide a perfect foil for the scarlet flowers of the flame creeper,* Tropaeolum speciosum, *a perennial which dies back in winter.*

the popular phormiums, yuccas, bergenias, irises and most ornamental grasses and bamboos. Use the outline, colour and shape of each to build up a group.

Use of colours
Bright colours advance towards the viewer, and paler colours recede. In the same way as the ground plan, the construction materials, layout, siting of features and plants have been controlled, so the use of colour should be restrained to avoid a garish, scattered effect.

By the controlled use of colour plants can be selected by elimination, if nothing else. All-white gardens have long been in fashion, but if this is thought too extreme, try shades of yellow, with orange, a dash of grey and white for freshness. Blue, pink and grey have a cool aura, purple and scarlet-red give a hot, tropical effect, while cream and green flowers are quietly soothing. In conjunction with flowers, consider also foliage and berry colours.

Ground covers
As a means of reducing bed maintenance, ground covers on

A small formal pool (left) cleverly combines still and moving water. The fountain spills softly into a drip basin raised above a quiet pool of floating water lilies.

Clematis 'Jackmanii Superba' (above) is justly one of the most popular wall draperies. From summer to autumn, the large rich purple flowers glow exuberantly against mellow brickwork.

various scales work efficiently. The mixed type of shrub planting already described will cover the ground and keep down weeds.

The massed use of low, evergreen plants to pick out a shape is an ideal technique for making up a garden pattern. Initially, the area must be kept clean of weeds until the ground cover knits together, a considerable time in the case of the slow heathers.

In established covers, pernicious weeds, like couch grass, are extremely difficult to eradicate.

As with other plant selections, be careful in the choice of ground covers; quick growers continue to spread long after they have achieved the ideal and may eventually defeat their original purpose. Ground-cover plants, notably the vigorous ivies (*Hedera sp.)* beneath shrubs

can also become a nuisance when they begin to spread and climb.

Wall covers

Climbers and wall shrubs provide a wealth of interesting material. Deciduous climbers can be chosen for their different flowering seasons, from spring until winter, and many of the evergreen wall shrubs have handsome foliage.

131

Do not worry about siting climbers on house walls; the popular belief that they damage masonry is unfounded. Pre-Victorian houses in which soft mortar was used between the joints may be susceptible, but present-day building techniques use harder mortar. Provided that wall climbers are pruned of old growth and dead leaves, damp is not likely to build up behind them.

For climbers which need support, use wires stretched between eyes bolted to the wall rather than trellis. Wooden trellis rots very quickly and unless carefully chosen tends to dominate the wall. Self-clinging climbers, such as ivies, need only initial training and tying in at ground level before they clamber freely up walls and fences.

Vegetable areas

In the suburban garden it can be difficult to site the vegetable plot within the overall design. Ideally it would be located near the kitchen and be approached by hard paving. Unless rows of potatoes or sprouts are planted, there is no reason why the kitchen garden should not be as decorative as the ornamental garden proper.

Cordon or espalier fruit provide a suitable hedge or screen and so do runner beans grown up tall bamboo poles. For a lower, but evergreen screen use herbs such as rosemary or lavender, or a useful mixed planting of sage and thyme.

Globe artichokes are spectacular, as screens or in the herbaceous border. At ground level, edge beds neatly with parsley.

As an entirely different approach, make no attempt to screen off the kitchen garden, but design it as a series of open, square beds arranged in a suitable pattern. You can plan the beds round a central feature—a beehive or large ornamental urn, perhaps, or a small white-painted bench seat.

A broad gravel path separates circular grass areas. The chippings graduate to chunks arranged as a stony field, and the arid landscape is accentuated with groups of foliage plants. The gravel also acts as a drainage bed for the grassy bank.

However, the compost heap, which should be adjacent, can never be a thing of beauty. Well-built, of brick, stout logs or railway sleepers, it can at least be tidy and acceptable. If possible, site log piles and dustbins close by so that all the features which are least appealing are concentrated in one low-key service unit.

Water and rock gardens

A formally shaped pool works well in suburban and town gardens, in association with a paved terrace. The water can be still, empty to mirror the sky or planted with floating water lilies. It can also have movement, from a fountain placed in the centre or from a spray at the side.

On a smaller scale, water can fall from a retaining wall into a basin and recirculate by means of a small electric pump.

Free shapes, simulating natural ponds and running water as in streams and cascades, are more suited to large gardens. Preformed fibreglass pools attempt to imitate large-scale water features, and rarely succeed.

Like natural water sheets, rock gardens proper need wide surroundings, and much attention. They

Dimorphothecas, petunias and other annuals flourish in paving pockets and urns. A yucca (left) adds an exotic touch.

should rise naturally from the site and be constructed from local stone. Ultimately, a rock garden should appear as pockets of earth and plants within natural outcrops of rocks relative in size.

Plants for suburban gardens

The choice of suitable plants depends on location, soil and size. For large, open gardens, plants can be selected from the lists for Country Gardens (p. 82-3) and Cottage Gardens (p. 98-9), while the suggestions for Town Gardens (p. 145) will probably be more appropriate for small enclosed suburban gardens.

TOWN GARDENS 1

Much of the advance thinking in designing a town garden is similar to that for the suburban garden, at least as far as pattern-making is concerned. It is the scale and limitations imposed by the surroundings which differ. Probably few town gardens start as bare plots. The surrounding walls and tall overhanging trees give a sense of maturity, irrespective of design changes.

More often than not the design will be inward-looking, and the ultimate plan will be static rather than fluid. Very occasionally the pattern can be sideways, to a view outside of the garden.

Begin by assessing existing features. One blessing of a town garden is often its enclosure within walls. However, this sense of security can be eroded where other houses

or flats overlook the garden. Surrounding structures will invariably obscure the light, and in the very small garden can induce a feeling of claustrophobia. Earlier attempts to shut out prying eyes have often resulted in trees which are too large, for their sites and for the garden, and which throw too much shade.

Established trees are generally protected by a Tree Preservation Order. However, if the shade problem is severe, and you can claim that light is seriously minimised, the Local Council will usually permit thinning of the head of the tree. The operation will be carried out by a tree surgeon, at your cost.

Gardens in shade
Few obstacles are insurmountable in town gardening, and the problems

are best solved by settling for plants which appreciate shade. They should preferably also be drought-resistant, as the surrounding masonry soaks up a great deal of ground moisture. A town garden will be different in character to one in an open position, and it is futile to attempt to create a country garden.

Accept the limitations of enclosure and capitalise on the fact that these result in more shelter and less frost. The vegetation can therefore be comprised of an entirely different range of plants.

Foliage plants flourish in shady town gardens (above); woolly lamb's ear, rue, tarragon and fragrant tobacco plants cluster close to an exotic yucca. In larger areas – and acid soil – azaleas and rhododendrons create a dazzling late-spring display (opposite).

134

TOWN GARDENS 2

A sunken lawn lies like a rug beneath large-leaved rodgersias, New Zealand flax and silver Senecio greyi.

A basement area, opened up with stepped levels, illustrates the harmonious relationship between planting and paved areas. Such a pattern leads the eye away from the high walls (see also opposite).

Scale restrictions will probably mean that the ground plan will be chiefly architectural. Within the strict boundary lines you can plant luxuriously – to the extent of creating a private jungle – so as to overcome the potential rigidity of the layout.

In a town, you live in closer contact with the garden than elsewhere, and it may well be the only pleasant view. The smaller space should be seen as an extension of the home, and the pattern is as important as in large areas.

Essentially, a well-designed town garden becomes one usable space. One of its joys is its immediate transition from the house, and its

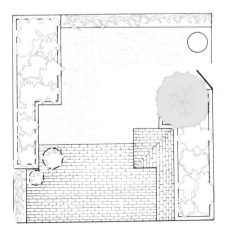

In small town gardens, grass functions best as a supplementary rather than a basic surface medium. Here it abuts from brick paving, skirting raised beds and climbers.

manageable size. Being sheltered, it is a perfect place for sunbathing and lounging and, as an extension of the living room, for entertaining.

Before designing the garden, draw up a list of the leisure and functional elements the garden should contain, then on a scaled plan mark in existing features you wish to retain. Round this evolves the pattern on the patchwork principle as described in Suburban Gardens (p.110-133).

Steps and raised beds

Changes of level become important in a reduced area. Structural details – a seat, barbecue or piece of sculpture – have even more visual impact, for they keep the eye inside the garden and stop it from wandering to the walls. The more you add to or elaborate on the structure the better, so that the whole pattern appears naturally in context.

Changes in level may consist of built-up beds so that plants can be raised towards the light; avoid making the beds too small or they will dry out quickly.

The best types of steps in small town gardens are shallow flights where the treads are wide enough to

Visually deceptive, the diagram opposite is here translated into a series of brick-paved levels and seating areas edged with raised beds and planting pockets for shade-lovers.

137

TOWN GARDENS 3

Small is beautiful, and a tiny, sunny garden becomes a tranquil retreat centered round a pool. Hemmed in by trees, the small garden opposite is largely given over to a paved terrace; hydrangeas and Begonia semperflorens *(foreground) are well suited to light shade.*

hold pots and other containers and with odd seating areas.

As in the suburban garden, the pattern can be at an angle of 45 degrees to the house, or the layout may consist of circles. However, a garden of flowing curves is difficult to achieve in a limited area. Peg out the final pattern and leave it for a day or two to check that it works.

Boundary lines
It will probably not be necessary to construct a boundary, but you may wish to heighten an existing one. Often a form of trellis or simply a horizontal rail along the top of a

wall will be sufficient, depending on the character of house and garden. Lattice work is traditional, but horizontal rails have cleaner lines.

Think carefully about colouring walls and the small outhouse which many town gardens still retain. Once painted, walls must be regularly treated, and self-clinging climbers will consequently be unsuitable. White is a popular choice for walls, but it turns grey when wet, and warmer colours, such as corn, gold or ochre, give a much more dramatic effect.

Overhead beams in the manner of a pergola are sadly neglected in

town-garden designs, in spite of the fact that they give a degree of privacy from above. Any overhead structures should follow the character of the house: a modern pergola might have white horizontals on black-painted upright poles while the more traditional approach uses stained wood. Grape vines and clematis can clamber through the beams; deciduous climbers are preferable to evergreens which make the garden too dark in winter.

Paving materials
The amount of light a garden receives will affect the selection of

Gravel and brick provide a warm and unifying surface for a basement garden kept in a green and white colour scheme. A eucalyptus tree blurs the outline of the house next door.

paving materials – and the plantings. Many gardens have little bright light in summer and even less in winter when the sun does not rise above the surrounding rooftops. Others have full sun in summer, but again heavy shade in winter.

In dark gardens, use light-coloured paving, possibly concrete in some form, interspersed with gravel in warm browns. In certain cases white gravel against dark-coloured walls can look spectacular. Old brick paving to match surrounding walls looks well in good light, but dull and dark in a garden constantly in shade.

Glazed tiles come into their own in a sheltered town garden, particularly when used on both sides of a connecting sliding glass door.

Pools and fountains

Moving water creates an enchanting sound splashing from a wall fountain into a stone basin. It is also useful in reducing outside noise.

If a pool is feasible – and remember that water is also valuable in attracting light from the sky – be bold in its usage and let the pool take up one whole section of the ground plan. A pool can also be raised, within a wall high enough to

prevent children from falling into the water and wide enough for the edge to be used for seating.

Lawns

Once the pattern is evolved and suitable paving selected, consider the question of grass. A lawn is pleasant to sit or lie on in summer, but small grass areas are boring to maintain and become worm-ridden and muddy in shaded gardens.

An immaculate piece of lawn can well be in keeping with a town garden, but it should appear more as a rug laid on a larger carpet than as the carpet itself. The concept of a

TOWN GARDENS 4

town garden is a form of interior design, with the major features representing furnishings, the plantings and levels room shapes and wall-treatment.

Trees and shrubs

It is the profuse plantings which give a town garden its special character and transform it into a surprise element. Contrary to popular belief, plenty of plants will flourish in shade. Their natural adaptation may result in large-leaved foliage, with less spectacular flowers, but the effect can be highly pleasing.

The trees – or probably *the* tree for few town gardens have space for more than one – can be quite exotic. It will be planted in an unnatural situation and will have to relate only to personal taste.

A town garden is the place for the eucalyptus and golden robinia, for the flowering almond and the amelanchier, the magnolia and catalpa and for the dracaena of startling silhouette. The winter-flowering cherry, *Prunus subhirtella* 'Autumnalis' is comparatively dull in leaf, but the white autumn blossom amply compensates for this.

Suggested planting scheme for a 10 metre square town garden: 1. x Fatshedera lizei 2.Jasminum nudiflorum 3.Hydrangea paniculata 'Grandiflora' 4. Choisya ternata 5. Hedera canariensis 'Gloire de Marengo' 6. Anemone x hybrida 'Alba' 7. Shrub rose 'Nevada' 8. Helleborus lividus corsicus 9. Hosta sieboldiana *10.* Pyracantha rogersiana *11.* Polygonatum x hybridum *12.* Santolina chamaecyparissus *13.* Magnolia x soulangiana *14.* Agapanthus campanulatus *15.* Viburnum tinus *16. Rambler rose 'Albéric Barbier' 17.* Salvia haematodes *18.* Ceanothus dentatus

Next select the skeleton shrubs in the same way as building up the suburban garden, but on a smaller scale. Fatsia, buddleia, forsythia, philadelphus and syringa (lilac) all make excellent background shrubs; the heady scent of their flowers is particularly pronounced in the enclosed space of a small garden.

Hebes, choisyas and senecios, among others, provide interesting evergreen foliage in addition to flowers in summer. Camellias, *Fatsia japonica*, daphnes, azaleas,

Leaf colours keep town gardens alive through the year. The composition (left) includes silvery Senecio bicolor, *dark green leathery bergenias, grey-blue euphorbias and pale green, white* Chrysanthemum parthenium. *Above, erect white flower spikes of* Acanthus spinosus *lend emphasis to a huge pot-bellied urn.*

olearias, kerrias and winter-flowering viburnums also do well in shade. They can be underplanted with hostas, if the slugs can be kept at bay, or with Solomon's seal, lily-of-the-valley and spring bulbs.

Clothe the walls with ivies of gold and silver variegations, with winter and summer jasmines, roses, wisteria, clematis or scented honeysuckle. Plant closely so that the effect is dense and bushy as a relief to the surrounding masonry. At the foot of the walls set lilies or white, fragrant tobacco plants.

Front gardens

Small front gardens can be depressing. They are often polluted from car fumes and fouled by pets.

Consider surfacing the whole area with some form of decorative paving, slabs of stone or concrete through cobbles, for instance. The paving should be non-slip and well-lit where changes of level occur. Use containers for the plants in keeping with the style of the house.

In larger front gardens you might choose gravel as the surface material, either with low plantings or one or two types of gravel laid in a pattern. Alternatively, plant the entire area with a ground cover punctuated with striking focal points, such as acanthus or the floppy-leaved *Yucca flaccida*.

Basement areas

Often dark and damp, basement areas sometimes lead to a garden above, but are usually low-lying

TOWN GARDENS 5

enclosed spaces. The character of such basement gardens must concentrate on treatment of the walls. They can be painted in bright colours, and a large mirror can be fixed to reflect the light.

Use plants as in the front-garden approach if there is enough space and light to do so. Clumps of ferns will also flourish.

The soil is usually impervious clay. When you excavate to provide planting spaces, take out holes about a metre deep and line them with a good drainage layer of broken bricks or tiles. Cover these with leaf-mould or turves laid grass-side down. Fill up with good compost, firm well before planting and water regularly.

Balcony gardens can hold a great variety of plants. In summer, this small space is bright with pots of annuals, kitchen herbs and roses. At other times, ivies and an alpine sink bed provide interest until bulbs and bedding plants take over in the spring.

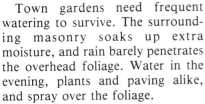

Roof gardens (opposite) need solid foundations and good drainage. Low foliage cover alternate with feathery herbs (fennel), variegated evergreens and white and purple buddleias. *A window box looks attractive with all-foliage plants, such as small-leaved variegated ivy, flame or painted nettle* (Coleus) *and* Senecio *'White Diamond'.*

Town gardens need frequent watering to survive. The surrounding masonry soaks up extra moisture, and rain barely penetrates the overhead foliage. Water in the evening, plants and paving alike, and spray over the foliage.

Roof gardens

The problem of watering, followed by drainage and weight, is the most inhibiting factor to roof-gardening. Plants are invariably grown in too small soil areas which quickly dry out under the combined effects of sun and wind. Before you begin the creation of a roof garden, bear these limitations in mind; in midsummer a roof garden may need watering at least twice a day.

The concept of a roof garden as such is impractical in all but the largest areas where a roof can be specially constructed to take the necessary soil load. The average roof garden is basically an outside room furnished with plants. Even this concept, which may well involve additional weight, particularly towards the centre of the roof, must be checked with an architect.

Before substituting one form of roof surfacing for another, seek professional advice as to its suitability and drainage. If you are thinking of erecting barriers or windscreens which can be seen from below, you may have to obtain permission from the Local Council who will usually insist on a survey.

Once the practical problems have been overcome, a garden high above the city can be a marvellous place for entertaining and relaxing in summer. Arrange overhead beams and windscreens, lighting and furniture for the purpose of creating an atmosphere of being *in* the roof, not perched precariously *on* it.

Plantings should be tough and wind-resistant; broom (*Cytisus*), gorse (*Ulex*), ivies, yuccas, cistus, heathers and low potentillas as well as most shrubby herbs will thrive in hot and dry situations. Concentrate on quantity rather than quality and plant in pre-packaged, well-drained compost in light containers; plastic hanging baskets, glassfibre and asbestos cement pots are ideal.

TOWN GARDENS 6

Town garden approaches *should be in keeping with the house. The stark lines of an open-
plan development (top) are given flamboyant
treatment with a wealth of bedding plants:*
*fuchsias, pelargoniums, coleus, and hanging
baskets of petunias. The transition from a
public to private garden (above left) is punctuated with a huge urn containing* Fatsia
japonica, *spotted laurel and other foliage
plants; on a smaller scale a sink garden, with a
collection of houseleeks* (Sempervivum),
maintains a sense of proportion.

PLANTS FOR TOWN GARDENS

(† = deciduous; § = evergreen; *suitable for shade)

TREES AND SHRUBS

Acer palmatum †
Amelanchier †
Aucuba japonica § *
Berberis † § (some *)
Buddleia †
Buxus §
Calluna §
Camellia § *
Catalpa †
Chaenomeles † *
Cistus §
Cotoneaster † § *
Crataegus † *
Daphne † § *
Elaeagnus pungens § *
Erica §
Euonymus fortunei § *
E. japonicus § *
Fatsia japonica § *
Forsythia † *
Hebe §
Hedera § *
Hydrangea † *
Juniperus § (dwarf cultivars)
Kerria japonica † *
Laburnum †
Laurus nobilis §
Ligustrum § (some *)
Lavandula §
Magnolia † §
Mahonia aquifolium § *
Olearia x *haastii* §
Philadelphus †
Prunus species † (flowering
    almond, cherry, peach,
    plum)
P. laurocerasus § *
    (common laurel)
Pyracantha § *
Ribes † *
Rosa †
Rosmarinus §
Senecio laxifolius §
Skimmia § *
Sorbus aucuparia †
S. vilmorinii †
Symphoricarpos † *
Syringa †
Viburnum † § *
Weigela †
Yucca §

CLIMBERS

Campsis radicans †
Clematis †
    (*C. alpina* *)
Eccremocarpus §
Hedera § *

Hydrangea petiolaris † *
Jasminum nudiflorum † *
J. officinale † *
Lonicera fragrantissima § *
L. japonica § *
L. periclymenum † *
Polygonum baldschuanicum
    † *
Rosa † (some *)
Solanum crispum §
Vitis coignetiae †*
Wisteria †

BEDDING PLANTS

Antirrhinum *
Begonia semperflorens *
Bellis *
Calendula
Cheiranthus
Coleus
Dahlia (pompoms)
Dianthus barbatus
Fuchsia *
Impatiens *
Myosotis *
Nicotiana (some *)
Pelargonium
Penstemon *
Petunia (some *)
Primula (primrose & polyan-
    tha *)
Reseda *
Salvia *
Tagetes *
Tropaeolum *
Verbena
Viola

BULBS

Allium
Colchicum *
Crocus
Cyclamen *
Eranthis *
Fritillaria (some *)
Galanthus *
Gladiolus
Hyacinthus
Lilium candidum *
L. regale
L. Asiatic hybrids (some *)
Muscari
Narcissus
Scilla *
Tulipa

GROUND COVERS (all
shade-tolerant)
Ajuga reptans

Alchemilla mollis
Athyrium
Bergenia cordifolia
Brunnera macrophylla
Convallaria
Cornus canadensis †
Cotoneaster dammeri §
Dryopteris
Epimedium grandiflorum
Galium odoratum
Hedera §
Hosta
Hypericum calycinum
Lamium galeobdolon
L. maculatum
Lysimachia nummularia
Pachysandra
Polygonatum multiflorum
Polygonum affine
Vinca

HERBACEOUS PEREN-
NIALS (all suitable for
shade)
Acanthus
Aconitum
Anenone japonica
Anthericum liliago
Aquilegia
Aruncus
Aster
Astilbe
Campanula
Centranthus
Dicentra
Doronicum
Euphorbia characias
Geranium
Helleborus
Hemerocallis
Heuchera
Hosta
Iris
Kniphofia
Lunaria
Lupinus
Macleaya
Mertensia
Oenothera
Paeonia
Physostegia
Polemonium caeruleum
Pulmonaria
Rudbeckia
Salvia
Solidago
Stachys macrantha
Tradescantia

PLANTS FOR TUBS AND
CONTAINERS
Agapanthus 'Headbourne
    Hybrids'
Begonia x *tuberhybrida*
Camellia § *
Chamaecyparis (dwarf) §
Choisya ternata §
Elaeagnus pungens
    'Maculata' §
Fatsia japonica §
Fuchsia † *
Heliotropium
Hydrangea † *
Juniperus (dwarf) §
Laurus nobilis §
Lilium regale
Narcissus
Nicotiana
Pernettya mucronata § *
Rhododendron § *
Rosa † (some)
Tulipa
Viburnum davidii §
Yucca §

PLANTS FOR WINDOW
BOXES
Ageratum
Alyssum
Antirrhinum
Aubrieta
Begonia *
Calceolaria
Campanula
Cheiranthus
Chrysanthemum (dwarf)
Coleus
Crocus
Erica carnea
Herbs
Hyacinthus
Lobelia
Matthiola
Muscari
Myosotis *
Narcissus
Pelargonium
Petunia
Primula (polyanthus) *
Rosa (miniature)
Salvia splendens
Senecio bicolor
Tagetes
Tulipa (dwarf)
Vinca *
Viola

SWIMMING POOL GARDENS

A private swimming pool is no longer an absolute luxury and can become a real possibility for the average householder who is prepared to sacrifice part of the garden proper and face installation and maintenance costs.

Swimming pool installation is never cheap, and the final cost will depend on several factors. There will be a considerable difference in cost between a site which offers ready access for excavating machinery and lorries, and one where the pool excavation will have to be done manually and the dug out soil removed by hand.

Costs also vary considerably, for pools to be sunken, partially sunken or above ground, and the lie of the land also influences costs: excavation is obviously faster and therefore less expensive on a level than on a sloping site.

The most durable pools are those made from concrete blocks or semi-liquid concrete sprayed *in situ* on to a steel framework. They are, however, more expensive than prefabricated glass-fibre shells and metal/vinyl lined pools.

Installation costs
In addition to installation of the pool itself, some form of heating is almost obligatory in our climate. Certainly filtration, automatic sweepers and circulation systems, all operated from electrical pumps to keep the water clean, are essentials. The size of the pool will usually be determined as a compromise between the probable number of users, the area available to accommodate it, and the installation cost.

Running and normal maintenance costs, which are constant but often overlooked in the initial stages, can add up to a considerable sum over the life of the pool; they must be taken into account from the start.

Before you commit yourself, obtain several estimates from reput-

able swimming-pool contractors as well as information on the likely running costs. Find out, too, what genuine extras will cost, such as automatic pool sweeps, springboards, water-slides, etc.

Check at your local planning and rates offices about existing by-laws. Usually swimming pools are not subject to planning permission unless they are being installed close to the house, i.e. in distance less than the equivalent to the pool's depth; associated buildings housing pump filtration units and saunas may well need permission.

Pool shapes and sizes
The outline shape of a pool is either formal (e.g. rectangular) or informal (free-form). From the point of view of use, a rectangular pool is preferable as it provides the largest uninterrupted swimming area compared size for size with a free-form pool. It usually shows to best advantage in a formally designed landscape.

A free-form pool, on the other hand, can look highly attractive if the surround too is in free-form. Generally, allow the lines of the pool surround to reflect or harmonise with the lines of the pool.

The pool position is usually determined by the availability of space and the optimum shelter and sunshine within the garden. If a natural sun trap exists this will be the obvious choice, but it is worthwhile to consider at which times of day the pool will be most frequently used. You might well find that a site which catches the late afternoon and evening sun will be better than one that heats up at midday.

Above-ground pools usually have a uniform depth of around 1 metre, but sunken and partially sunken pools, whether concrete or vinyl-lined, have a shallow and deep end. A water depth of 0.75 metres is sufficient for swimming, but for diving in from the edge or for a water slide,

A formal swimming pool, sited in a suntrap, is hidden from this large country garden with a handsome stone and wrought iron screen supporting climbing American Pillar roses. The soft-toned, wide paving surround complements the stone pillars.

1.25 metres are better, and for a diving board a depth of at least 2.4 metres is necessary.

Where space and finances permit, the swimming-pool site can be conceived as one combined leisure area, with sauna, changing rooms, barbecues and lounging facilities positioned or planned for later inclusion near the pool.

To extend the useful life of a pool into autumn, several overhead covers are available, one of the most ingenious being an inflatable plastic covering. The advantages of this is that the warm air, which is trapped inside, keeps the water temperature fairly constant and comfortable. In summer the cover can be

disassembled to restore the pool to its proper place in the garden.

Pool surrounds

Despite often clever attempts to make a swimming pool look like a natural pool, it never quite succeeds. The overall visual effect is of a large area of intense blue. Neither naturally occuring pools nor the sea of the British coasts show the same clarity and purity of colour even on a sunny day, and a swimming pool cannot truly resemble anything but a swimming pool.

In a large garden, it is sensible to have the pool installed some distance from the house, in a warm and sheltered spot which can be partly or wholly screened from the rest of the garden.

In a smaller garden, a well-designed pool will fit more naturally into the garden-house picture if it is installed as an extension of the main house and terrace complex to become the centre-piece.

Above-ground, prefabricated pools are usually circular because this shape withstands water pressure best. They are difficult to integrate into any garden design and should preferably be screened from view as other utilitarian features. The ideal surround is a wooden deck, with a matching palisade screen.

The style and make of pool will have a bearing on the treatment of its surround to ensure that it harmonises with the garden and the house. The surround may be a wooden deck, but is most likely to be paving with a non-slip texture. Surprisingly often purpose-made paving slabs are laid the wrong way up to reveal a smooth and shiny surface, disastrous to bare wet feet in summer and equally dangerous in winter when ice forms.

Subdued natural colours are best, with the number of different colours kept to a minimum. One-colour stone will expand the impression of space, while a mixture of bright and unrelated colours soon palls, makes the surround look fussy and distracts from the pool itself. The bright, almost flambuoyant paving colours encountered in Mediterranean climates need a high light intensity to be appropriate.

Pool screens and plants

Screening is often essential for the sake of privacy and as a means of sheltering the immediate pool area. This may be achieved with either a fence, hedge or wall or a combination of two of these.

A solid wall or fence has one drawback as winds can cause turbulences to the supposedly protected side; a slatted fence or pierced screen-wall must be erected to minimise the effect or as an alternative to a solid wall. This will reduce the wind force on impact and will filter it. If a fence or wall can be used in conjunction with a hedge, on the windward side, this will have an even greater filtering effect.

As with paving, consider the hedge, screen or wall as part of the total picture and choose plant material of a style and texture which will be in keeping with the paving and associated buildings. The good appearance of a pool can easily be spoiled by its surrounding.

The relationships of colours play a major part in garden design. Ideally the colours of the paving or deck, buildings and even plants should complement or harmonise with the large blue water area. Brown and coffee-coloured paving associate particularly with white pool coping.

Flower colours rarely clash, except occasionally with each other, but greys and silvers are particularly good colour subjects near a pool. As for the plants themselves, choose types which are either associated with water or appear to be so. Small weeping trees, ferns, grey and silver foliage plants, bamboos, rushes and other grasses are good examples of pool plantings.

All look better in groups rather than as isolated specimens, and most should be set well away from the pool's edge. The chlorinated water splashing on leaves and infiltrating the roots causes chemical burns and bleaches and also works out essential iron from the soil.

Avoid flowering plants which attract swarms of bees, set prolific seed or drop berries and sticky resin. Deciduous and evergreen shrub plantings are the most suitable, with perhaps a few water irises and rushes set in planting pockets in the pool surround.

Willows and poplars should never be planted near a pool, and other trees should be at least 3 metres from the edge. Fallen leaves foul the water, and the needles of conifers clog up the filtration system.

GARDENS FOR CHILDREN

A small sandpit in a preformed concrete shell can later be used as a shallow sunken pool. Free-standing climbing frames **(right)** must be securely anchored in the ground; swings can be fashioned from old car tyres suspended at different heights.

One of the great things about children is that they do grow up. This may be easy to forget when parents are struggling to keep a garden tidy and productive, and the children are energetically turning it into an adventure playground.

One day the lawn will be uncluttered with bikes and balls. Bulbs will naturalise in the grass, without danger of them being trampled into the ground. There will be choice plants in the borders and glass in the greenhouse. Until that happy day it is a waste of time to nag and worry and far better to think of the garden as of the home: a place for relaxation and play.

Depending on the size of the garden, it may well be possible to create a small retreat for the grown-ups and leave the rest of the site fairly uncluttered for the children. A paved patio or terrace, preferably adjoining the house, furnished with tubs of flowers, evergreen and deciduous climbers and wall shrubs, can become a haven of peace.

Such a paved area is also an ideal playground for young children after rain when the grass is too wet to play on. It can be even more useful if roofed over with clear PVC (polyvinylchloride) sheeting and if sheltered from the wind.

Even if the rest of the garden is turned over to the children, it need not be unattractive. Plants of neat and compact growth habit can be set in narrow borders along the boundary fences or walls to soften the lines. Climbers are obvious examples as are shrubs that grow naturally upright. Espalier and fan-trained fruit trees do not take up much room at ground level, and provide blossom and fruit. Avoid plants with spiky leaves or brittle stems which may die back if their branches are broken. Leave the centre of the garden open for play, but if possible provide also retreats and hiding places—mini-arbours and dense shrubs which will also encourage birds to nest.

Grass is kinder to young knees than paving, and cheaper. If you are starting a lawn from scratch, choose a grass seed mixture specially blended for hard wear or a slow-growing type such as 'Hunter'. A path of paving or forest bark round or alongside the lawn makes a suitable track for tricycles, wheelbarrows and other toys on wheels.

Pets and wildlife

With children there are almost bound to be pets, and one lively dog can create as much havoc as a couple of high-spirited children. Even a playful cat will streak through a border leaving a trail of broken stems and flattened leaves. However, if the garden is designed and planted with children in mind, it will also be proof against pets.

The most important defence is safety. Toddlers and dogs are in danger if they can get out on to a road, and fences should be in good repair and too high for them to escape over. Gates must be securely fastened with toddler-proof catches, bolts or locks, and hedges should be dense and impenetrable.

Pet rabbits are usually kept in hutches, but it is fun for them and their young owners if they are let out every day to play. However, as they can devastate the vegetable garden, dig under fences and climb wire netting, it is safer to keep them in a portable pen or run when they are let out.

Water fascinates children, and a pool with lilies and lively, colourful fish will enthrall them for hours. Birds come to drink and catch insects, frogs to mate and spawn, and shining dragon-flies to dart over the water surface. The smallest pool is a varied miniature conservation area where children can learn much about wildlife.

Small children should never be allowed to play unattended near a pool or pond, however small or shallow. A raised pool is the safest; alternatively you can fit rigid garden mesh over the pool, secured firmly round the edges, and strong enough to take the weight of a child. A dark colour is unobtrusive, and water plants will grow through the mesh.

Outdoor toys

If the garden is large enough, play equipment can be installed. Climbing frames, swings and Wendy houses will keep children occupied for hours, but are rather expensive if they are bought as amusement for only a couple of children. They are probably worthwhile if you have several children or can pass the equipment on to friends.

A sandpit, however, is relatively inexpensive and a safe playground for toddlers. It should be sited in the sun, close to the house so that the children can be supervised. A wooden surround should be planed smooth to avoid splinters and scratches, and the pit should preferably be equipped with a cover to keep out rain and the neighbourhood cats. Provide seating in the sand, with sawn-off logs or cross planks.

In small gardens a sandpit can be incorporated in the terrace. Leave a small area free of paving material, box it in with timber and fill it up with clean sand. Later on, soil can replace the sand, and the pit become a suitable planting pocket.

Toddlers and young children also enjoy splashing around in a paddling pool. These are available in a range of shapes and sizes, all made from heavy-duty plastic, easy to erect, and pack away for the winter.

As the children grow they graduate to swings, slides, seesaws and climbing frames which they prefer to be sited some distance from prying faces in the kitchen window. These types of equipment must be sensibly sited and firmly anchored: swing chains should be securely locked and seesaws fitted with shock absorbers.

Tree houses and frames

Generally though, children soon grow bored with purpose-made toys, and prefer to use their imagination in making their own.

If you have a large robust tree, the kids can climb it, build a tree house, with your help, attach a rope ladder and fix a swing from one of the sturdy boughs with strong rope and an old car tyre.

Lacking a suitable tree, a sturdy frame, home-made or purchased, can be adapted with nets and rubber tyres for climbing, scrambling or swinging. Imaginative children will play house or Indians in a tent improvised from old blankets or curtains and a pole; a bought tent, even a tiny one, invites the adventure of sleeping out on warm nights. Old boxes, milk crates, planks of wood, large drain pipes, logs of different heights sunk into the ground become tables and chairs, or caves, tunnels and mountains for imaginary explorations.

Children's gardens

Children who show an interest in tending the garden could well be at the beginning of a satisfying, life-long hobby. Encourage their interest, but do not push them too hard or allow them to take on too much in the beginning, however en-thusiastic they seem. Give them a patch of their own, by all means, but do not be surprised if you end up looking after it. Show them how to grow quick-germinating seeds—radishes and stocks are the classic examples—but other vegetable seeds are fairly quick.

Runner beans are plump and easy for young hands to handle, and alpine strawberries fruit over several months. Bulbs, especially the small ones like snowdrops, crocus and bluebells, are full of magic for young children.

Help them with the heavy work to avoid strain on young muscles and tiredness from using heavy, grown-up tools. Dig over the patch, level and firm it, then let the children take over and make a seed bed with a hand cultivator, rake or hoe. From then on they can probably manage with a hand fork and trowel. Supervise them when they are using sharp tools, particularly secateurs and shears, until you are sure they can handle them safely. The same applies to garden chemicals, which should always be kept under lock and out of reach of small children and pets.

Dangerous plants

Many parents worry about poisonous plants. Several garden plants, including lily-of-the-valley, laburnum and yew, are poisonous in all or some of their parts and are better not introduced to the garden while the children are young. However, it is safer to impress on children from the earliest possible age, that they must not touch or eat any part of any unfamiliar plant unless told it is safe.

Use the garden as a place to teach the children about nature, wildlife and conservation. Include them when you tend the plants and explain why certain jobs have to be done; encourage them to be careful and observant.

LABOUR-SAVING GARDENS

People who look for a labour-saving garden usually mean that they want a time-saving garden. It is possible that they are not interested in the garden as a hobby and relaxation, but as it came with the house they are duty-bound to look after it. They want to pay it as little attention as possible and will be content if it is neat and tidy enough to satisfy the neighbours and visitors.

However, it is more likely that work—and family life—is a full-time occupation and that gardening has to be crammed into a few hours over the weekend. In other instances, gardeners, though healthy, no longer have the enthusiasm or stamina to do the heavy work they once enjoyed. If you come into one of these categories you will want a garden that always appears attractive—but asks little effort.

Labour—and time—saving is not difficult if the garden is small. This can be achieved with paving, containers and a few plants carefully chosen for their ease of cultivation. For anyone who loves growing things, the most difficult part will be to stop. A garden is a great seducer, and as long as it tempts with jobs to be done, it will be almost impossible to resist the challenge.

Greenhouses and frames
A greenhouse or even a modest cold frame should be resisted. Once installed you will invariably be buying seeds, compost and pots, and before long the greenhouse will be overflowing with rooting cuttings, annuals at varying seedling stages and tomatoes ready for potting-on.

A greenhouse is a marvellous aid for the dedicated gardener, but it demands labour, time and money. Once a year the structure will need painting or cleaning, the glass must be cleaned frequently, shading put up and taken down again, in addition to the regular chores of fumigating and spraying against pests and diseases which thrive in the warm humid atmosphere. And that it just the house; seedlings must be pricked out and potted-on, watered, sometimes twice a day, fed and tied in.

A labour-saving garden means doing without a greenhouse or frame, amongst other things. However, with thought and careful planning the garden can become a useful extension to the house, and be just as attractive as a conventional lawn and flower-border type.

Paving versus grass
Be prepared to spend a fair amount of time and money, at the beginning. Good paving is comparatively expensive and takes time to lay properly, but once down it is there for good and thereafter needs little or no upkeep. With the vast choice of paving types and materials, it is easy to combine different textures and colours to give warmth and interest and avoid a cold flat look. Keep the colours neutral and complementary to the house and terrace.

Boundary walls are vastly more expensive to install than fences and hedges, but they do not need clipping, painting or replacing. Walls also give better shelter and support to many plants.

A lawn sets the style of the conventional garden and is the first to show neglect. Although mowing is quick and easy with powered rotary or cylinder mowers, a lawn must still be fed, weeded, top-dressed, raked, aerated, and the edges trimmed. Grass clippings must be disposed of—probably on to a compost heap which entails more work and time.

Herbaceous borders take time to plan and plant to achieve a pleasing blend of colours and heights throughout summer and autumn. No sooner are they established and looking stunning than it is time to lift the plants, divide them, fork over the ground, feed and cultivate it, and replant the divisions and newcomers. In between there is staking, tying, dead-heading, cutting back and weeding.

Kitchen gardens
Fruit and vegetable growing demands more time, effort and regular attention than any other garden activity. Trees, bushes and cane fruit need pruning, training and tying in, spraying, feeding, netting and winter-washing. Trained fruit trees and outdoor vines are even more demanding—spur-pruning takes many hours of concentration.

Vegetables are the true tyrants of the garden. They need well-prepared, well-fed, regularly watered ground. They must be sown at intervals for a succession of crops or they will mature together, which entails several evenings preparing them for the freezer. When they need thinning out and transplanting, this must be done then and there, not when time can be found.

Cutting down on weeding
Weeding is a labour that cannot be avoided altogether, but it can be cut down by covering all bare soil with a thick mulch of peat or shredded, composted tree bark. Naturally all traces of perennial weeds must first be removed, by forking over the ground and picking out every scrap of weed.

Alternatively wait until the weeds have made a fair amount of growth, then water them with a glyphosate weedkiller, which moves through all parts of the plants within a few weeks, finally killing them completely. The advantage of this kind of weedkiller is that it does not contaminate the soil, and the area can be planted when the weeds are dead and cleared away.

Once the plants have been positioned and a mulch laid between

Minimum upkeep is needed for this restful garden. The lawn has yielded to a covering of stone chippings which remain weed-free for months after a weedkiller application in spring. Plantings consist of a few specimen trees and low evergreen foliage shrubs.

them, leave the soil alone. Do not use the hoe or fork the ground over as this will bring buried dormant weeds to the surface, and they will immediately grow and spread. An undisturbed mulch keeps the soil moist and friable and smothers most annual weeds that do germinate.

Containers and statuary

Having reduced a time-consuming garden to one of bare practicalities, it will need some ornamental touches. Invest in hand-thrown, frost-proof earthenware containers; in classical shapes and designs they are as attractive empty as when they are planted up.

Fill your containers with slow-growing evergreens or a succession of spring bulbs, followed by annuals. Buy the annuals as seedlings from a reputable nursery or garden centre which can also supply the potting compost.

It will be necessary to water all containers, probably twice a day in a hot summer, feed them weekly during the growing season and do a

little dead-heading, but these jobs take minutes and do not involve getting down on hands and knees. Tubs crammed with brightly coloured annuals make a tremendous impact for the small amount of effort involved.

Statues, sundials and birdbaths discreetly placed also dress a garden. So does attractive weatherproof furniture, lounging beds and softly playing wall fountains.

Walls and borders

Cover the boundary and house walls with self-supporting climbers, such as ivy which can be plain green or variegated and adds colour throughout the year.

Ivy and another rampant climber, *Parthenocissus tricuspidata* 'Veitchii' (Virginia creeper), should be checked periodically before they reach guttering and roofing tiles. The climbing hydrangea, *H. petiolaris*, clings by itself and quickly softens the hard look of brickwork. In summer it is clothed with large clusters of creamy flowers, and it is almost as beautiful

in winter with its bare shiny chestnut-brown stems.

Fill the borders with shrubs and small-growing trees. Select those that are handsome at various times of the year, whether in leaf, flower, autumn foliage or bare outline. Silver birches, for example, staghorn sumach, though it does sucker, Japanese maples, crab apples or one of the purple-leaved cultivars of *Cotinus coggygria* are all easy-growing trees.

Choose shrubs which need no pruning, or just a trim once a year; philadelphus and lilac, for example, need only the flowering stems shortened when the blooms have faded. Rhododendrons and camellias, where the soil is right, also need little attention. In general, it is safe to assume that shrubs which thrive locally are easy to care for.

Plant a fair number of evergreens to provide some foliage to soften the outlines of paving and walls and to make a backcloth for flowering shrubs. Set clumps of bulbs under the deciduous shrubs and leave them to increase. Most of them will flower year after year.

Ground covers and mulches

The shrub border will have to be fed and perhaps watered in dry spells until it gets established. A mulch will have to be renewed annually, and it may be a good idea to underplant the shrub border with an evergreen cover which is even more effective in smothering weeds. Heathers, *Vinca minor, Cotoneaster microphyllus, C. salicifolius*, hypericums, ivies and junipers are all suitable.

Large gardens are more difficult to transform. It is only feasible to have so much concrete or paving. One way to cut down the work is to construct a large paved, formal area round the house and treat this as a small garden, with the remainder as a wild garden (see p.84-89).

151

GARDENS FOR THE DISABLED 1

Go into any office on a Monday morning, and the odds are that there will be a fair proportion of people complaining of backache and sore muscles. They are the weekend gardeners, the ones who spent the previous two days bending, kneeling and stretching for far too long.

In the course of a weekend, these gardeners have probably dragged or lifted heavy, unwieldy bags of compost a good distance, or perched tensely on ladders while they pruned away at the climbing roses or the apple tree. Often they have worked with their backs unprotected from cold winds.

With luck the aches and pains will be soothed away by a couple of hot baths and nights of good sleep, but these unwise gardeners could be laying the foundations for permanent back or muscular trouble.

Such gardeners could take a few tips from the many disabled people

Pre-fabricated beds are ideal for handicapped gardeners. Available in moulded plastic, in a range of sizes and heights, they are instantly ready for planting up.

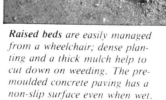

Raised beds are easily managed from a wheelchair; dense planting and a thick mulch help to cut down on weeding. The pre-moulded concrete paving has a non-slip surface even when wet.

Drystone walling being constructed for a free-standing raised bed. Trailing alpines are inserted in planting pockets, and sharp drainage is provided with broken pot chards.

in this country. Because of their disabilities they have been forced to adapt traditional working methods and to eliminate many of the jobs and movements that leave able-bodied gardeners sore and aching.

Ingenuity and sound common sense are the disabled gardeners' most useful tools, and with them they derive immense pleasure and satisfaction from their hobby.

Depending on the type and extent of the disability, it is comparatively simple to adapt a garden and gardening methods. Many of the ideas on easy maintenance, outlined in the chapter on labour-saving gardens (pages 150-151) can be adapted and extended.

Lawns and paving

Although it is possible for disabled people, even those confined to wheelchairs, to mow a lawn given a small area and suitable mower, general lawn care can be taxing. Paving is easier to look after than a lawn; it should have a non-slip surface—concrete paving slabs are the safest—and be kept free of leaves and slimy algae, by brushing and treating with a proprietary algicide.

All paving should also be level to allow wheelchairs to run over it smoothly; even a slight unevenness may trip anyone who is not too steady on their feet or who uses a walking aid.

Paths, too, should be non-slip, level and about 1 metre wide so as to accommodate a wheelchair comfortably, two people walking side by side, or a gardener with a walking frame or sticks.

Steps may have to be done away with and replaced by gentle ramps, with a gradient of no more than 1:15. For agile gardeners steps with wide treads are suitable provided they do not rise too steeply. They should be provided with a sturdy hand rail, on one side at least, to hold on to.

Trouble-free plants

Trees and shrubs that need little attention, especially in respect of pruning, are the most suitable. Slow-growing conifers, silver birches, laburnum and lilac require little care. The same is true of shrubs such as mahonias, skimmias, euonymus and cotoneasters.

If you work fairly slowly it is a good idea to keep chores to a minimum, otherwise the garden will get out of hand. Ground-cover plants smother weeds, but choose them with care; those that do the job most efficiently are usually vigorous and, unless chopped back or uprooted, will swamp everything in the border.

Evergreen ground covers— winter-flowering heathers, vincas and creeping junipers—cause few problems. You could also try perennials such as *Ajuga reptans, Geranium endressii*, sedums, hostas, galiums or soapworts (*Saponaria ocymoides*).

Beds and borders

Flower beds should be fairly narrow, no more than 60cm wide, so that the far side can be reached with a long-handled hoe or cultivator from the path. Large paving slabs can alternatively be set firmly in a wide border to act as stepping stones. Provided that they are stable and non-slip you can generally work from them in safety.

Choose plants that do not need staking, to avoid the chore of tying in and the danger of falling on sharp stakes. Climbers should be of the self-supporting kind to save erecting trellis and climbing ladders to prune and train them.

If you cannot resist growing climbing roses and feel you can manage to control them, choose one with few or no thorns. The thornless 'Zepherine Drouhin' and 'Kathleen Harrop' are excellent and easy to manage. The popular climbing

'Mermaid' is not only extremely vigorous, but also has the most vicious thorns that lock firmly in clothing and inflict painful flesh wounds. Standard roses are easier to care for than bush hybrid teas and floribundas.

As with a labour-saving garden, avoid fussy, fiddly borders, narrow paths and sharp corners that are difficult to negotiate.

Raised beds

Rock gardens are definitely for those nimble of hand and foot, but raised beds and troughs are perfect alternatives for anyone whose movements are restricted or who works from a wheelchair.

A raised bed should be approximately 60cm high to give a comfortable working level. If it is built against a wall, the width should be no more than 60cm; a free-standing bed can be twice that if there is space for a wheelchair on both sides of the bed.

Raised beds can be built from paving slabs stood on end, or purchased with a recess which accommodates a chair. Raised beds can also be constructed from peat blocks, suitable for lime-hating alpines; they can be built as drystone walls or consist of troughs and trays raised to waist height.

Such beds are easy to sow, plant and weed, but as they tend to drain quickly they need more watering than a bed at soil level. Good quick drainage suits plants that like dry conditions, notably most true alpines. Practicalities apart, a raised bed enables the gardener to observe plants and flowers almost at eye level and savour their fragrance far better than at ground level.

Garden equipment

Watering can be a problem for the handicapped as water, even carried in a light plastic can, is heavy. A

GARDENS FOR THE DISABLED 2

permanent hose-based system or trickle irrigation that is laid in the soil and has several supply points is the ideal solution, especially if it can be automatically controlled.

A simpler and cheaper idea is to have large containers or water butts placed round the garden. These reservoirs can be topped up from a hose and you can fill small watering cans from them quite easily.

A wheelbarrow will be necessary for moving larger pieces of equipment or bags of compost. Several makes have been designed specifically for disabled gardeners. The Remploy Gardenmate has a removable galvanised container, and the frame can be used as a walking aid or for moving heavy sacks and other articles.

There is also a barrow with a single handle that hitches, like a trailer, on to the back of a wheelchair. There is another type with a pram handle that supports the user as it is pushed along.

For sitting or kneeling, there is the Easy-kneeler stool. It has handles at either side to hold on to as you lower yourself to a kneeling position or push yourself upright. A thick foam mat protects knees from cold and damp. Turned over the Easy-kneeler makes a useful stool.

Hand tools

Most cultivation chores can be done, even from a wheelchair, using lightweight, long-handled tools. Before purchasing try them out for comfortable, easy grip and good balance. Do not buy too many tools at the beginning because one can often do several different jobs.

A Dutch hoe, for instance, skims off surface weeds, and pushed through the top layer of soil, keeps it open and weed-free. It can also be used to break down small lumps of soil, draw out seed drills, cover and firm them down as well as taking out shallow planting holes and fill-ing them in. There are also special hoes, such as the scuffle hoe; its diamond-shaped blade makes it easy to thin out seedlings without damage. Another type of hoe has a cranked handle, and is designed for the use of only one hand.

Many tools can be adapted: a trowel, fixed to a long handle, makes planting easy and can be used to dig out the holes, drop the plants in and position them correctly. Without bending, the soil can be replaced and firmed round the plants with the back of the trowel.

A small cultivator or tiller, like the Merry Tiller or the Garden Weasel, are easy to use on light soils and do an excellent job of breaking them down to a fine tilth. As the handle is pushed forwards and backwards, from a standing or sitting position, a row of starshaped wheels bite into the soil. These cultivators are also efficient for weeding between rows, and the Weasel can have one or two of its heads removed, so that it will fit into small gaps or narrow spaces between rows.

A wheel-type seed sower set to release a given number of seeds per row is easy to use from a sitting position if the handle is strapped to a wooden coat hanger. It is also possible to grow most vegetables and herbs in raised beds. Pelleted seeds are easy to distribute, but the seed drills must be kept moist.

Packets of seeds and small tools can be carried in a basket fixed to a walking stick, or a carrier bag or plastic tray hung from a walking frame. For straight seed drills without bending, fix a garden line wound on a fishing reel to the top of one long stick. Feed it through two screw eyes to the lower end of the stick and tie it to an eye at the bottom of another stick. A marked ruler can be fixed to a light rod and used for measuring the width of rows and plant spacings.

Spades and forks can be adapted by fitting a handle grip on the shaft, so that they can be used from a wheelchair, and the Wolf Terrex spade is one of the best tools for a gardener who finds it difficult to bend and to lift spadefuls of turned over soil. It has widely spaced handles and a spring lever action which pushes the blade into the soil and propels it forwards.

Pruners and secateurs

For pruning, choose ratchet-operated secateurs. They need only light pressure to cut through stems up to 2cm thick. Long-handled ratchet pruners are a little heavier, but they can be operated for short periods from a sitting position by a lever action on the handle. It is best to avoid powered tools unless you are absolutely sure that you can handle them.

For hands with weak grip, there are special aluminium hand trowels, forks and planters. They are moulded in one piece with a preformed grip for finger and thumb; they are light and strong, though rather cold to the touch.

A greenhouse is a boon for disabled gardeners, especially if it is all automatic. You can garden in it all year round, except on the very coldest days, and be protected from wind and rain. A much wider range of plants can be grown with ease and comfort. Choose a type with an easily negotiable door—a sliding door for a wheelchair gardener. Keep the centre aisle free; it should leave room to manouevre and be at least 75cm wide. Have the staging at a comfortable height and no more than 60cm wide.

Clothing that keeps feet and back warm and dry makes sense for all gardeners, and particularly so if you are disabled by arthritis or rheumatism. A hat is sensible too, keeping in warmth on cold days and giving shade from hot sun.

ALLOTMENT GARDENS 1

Allotment gardens are usually fine examples of good cultivation and tidiness. Neat rows of potatoes, lettuce, spinach and carrots *alternate with netted cane fruits and odd clumps of delphiniums. By midsummer individual plots will be demarcated with* *screens of scarlets and white runner beans. Each allotment is divided into three strips for a three-year cycle of crop rotation.*

ALLOTMENT GARDENS 2

The history of allotments in Britain can be traced back to the Middle Ages, but the Small Holdings and Allotments Act of 1908 is the basis for the present-day allotment system. The act placed obligations on local authorities to provide allotments for the working population if land could not be obtained by private agreement and also gave them the right to purchase land compulsorily for allotments.

The Allotments Act of 1922 defined an allotment garden as "not exceeding forty poles in extent which is wholly or mainly cultivated by the occupier for the production of vegetable or fruit crops for consumption by himself or his family".

A further Allotments Act, in 1925, stipulated that allotments should be considered in every town-planning scheme. Land purchased or appropriated by a local authority for use as allotments must not be disposed of or used for other purposes without Ministerial consent.

In 1965, a committee, appointed by the then Minister of Land and Natural Resources, was set up to review general policy on allotments. The committee recommended among other things that allotments be abolished as a term of law because of its economic overtones, and that the term "leisure gardens" be substituted.

These recommendations still await consideration by Parliament, but many people have become aware of the need for improvements in allotment gardening, and Leisure Garden Sites have become a reality in many parts of the country.

The demand for leisure gardens, where the cultivation of flowers, herbs, ornamental shrubs and trees is encouraged, along with lawns and the erection of garden chalets, shows no evidence of reducing the need for the more conventional type of allotment garden devoted to fruit and vegetables.

Allotment tenancies

An express duty is placed on every parish and community council and on every district council, where they are of the opinion that there is a demand for allotment gardens in their area, to provide a sufficient number for letting to persons resident in their area.

At the end of September 1978, the date of the latest allotment statistics issued by the Department of the Environment, 121,000 people throughout the country were on official waiting lists. With the original stipulation of "labouring poor" being long abolished, gardeners of both sexes and of every profession are steadily increasing the demand for allotments.

Most people rent their allotment gardens from the local councils, and having been granted a tenancy, the term is usually assured for one year, and thereafter on an annual renewal basis. Many Allotment Associations have taken over the management of the sites and allocate plots on behalf of the council.

It is geneally useful to make enquiries to local Allotment Associations which are less tied up in official red tape. Some landowners and various statutory undertakings also provide allotment plots, and several industrial concerns offer sites round their premises for the use of their employees.

Allotments vary considerably in age, status and characteristics. Many provide the only open spaces in a built-up environment, constituting a measure of fresh air and attractive visual features.

Tenancy agreements

Model rules regarding allotment gardens are available to local authorities from the Department of the Environment, and these are issued to individual tenants or to Allotment Associations as tenancy agreements. After identifying the particular allotment garden, a tenancy agreement generally states the date of the commencement of the tenancy and the annual rental, and sets out the conditions under which the tenancy may be held.

There is complete prohibition on any trade or business being carried out from the produce of an allotment garden. Home freezers, whereby most of the excess crop grown can now be preserved, has in any case reduced the temptation for this form of activity.

The keeping of animals on allotment gardens is prohibited, except for hens (but not cockerels) and rabbits, other than by way of trade. The consent of the local council must be obtained in each instance.

No planning permission is needed for the use of land as allotments. The General Rate Act of 1967 declares that no agricultural land or agricultural buildings (which includes allotment gardens within the meaning of the Allotments Act 1922), shall be liable to rating or be included in any valuation list.

Allotment crops

The emphasis on vegetable growing is so strong on allotment sites that few flowers are cultivated. Many local authorities impose a complete ban on the growing of flowers or any plant, bush or tree that takes longer than 12 months to reach maturity.

There appears to be no restriction on the type of vegetables that may be grown. Many allotment tenants from other countries have introduced their native vegetables, and these can be seen growing side by side with more usual crops. A considerable amount of asparagus is now grown on allotment sites, along with celeriac, chicory, garlic, kohlrabi, salsify, scorzonera and many other unusual vegetables.

The overall appearance of allotment-garden sites is influenced by the presence, condition and positioning of individual structures on the plots, such as sheds and greenhouses. Standards are set by most local authorities, and tenants are not allowed to erect any structure without written consent.

General amenities are constantly being improved by local authorities, although the provision of toilet facilities has extremely low priority. Only on larger sites have communal buildings been erected.

Rules and regulations

Many allotment sites are fenced in and provided with lockable gates, each tenant being provided with a key, in an effort to reduce vandalism which is prevalent in some areas. The families of allotment gardeners are allowed access to the sites, but car parking is banned. Children and pet animals are not permitted to wander at will. In many cases, dogs are not allowed on the site unless on a lead.

Water and the high cost of installing it also presents difficulties. Sites which are provided with water points rarely have enough of these and fetching and carrying becomes inevitable. On most sites the use of hoses is banned, and water is normally turned off during winter.

Many allotment sites are adjacent to residential properties, and nearby householders may complain about smoke nuisance from the burning of spent crops. Most waste material can be composted to form organic matter to feed successive crops, and the plot is easily kept tidy if the compost material is contained in bins or bounded by wire-netting. In some instances garden rubbish can be deposited in a communal dump which is cleared by the local council at certain intervals.

The delivery of farmyard and other bulky manures can present difficulties; the tenant is usually required to be present at delivery to ensure that it is not deposited on the wrong plot.

Soil conditions vary from site to site and even within one site. Some soils are of heavy clay, and the drainage can be more than poor during the winter season. However, allotment soil is required to be suitable for spade husbandry, and where this is in doubt the site may be visited and subsequently reported on by a Regional Surveyor of the Ministry of Agriculture, Fisheries and Food.

An allotment site is also expected to be within reasonable travelling distance of a tenant's home. This was originally estimated at ¾ mile (approx. 1km), but with greater mobility resulting from increased car-ownership, a distance of up to 1½ mile (approx. 2.5km) would now be considered reasonable.

Costs and sizes

Local authorities are supposed to assess the rents allotment-garden tenants may reasonably be expected to pay, although they may charge a lower rent if the personal circumstances of a tenant warrants it, as in the case of Senior Citizens.

There appears to be no basis on which local authorities let their plots: a 10 pole (250 square metres) plot in Cardiff may at present be rented for £2.70 per annum; the same-sized plot in Oxford costs £1.85, but in Bristol it would cost £8.00.

The standard allotment garden consists of 250 square metres (300 sq. yds.). An area of this size is necessary for the proper rotation of crops to ensure that the utmost use is made of whatever manures or fertilizers have been put into the ground, and to prevent the build-up of soil-borne plant diseases.

The practice of dividing a standard plot into two of 125 square metres in order to reduce the waiting lists of tenants, without providing additional land, does not benefit the land in any way as proper crop rotation is curtailed.

Termination of tenancies

Allotment-tenancy agreements usually have a provision that the tenancy may be seen to have expired in the event of the rent remaining unpaid for at least 40 days, on giving one month's notice in writing.

Normally, an allotment tenancy can only be terminated by serving 12 months or longer notice to quit, on or before 6th April or on or after 29th September in any year.

On the termination of a tenancy and on quitting the land, the tenant, irrespective of any agreement to the contrary, is entitled from his landlord to compensation for crops growing on the land in the ordinary course of cultivation.

Few statistics are available, but it is estimated that the standard-size plot can keep a family of four in vegetables for the full year.

At the end of the tenancy, there may also be some compensation for manure applied to the land and for any disturbance, amounting in total to one year's rent at the rate payable immediately before the termination of the tenancy.

Allotment Associations

Most allotment gardeners as well as many non-allotment gardeners belong to a local Allotment Association. In addition to mutual aid, these are able to obtain gardening equipment, such as seeds, fertilisers and tools, below retail prices.

Most associations amalgamate in federations within local authority areas, and federations together form county organisations. Many are organised in 23 area bodies, affiliated to the National Society of Allotment and Leisure Gardeners Limited, the only national organisation existing for the benefit of all allotment gardeners.

GARDEN UPKEEP

Young or mature, a garden is constantly
developing.
It falls to the gardener to direct,
alter or stem its growth
by timely and frequent attention.

GARDEN UPKEEP 1

A well-ordered, profitable and pleasure-giving garden is achieved only through regular care, throughout almost the full 12 months, year after year. True, there are several short-cuts to successful gardening: powered machinery takes the backache out of mowing and hedge-trimming, sprinkler systems cut to a minimum the chore of watering, and mulching suppresses most of the annual weeds.

Even so, vegetable plots and flower borders need annual digging or forking over, manures and fertilisers must be applied to maintain soil fertility, and the battle must be fought against pernicious weeds, garden pests and diseases. Roses and fruit trees must be pruned and trained, lawns regularly mown, and faded flowers dead-headed.

Digging and forking

Why dig or fork the garden? Some gardeners, keen on avoiding this arduous chore, maintain it is a waste of time and spread garden compost instead. They insist that compost-grown fruit, vegetables and flowers not only taste and look better, but are easier to manage and grow

faster. This claim is generally true, but most gardeners simply lack large quantities of leaf-mould, rotted manure or garden compost to spread around. They have to grow plants in the existing soil and enrich it with organic manures.

A heavy clay soil is best dug in autumn, to the depth of a spade blade (or spit). Throw the soil up into even layers of chunky clods for frost to break it down to a tilth in spring. You can assist this pulverising action by sprinkling the soil with hydrated or garden lime (ground chalk) or with gypsum (calcium sulphate).

Light sandy soils, though constantly needing food in the form of bulky organic manures, are a pleasure to cultivate. No need to dig them in winter—a light forking over in spring is all that is necessary. However, if you are thinking of adding manures do this in the autumn, using a spade, so that the organic matter can rot down fully and release their plant foods. Faced with a patch thickly carpeted with weeds, slice these off before digging and place them in the bottom of the digging trenches.

In early spring, prick round border plants with a border fork, slightly smaller than a digging fork, to nick out germinating weeds. This operation also aerates the soil, and it is aesthetically satisfying to view a neatly forked plot. Fork over also the soil between rows of potatoes, to encourage the roots to spread and produce a heavier yield. Lightly prick the soil between rock plants and close-set spring bedding with a long-handled weeding fork.

Liming and feeding

Throughout the growing season all plants draw on nutrients in the soil. Nitrogen, phosphates and potash are essential; other chemicals, such as calcium, magnesium and iron are also necessary but in smaller amounts. At the time of sowing, scatter a 5cm wide band of complete fertiliser, at 100g. per square metre, along the seed drills for rain water to wash it in.

Lime, like calcium, is needed to ensure balanced growth in all but lime-hating plants, to prevent the soil from becoming too acid and to reduce the incidence of club root disease in brassicas. Lime is best

Autumn digging, leaving the soil rough, exposes the greatest volume of heavy clods to the beneficial effects of winter frost.

Farmyard manure, spread over the bottom of trenches, not only converts into humus but also releases valuable plant nutrients —

nitrogen, phosphoric acid and potash, with magnesium and calcium. Freshly manured soil is suitable for brassicas, not root crops.

scattered over the soil in autumn, once every three years (see also p.167).

Liquid feeds of high potash fertiliser should be given when tomatoes and other fruits start to form. Potash encourages good fruit development and flavour. Do not feed tomatoes until they have formed their lower truss, or they may grow so vigorously that they forget to form fruit.

In late winter, spring cabbages benefit from a top dressing of sulphate of ammonia or nitrate of soda; give each plant about 1 dessertspoonful sprinkled over the root area. Make sure to keep crystals or granules off all plant leaves.

After an initial feeding in spring, repeat top dressings for vegetables, such as lettuces, beetroot and cabbages, every 6 – 8 weeks throughout the growing season. Cease feeding in autumn when the soil grows cold and plants become inactive.

Lime-induced chlorosis—a yellowing of the leaves between bright green veins—is caused by iron being locked in the soil by excess calcium. Sequestered iron provides plants with soluble iron and magnesium necessary for general plant health.

See also the chapter on soil (pp. 22 – 37).

Watering
No dribbles. If watering becomes necessary because flowers and vegetables are on the point of wilting, be generous. An occasional light watering, merely wetting the surface of the soil, does more harm than good and encourages roots to probe upwards, where they are liable to be scorched by the sun.

Forget the watering can, except for pot and greenhouse plants, and invest in a hosepipe, complete with T-junctions, so that a sprinkler can be attached to one offshoot, to

Young Brussels sprouts in a protective straw mulch. Weeds are suppressed and mud is less likely to splash on to the sprouts.

water the lawn, and another branch can feed water to the vegetable plot. A perforated hosepipe which sends up a fine mist spray ensures that the soil is evenly watered without becoming compacted.

Always water in the evening or early morning, when the sun, and therefore transpiration, is at its weakest. If using a hand-held hosepipe avoid strong jets of water which can bruise leaves and stems and compact the soil.

Marrows, tomatoes and other plants with a large spread of leaves can be watered the easy way: by sinking flower pots close to each plant and filling these. This ensures that all the water goes straight to the roots; later in the season, liquid feeds can be added to the water. Runner beans appreciate a fine spraying over after hot days; this also encourages flowers to set.

Water-in transplanted seedlings so that the soil settles firmly round their roots. Leek seedlings, for example, are usually placed in deep holes made with a dibber, then filled with water. As the water drains away it washes the soil over the fine roots and anchors them.

During prolonged droughts, dig out shallow trenches round surface-rooting shrubs; fill these with water, then replace the soil and cover with black polythene. Lawns watered with a hand-held hosepipe can be fertilised at the same time by fitting to it a plant food distributor.

Newly arrived, bare-rooted fruit trees, shrubs or roses which seem limp can be plumped up by soaking them in a large bucket or tub of water until the bark is sleek.

Damping down the greenhouse, which means spraying water so as to wet pots, staging and floor, is essential in summer to stop plants wilting. Do this in the morning to create a humid atmosphere.

Mulching
The need for watering in summer can be greatly reduced where the soil is mulched to keep it cool and evenly moist. Basically a mulch is a thickish, about 10cm, layer of peat, garden compost, forest bark, leaf-mould, decomposed sawdust or other organic refuse spread over the soil. A mulch insulates roots against the drying effects of the sun, prevents ruptures of the cells by frost and smothers germinating weed seeds.

In short, a mulch ensures that soil temperatures remain stable and that sturdy top growth is unchecked by fluctuating air temperatures. However, precisely because of its insulating effect a mulch must be spread at the proper time. The best time to summer-mulch roses, herbaceous perennials, trees, shrubs and bulbs, is in spring when the sun has warmed up the soil. For a winter mulch to frost-tender plants spread a protective layer of peat in autumn before the soil becomes cold. Never mulch frosted or dry soil.

Before mulching, fork out all perennial weeds and hoe off annual weeds such as groundsel and chickweed. Alternatively douse the area with a dilute selective weedkiller. Water the soil copiously, without flooding, then spread the mulch evenly.

GARDEN UPKEEP 2

Use a hoe to create a dust mulch between rows of vegetables and between flowering plants. This disturbed layer helps to check the upward evaporation of water from the subsoil, and also keeps down weeds.

An evenly cool and moist soil can also be maintained by laying black plastic between and around plants. Weeds, too, are prevented from germinating. Keep the plastic in position by inserting the edges in slit trenches along the rows or around the root spread.

Spring bedding plants

These include wallflowers, forget-me-nots and polyanthus. The latter is a true perennial, but the others are grown as biennials, from seed sown in May or June.

Prepare a nursery bed in reasonably fertile soil, and sow seeds 1cm deep in drills 15cm apart. When the seedlings are about 15cm high, lift them with plenty of soil round their roots and transplant them to a nursery bed, 15cm apart.

In autumn, after they have made strong growth, set the young plants where they are to flower, spacing them 15cm apart each way. Nip out the growing tips if side-branching has not occurred naturally to help to develop stocky plants.

When the blooms of wallflowers and forget-me-nots fade, dig up the plants and relegate them to the compost heap.

Dead-head polyanthus by cutting out the faded flower stems so as to divert energy into new leaf growth. Lift the plants carefully and set them in a cool, moist spot for the summer. Large clumps can be pulled apart to increase the stock.

Spring and summer bulbs

Gay and cheerful from late winter through the spring, the tulips, daffodils and crocuses planted in the autumn can present a dismal sight as the blooms fade.

Daffodils and crocuses can be left where they are, assuming they have been set among shrubs and patches in the lawn or herbaceous border. But tulips are different. They are often planted as spring bedding, and the ground will be needed for summer-bedding plants.

As soon as the petals drop, lift the tulips carefully with a fork and heel them in in a reserve border where the sun can ripen the bulbs and where they can be left undisturbed. In autumn, lift the tulips, remove the tiny bulblets and plant them in a nursery bed to mature. Plant the mature bulbs once more to provide a colourful spring show. If it is not possible to spare a piece of ground, lift the heeled-in tulips when the leaves and stems have withered. Sort through the bulbs and store them in a cool and dry place until replanting in autumn.

Gladioli, planted in spring to flower in summer, must also be lifted when the great spikes of blooms begin to fade. When the leaves have yellowed, dig up the corms from the ground and cut the stems back to 5cm from the top of the corm, at the same time pulling off the shrivelled, used-up corm beneath. Pack the new corms, dusted with a fungicidal powder, side by side in boxes and store them in a frost-free greenhouse or shed for the winter. Replant them the following spring.

Beds and borders

A bed of hardy annuals sown in March, or a little later if the weather is cold, will yield colour all summer long. Broadcast the seed thinly and cover with a shallow layer of soil. When the seedlings are large enough to handle, thin them to stand 10-15cm apart; thinnings can be replanted to increase the display.

Like herbaceous perennials, annuals tend to flop unless staked, but as the latter seldom attain the heights of perennials short twiggy props can be used. Alternatively, make up rings of rigid plastic mesh, fix them to canes and set them over clumps of plants to support them.

Dead-heading encourages a second show of colour in late summer. Simply shear off the flowered stems with hedging shears. Sweet peas, grown for long-stemmed blooms, can be trained as cordons. Allow one stem only per cane and remove all tendrils. This directs more energy into flower formation, and the task of tying stems to the canes is not difficult. Sweet-pea rings can be used for fixing stems in position.

Herbaceous borders

In spring, delphiniums, Michaelmas daisies, phlox and other clump-forming perennials benefit from having crowding shoots thinned to four or six in each clump. They will grow on strongly and produce larger flowers.

Except for self-supporting plants like coreopsis, dicentras, *Aster frikartii* and kniphofias (red hot poker), support of some kind is necessary. This can be two or three canes inserted round the edge of the clump, with string wound round them, or special 'grow-through' wire rings supported on legs. Hazel sticks inserted among the plants early in the season are ideal supports, but difficult to come by now. Tie up plants progressively as they grow.

If the plants are mulched with garden compost or rotted manure annually in spring, no feed is needed apart from a spring dressing of National Growmore.

Prolong the flowering period by cutting out faded flowers, thus preventing seed formation and encouraging new flower shoots.

Every third or fourth year a herbaceous bed needs an overhaul. In autumn, lift all plants and heel them in in a reserve border. Dig over the soil, and use healthy outer portions from the old clumps to make the new border. Discard the worn centres of the divisions.

Inevitably gaps appear between established perennials, but these can be filled temporarily with hardy annuals, such as godetias, clarkias or calendulas, sown *in situ*.

In late autumn or early spring cut down to ground level all dead shoots and faded flowers, and fork between the clumps to remove weeds. Scatter slug bait round delphinium crowns, which are favourites with this pest.

ANNUAL LAWN CARE

A lawn which is a healthy deep green in winter is a hallmark of perfection. A patch of grass in perfect condition at the worst time of the year indicates that it will be truly superb throughout the spring and summer—provided it receives regular and careful attention.

In January there is little work to do, and this is the time to have the mower blades sharpened. Check over the machine; oil will almost certainly be needed round the chain and control linkage. Sand away spots of rust and paint the metal.

With the mower in good order, with sharp shiny blades, do not be afraid to shear off shaggy grass in February if a mild spell spurs growth. This will make the lawn less retentive of water and more pleasant to walk on.

In March give the grass a good raking to tease out dead and yellowing growth. Use a springy wire rake or a steel rake with thin, flat cutting blades that pivot as you push and pull. Comb the lawn thoroughly and compost the debris.

After raking, spike any areas that were seen to collect puddles after heavy rain; brush into the holes a mixture of half peat and half sharp sand to improve surface drainage. Spiking can be done with a garden

LAWNS: WEEDKILLERS AND FERTILISERS		
Weeds	**Chemicals**	**Brand names**
Plantains, daisies, clover, dandelions	2,4 – D + mecoprop	ICI Lawn Plus Fisons Velvetone Verdone (spot treatment)
Speedwell	Ioxynil/mecoprop	Iotox (May & Baker) Clovercide Extra (Synchemicals)
Annual weeds (new lawns)	Ioxynil	Actrilawn (May & Baker)
Moss	Mercurous chloride Ammonium sulphate + ferrous sulphate	MC Mosskiller Fisons Lawn Sand
Diseases		
Red thread	Dichlorophen	Super Mosskiller and
Fusarium	Dichlorophen	Lawn Fungicide (Murphy) Mosstox Plus (May & Baker)
Fertilisers: Spring	**Fertilisers: Summer**	**Fertilisers: Autumn**
ICI All Seasons Lawn Food National Growmore Peat and sand	ICI All Seasons Lawn Food National Growmore Murphy Lawn Food Bio Lawn Tonic	ICI All Seasons Lawn Food National Growmore PBI Toplawn Peat and sand

fork, along a guideline, inserting the tines 15cm deep and 15-23cm apart. Alternatively use a rotary lawn aerator, a machine fitted with a spiked drum-shaped device which effortlessly perforates the surface.

Spiking and top-dressing completed, the next job is a spring feed to the lawn during mild weather. Use a balanced lawn fertiliser or National Growmore at 100g per square metre. This will spur rapid growth and help to build up strong roots.

When the grass is ready for the first proper cut of the season, set the roller on the mower so that the blades leave about 2cm of grass standing. If frost has raised the lawn surface or made it uneven, give it a light rolling before you mow. You can use the heavy roller on a cylinder mower with its blades in the air. Another good reason for rolling before the first mowing is that otherwise the blades may pull the loosened grass from the soil.

As the weather warms up, the grass will need cutting once a week. Weeds will make their appearance and should be dealt with at once. Destroy them with a combined weed-and-feed fertiliser, to eradicate common nuisances such as plantains, daisies, clover and dandelions. Blue-flowered speedwell must be tackled with an ioxynil-based weedkiller specially formulated to destroy persistent small-leaved weeds.

Isolated large, broad-leaved lawn weeds can be destroyed by spot-treatment with a 2,4-D/mecoprop based aerosol spray.

Lawn edges will need a regular trim every ten days. Use long-handled edging shears rather than hedging shears or, if the lawn is large, invest in a rotary edging machine, which can be operated by hand or electric power. For a new lawn edge, stretch a guideline tautly and work along it with a half-moon

GARDEN UPKEEP 3

Spiking a lawn in spring (above) aerates the soil and helps to improve drainage of compacted areas. For turfing, prepare the ground thoroughly and rake it level (right); lay the turves in strips, working from a plank, and press them firmly together.

edging tool in preference to a spade. Curved edges can be achieved by cutting to a flexible hose pipe.

By June, the roller can be lowered so that the mower blades leave barely 1cm of grass. Give a further feed of balanced lawn fertiliser, or a combined weed-and-feed dressing, ideally when rain is imminent so that the plant foods are quickly dissolved and absorbed.

Droughts may occur in late June, and with a ban on watering the lawn must be left to its fate. You can prevent serious damage by curtailing mowing. When watering is necessary and permissable, it should be done thoroughly. The easiest way to soak the whole area evenly is with a hosepipe attached to an oscillating sprinkler. For large lawns there are sprinklers which 'walk' slowly across the lawn, distributing the water. It may also be worthwhile to install an underground sprinkler system with strategically placed sprinkler heads which pop up when water is turned on.

By late summer, the grass is growing less quickly, and a cut every ten days is adequate. In warm weather it is advisable to mow without the grass box so that the fine spray of clippings falls on to the grass and keeps the roots cool.

New and repaired lawns

Heavy dews forecast the end of summer and the start of autumn. This is the time to sow or lay a new lawn or patch up balding spots. Lawns can also be sown in spring, and turfing can continue during winter in mild spells.

Ground for a new lawn should have adequate drainage. Use a fork or rotary cultivator to loosen compacted soil; rake out stones and debris and, if necessary, firm the area by treading or rolling. Level the site with a rake as a final preparation for seeding or turfing.

Choose a calm day for sowing and use seed treated with a bird repellant; sow at 40-50g per square metre. An old cup or tin, marked to show the level of 40g of seed, makes a simple and reliable measure. Scatter each measure of seed as evenly as possible over each square metre.

Large lawn areas can be sown with a mechanical seed distributor, which is also useful for applying fertilisers.

Rake the seed in evenly and give a light rolling if the soil is dry.

Turves give an almost instant lawn, but are expensive compared to seed; purchase turves, grown for lawns, from a reputable source—cheap turf is likely to consist of coarse grasses and to contain weeds. Most turves are 2.5–4 cm thick and sold in 30cm squares or in 1 metre long rolls, 30cm wide. Start laying the turves from one of the outer edges, working towards the centre; stagger the turf joints in each row as in brickwork, and ideally work on a plank laid over the already turfed area to avoid compacting the bare soil in front.

Press each turf firmly and pack in soil if necessary to maintain a true level. Take care that turf pieces on the lawn edges are of reasonable size; filling in with small pieces is unsatisfactory as they tend to crumble and break away. As each row of turves is completed, tamp it firm with the back of a spade or a special turf beater. Rolling of the finished lawn, though not essential, helps to weld the turves together.

Repair work of worn-out lawn patches can begin in late autumn. Hollows and hummocks in the lawn can be levelled simply by slicing through and peeling back the turf, then adding or removing soil to get the area level.

If the lawn edge has crumbled in places, cut out squares of turf round the damaged area and reverse them. Fill the resultant holes with sifted compost and sow thickly with grass seed. Do the same to bald patches worn thin by the summer's activities: fork over the compacted soil, rake it to a tilth, working in a little balanced fertiliser, and sow.

Autumn is also the best time to give the lawn a nourishing top dressing of equal parts sifted garden soil, peat and sharp sand, together with an autumn lawn fertiliser. Spike the lawn first then scatter the soil and fertiliser mixture over the lawn at the rate of one bucket per square metre and brush it into the holes.

In late autumn, red thread and fusarium diseases may appear, especially if a high-nitrogen fertiliser was used earlier in the year. These lawn fungi can brown off large areas of turf and weaken the grass unless treated in time. Overcome them by treating the affected areas with dichlorophen.

A new lawn sown in early August or September will need a light mowing in early November. Roll it lightly first, with the rear roller of the mower, and set the blades to leave the grass about 2.5cm high. If weeds are coming up strongly and tend to stifle the grass, use a mild selective weedkiller such as Actrilawn; 2,4-D/mecocrop weedkillers should not be used until the following late spring or the young grasses may be checked.

By December, little routine work is necessary, and apart from a very occasional cut to keep the turf in trim the only other jobs should be an overhaul of tools and machinery.

HEDGES

Once a hedge has reached its required height, it needs annual clipping to keep it healthy, bushy and at a suitable height. Hedges serve a number of purposes, such as wind or privacy screens, boundary markers or bed edging; they may be close and formal or loosely arching and informal in habit. All need some maintenance.

A number of flowering shrubs make good, if fairly loose hedges, but the more popular hedging plants are foliage shrubs or trees, deciduous or evergreen, including many conifers. However, certain plants are best avoided in certain situations. A dairy farmer, for instance, would hardly appreciate a hedge of yew whose leaves and berries are poisonous, planted next to a field in which his herd of cattle graze. Similarly, it would be unwise to grow a barrier of laburnum, poisonous in all its parts, near a public footpath.

Although your hedge is growing within your boundaries, a neighbour is legally entitled to cut off any shade-casting branches, and soil-invading roots which cross the boundary, and, in theory, he must return the pieces removed.

Theoretically, any woody-stemmed plant could be used for hedging, but in practice only those which respond well to hard clipping are suitable. Many shrubs die back if pruning cuts reach into old wood. This is particularly the case with flowering hedge plants, and for this reason they are chiefly used for informal hedges and given a light trim only, after flowering. Hedges of lavender rarely survive for long excessively hard pruning, and while forsythia and snowberry can be cut back several times during the growing season, this will be at the expense of next year's flowers.

Hedge shaping
The purpose of any formal hedge is to form a dense barrier, from ground level up. In general, hedging plants, excepting some conifers, are supplied as 45-60cm high, young shrubs and planted at similar distances. They should all be cut back by at least half—informal flowering hedges of loose habit need only be shortened by one third at planting time.

As a hedge grows, reduce the new shoots by half, annually in summer, until the required height is reached. At the same time as pruning for bushiness, shape the developing hedge so that the sides taper slightly inwards, and the top becomes narrower than the base. It is also a good idea to leave the top slightly rounded so that rain and snow are shed more easily.

Once established, hedge shaping is governed by the growth rate. The fast-growing privet (*Ligustrum japonicum*) may need three cuts during the season unless the hedge is sprayed, after the first trimming in late spring, with a proprietary growth retardent. Most other hedges, including informal flowering ones, will usually do with one annual trimming. The best time is high summer, when new growth has matured and hardened; earlier trimming will result in abundant new shoots requiring a second shaping later in the summer.

Do not prune hedges after late August/early September or the young shoots may not have hardened sufficiently to withstand autumn and winter frost.

For small-leaved hedges, use hand or electric shears, kept sharp and with notched positions on the blade for extra tough shoots. Broad-leaved (Portugal laurel and holly)

GARDEN UPKEEP 4

HEDGE PLANTS

Name	Type	Growth rate	Trim
EVERGREEN			
Berberis x *stenophylla*	Informal	Medium	June, after flowering
Buxus sempervirens 'Suffruticosa' (box)	Dwarf formal edging	Slow	August
Chamaecyparis lawsoniana and cultivars	Formal (hedges & screens)	Fast	Late spring
x *Cupressocyparis leylandii* and cultivars	Formal (hedges & screens)	Fast	Late spring
Escallonia macrantha	Informal (maritime gardens)	Medium	After flowering
Euonymus japonicus cultivars	Formal (maritime gardens)	Slow	July
Ilex aquifolium (holly)	Formal	Slow	July
Lavandula latifolia	Dwarf informal edging	Slow	August, after flowering
Ligustrum japonicum (privet)	Formal	Fast	Late spring to late summer
Lonicera nitida	Formal	Fast	Late spring to late summer
Prunus lusitanica (Portugal laurel)	Formal	Slow	April/May
Pyracantha coccinea & *P. rogersiana*	Formal or informal	Fast	Spring (before flowering) or summer (loss of berries)
Rosmarinus officinalis	Informal edging	Slow/medium	April or September
Taxus baccata (yew)	Formal	Slow	Late spring
Thuja plicata	Formal	Medium	Late spring
DECIDUOUS			
Carpinus betulus (hornbeam)	Formal (brown winter leaves)	Medium	August
Crataegus monogyma & *C. oxyacantha* (hawthorn)	Formal/informal	Medium	August / Lightly after flowering
Fagus sylvatica (beech)	Formal (brown winter leaves)	Slow/medium	August
Forsythia x *intermedia*	Informal	Medium/fast	Late spring
Fuchsia magellanica cultivars	Informal	Medium/fast	Autumn or spring
Prunus cerasifera (cherry plum)	Formal	Medium	June/July
Rosa 'Queen Elizabeth'	Informal	Fast	October or March
Symphoricarpos albus 'White Hedge'	Informal	Medium	March

hedges are better trimmed with secateurs to avoid cuts in the leaves. For an even hedge top, fix a taut line, between two stakes, at the required height and clip to this.

Overgrown hedges, or those thin and weak at the bottom can often be rejuvenated by cutting them back to 15cm above ground level in spring.

ROCK GARDENS

Rock gardens are at their most exciting in spring when they are a mass of colour in almost every conceivable hue. But before that, firm any plants loosened by frost and remove piles of drifted leaves. Fork the rock garden over lightly, taking care not to damage surface roots; remove weeds and top dress with sifted, good garden compost or John Innes No. 1 potting compost.

Cut back invasive mossy saxifrages before they swamp less vigorous plants near them. Set out new plants and divide and replant others which are in need of rejuvenation. Woodruff (*Asperula odorata*) benefits from having last year's dead shoots pulled off.

Place a layer of stone chippings round the plants to improve drainage and suppress weeds. In periods of drought water with a fine spray so that the soil will not be washed down to lower levels.

WATER GARDENS

Hours of sheer pleasure can be distilled from a garden pool, complete with lily pads, lazing fish and enchanting marginal plants. However, certain jobs must be done to ensure this related environment.

In early summer, blanketweed, a long stringy type of algae, grows quickly and may fill the pool unless removed with a rake.

If a pool has just been installed and filled up with fresh water for the first time do not be alarmed by the pea-soup consistency which may develop a few days later, especially in bright sun. This is caused by algae feeding and multiplying in water rich in mineral salts. In time, when the pool balance is right, the green scum will disappear.

Cut off rotting lily leaves to prevent them from contaminating the water. Repot overcrowded lilies and marginal plants such as sedges and irises if their crowns are spilling over the edges of pots or baskets. When repotting, use heavy clay soil packed thickly and solidly round the roots. Light soil disperses in water as clouds of fine particles.

Water lilies are best planted in special perforated aquatic baskets; do not set these directly on the floor of the pool, but support them on bricks or upturned pots. As growth progresses, remove the supports and lower the baskets so that the lily pads float on the surface.

In autumn, cover the pool with fine netting to catch falling leaves; later protect it against ice with boards or rush matting.

KITCHEN GARDENS

The ideal site for a kitchen garden is sunny and open, with a fertile, well-drained soil that is neither light nor heavy. Acid soils generally need liming—a deterrent against club root disease in brassicas, but detrimental to potatoes and some cane fruits.

The vegetable plot should be dug annually, in autumn for heavy soils and in spring for light soils. Organic

A rocky outcrop in the making. Large stones outline the informal shape, complementary to the surrounding lawn. Smaller stones infill the centre, and the whole area is topped with a layer of grit before true alpines and slow-growing conifers are set in position.

materials should be incorporated to maintain fertility, but many root crops — carrots, beetroot and parsnip tend to fork in newly manured soils.

Precisely because various types of vegetables need various growing conditions, it is sensible to practise crop-rotation. Usually this is done in a three year cycle, the whole plot being divided into three sections—one for peas, onions and salad crops, one for brassicas (cabbages, cauliflowers, etc.) and one for potatoes and other root crops.

In one year the salad crop area is double-dug and heavily manured, the brassica section is forked over and limed while the root crop section is lightly dug and fertilised prior to sowing. The following year brassicas are grown in the plot previously occupied by salad crops, potatoes, etc., in the brassica bed, and salads in the root crop bed. Similarly in the third year, brassicas move to the 1st year root crop section, salad crops to the original brassica plot, and root crops to the area occupied by salad crops in the first year.

In this way, one third of the vegetable garden is double-dug and heavily manured once a year, another third is limed and the final third is topdressed with fertiliser in spring. Annual care includes sowing and planting, thinning seedlings, spurring growth with granular, liquid or foliar feeds, keeping weeds down and safe-guarding against pests and diseases. In dry weather, watering, preferably from an overhead sprinkler system, is essential, particularly at the seedling stage. Certain vegetables—peas, beans, tomatoes—need staking.

Fruit gardens

The ground for fruit trees and bushes should have been thoroughly dug and manure added at planting

GARDEN UPKEEP 5

time. Once the fruit are established avoid disturbing the soil as most feeding roots grow close to the surface. In spring and autumn apply appropriate fertilisers and keep weeds down with a summer mulch or by shallow hoeing. For fruit trees and bushes follow a regular spraying and pruning programme: cane fruits need old canes removed at the end of the season and the new canes tied in their place.

It is worthwhile protecting cane and bush fruits, grown on a large scale, with fruit cages against birds; otherwise cover individual plants with fine netting.

Early flowering peaches and apricots often produce poor crops because pollinating insects are not yet about. It is essential to hand pollinate these trees, with a stick tipped with cotton wool, or a soft paintbrush. Choose a warm sunny day and dip the brush into every open flower, transferring pollen from bloom to bloom. Continue this every other day for a fortnight to ensure that all the blooms have been cross-pollinated.

Other tree-fruits—apples, pears and plums—flower later in spring when pollinating insects are around, and by early summer (June) it should be possible to gauge the eventual fruit crop. At this stage the fruits will be small, and while many will drop naturally from overcrowding, the remainder must be thinned out. Start by removing all mis-shapen or bruised fruits in each cluster, then thin the remainder to 5cm apart each way.

GARDEN FENCES

A solid and well-constructed fence should last for many years, given some regular attention. If you are in doubt as to the ownership of a boundary fence, a quick glance at the rails, posts and nails should tell you. If the posts and rails are facing away from your land, the fence belongs to your neighbour; towards you it is your fence.

Wooden fence posts often rot at ground level after some years. To save a post, clear away the soil and cut the rot back to sound wood. Drench the portion of post below ground level with creosote and insert a wooden, ideally oak, brace upright or at an angle, again bolted to the post.

Alternatively, excavate soil to a deeper level round the post and support this with an infill of concrete mixture of 1 part cement (by volume) to 4 parts aggregate of fine shingle and sand. Sometimes fence posts are past repair and need replacing completely. In this case, concrete posts, drilled to take the horizontal rails to which the fencing panels are nailed, are preferable, on fences less than 2m high. A modification of this is concrete supports sunk in the ground and drilled to take wooden posts.

Use a plumb line or spirit level when erecting fence posts, with another person holding them in place so that you can align them

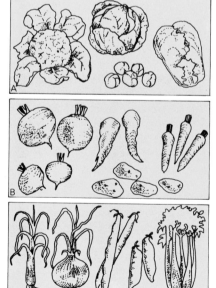

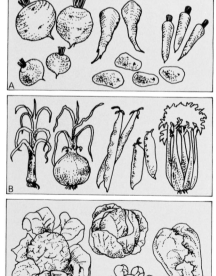

Three-year crop rotation: plot A, double-dug and manured, contains legumes (peas, beans), onions, leeks and salad crops; plot B, lightly dug and limed, is devoted to brassicas (Brussels sprouts, cauliflowers, cabbages); plot C, single-dug and fertilised, is occupied by root crops. In the second year, plot A is occupied by brassicas, plot B by root crops and plot C by legumes and miscellaneous crops. In the third year, root crops move to plot A; legumes to plot B and brassicas to plot C.

with your eye from a distance. Keep the aligned posts in position with bricks or rubble before pouring concrete round them. Allow the concrete to set before fixing the panels.

Wire netting or chain-link fencing may eventually rust through and need replacing. Use bolt strainers to get the horizontal wire supports perfectly taut. Vaseline or grease smeared over the threads prevents them from rusting.

The life of wooden fencing is prolonged with an annual preservative applied in autumn or early spring. Creosote is the cheapest but also harmful to plants, and a proprietary wood preservative is preferable.

Modern fencing materials are usually treated with a special preservative which lasts for several years before the fence needs new treatment. Always use galvanised nails to fix planking to a fence, and avoid piling soil round the posts and the base gravel boards. Vigorous shrubs and climbers should be avoided on fences exposed to high winds.

Cedarwood garden chalets and toolsheds also need some maintenance to prevent them from taking on a bleached appearance. If treated annually with a special cedarwood oil one coat is usually sufficient. Cold frames with wooden surrounds need similar treatment.

Teak tables and chairs are best brought inside for the winter to protect them from injurious frost and soaking rain. If they do need to have their colour restored, wait until the wood is perfectly dry, then rub them down lightly with fine sandpaper and wipe them with a soft cloth dipped in teak oil.

PRUNING FOR HEALTHY PLANTS

Why prune? In the wild, shrubs and trees grow naturally without interference, and so, theoretically, should garden plants. But unpruned plants do not produce their best, dead and dying wood will attract

disease and new growth might be badly placed. Crowding would result in reduced vigour, smaller flowers and limited crops. In gardens, some degree of pruning must be practised in most years, to ensure healthy balanced growth and to maintain vigour and cropping.

Roses
Newly planted hybrid tea and floribunda varieties should have all shoots cut back to outward-facing buds 15cm from the ground; remove entirely spindly, broken or diseased shoots.

After a season's growth, roses must be pruned again, in autumn to shorten by half tall, whippy stems that catch the wind and thus tear the roots from the soil. February or March is the main season for dealing with rose-pruning proper. Aim at creating a cup-shaped bush through which air can circulate freely. Shorten all strong shoots by half to two-thirds their length; reduce side shoots to two buds of the main branches and cut out completely all weak and worthless wood. Remove, too, shoots that are crossing others, causing the bark to chafe, and any growing into the centre of the bush.

In time, old and worn-out wood builds up and should be cut back close to the graft union. This will spur the development of strong new shoots from the base.

During the summer, cut back spent flower trusses to shoots or buds lower down from which more flowering shoots will break. Remove thorny suckers from the graft union, tracing them back to their point of origin on the stock and pull them out.

Climbing roses are best pruned in late summer. Simply cut back the flowered shoots to within two buds or so of the principal leaders. Cut out spent leaders and train in new shoots to replace them and to cover the allocated space. Remove any

Protection against birds. Raspberries, currants and strawberries are favourites with birds. Protection can consist of fine-mesh nylon netting thrown over individual bushes, but a permanent cage of wire or plastic netting attached to a wooden frame is even better. A cage also ensures that birds cannot get at the young fruit buds.

weak and soft tips from the main branches. On newly planted climbers, shorten the shoots to half their length and tie them upright to supporting wires. Thereafter, train and tie the shoots horizontally when they will flower more freely.

True rambling roses form long whippy cane-like shoots; these are cut right back to ground level each autumn and the new canes are trained in every year to replace those which have flowered.

Standard and shrub roses

Standard hybrid tea and floribunda roses should not be pruned hard. Aim at creating a shallow cup-shaped arrangement of branches. Standards are seldom very vigorous, and the 15-20cm of new growth that they usually make each year should be shortened by one third, occasionally cutting hard back a dark-wooded, old shoot in the hope of spurring strong new growth.

Species roses, such as the climbing *Rosa filipes*, need no pruning at all, except to remove dead and damaged shoots. Shrubby species roses, such as *R. moyesii* valued for its shining scarlet hips, are usually left to perform naturally, apart from the occasional shortening of an old branch to near ground level.

Cabbage roses, musk roses, damask and other shrub roses should be pruned lightly in autumn, removing any long wind-catching shoots. In February or March take out crowding and weak shoots, leaving intact the main framework of branches, evenly spaced. Prune back to strong, outward-facing buds any stems which are excessively long and out of balance with the rest of the bush.

Trees

Unfortunately, trees do not always grow with their branches evenly spaced and symmetrically arranged, and sometimes an ill-positioned branch must be removed. This is easiest done by cutting it off in two sections, first the outer bulk of the branch, then the stump close to the trunk. On both occasions, under-cut before sawing through from the top, to prevent the bark on the trunk from tearing. The last cut should be made flush with the trunk, and the wound pared with a sharp knife, then painted liberally with a sealer to speed healing and callousing and keep out disease.

Leaf-shedding trees, such as hornbeam, beech, oak and lime, are best pruned in winter, evergreens in spring or early summer.

If a tree's lower branches cast so much shade that gardening beneath becomes impossible or a window is in permanent shadow, the crown can be lifted simply by removing all the lower branches flush with the trunk to a point where the tree shape is acceptable. Pare all pruning cuts with a sharp knife and paint with a wound sealer.

Bracket fungi pushing out from the base of a tree usually indicate core rot which makes the tree a hazard and unsafe in windy weather. Call in a tree surgeon who may carry out an auger test on a narrow core of tissue from the trunk. If rot is found, the tree must be felled.

Shrubs

Evergreen shrubs — and trees — generally need little or no pruning apart from removing dead or damaged branches or shortening back any that spoil the symmetry. Flowering deciduous shrubs are pruned according to their mode of flowering: shrubs which flower on shoots made the previous season are generally pruned as soon as the flowers are faded; those which flower on current year's extension shoots are pruned in early spring.

Some of the more familiar garden shrubs are pruned as follows:
Buddleia davidii (butterfly bush). Cut back all the previous year's long flowered shoots to within a few centimetres of older wood in February or early March.

Pruning floribunda roses. In March (1), cut new bushes back to 15cm and in autumn (2) tip all thin shoots. Thereafter, prune annually in spring (3), reducing 1-year shoots by a third, older shoots to 15cm and laterals to 2 to 3 buds. In autumn (4), tip the main shoots again and take out weak and thin side-shoots.

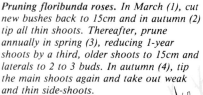
1

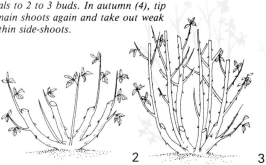
2

3

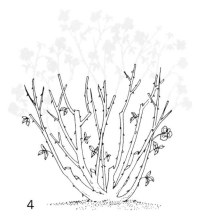
4

Caryopteris. Shorten last year's shoots to within 3cm of the base when frosts have finished; thin out crowding branches.

Ceanothus. Evergreen types, such as *C. dentatus* and *C. impressus*, are pruned after flowering, cutting back spent flowered stems by half to encourage strong new growth. The deciduous kinds, such as 'Gloire de Versailles', should have their shoots reduced to about 10cm of the main branches in April or May.

Clematis. There are numerous types, and it would be confusing to enumerate their individual requirements. A simple guide is to remember that *C. montana* and other true species are not pruned at all, apart from removing shoots that have outgrown their allotted space, in spring or summer when the flowers have faded. The large-flowered clematis hybrids which bloom in late summer are best cut back to near the base of strong shoots in February or March. Those that flower in early summer need only have flowered stems cut back to healthy buds, after flowering.

Cornus (dogwood). *C. alba* 'Sibirica' and *C. stolonifera*, grown for their red and yellow bark respectively, are cut back to just above the ground each spring.

Cytisus (broom). Use sharp shears to trim off faded flower heads in late spring. Do not cut back into the older wood as this may cause the shoots to die back.

Deutzia. Prune out entirely flowered stems in summer, retaining new growth from the base. Take out any crowding shoots.

Forsythia. Prune flowered stems hard back to strong new shoots when the blooms fade in spring.

Hydrangea (mophead type). Leave faded blooms to protect new shoots and flower buds over winter; in early April remove spent blooms and congested shoots.

Lavandula. Shear off faded blooms

Buddleia davidii and other shrubs which flower on shoots of the current season can be pruned back to 2-3 strong buds from the base in early spring. New growth is rapid.

Cornus alba and certain willows are grown for their bright winter stems. For the best display, prune the previous season's shoots back to just above base in spring.

in late summer. Trim lightly to shape in early spring, but do not cut into older wood, which seldom breaks again.

Philadelphus. Cut back flowered shoots in summer to new growth lower down; rejuvenate old bushes by cutting out thick, dark-coloured branches in spring.

Potentilla fruticosa. Keep bushes young and freely flowering by shortening all shoots to just above ground in spring. Alternatively, leave the shrubs to grow naturally, merely thinning out congested shoots in May. Prune hard back, in spring, when the plants become gaunt and flower less freely.

Sambucus. Prune back all shoots to within 5cm of the ground in spring, to encourage strong new growth.

Syringa (lilac). Cut back flowered shoots in early summer to strong buds below the faded flowers. Remove all suckers.

Weigela. Keep plants young and flowering profusely by shortening flowered shoots to young growth lower down. Prune in early summer, and at the same time remove crowding and crossing branches to help air circulate freely.

Fruit trees and soft fruit
All types of fruit should be pruned annually, to contain the plants and to encourage and maintain good cropping.

Black currants. These fruit best on strong shoots rising from below ground. After planting, prune all shoots back to within three buds of the base. The shoots that form will fruit the following year. Thereafter prune out completely fruited shoots or cut back to young shoots near the base. Keep the centre of the bushes open by removing crowding and crossing branches and weak shoots.

Red currants and gooseberries. These are usually grown on a short 'leg' and pruned by shortening all side shoots on the main framework

GARDEN UPKEEP 7

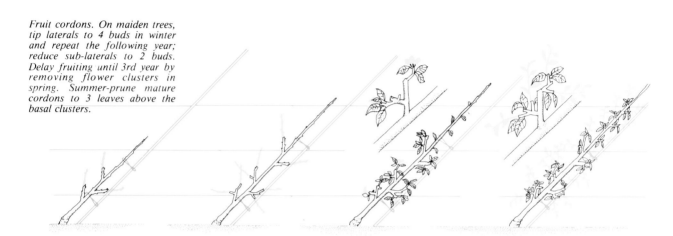

Fruit cordons. On maiden trees, tip laterals to 4 buds in winter and repeat the following year; reduce sub-laterals to 2 buds. Delay fruiting until 3rd year by removing flower clusters in spring. Summer-prune mature cordons to 3 leaves above the basal clusters.

to within five or six leaves in July, after fruiting. Keep the centre of the bushes free from in-growing shoots, taking out at base crossing and crowded, broken and diseased branches. Mildewed tips should be pruned back to healthy buds and burnt as soon as noticed.

Blackberries and loganberries. These, like black currants, fruit on one-year old shoots. Train the canes fan-wise or in espalier fashion, with canes trained horizontally to left and right on taut wires. After fruiting, cut all fruited canes back to base. Ideally, tie the new canes up through the centre of the plant, arranging the fruiting canes to either side of them so that disease will not be transferred to the new canes.

Raspberries. Fruits are borne on one-year old canes. These should be cut out from the base when all the fruits have been picked; allow up to six strong new canes on each plant, tied to wires (15cm apart) secured to strong posts. Weak and excess canes should be removed completely.

Apples and pears. These are often grown as space-saving, single-stemmed cordons, planted at an angle of 45 degrees to a post and wire-supporting framework, or as espaliers with several tiers of branches trained horizontally to left and right of the trunk. Both apples and pears can also be grown as bushes or

dwarf pyramids and are pruned according to the trained habit.

Cordons are summer-pruned in July or August, when the tissues are beginning to mature. Cut back all side-shoots to three leaves above the basal leaf cluster. No regular winter pruning is necessary, but over-crowded spurs should be thinned in December. When the leading shoot has reached the required height, shorten new growth to within 1cm of the older wood in May.

Established espalier trees are pruned like cordons, treating each horizontal arm by shortening new side shoots to within three leaves of the basal cluster. If an espalier is still being trained, and new arms are needed, make a tiny notch above each of two close buds on the leader, about 30cm above the lower tier of branches. This will encourage the buds to grow strongly and the resulting laterals can be trained as the next tier. Tie the shoots to canes, at an angle of 45 degrees to the supporting wire, then gradually bring them down parallel with the wires.

Fully trained espaliers usually have four or five tiers, about 45cm apart. In May, reduce the new growth of branch leaders by one third to one half their length.

Dwarf pyramids are pruned in summer to develop a close-knit system of fruiting spurs on branches

forming a steep pyramid. In July, or when the leaves are deep green and the shoots are becoming woody, shorten main laterals to six leaves from the basal cluster and cut back side shoots to three leaves. When the tree is about 2 metres high, cut out the growing tip. Thereafter, shorten new growth to within 1cm of the older wood in May.

Plums and cherries. Plums are usually grown as bushes, half-standards or fans. On bushes and half-standards cut out all crowded and crossing shoots and prune broken or dead shoots back to healthy buds lower down in early autumn. Any large, badly placed branches should be removed in late summer, after harvesting.

Fan-shaped plums, on walls or fences, should have their branches trained in evenly over the allotted area. Leave at full length all healthy one-year old shoots to form fruit buds, but cut back to three leaves all other side shoots. Prune in autumn, never in winter when spores of the silver leaf fungus are active and may contaminate wounds.

Bush and fan-trained cherry trees are pruned like plums for the first few years. Once established, pruning should be done in spring, cutting two-year wood back by a quarter, older branches by up to half.

Peaches and apricots. These are best

172

fan-trained against a warm, sunny wall where their early blossom, in February, can be pollinated by insects or by hand. Prune in early spring, shortening long flowerless shoots to half their length to encourage new wood which will flower and fruit the year after. Cut back diseased and dead wood to healthy buds, and rub out any shoots which are growing towards or away from the wall and which cannot be trained in easily. Aim at keeping growth on the young side, to encourage flowers and fruits every year, by removing a proportion of old unfruitful shoots each year. Too many leaves usually form on fan-trained trees, so remove all but three leaves, retaining one at the base, one in the middle and one at the tip of every fruiting side shoot.

Bush-trained peaches and apricots need only have their centres kept free of crowded branches; shorten bare lengths of stem occasionally to maintain production of young fruiting wood.

PROPAGATION

Multiplying favourite perennials and shrubs to increase existing stock, fill in gaps or exchange treasures with friends, is one of the most creative and inspiring aspects of gardening. Propagation involves little effort, and the plants will have cost a fraction of those purchased.

Herbaceous plants

All types with tufted rootstocks, such as acanthus, achilleas, agapanthus, alchemillas, asters, brunneras, campanulas, helianthus, hostas and sedums can be divided in autumn or early spring, provided the ground is not frozen. Lift the plants with a fork, split them into well rooted portions and replant the outer young and healthy portions.

Irises of the bearded flag type (*I. germanica*), which flower in May and June, should be lifted and divided after blooming. Use the outer parts of a rhizome, complete with roots and healthy leaves; cut the leaves across to half their length, and replant sections of the rhizomes in lime-laced soil. Cover the roots only and leave the fleshy rhizome exposed above soil level.

Delphiniums and lupins can be increased by basal cuttings of young shoots in early spring. Trim away the lowest leaves, insert the cuttings 8cm apart round the edge of a pot filled with potting compost and leave in a heated frame or propagator to root. Keep the soil evenly moist, but not wet enough to rot the tissues. When new growth is apparent, move the young plants to a sheltered nursery bed and transplant to their flowering quarters the following autumn.

Plants with fleshy roots can be increased from root cuttings taken in autumn. Lift the plants, cut off healthy roots, 10-15cm long, and insert in boxes of compost. Leave the cuttings in a cold frame to root during the winter.

Border carnations and pinks are easily propagated from layers and cuttings in July and August. For layering, select a flexible shoot about 20cm long and strip away the lower leaves. Make a sloping cut halfway along the stem to leave a 1cm tongue, wedge this open with a match and peg the open cut into the soil. Cover with 1cm of mixed peat and sharp sand. Roots should form within a month or so, and the new plant can be severed from the parent in early autumn.

Cuttings are taken by pulling a shoot, 10cm long, from its socket. Remove the lower leaves and insert the cuttings in pots of gritty compost. Keep in a closed frame or slip a plastic bag over each pot. When rooted, pot each plant up separately. Overwinter in a cold frame and plant out in spring.

Shrubs

Many shrubs, including deciduous berberis, buddleias, *Cornus alba* and *C. stolonifera*, deutzias, forsythias, ribes, philadelphus and weigelas, can be increased from hardwood cuttings of pencil-thick shoots taken after leaf-fall in late autumn. These should be 15-23cm long, trimmed to just above a bud at the top and just below a bud at the base, and inserted to half their depth and 15cm apart in a shallow trench lined at the bottom with sharp sand. Firm in the cuttings, and again if heavy frost lifts them.

Some shrubs, such as amelanchier, flowering quince and others which sucker freely, can be propagated from well-rooted suckers dug up and replanted. This is best done in late autumn or early spring; do not use suckers from grafted plants such as lilac.

The majority of shrubs can be increased from softwood or semi-hardwood cuttings, taken in early or mid to late summer respectively. Use non-flowering shoots, about 15cm long, cut off just below a node. Trim off the lower leaves; dip the cuttings in a hormone rooting powder and root in pots of good compost. Some cuttings, such as those of lavender and santolina, root easiest if semi-hardwood cuttings are taken with a heel. Pull off healthy shoots so that each has a sliver or heel of older wood at the base. Pare this back to within 1cm of the cutting and treat as already described.

Softwood and semi-hardwood cuttings will usually form roots by late autumn. In early spring or the following autumn transplant them to their flowering positions or to a nursery bed in which to grow on.

Clematis is usually propagated by layering in late summer. Choose a flexible shoot and bend to ground level. Take out a depression in the soil, about 15cm deep, and fill with

Heel cuttings. Semi-hardwood cuttings often root better with a so-called heel, or sliver of woody stem. Cuttings, 8cm long,

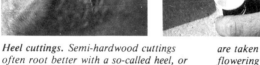

are taken in late summer from non-flowering side-shoots. Slice the shoot from the stem, with a portion of bark attached.

Dip in hormone rooting powder before inserting the cuttings in a propagating frame. Pot the cuttings when properly rooted.

moist peat and sharp sand. Make a nick halfway through a node on the underside of the shoot; wedge the cut open and peg it into the rooting mixture. Tie the tip of the shoot to an upright cane. Leave the layer to root and grow for a year before cutting it from the parent plant.

Rhododendrons can also be propagated by layering. Instead of slitting through the shoot, give it a twist to tear, without breaking, the stem tissues. Peg the shoot down and tie the tip section to a cane to keep it upright. Sever and plant out when roots have formed.

Heathers root easily if the lower or outer part of a clump is mounded with soil. In time, roots will sprout from the buried stems, and these can be severed and planted out.

Soft fruit
Strawberries are best replaced after two or three years, from runners

rooted in pots of good soil sunk to rim level close to the parent plants. Use pieces of bent wire to peg the first and second plants that form on a runner into pots. Remove all other plantlets. In late summer the new plants can be severed and planted out to fruit the following year. For stronger plants, remove all the flowers in the first year.

Black currants are easily multiplied from hardwood cuttings in early autumn. The cuttings, up to 30cm long, should have plenty of buds from which shoots will form from below the ground. Insert them to half their depth in a trench lined with sand and firm the soil.

Red currants and gooseberries are also increased from hardwood cuttings, 30cm long, in late autumn. As these fruits are grown on a short leg, pinch all but the top four buds on each cutting. Treat as black currant cuttings and transplant, if growing

strongly, to a nursery bed for a year or two before setting them out.

Blackberries and loganberries root readily by layering in late summer. Bend young shoots to ground level and keep the tips in contact with the soil with pegs or stones. When roots have formed sever the young plants.

BATTLING AGAINST PESTS, DISEASES AND WEEDS
Regular garden maintenance involves a greater or lesser fight against harmful insects, crippling diseases and invasive weeds. While there is never a clear victory over these enemies, the battle can be confined to a few annual skirmishes if precautions are taken in time. Keep your eyes open for the first signs of pest or disease. Stunted shoot tips can mean a colony of greenfly, oddly white leaf surfaces

Hardwood cuttings are the easiest of all. They are taken in autumn from 1-year old shoots of hardy shrubs and trees and

trimmed to 25-30 cm lengths. Insert the cuttings in a sheltered trench lined with sand for drainage. Bury the cuttings, spaced

10cm apart, to half their depth and firm the soil round them. Most hardwood cuttings will be ready for transplanting 1 year later.

Root cuttings from herbaceous perennials are taken during winter. Lift a plant and cut off healthy roots close to the crown. On *fibrous-rooted perennials like phlox, trim the thin roots to 10cm, lay them in boxes of compost, cover lightly and place in a closed* *cold frame to root by spring. Cuttings from fleshy-rooted plants are cut into 5cm pieces and inserted vertically in pots of compost.*

may indicate powdery mildew, and the delicate flower trumpets of bindweed belie its strangler instinct.

Certain disorders afflict the garden as a whole, but the most common offenders congregate on typical host plant groups.

The kitchen garden

Broad, runner and French beans attract blackfly (aphids) which cluster on soft shoot tips. Control by nipping out and burning affected shoots and spray with permethrin, dimethoate or malathion.

Brassicas are hosts to several nuisances, such as aphids (see above) and white caterpillars which can skeletonise cabbage leaves. Remove the latter by hand or spray infested plants with trichlorphon. Cabbage root fly, whose grubs feed on roots and stems of young plants, is best checked by sprinkling bromophos or diazinon granules along the seed drills or planting holes or watering the root area with a spray strength, diazinon-based insecticide.

Club root disease, a serious trouble on the cabbage family, is controlled by crop rotation, by liming acid soil regularly, and by dipping roots of seedlings in a paste of calomel (mercurous chloride) and water, or by dusting planting holes with calomel.

Carrot fly, whose grubs bore into carrots, parsnips, parsley and celery, is controlled by dusting the seed drills with diazinon and repeating the dressing when the plants are about 15cm high. When thinning seedlings, take care to firm the soil well round the roots to block entry by the flies.

Potatoes are likely to be beset by the following troubles: blight, which strikes in warm, muggy weather in mid-to late summer, keeled slugs, which bore into the tubers, and scab disease which blemishes the potato skins.

Overcome blight by earthing up rows so that rain washes spores on infected leaves to the sides of the ridges and away from the tubers. Prevent attacks by spraying the foliage, in mid-July and again a fortnight later, with a copper-sulphate based Bordeaux mixture or Dithane 945 based on mancozeb. If necessary continue fortnightly treatment until mid-September. Usually only maincrop varieties need protection, as early potatoes are lifted before attacks are likely.

Keeled slugs can be checked by watering the drills at planting time with a liquid metaldehyde slug killer, to a depth of about 15cm. If necessary, repeat every three weeks.

Scab is an unsightly skin disease which penetrates into the surface flesh of potatoes. Prevent infection

Stem cuttings. In most cases, one new plant results from one cutting, but several can be obtained from leaf-bud cuttings. Choose a *semi-ripe, non-flowered shoot with strong buds in the leaf axils and cut this into sections. Trim each small cutting so that it* *retains a sliver of wood and one leaf. Root in pots of compost and cut each leaf in half to minimise moisture loss by transpiration.*

by withholding lime and incorporating plenty of manure prior to planting; or grow scab-resistant potato varieties.

Onions are prone to two major troubles: onion fly and white rot disease. Calomel acts as a combined insecticide and fungicide. It can be sprinkled in powder form round the base of onion sets or along the seed drills to control both problems. Alternatively, diazinon granules can be used to control onion fly, in the seed drills and round the seedlings when they are 4cm high.

Lettuce, beetroot, potatoes and tomatoes may be crippled with greenfly (aphids), signposted by distorted leaves and stunted growth. Treat as for beans.

Cutworms feed at night and chew through the stems of many vegetables, especially lettuce. Keep these bloated caterpillars at bay by sprinkling bromophos or diazinon granules round plants.

In autumn and winter, overwintering lettuce seedlings, outdoors or in cold frames and unheated greenhouses, can be troubled by grey mould fungus (botrytis). Prevent attacks by dusting the soil, before planting, with quintozene, or by fumigating the greenhouse with tecnazene.

Scab disease in the shape of blemishes and cracks, is common on apples and pears. It is not difficult to control if regularly sprayed. In mid-December winter-wash trees with tar oil; at bud burst, spray with a systemic fungicide based on dimethoate. When the flower buds show green, spray again with a combined systemic insecticide and fungicide. Give a repeat application when the flower buds turn pink, when the petals have fallen, and again as the tiny fruits form.

This extended spray treatment will control not only scab, but also greenflies, capsid bugs, sawflies, woolly aphids, red spiders, winter moths, and mildew that can cripple and whiten the leaves and stems. On pears, pear suckers and midges will also succumb.

Peach leaf curl is a serious disease that bloats and distorts the foliage. Spray twice with Bordeaux mixture or Dithane 945 (mancozeb) when the leaves start to fall in early autumn, and again in late January or early February, before the buds start to burst. Repeat treatment every year to keep trees free from infection.

Raspberry beetle, whose grubs may be found in ripe fruit, is best dealt with by dusts of derris just before the blooms open, and again 10 days later.

The flower garden

The greatest enemies are slugs and snails, those nocturnal pests that can reduce newly set-out bedding plants to mere skeletons. Keep them at bay with baits, such as methiocarb or metaldehyde-based pellets and renew these frequently. Alternatively, set a couple of saucers in the garden and fill them with beer; this will lure countless slugs to their death. Circles of lime or soot round plants also deter slugs and snails. Clean up piles of rotting wood, old cracked pots and other debris that harbour these creatures; in winter, destroy snails where they cluster at the foot of dry walls or under dense ivy.

Caterpillars are another pest often difficult to track down. A few holes appear in geranium or nasturtium leaves, and before long they take on a perforated appearance. Dust with derris or spray with trichlorphon.

Dense colonies of greenfly (aphids) cluster at the shoot tips of many flowering plants. Spray as soon as possible with a systemic insecticide based on dimethoate. This is absorbed into the sap stream and will keep the tissues immune from attack for about three weeks or so. Repeat this treatment if the weather is hot and dry and conducive to a greenfly explosion.

Dahlias and chrysanthemums are favoured by earwigs which shred the petals. Formerly these pests were trapped in small pots stuffed with straw and propped on canes among the plants, but a dusting of gamma-HCH, or a spraying of pirimiphos-methyl is infinitely quicker and just as effective.

The lovely roses are unfortunately afflicted by a goodly share of pests and diseases. A small green beetle, the rose chafer, nibbles the petals so that the blooms open torn and dishevelled. Spray at once with malathion or gamma-HCH (Lindex).

Leaf-rolling sawfly is first seen when the leaves take on the shape of cigars inside which the larvae are busily feeding. Hand-pick and destroy the leaves or control with sprays of dimethoate.

The worst diseases are mildew, black spot and rust. The first two are vanquished without too much difficulty by spraying with bupirimate plus triforine as soon as the diseases appear. Gather fallen leaves infected with black spot and burn them so that the spores are killed. Black spot spores overwinter in the soil; destroy them by spraying with tar oil in mid-December, drenching the shoots and the soil.

Rose rust, seen as brownish-reddish pustules on the upper leaf surfaces, weakens growth and is difficult to control. Generous mulches of well-rotted manure in spring and top dressings of rose fertiliser during spring and summer have some remedial effects. Severe attacks can be treated with sprays of copper fungicide or thiram.

Paeony blight can build up quickly unless checked. Characterised by young shoots turning brown and shrivelling in early summer, the disease is best controlled by dusting the crowns with copper sulphate Bordeaux mixture in April, and digging up and burning infected plants.

Phlox eelworms, which reduce leaves to skeleton proportions, live in the stems of the plants. To destroy the pests slice away the crowns just below soil level and burn them. Alternatively, propagate by root cuttings, which will produce healthy plants.

Narcissus fly is a serious pest of daffodils and occasionally attack other bulbs, such as bluebells, hyacinths and snowdrops. The flies lay their eggs close to the neck of the plants, and the larvae burrow down and into the bulbs rotting them: gamma-HCH, made up to spray strength, should be watered round the necks of bulbs fortnightly from mid-April to early July, to deter the winged flies. Alternatively, dust with gamma-HCH dust.

Keeping down weeds
A quick thrust with a Dutch hoe between rows of vegetables—and among annuals — is the best way of keeping down weed seedlings. Once they have got out of hand, it is quicker to apply weedkillers.

Annual weeds, such as chickweed, groundsel and shepherd's purse, are readily destroyed with a paraquat-based weedkiller (Weedol). Water this on through a sprinkler bar attached to a watering can so there is no danger of spray drift harming other plants. Weedol destroys the green parts (leaves and stems) of a plant and is inactivated on contact with the soil.

The weedkiller based on glyphosate (Tumbleweed) works similarly and is also inactivated by soil, but being systemic it is absorbed by the leaves and taken to all parts of a plant. It is highly effective against perennial weeds, such as docks, dandelions and nettles, and against all annuals.

Prevent long grass and broad-leaved weeds, such as dandelions, speedwell and docks, round soft fruit bushes and fruit trees by treating with Weedol or Tumbleweed. These weedkillers are most effective when applied during sunny weather.

Greenhouse troubles
Wilting cyclamen, rotting primulas and other ornamentals with yellowing leaves and of stunted growth are almost invariably due to the feeding activities of one of the worst pests of house and greenhouse plants—vine weevil. The dirty, creamy-coloured grubs feed voraciously on the roots of many plants, and diagnosis often comes too late for any remedial action. On suspicion alone, knock the plant from its pot, examine the roots, pick out grubs and destroy them. Repot in fresh, sterilised compost with a pinch of gamma-HCH dust. Alternatively, water the compost with Lindex.

Another menace is whitefly. The adults—minute, winged moth-like creatures that rise in clouds as you touch an infested plant—are the only vulnerable phase. Eggs and nymphal stages are resistant to insecticides, and it will be necessary to spray with bioresmethrin for a fortnight or more to catch the hatching adults. Whiteflies suck sap like aphids and quickly cripple growth, especially on tomatoes and cucumbers. The sticky honeydew deposited by them attracts sooty mould which smothers the leaves and interferes with photosynthesis.

Damping-off disease, caused by a fungus, affects crowded seedlings, especially in unsterilised compost. Use a good brand of seed or potting compost, sow thinly and prick out the seedlings as soon as large enough to handle. Outbreaks can sometimes be controlled and isolated by spraying or watering with Cheshunt compound.

Lawn problems
Worm casts appear in spring and autumn and if numerous the worms can be destroyed by watering with chlordane. This chemical will also deal with leatherjackets, the fat, slate-grey grubs that feed on grass roots and cause patches of turf to die out completely.

Diseases are worst in autumn, especially if fertilisers high in nitrogen were given in spring and summer in an attempt to green-up the lawn. Such treatment results in soft growth vulnerable to attack by fusarium, which causes slimy yellow-brown patches, or corticium, where pinkish-red threads can be seen. Control both by sprinkling 100g of mercurised lawn sand per square metre when the diseases are first noticed.

Moss can be a serious problem. Do not attempt to rake it out, but scatter calomel dust (mercurous chloride) or dichlorophen in early spring when the grass is growing vigorously. See also chart on p. 163.

Clover is another lawn nuisance. Treat it with ioxynil and mecoprop, mecoprop, or 2,4-D and mecoprop. Chalky soil encourages clover, and if a soil test reveals that your soil is limy, use sulphate of ammonia at 25g per square metre in spring and again in summer to lower the pH.

Speedwell and other small-leaved weeds are best tackled with an ioxynil or mecoprop-based weedkiller. Repeat applications may be necessary to remove long established colonies. Dandelions, daisies and plantains can be spot-treated with a 2,4-D/mecoprop weedkiller.

Gravel paths can be watered with a total weedkiller effective for up to 12 months. Those based on aminotriazole/MCPA/simazine are preferable to sodium chlorate which 'creeps' sideways into lawns, hedges and borders. Even so, keep a wide margin between weedkiller and cultivated plants.

POPULAR GARDEN PLANTS

The following brief profiles
represent some of the most popular
in a vast range of garden plants

THE ORNAMENTAL GARDEN 1

Acer palmatum (autumn)

Abies (fir)
HARDY EVERGREEN CONIFEROUS TREES
Soil/aspect: Preferably neutral to acid, moisture-retentive. Sun, partial shade.
Culture: Plant dormant season. Propagate by seeds in spring; dwarf cultivars by cuttings in autumn. No pruning.
Flowers: No true flowers; immature cones of some species coloured.
Species/cultivars: *A. balsamea* 'Hudsonia', slowly to 60 cm, good for rock gardens. *A. koreana*, to 10 m but slow-growing, dark green, white-banded foliage, blue cones.
Remarks: Good specimen conifers for small gardens.

Acanthus (bear's breeches)
HARDY PERENNIALS
Soil/aspect: Ordinary fertile. Sun or partial shade, sheltered.
Culture: Plant autumn/spring. Propagate by division or by root cuttings late winter/spring.
Flowers: Summer.
Species/cultivars: *A. mollis*, 90 – 120 cm, erect flower spikes white and dull purple; *A.m.* 'Latifolius', taller and more robust; the form usually seen in cultivation. *A. spinosus*, similar to *A. mollis*, but leaves dark glossy green and more deeply lobed.

Acer (maple)
HARDY DECIDUOUS TREES
Soil/aspect: Ordinary, but see individual species. Sun or shade.
Culture: Plant dormant season. Propagate from ripe seeds; cultivars by grafting, early spring. No pruning except for initial shaping of young trees.
Flowers: Spring/early summer.
Species/cultivars: *A. davidii*, to 6 m, bark olive-green, white-striped, flowers yellow-green. *A. griseum* (paper bark maple), to 6 m and slow-growing, bark red to coppery-brown, peeling; leaves trifoliate, red to orange in autumn. *A. hersii (A. grosseri hersii)* similar to *A. davidii*, but leaves lobed and seed-wings pink. *A. negundo* (ash-leaved maple, box elder), to 7.5 m, leaves ash-like with 3 – 7 leaflets, flowers yellow-green; *A.n.* 'Elegans' ('Elegantissimum') leaves yellow margined; *A.n.* 'Variegatum' ('Argenteo-variegatum'), white-margined. *A. palmatum* (Japanese maple), large shrub or small tree to 3 m, flowers purplish, leaves 5 – 7 lobed, red in autumn; neutral to acid soil; *A.p.* 'Dissectum', low shrub, leaves finely cut; *A.p.* 'Dissectum Atropurpureum', red-purple leaves; *A.p.* 'Heptalobum', larger, 7-lobed leaves bright scarlet in autumn. *A. platanoides* (Norway maple), to 15 m or more, leaves large, yellow in autumn, flowers bright green-yellow; *A.p.* 'Columnare', columnar habit; *A.p.* 'Crimson King', summer leaves ruby-red, often confused with the red-purple 'Goldsworth Crimson'. *A. pseudoplatanus* (sycamore, maple-plane (Scotland)) to 25 m, yellow-green, catkin-like pendent flower spikes; too large for most gardens; *A.p.* 'Brilliantissimum', small, slow-growing, round-headed tree, young leaves pink. *A.p.* 'Worleei', soft gold-green.

Achillea (yarrow)
HARDY PERENNIALS
Soil/aspect: Ordinary, well-drained. Sun.
Culture: Plant autumn. Propagate by division, autumn, or basal cuttings, spring.
Flowers: Summer.
Species/cultivars: *A. clypeolata*, 45 – 60 cm, leaves feathery, grey, flowers bright yellow. *A. filipendulina*, 90 – 120 cm, yellow, plate-like flower clusters; *A.f.* 'Gold Plate', rich yellow, 'Coronation Gold', shorter, foliage

Adonis vernalis

greyish, 'Lye End Lemon', similar, but lemon-yellow. *A. millefolium*, 60 – 90 m, flat flower clusters, white or pink tinged; can be very invasive; *A.m.* 'Fire King' and 'Red Beauty', flowers cerise-red. *A.* x *taygetea*, like *A. clypeolata*, but taller and greener; *A.* x *t.* 'Flowers of Sulphur', bright sulphur-yellow. *A. tomentosa*, 20 – 25 cm, feathery foliage mats, flowers bright yellow.

Aconitum (monkshood)
HARDY PERENNIALS
Soil/aspect: Ordinary, moisture-retentive. Sun or partial shade.
Culture: Plant dormant season. Propagate by division at planting time.
Flowers: Summer/autumn.
Species/cultivars: *A.* x *cammarum (A. bicolor)*, 90 cm; similar to *A. napellus*, but with denser spikes opening later; *A.* x 'Blue

Agapanthus Headbourne Hybrids

evergreen strap-shaped leaves, blue flowers; *A.p.* 'Maximus Albus', large white; 'Blue Giant', large rich blue; 'Argenteo Vittatus', leaves striped white; 'Flore Pleno', double.

Ageratum (floss flower)
HALF-HARDY ANNUAL
Soil/aspect: Ordinary, well-drained. Sun.
Culture: Plant out when frost is past. Propagate by seeds at 15 – 18°C, mid-spring.
Flowers: Summer/early autumn.
Species/cultivars: *A. houstonianum (A. mexicanum)*, to 30 cm, powder-blue dense flower clusters; dwarf cultivars to 15 cm in shades of blue, purple, pink and white.

Ajuga (bugle)
HARDY EVERGREEN PERENNIALS
Soil/aspect: Ordinary, moisture-retentive. Sun or partial shade.
Culture: plant dormant season. Propagate by division at planting time.
Flowers: Spring/summer.
Species/cultivars: *A. pyramidalis*, to 30 cm, pale violet-blue, tubular flowers with purple bracts; *A.p.* 'Crispa', leaves crinkly, metallic purple-green flowers. *A. reptans*, 15 – 30 cm, blue to blue-purple; *A.r.* 'Alba', flowers white; 'Atropurpurea', leaves flushed red-purple; 'Burgundy Glow', leaves wine-red; 'Multicolor', ('Rainbow'), leaves variegated bronze, yellow and pink; 'Variegata', leaves grey-green and white.

Alchemilla (lady's mantle)
HARDY FOLIAGE PERENNIALS
Soil/aspect: Ordinary. Sun or partial shade.
Culture: Plant dormant season. Propagate by division at planting time or by seeds in spring.
Flowers: Summer.
Species/cultivars: *A. conjuncta*, to 20 cm or more, leaves narrow, dark above, silvery beneath, sometimes sold as *A. alpina*, a smaller, less garden-worthy plant. *A. mollis*, 30 – 45 cm, leaves grey-green, downy, lobed, 15 cm wide; flowers lime-green.

Allium (ornamental onion)
HARDY, MAINLY BULBOUS PERENNIALS
Soil/aspect: Ordinary, well-drained. Sun.
Culture: Plant dormant season, preferably autumn. Propagate by division in autumn or from ripe seed.
Flowers: Late spring/summer.
Species/cultivars: *A. christophii (A. albopilosum)*, to 50 cm, flowers starry, metallic purple. *A. cyaneum*, to 15 cm, leaves grassy, flowers deep blue. *A. cyathophorum farreri (A. farreri)*, 25 cm, red-purple, pendent. *A. giganteum*, 90 – 120 cm, leaves blue-green, flowers metallic-lilac. *A. karataviense*, 15 cm, broad leaves grey-green, purple beneath, flowers white or purplish, late spring. *A. moly*, to 25 cm, leaves grey-green, flowers bright yellow. *A. narcissiflorum*, 20 – 30 cm, flowers pink to rose-purple, bell shaped, nodding. *A. ostrowskianum*, 10 – 15 cm, pink, *A.o.* 'Zwanenburg', carmine-rose. *A. rosenbachianum*, 60 – 90 cm, starry, violet-purple. *A. siculum*, 60 – 90 cm, leaves sharply keeled; maroon and green, large bell-shaped flowers.

Sceptre', blue-purple and white; *A. napellus*, 90 – 150 cm, clump-forming, leaves deeply lobed, flowers hooded, purple-blue.

Adonis
HARDY PERENNIALS
Soil/aspect: Ordinary, well-drained. Sun.
Culture: Plant late summer. Propagate by division, dormant season, or ripe seeds.
Flowers: Late winter/spring.
Species/cultivars: *A. amurensis*, 15 – 30 cm, clump-forming, leaves deeply cut, flowers yellow, late winter; *A.a.* 'Fukujukai', flowers larger, golden-yellow. *A. vernalis*, like *A. amurensis*, but flowers in spring.

Aesculus (horse-chestnut, buckeye)
HARDY DECIDUOUS TREES AND SHRUBS
Soil/aspect: Ordinary, moisture-retentive. Sun or partial shade.

Culture: Plant dormant season. Propagate by seed when ripe or by suckers in autumn; cultivars by grafting on *A. hippocastanum* or nearest species, late winter.
Flowers: Early to late summer.
Species/cultivars: *A.* x *carnea* (red horse chestnut), 6 m or more, round-headed, light red, yellow-eyed flowers early summer; *A.* x *c.* 'Briotii', flowers bright red, growth compact. *A. hippocastanum* (common horse chestnut), 10 m or more, flowers white, with yellow to red throat; suitable only for largest gardens; *A.h.* 'Baumannii', double flowers. *A. parviflora*, to 3 m, spreading by suckers, flowers white, late summer.

Aethionema (stone cress)
HARDY EVERGREEN ROCK GARDEN SUB-SHRUBS
Soil/aspect: Ordinary, well-drained. Sun.
Culture: Plant autumn or spring. Propagate by seeds in spring, cuttings in summer.
Flowers: Early summer.
Species/cultivars: *A. grandiflorum (A. pulchellum)*, to 30 cm, flowerheads rose-pink. *A. schistosum*, similar, but leaves blue-grey and flowers smaller. *A.* x 'Warley Rose', like *A. grandiflorum*, more compact with richer pink flowers.

Agapanthus (African lily)
HARDY OR HALF-HARDY DECIDUOUS AND EVERGREEN PERENNIALS
Soil/aspect: Ordinary, well-drained. Sun, sheltered.
Culture: Plant spring. Propagate by division or seeds under glass in spring.
Flowers: Summer/autumn.
Species/cultivars: The following are hardy and deciduous; Headbourne Hybrids, 90 cm or more; 'Isis', deep blue; 'Blue Moon', ice-blue, 'Luly', light blue. *A. praecox (A. umbellatus)*, 90 cm or more, half-hardy,

181

THE ORNAMENTAL GARDEN 2

Alstroemeria x Ligtu Hybrids

Amelanchier canadensis

Alstroemeria (Peruvian lily)
HARDY OR NEAR HARDY TUBEROUS-ROOTED PERENNIALS
Soil/aspect: Ordinary, well-drained. Sun, sheltered.
Culture: Plant spring. Propagate by careful division at planting time or seeds in spring under glass.
Flowers: Summer.
Species/cultivars: *A. aurantiaca,* to 90 cm, orange, streaked red trumpet flowers; *A.a.* 'Dover Orange', rich orange; 'Lutea', yellow. *A.* x Ligtu Hybrids, similar to *A. aurantiaca,* larger flower trusses in shades of pink to orange-red and yellow.

Althaea (Alcea) (hollyhock)
HARDY PERENNIAL, OFTEN GROWN AS ANNUAL OR BIENNIAL
Soil/aspect: Ordinary, well-drained. Sun, wind-sheltered.
Culture: Plant late summer to autumn. Propagate by seeds in summer, *in situ* or boxes. As annuals sow under glass early spring.
Flowers: Summer/autumn.
Species/cultivars: *A. rosea,* 2 m or more, pink to red; numerous cultivars, shorter and sturdier, and/or disease-resistant, in shades of red, pink, orange, yellow and white; single or double.

Alyssum
HARDY ANNUALS AND ROCK GARDEN PERENNIALS
Soil/aspect: Ordinary, well-drained. Sun.
Flowers: Spring/summer.
Culture: Plant autumn/spring. Propagate by seeds in spring, cuttings late summer.
Species/cultivars: *A. maritimum* (*Lobularia maritima*) (sweet alyssum); annual, 8 – 15

cm, white, pink, purple. *A. saxatile* (gold dust), 20 cm, mat-forming perennial, leaves grey-green, flowers bright yellow; *A.s.* 'Citrinum', lemon-yellow, 'Dudley Neville', biscuit-yellow. *A. spinosum* (*Ptilotrichium spinosum*), 7 – 15 cm, hummock-forming perennial, leaves silvery-grey, flowers white; *A.s.* 'Roseum', pink-tinted.

Amaranthus (love-lies-bleeding)
HALF-HARDY ANNUALS
Soil/aspect: Ordinary fertile soil. Sun or light shade.
Culture: Plant when frost is past. Propagate by seeds at 15 – 18°C, mid-spring.
Flowers: Summer/autumn.
Species/cultivars: *A. caudatus,* to 90 cm, red flowers in catkin-like, pendent spikes; *A.c.* 'Viridis', flowers pale green. *A. hypochondriacus* (prince's feather), as above, but taller, with erect flower spikes. *A. tricolor (A. gangeticus),* 90 cm, oval large leaves, flushed red, yellow, bronze (Joseph's coat); *A.t.* 'Molten Fire', leaves coppery-crimson, scarlet when young; *A.t.* 'Salicifolius', 60 cm, leaves narrow and drooping.

Amelanchier (June berry, snowy mespilus)
HARDY DECIDUOUS SHRUBS OR SMALL TREES
Soil/aspect: Ordinary, moisture-retentive; autumn colour best on neutral to acid soil. Sun or partial shade.
Culture: Plant dormant season. Propagate by seeds when ripe, by suckers in autumn.
Flowers: Spring.
Species/cultivars: *A. canadensis,* 3 – 5 m, suckering; young leaves white-felted, starry flowers white. *A. laevis,* 3 m or more, non-suckering, young leaves smooth and coppery-

red, flowers white. *A. lamarckii* (*A.* x *grandiflora, A. confusa*), similar to *A. laevis,* but leaves silky-haired.
Remarks: All species have edible fruits and outstanding autumn colours.

Anagallis (pimpernel)
HARDY OR NEAR-HARDY ANNUALS AND PERENNIALS
Soil/aspect: Ordinary, well-drained. Sun.
Culture: Plant perennials late spring-early summer; sow annuals *in situ.* Propagate perennials by seeds under glass, early spring.
Flowers: Summer.
Species/cultivars: *A. arvensis* (scarlet pimpernel), prostrate annual, usually red, but pink, lilac, purple and blue forms occur; *A.a.* 'Caerulea' is the best blue. *A. linifolia,* prostrate short-lived perennial, flowers large and gentian-blue.

Anaphalis (pearl everlasting)
HARDY PERENNIALS
Soil/aspect: Ordinary. Sun or partial shade.
Culture: Plant dormant season. Propagate by division, autumn or spring.
Flowers: Late summer.
Species/cultivars: *A. margaritacea,* 45 – 60 cm, leaves slender, flowers pearly-white. *A. nubigena,* 20 cm, leaves lance-shaped, flowers white. *A. triplinervis,* 30 – 45 cm, leaves obovate, flowers white; *A.t.* 'Summer Snow', more compact, flowers pure white.
Remarks: Flowers excellent for drying.

Anchusa (alkanet)
HARDY PERENNIALS AND ANNUALS
Soil/aspect: Ordinary, well-drained. Sun.
Culture: Plant dormant season. Propagate by division or root cuttings late winter.

Flowers: Late spring/summer.
Species/cultivars: *A. azurea* (*A. italica*), perennial, blue panicles; 'Little John', 45 cm, deep blue; 'Loddon Royalist', 90 cm, gentian-blue, large; 'Opal', 2 m, sky-blue. *A. capensis*, 30 – 60 cm, annual or biennial, red, blue or white.
   A. myosotidiflora, see *Brunnera*.

Androsace (rock jasmine)
HARDY ROCK GARDEN PERENNIALS
Soil/aspect: Well-drained, but moisture-retentive. Sun or partial shade.
Culture: Plant autumn or spring. Propagate in summer by rooting rosettes.
Flowers: Spring/summer.
Species/cultivars: *A. lanuginosa*, mat-forming, leaves silky, flowers lilac-pink. *A. primuloides*, mat-forming, stoloniferous, winter rosettes small and woolly, flowers pink; *A.p.* 'Brilliant', deep pink. *A. sarmentosa*, similar to *A. primuloides*, but larger in all its parts. *A. sempervivoides*, mat-forming, rosettes smooth, flowers pink.
Remarks: In areas of high rainfall, all but *A. sempervivoides* need protection from winter wet.

Anemone (windflower)
HARDY BORDER PERENNIALS
Soil/aspect: Ordinary. Sun or partial shade.
Culture: Plant dormant season. Propagate by division in autumn; seeds when ripe.
Flowers: Spring/summer/autumn.
Species/cultivars: *A. apennina* (tuberous), 15 cm or more, clump-forming, blue, purple, white (spring). *A. blanda*, similar to *A. apennina*, but colour range also includes red and pink. *A. coronaria* (tuberous), 30 cm; large red, purple, blue, pale yellow or white flowers can be had throughout the year by planting tubers at monthly intervals and using cloches or frames in winter; De Caen (single) and St. Brigid (double) are popular strains. *A.* x *hybrida* (*A. japonica*, *A. elegans),* 90 cm, shades of red-purple, pink, white, late summer/autumn. *A. narcissiflora*, 30 cm or more, white, sometimes flushed purple, summer. *A. nemorosa* (wood anemone), 15 cm, as *A. apennina*, but with creeping rhizomes, white, spring; *A.n.* 'Allenii', soft purple-blue; 'Blue Bonnet', pale blue, 'Robinsoniana', lavender-blue, 'Vestal', white with central boss of petaloids.
   A. pulsatilla, see *Pulsatilla*.

Antennaria (mountain everlasting)
HARDY ROCK GARDEN PERENNIALS
Soil/aspect: Ordinary, well-drained. Sun.
Culture: Plant dormant season. Propagate by division after flowering or in autumn.
Flowers: Spring/summer.
Species/cultivars: *A. aprica*, as *A. dioica*, leaves silvery-grey. *A. dioica*, mat-forming, grey-white hairy leaves, flowers white or pinkish; *A.d.* 'Rosea', deep pink.

Anthemis (chamomile)
HARDY BORDER OR ROCK GARDEN PERENNIALS
Soil/aspect: Well-drained, fertile. Sun.
Culture: Plant dormant season. Propagate by division or cuttings in autumn.

Androsace primuloides

Arbutus unedo 'Rubra'

Flowers: Summer.
Species/cultivars: *A. cupaniana*, 15 cm or more, mat-forming, leaves dissected, silvery, flowers white and yellow; needs sheltered site. *A. sancti-johannis*, to 60 cm, clump-forming; leaves grey-hairy, flowers bright orange. *A. nobilis* (true chamomile), 10 – 15 cm, mat-forming, leaves dissected, bright green, aromatic; flowers white and yellow; 'Plena', double; 'Treneague', dense mossy foliage, non-flowering, suitable for lawns. *A. tinctoria*, 60 – 90 cm, as *A. sancti-johannis*, but foliage green and flowers yellow; the cultivars are mainly hybrids of these species: 'E.C. Buxton', lemon-yellow; 'Grallagh Gold', bright orange-yellow; 'Wargrave', creamy-yellow.

Antirrhinum (snapdragon)
NEAR-HARDY PERENNIALS GROWN AS ANNUALS
Soil/aspect: Ordinary. Sun.
Culture: Plant late spring/early summer. Propagate by seeds at 15°C late winter, early spring. Can be sown outside in summer for overwintering in sheltered sites.
Flowers: Summer/autumn.
Species/cultivars: *A. majus*, 60 – 120 cm, red-purple to pink; numerous cultivars listed

in groups: Pumilum, 10 – 15 cm ('Tom Thumb', 'Magic Carpet'); Nanum, 45 cm ('Monarch' single colour strains); Maximum, 90 – 120 cm ('Harrison's Rust Resistant'). In addition there are large flowered tetraploid cultivars (Tetra Snaps) and the open-mouthed Penstemon-flowered strain, 'Bright Butterflies'.

Aponogeton (water hawthorn)
HARDY AQUATIC PERENNIAL
Soil/aspect: Loam or natural pond mud. Sun or partial shade, sheltered.
Culture: Plant spring in water 15 – 60 cm deep. Propagate by division in spring.
Flowers: Late spring to autumn.
Species/cultivars: *A. distachyos*, leaves oblong-elliptic, floating; flowers white, fragrant, in forked clusters.

Aquilegia (columbine)
HARDY BORDER AND ROCK GARDEN PERENNIALS
Soil/aspect: Ordinary, well-drained but moisture-retentive. Sun or light shade.
Culture: Plant dormant season. Propagate by division October-March, seeds when ripe.
Flowers: Spring/summer.
Species/cultivars: *A. alpina*, to 30 cm, deep blue, or blue and white. *A. bertolonii*, 10 – 15 cm, bright deep blue; good rock garden plant. *A. canadensis*, 30 cm or more, yellow and red bicolour. *A. flabellata pumila*, 10 cm, violet and white; *A.f.* 'Nana Alba', white. *A.* x Long-spurred Hybrids, to 90 cm, in a variety of colours, e.g. 'McKana' and 'Mrs. Scott-Elliot'. *A. vulgaris* (granny's bonnet), 45 – 60 cm, short-spurred, purple, red and white flowers, often double.

Arabis (rock cress)
HARDY ROCK GARDEN PERENNIALS
Soil/aspect: Ordinary, well-drained. Sun.
Culture: Plant dormant season. Propagate by seeds in spring, division after flowering.
Flowers: Spring/early summer.
Species/cultivars: *A. blepharophylla*, similar to *A. caucasica*, but flowers red-purple; not reliably hardy. *A.* x 'Rosabella' and *A.* x 'Rosea', flowers pink. *A. caucasica* (*A. albida*), 15 – 20 cm, mat-forming, white.

Arbutus (strawberry tree)
HARDY EVERGREEN SHRUBS AND TREES
Soil/aspect: Ordinary, well-drained. Sun, sheltered.
Culture: Plant autumn or spring. Propagate by tip cuttings in summer, layering in spring or seeds when ripe.
Flowers: Autumn/winter/spring.
Species/cultivars: *A. andrachne*, to 5 m, bark reddish, smooth; flowers white, spring; fruits orange. *A.* x *andrachnoides*, 3 m, bark smooth, cinnamon-red; flowers ivory-white, autumn to winter. *A. unedo*, to 6 m, bark deep brown, fibrous; flowers white or pinkish, autumn to early winter; fruits red; *A.u.* 'Rubra', deep pink.
Remarks: Tolerant of limy soil.

Arctotis (African daisy)
HALF-HARDY ANNUALS
Soil/aspect: Ordinary. Sun, sheltered.

THE ORNAMENTAL GARDEN 3

Culture: Plant early summer or when frost is past. Propagate by seeds at 18 – 21°C in early spring or cuttings late summer under glass.
Flowers: Summer, autumn.
Species/cultivars: *A. stoechadifolia*, 60 – 90 cm, leaves grey-green, daisy flowers white with blue disks, lavender in bud.

Arenaria (sandwort)
HARDY ROCK GARDEN PERENNIALS
Soil/aspect: Ordinary, well-drained. Sun.
Culture: Plant dormant season. Propagate by seeds spring, division autumn to spring.
Flowers: Spring/summer.
Species/cultivars: *A. balearica*, prostrate, forming dense filmy mats of minute leaves, starry flowers white; needs partial shade and soil that does not dry out. *A. purpurascens*, mat-forming, pale purple flowers.

Armeria (thrift)
HARDY ROCK GARDEN AND BORDER PERENNIALS
Soil/aspect: Ordinary, well-drained. Sun.
Culture: Plant dormant season. Propagate by division autumn – spring, cuttings late summer, seeds spring.
Flowers: Late spring, summer.
Species/cultivars: *A. alliacea (A. plantaginea)*, tufted, 20 – 25 cm, red-purple flower globes. *A. juniperifolia (A. caespitosa)*, hummock-forming, 5 cm, leaves greyish green, flowers pink. *A. maritima*, mat-forming, 10 – 30 cm, pink; *A.m.* 'Alba', white; 'Bloodstone', red.

Artemisia (wormwood)
HARDY FOLIAGE PERENNIALS AND SHRUBS
Soil/aspect: Ordinary, well-drained. Sun.
Culture: Plant dormant season. Propagate perennials by division autumn – spring, shrubs by cuttings late summer.
Flowers: Summer.
Species/cultivars: *A. abrotanum* (southernwood, lad's love, old man), shrub to 1 m, leaves grey-green, finely cut, aromatic. *A. absinthium* (common wormwood), woody-based perennial to 90 cm, leaves grey-green, deeply cut; *A.a.* 'Lambrook Silver', leaves silvery-grey. *A. lactiflora*, clump-forming perennial to 150 cm, leaves deeply lobed, terminal, plume-like flower panicles late summer. *A. ludoviciana*, rhizomatous perennial, to 120 cm, leaves narrow, densely white-felted. *A. schmidtiana*, perennial to 20 cm, leaves deeply cut, silvery and downy.

Aruncus (goat's beard)
HARDY PERENNIAL
Soil/aspect: Moisture-retentive. Sun or partial shade.
Culture: Plant dormant season. Propagate by division autumn-spring.
Flowers: Summer.
Species/cultivars: *A. dioicus (A. sylvester, Spiraea aruncus)*, 1.5 m, tiny white flowers in slender plume-like clusters.

Arundinaria (bamboo)
HARDY SHRUBS (WOODY-STEMMED GRASSES)
Soil/aspect: Ordinary, moisture-retentive. Sun or partial shade.

Aruncus dioicus

Asarum caudatum

Culture: Plant spring. Propagate by division in spring.
Flowers: Insignificant or rarely produced.
Species/cultivars: *A. japonica (Pseudosasa japonica)*, 3 m or more, rhizomatous, canes olive-green, narrow leaves to 30 cm long; can be invasive. *A. murielae*, to 4 m, clump-forming, canes yellow-green, leaves 10 cm long. *A. nitida*, like *A. murielae*, but with purple canes.

Asarum (wild ginger)
HARDY EVERGREEN PERENNIALS FOR GROUND COVER
Soil/aspect: Ordinary, moisture-retentive. Shade, but tolerate sun.
Culture: Plant autumn to spring. Propagate by division.
Flowers: Late winter/spring, hidden by foliage.

Species/cultivars: *A. caudatum*, leaves glossy, kidney-shaped, flowers brown-purple, tailed. *A. europaeum*, leaves glossy, rounded, small brown flowers. *A. shuttleworthii*, leaves mottled, large dark-purple flowers.

Asperula
HARDY ANNUALS AND PERENNIALS
Soil/aspect: Ordinary, well-drained. Sun or partial shade.
Culture: Plant autumn or spring. Propagate by division while dormant, seeds in spring, cuttings summer.
Flowers: Late spring, summer.
Species/cultivars: *A. lilaciflora caespitosa*, perennial, 6 cm, dark green mats, carmine-pink flowers. *A. orientalis (A. azurea)* annual, 20 – 30 cm, blue, fragrant. *A. suberosa*, prostrate and hummock-forming perennial, silver, hairy foliage, flowers pink; needs protection from winter wet.

Asplenium (spleenwort)
HARDY FERNS
Soil/aspect: Ordinary, moisture-retentive. Shade.
Culture: Plant dormant season. Propagate by careful division autumn-spring or spores in spring.
Flowers: None.
Species/cultivars: *A. scolopendrium (Phyllitis scolopendrium)* (hart's tongue fern), 30 – 60 cm, evergreen, strap-shaped, wavy fronds. *A. trichomanes* (maidenhair spleenwort), 20 cm, evergreen, pinnate fronds, black mid-ribs; good for dry walls and rock gardens.

Aster (Michaelmas daisy)

HARDY PERENNIALS

Soil/aspect: Ordinary, moisture-retentive. Sun.

Culture: Plant early spring. Propagate by single-shoot divisions in spring.

Flowers: Summer/autumn.

Species/cultivars: *A. amellus,* to 60cm, purple, late summer; *A.a.* 'Brilliant', bright pink; 'King George', violet-blue. *A. ericoides,* to 90 cm, white, tinted pink or blue, small but in profusion, autumn; *A.e.* 'Cinderella', blue; 'Ringdove', rosy mauve. *A. x frikartii,* 80 cm, satiny purple-blue and orange-yellow, late summer. *A. lateriflorus (A. lateriffolius),* 60 – 90 cm, white or pink tinted, autumn; *A.l.* 'Horizontalis', widespreading, larger flowers. *A. novae-angliae,* 1.5 m, violet-purple to pink, autumn; *A.n.* 'Harrington's Pink', clear pink; 'Lye End Beauty', phlox-purple. *A. novi-belgii,* purple-blue, autumn; hundreds of cultivars in shades of blue, purple, red, pink and white, 15 cm to 2 m tall, are readily available. *A. sedifolius (A. acris),* 60 – 90 cm, blue-mauve, in profusion, late summer. *A. tongolensis (A. yunnanensis),* 30 – 50 cm, blue and orange-yellow, summer. *A.t.* 'Napsbury', rich purple-blue.

Astilbe (false goat's beard)

HARDY PERENNIALS FOR BORDERS AND ROCK GARDENS

Soil/aspect: Moisture-retentive to wet. Sun or partial shade.

Culture: Plant dormant season. Propagate by division autumn to spring.

Flowers: Summer.

Species/cultivars: *A. x arendsii,* 60 – 150 cm, name covering numerous cultivars; dissected leaves, tiny flowers in terminal plumes in shades of red, pink, white and purple. *A. chinensis pumila,* 30 cm, wide-spreading, mauve pink, late summer-autumn. *A. simplicifolia,* 10 – 20 cm, leaves entire, flowers white.

Astrantia (masterwort)

HARDY PERENNIALS

Soil/aspect: Ordinary, moisture-retentive. Partial shade or sun.

Culture: Plant dormant season. Propagate by division autumn to spring, seed when ripe or in spring.

Flowers: Summer.

Species/cultivars: *A. major,* 60 – 90 cm, leaves pinnate, starry flowers and bracts green, tinted white, pink or purplish; *A.m.* 'Rubra', plum-red; 'Sunningdale', yellow variegated foliage. *A. maxima,* 40 – 60 cm, leaves trifoliate, flowers rose-pink.

Athyrium (lady fern)

HARDY FERNS

Soil/aspect: Ordinary, moisture-retentive. Partial shade.

Culture: Plant dormant season. Propagate by careful division autumn to spring, or spores.

Flowers: None.

Species/cultivars: *A. felix-femina,* to 1 m, deciduous fronds, bi-or tripinnate, arching, bright green.

Aubrieta

HARDY ROCK GARDEN PERENNIALS

Soil/aspect: Ordinary, well-drained. Sun.

Culture: Plant dormant season. Propagate by seeds in spring, cuttings in summer.

Flowers: Spring.

Species/cultivars: *A. deltoidea,* 10 cm, mat-forming, purple; several cultivars and strains in shades of purple, lilac, pink, red and white. *A.d.* 'Argenteovariegata', white variegated foliage; *A.d.* 'Aureovariegata', yellow variegated leaves.

Aucuba (laurel)

HARDY EVERGREEN FOLIAGE SHRUBS

Soil/aspect: Ordinary, moisture-retentive. Shade or sun.

Culture: Plant autumn or spring. Propagate by cuttings late summer or seeds when ripe.

Flowers: Spring, but insignificant.

Species/cultivars: *A. japonica,* 2 m, leaves lustrous rich green, flowers brown-purple, fruits bright red, 2 cm long; *A. j.* 'Crotonifolia' (male), leaves spotted yellow; *A.j.* 'Gold Dust' (female), leaves marked with golden-yellow.

Remarks: Plants of both sexes necessary for berries.

Baptisia (false indigo)

HARDY PERENNIALS

Soil/aspect: Ordinary, moisture-retentive. Sun or partial shade.

Culture: Plant dormant season. Propagate by division autumn to spring or seeds in spring.

Flowers: Summer.

Species/cultivars: *B. australis,* to 120 cm, clump-forming, soft indigo-blue flower spikes.

Begonia

TENDER PERENNIALS GROWN AS ANNUALS

Soil/aspect: Ordinary, moisture-retentive. Sun or light shade.

Culture: Plant when frost is past. Propagate by seeds late winter at 16°C, division of sprouted tubers or by cuttings in spring.

Flowers: Summer, early autumn.

Species/cultivars: *B. semperflorens,* fibrous-rooted, 15 – 30 cm, shades of red, pink, white, some doubles; glossy green or purple foliage. *B. x tuberhybrida,* large, double-camellia-flowered and Pendula type, tuberous-rooted begonias; many cultivars in shades of yellow, orange, pink, red or white, some picotees. Pendula types suitable for hanging baskets in sheltered sites.

Bellis (daisy)

HARDY PERENNIALS.

Soil/aspect: Ordinary. Sun or partial shade.

Culture: Plant autumn to late winter. Propagate by division while dormant or by seeds in spring.

Flowers: Spring, summer.

Species/cultivars: *B. perennis,* to 15 cm, clump-forming, white, red, pink; represented in cultivation by two double-flowered cultivars: Monstrosa, with large daisy flowers, available in separate colours or as mixtures; and Miniature, small pompon-like blooms in white, pink or red, named cultivars.

Berberis (barberry)

HARDY EVERGREEN (e) AND DECIDUOUS (d) SPINY SHRUBS

Soil/aspect: Ordinary. Sun or partial shade.

Culture: Plant dormant season. Propagate by heel cuttings late summer or seeds when ripe.

Flowers: Spring/summer; mainly yellow.

Species/cultivars: *B. candidula* (e) 60 cm, dense habit. *B. x carminea* (d), 1.5 – 2 m, vigorous, berries freely; 'Buccaneer', erect, large deep red fruits; 'Pirate King', dense, fruits bright orange. *B. darwinii* (e), to 3 m, glossy foliage, bright orange-yellow abundant flowers in spring. *B. julianae* (e), to 3 m, fruits blue-black; good hedging shrub with long spines. *B x lologensis* (e), hybrid of *B. darwinii,* bright reddish-orange flowers. *B. x rubrostilla* (d), 1 – 1.5 m, fruits coral-red, large. *B. x stenophylla* (e), to 3 m, arching habit, light orange-yellow flowers, good hedging shrub. *B. x s.* 'Corallina', dwarf, spreading habit, red buds, yellow flowers. *B. thunbergii* (d), to 2 m, leaves bright green, brilliant autumn colours, fruits glossy red; *B.t.* 'Atropurpurea', leaves red-purple; *B.t.* 'Atropurpurea Nana', 60 cm, purple foliage. *B. verruculosa* (e), to 1.5 m, slow-growing, dense, fruits violet-black.

Berberis x *lologensis*

Bergenia

HARDY EVERGREEN PERENNIALS

Soil/aspect: Ordinary, moisture-retentive. Partial shade or sun.

Culture: Plant autumn, winter. Propagate by division while dormant or by seeds in spring.

Flowers: Winter/spring.

Species/cultivars: *B. cordifolia,* to 40 cm, large leaves, heart-shaped at base, flowers pink; *B.c.* 'Purpurea', leaves purple-flushed. *B. crassifolia,* to 30 cm, paddle-shaped leaves, flowers rose-purple. Hybrids (40 cm): 'Abendglut' ('Evening Glow'), leaves flushed red, flowers deep purple; 'Silberlicht' ('Silver Light'), white flowers turning pinkish; 'Ballawley', leaves red, flowers magenta.

Betula (birch)

HARDY DECIDUOUS TREES

Soil/aspect: Ordinary. Sun or partial shade.

Culture: Plant dormant season. Propagate by seeds when ripe, or in spring.

THE ORNAMENTAL GARDEN 4

Flowers: Insignificant catkins in spring.
Species/cultivars: *B. albo-sinensis*, 10 m or more, reddish bark flaking. *B. ermanii*, 10 m or more, peeling bark, white flushed pink. *B. pendula* (common or silver birch), 10 m, bark brown, ageing to white with grey pattern; *B.p.* 'Dalecarlica', leaves deeply toothed; 'Fastigiata', narrow erect habit; 'Purpurea', leaves purple-flushed; 'Youngii', 3 – 5 m, weeping habit.

Brunnera (alkanet)
HARDY PERENNIALS
Soil/aspect: Ordinary, moisure-retentive. Sun or partial shade.
Culture: Plant dormant season. Propagate by division autumn to spring.
Flowers: Spring/summer.
Species/cultivars: *B. macrophylla*, (*Anchusa myosotidiflora*), 30 – 45 cm, bright blue forget-me-not flowers; *B.m.* 'Variegata', leaves broadly bordered with creamy white.

Buddleia (butterfly bush)
HARDY DECIDUOUS SHRUBS AND TREES
Soil/aspect: Ordinary. Sun or partial shade.
Culture: Plant dormant season. Propagate by cuttings late summer.
Flowers: Early to late summer.
Species/cultivars: *B. alternifolia*, to 6 m, arching to weeping habit, rosy-lilac flower sprays, early summer. *B. davidii* (*B. variabilis*), 3 – 5 m, smaller if pruned hard annually for larger flower trusses, lilac-purple, summer-autumn. *B.d.* 'Harlequin', reddish-purple, leaves variegated cream; 'Black Knight', deep violet; 'Peace', white; 'Royal Red', deep red-purple. *B. globosa*, to 3 m, semi-evergreen, orange-yellow flowers.

Buxus (box)
HARDY EVERGREEN SHRUBS AND SMALL TREES
Soil/aspect: Ordinary. Shade or sun.
Culture: Plant dormant season. Propagate by cuttings late summer.
Flowers: Insignificant; spring.
Species/cultivars: *B. microphylla,* 1 m, dense, slow-growing. *B. sempervirens* (common box), to 6 m, leaves leathery and glossy; *B.s.* 'Aureovariegata', leaves splashed creamy-white; 'Handsworthensis', vigorous, erect habit; 'Latifolia', large, glossy leaves, dense spreading habit; 'Suffruticosa', 90 cm, twiggy, dense, much used for edging.

Calendula (pot marigold)
HARDY ANNUALS
Soil/aspect: Ordinary. Sun.
Culture: Sow *in situ*, spring or autumn.
Flowers: Early summer to autumn.
Species/cultivars: *C. officinalis*, 30 – 50 cm, robust, sometimes short-lived perennial, pale yellow to rich orange flowers. Several cultivars available with double flowers.

Callistephus (China aster)
HALF-HARDY ANNUALS
Soil/aspect: Ordinary, preferably humus-enriched. Sun, sheltered.
Culture: Plant when frost danger is past. Propagate by seed in spring, at 16 – 18°C.
Flowers: Summer/autumn.

Bergenia cordifolia

Calluna vulgaris 'H.E. Beale'

Species/cultivars: *C. chinensis*, to 60 cm, purple and yellow, variable in habit and height, shape, colour and size of blooms. Classified after flower shape: Ball, neat and rounded, petals quilled; Chrysanthemum-flowered, double flowers, petals strap-shaped; Ostrich plume, large blooms, with long wavy petals; Paeony-flowered, rounded flowers with incurving petals; Pompon, dwarf plants, numerous small flowers, dense and rounded; Spider, long, slender, quilled petals. Numerous cultivars readily available, many wilt-resistant.

Calluna (heather)
HARDY EVERGREEN SHRUBS
Soil/aspect: Neutral to acid. Sun.
Culture: Plant dormant season. Propagate by cuttings late summer, layering in spring.
Flowers: Summer, autumn.
Species/cultivars: *C. vulgaris*, 60 cm or more, variable in colour of flowers, foliage and height. Hundreds of cultivars are available; the following are recommended: 'Alba Elata', flowers white; 'Beoley Gold', foliage rich yellow, flowers white; 'Blazeaway', foliage red to orange in winter; 'C.W. Nix', flowers deep crimson; 'Elsie Purnell', silvery-pink double flowers; 'Foxii Nana', dwarf, bun-like habit, bright green foliage, sparse pale purple flowers; 'Gold Haze', bright yellow foliage; 'H.E. Beale', icing-pink, double flowers; 'Hirsuta', silvery hairy foliage; 'Tib', compact habit, cyclamen-purple double flowers.

Caltha (marsh marigold)
HARDY PERENNIALS
Soil/aspect: Moist to wet. Sun or partial shade.
Culture: Plant dormant season. Propagate by division early spring or after flowering.
Flowers: Spring.
Species/cultivars: *C. palustris*, 30 cm, rich lustrous yellow buttercup-flowers; *C.p.* 'Alba', white; 'Multiplex', 'Monstrosa Plena' and 'Plena' all double-flowered yellow. *C. polypetala*, like *C. palustris*, but more robust and up to 45 cm.

Camassia (quamash, camass)
HARDY BULBS
Soil/aspect: Ordinary, moisture-retentive. Sun or partial shade.
Culture: Plant autumn. Propagate by offsets in autumn.
Flowers: Early summer.
Species/cultivars: *C. cusickii*, 90 cm, leaves narrow greyish-green, long blue flower spikes, needs support in windy sites. *C. leichtlinii*, 90 – 120 cm, leaves rich green, flowers violet to blue; 'Eve Price', 'Atroviolacea' and 'Onion', deeper purple-blue shades, wind-firm.

Camellia
HARDY EVERGREEN SHRUBS
Soil/aspect: Neutral to acid, moisture-retentive. Sun or partial shade, shelter from winds and morning sun.
Culture: Plant autumn or spring. Propagate by stem or leaf-bud cuttings, late summer; seed when ripe; layering in autumn. No pruning except dead-heading.
Flowers: Late winter/spring.
Species/cultivars: *C. japonica*, 3 m, foliage lustrous deep green, flowers red or pink. Variable in form and shade of flowers, with hundreds of known cultivars. The following are recommended: 'Adolph Audusson', red, semi-double; 'Alba Plena', double white; 'Alba Simplex', single white, yellow stamens; 'Drama Girl', salmon to rose-pink, large; 'Elegans', single, anemone-centred, bright pink; 'Magnoliaeflora', semi-double, shell-pink, magnolia-like; 'Tomorrow', semi-double, paeony-shaped, rose-pink, large; 'Tricolor' ('Sieboldii'), semi-double, white streaked carmine. *C* x *williamsii*, 3 m or more, graceful hybrid derived from *C. japonica*, with more freely produced, smaller flowers: 'Citation', semi-double, silvery-pink 'Donation', semi-double, orchid-pink; 'November Pink', single, phlox-pink, autumn to spring; 'St. Ewe', abundant, rose-pink, single flowers.

Campanula (bellflower)
HARDY BORDER AND ROCK GARDEN BIENNIALS AND PERENNIALS
Soil/aspect: Ordinary, well-drained. Sun or partial shade.
Culture: Plant dormant season. Propagate by division autumn to spring, basal cuttings and seeds in spring.
Flowers: Early to late summer.
Species/cultivars: *C. barbata*, 15 – 30 cm, pale blue bell flowers, hairy within, early

Campanula portenschlagiana

summer. *C. carpatica*, 30 cm, large erect blue cups, summer; *C.c.* 'Alba', white; 'Turbinata', compact, to 15 cm, *C. cochleariifolia (C. pusilla).* 10 cm, lavender-blue bells, summer/autumn; *C.c.* 'Alba', white. *C. garganica*, prostrate, blue with white centres, star-shaped, late spring-summer; *C.g.* 'Alba', white, *C.g.* 'Hirsuta', grey hairy leaves. *C. glomerata*, rhizomatous, to 50 cm, light violet-purple bells in erect heads, late spring through summer; *C.g.* 'Acaulis', dwarf to 15 cm; *C.g.* 'Nana' to 30 cm; *C.g.* 'Dahurica', robust, rich violet-purple. *C. lactiflora*, 1 – 1.5 m, clump-forming, milky-blue bells in clusters; *C.l.* 'Alba', white; 'Loddon Anna', lilac-pink; 'Pouffe', 15 – 25 cm, compact, lavender; 'Prichards', violet-blue.

    C. medium (Canterbury bell), biennial, best sown in late spring, to 90 cm, lilac-blue, pink, yellow or white bell flowers, summer; *C.m. calycanthema*, petaloid, saucer-shaped calyx, single or double flowered strains available. *C. persicifolia* (peach-leaved bell flower), to 90 cm, blue or white open bells, summer; 'Telham Beauty', rich purple-blue; 'Planiflora' (*C. nitida*), dwarf, 23 – 30 cm. *C. portenschlagiana* (*C. muralis*), semi-prostrate, lilac-blue bells, summer-autumn; best in light shade.

    C. poscharskyana, semi-prostrate and spreading, lavender-blue starry flowers freely borne; can be invasice. *C. rotundifolia* (harebell), 15 – 30 cm, blue or white bells, summer-autumn.

Campsis (trumpet creeper)
HARDY DECIDUOUS, SELF-CLINGING WOODY CLIMBERS
Soil/aspect: Ordinary, moisture-retentive. Sun, sheltered.
Culture: Plant dormant season. Propagate by cuttings late summer, layering or seeds in spring. Prune hard early spring.
Flowers: Late summer-autumn.
Species/cultivars: *C. grandiflora* (*Tecoma grandiflora, Campsis chinensis*), 10 m or more; deep orange and red trumpets; aerial roots sometimes sparse and need tying in. *C. radicans* (*Tecoma radicans*), to 15 m, orange and scarlet. *C. x tagliabuana*, hybrid between above species, more vigorous and freer-flowering; 'Madam Galen', salmon-red.

Carpinus (hornbeam)
HARDY DECIDUOUS TREES
Soil/aspect: Ordinary. Sun or partial shade.
Culture: Plant dormant season. Propagate by seeds when ripe. Trim hedges in summer.
Flowers: Spring; catkins insignificant.
Species/cultivars: *C. betulus*, 5 – 8 m, trunk ridged or fluted when mature, bark smooth, grey; catkins yellow; autumn leaves yellow to russet. 'Fastigiata' ('Pyramidalis'), narrowly pyramidal when young.
Remarks: Useful hedging plant.

Caryopteris (blue sage)
HARDY DECIDUOUS SHRUBS
Soil/aspect: Ordinary, well-drained. Sun, sheltered.

Culture: Plant autumn or spring. Propagate by heel cuttings, late summer. Prune hard in spring.
Flowers: Summer/autumn.
Species/cultivars: *C. x clandonensis*, to 1.5 m if not pruned, leaves grey-downy, aromatic; flowers blue. 'Arthur Simmonds', compact, to 60 cm, bright blue flowers; 'Ferndown', green foliage, dark blue flowers; 'Kew Blue', flowers even darker blue.

Catalpa (Indian bean tree)
HARDY DECIDUOUS TREES
Soil/aspect: Ordinary, moisture-retentive. Sun or partial shade.
Culture: Plant dormant season. Propagate by stem cuttings late summer at bottom heat, or by root cuttings late winter. No pruning.
Flowers: Late summer.
Species/cultivars: *C. bignonioides*, 8 – 10 m, round-headed, heart-shaped leaves 25 cm wide, flowers white, spotted yellow and purple within, long, slender, bean-like seed pods. 'Aurea', soft yellow leaves.
Remarks: Suitable for larger gardens only. Trees do not flower until mature.

Catananche (cupid's dart)
HARDY PERENNIALS
Soil/aspect: Ordinary, well-drained. Sun.
Culture: Plant spring or autumn. Propagate by seeds in spring, by root cuttings late winter. Seeds sown early under glass will flower same year.
Flowers: Summer/autumn.
Species/cultivars: *C. caerulea*, 50 – 80 cm, leaves mainly basal, narrow, flowers scabious-like, lavender-blue; 'Major', large flowers; 'Bicolor', white and blue; 'Perry's White', pure white, papery bracts.

Ceanothus (California lilac)
ALMOST HARDY, MAINLY EVERGREEN SHRUBS
Soil/aspect: Ordinary, well-drained. Sun, sheltered, best against walls.
Culture: Plant spring. Propagate by tip cuttings in spring, heel cuttings late summer, both with bottom heat; layering where possible in spring. In spring, prune deciduous types hard; evergreens can be trimmed lightly after flowering.
Flowers: Spring, summer, some autumn.
Species/cultivars: *C. x* 'Autumnal Blue', to 3 m, evergreen, mid-blue, summer-autumn. *C. x* 'Burkwoodii', similar to above, but rich, bright blue flowers. *C. x delinianus*, a group of deciduous hybrid cultivars, including 'Gloire de Versailles', 2 m, powder-blue in large clusters; 'Henri Desfosse', similar, but deep blue; and 'Topaz', light indigo-blue. The Pallidus group is similar and includes 'Marie Simon' and 'Perle Rose', both pink. *C. dentatus*, 2 – 3 m, evergreen, small dark green leaves, bright blue flowers; *C.d.* 'Floribundus', more profusely flowering. *C. impressus*, 3 – 4 m, evergreen, rich mid-blue, spring; 'Puget Blue', free-flowering.

    C. x lobbianus, similar to *C. dentatus*, but leaves broader and hardier, bright blue flowers, early summer; 'Russellianus', small-leaved and glossy. *C. thyrsiflorus* (blue blossom), to 6 m, evergreen, pale blue, in

Ceanothus impressus

profusion. *C.t. repens*, prostrate, forming low wide mounds; *C.t.* 'Cascade', arching branches, pale powder-blue flowers, early summer.

Cedrus (cedar)
HARDY EVERGREEN CONIFEROUS TREES
Soil/aspect: Ordinary, moisture-retentive. Sun.
Culture: Plant autumn or spring. Propagate by seeds in spring. No pruning.
Flowers: Autumn; catkins insignificant.
Species/cultivars: *C. atlantica*, to 20 m, pyramidical when young, broadening with age; *C.a.* 'Glauca', leaves blue-green. *C. deodara* (deodar), similar to *C. atlantica*, but with pendulous stem-tips. *C. libani* (cedar of Lebanon), much like *C. atlantica*, but longer and greyish-green leaves; dwarf cultivars, to 1.5 m, are available.
Remarks: Generally too vigorous for all but the largest gardens.

Celastrus (staff tree or vine)
HARDY DECIDUOUS, WOODY-STEMMED, TWINING CLIMBERS
Soil/aspect: Ordinary, moisture-retentive. Sun or partial shade.
Culture: Plant dormant season. Propagate by layering in spring, seeds when ripe. Prune to shape in spring.
Flowers: Summer, insignificant.
Species/cultivars: *C. orbiculatus* (*C. articulatus*), to 12 m; stems sometimes spiny when young; fruit capsules split in autumn to disclose glossy, scarlet seeds.

Centaurea (cornflower, knapweed)
HARDY ANNUALS AND PERENNIALS; TENDER SUBSHRUBS
Soil/aspect: Ordinary. Sun.
Culture: Plant hardy perennials dormant season, sow hardy annuals *in situ*, spring or autumn; plant tender bedding perennials when fear of frost is past. Propagate perennials by division autumn to spring, subshrubs by cuttings late summer.
Flowers: Summer.
Species/cultivars: *C. gymnocarpa* (dusty miller), tender foliage sub-shrub to 70 cm, silver-grey fern-like leaves, rose-purple flowers, sparsely on young plants. *C. cyanus* (cornflower), annual to 90 cm, shades of blue, purple, red, pink, white; 'Polka Dot', 30 cm, compact. *C. macrocephala*, robust perennial to 90 cm, large yellow flowers. *C. montana*, perennial to 60 cm, deep purple-blue, late spring-summer; 'Alba', white; 'Rosea', pink. *C. moschata* (*Amberboa moschata*) (sweet sultan), annual to 60 cm; *C.m. imperialis* most commonly cultivated, with fragrant, white, yellow, red-purple or pink flowers.

Centranthus (red valerian)
HARDY PERENNIALS
Soil/aspect: Ordinary, well-drained; good for dry sunny walls.
Culture: Plant spring. Propagate by division, basal cuttings or seeds, all in spring.
Flowers: Summer-autumn.
Species/cultivars: *C. rubra*, 45 – 90 cm, red, pink or white flower clusters.

Cerastium (snow-in-summer)
HARDY PERENNIALS
Soil/aspect: Ordinary, well-drained. Sun.
Culture: Plant dormant season. Propagate by division autumn to spring.
Flowers: Late spring-summer.
Species/cultivars: *C. tomentosum*, mat-forming, rhizomatous; leaves grey-silver,

downy; flowers white; *C.t.* 'Columnae', deep silvery-white.
Remarks: Invasive; not suitable for small rock gardens.

Ceratostigma (leadwort)
NEAR-HARDY DECIDUOUS SHRUBS AND PERENNIALS
Soil/aspect: Ordinary, well-drained. Sun, sheltered.
Culture: Plant spring. Propagate by heel cuttings late summer, careful division or removal of rooted suckers, spring.
Flowers: Summer-autumn.
Species/cultivars: *C. plumbaginoides* (*Plumbago larpentae*), hardy rhizomatous perennial, 30 – 40 cm, bright blue flower clusters, leaves red-tinted in autumn. *C. willmottianum*, near-hardy shrub, 60 – 120 cm, bright blue flowers; leaves sometimes red in autumn.

Cercis (Judas tree, redbud)
HARDY DECIDUOUS SHRUBS OR SMALL TREES
Soil/aspect: Ordinary, well-drained. Sun, sheltered.
Culture: Plant autumn or spring. Propagate by seeds under glass in spring (germination erratic, often prolonged). No pruning.
Flowers: Late spring.
Species/cultivars: *C. siliquastrum*, shrub or tree to 6 m, bright rose-purple pea flowers before leaves.

Chaenomeles (Cydonia, Japonica, Japanese quince)
HARDY DECIDUOUS SHRUBS
Soil/aspect: Ordinary. Sun or partial shade.
Culture: Plant dormant season, propagate by layering in spring, seeds when ripe—cultivars do not come true to type. Prune wall-trained shrubs after flowering.
Flowers: Winter to spring, sometimes later.
Species/cultivars: *C. japonica*, to 1 m, suckering habit, thorny, orange to blood-red flowers, fruits apple-like, small and yellow. *C. speciosa* (*C. lagenaria*), 2 m or more, spreading habit, scarlet, lightly fragrant flowers, fruit ovoid, greenish-yellow; 'Cardinalis', crimson-scarlet; 'Moerloosii', pink and white; 'Nirvalis', pure white; 'Umbilicata', deep pink. *C.* x *superba*, a group of hybrid cultivars, blending the characters of the previous species, but generally more vigorous: 'Boule de Feu', orange-red; 'Crimson and Gold', crimson with prominent yellow stamens; 'Hever Castle', shining pink; 'Knap Hill Scarlet', orange-scarlet; 'Rowallane', spreading habit, glowing crimson.

Chamaecyparis (false cypress)
HARDY EVERGREEN CONIFEROUS TREES
Soil/aspect: Ordinary, moisture-retentive. Sun or partial shade.
Culture: Plant autumn or spring. Propagate by heel cuttings late summer, seeds in spring. No pruning.
Flowers: Spring, barely noticeable.
Species/cultivars: *C. lawsoniana* (Lawson cypress), 20 m or more, greyish-green foliage in flattened sprays, tiny crimson male

catkins, sometimes in abundance. Numerous cultivars are available: 'Allumii', blue-grey, broadly columnar; 'Elwoodii', mossy juvenile foliage, slow-growing to 3 m, 'Fletcheri', similar to 'Elwoodii', but larger and foliage greyer; 'Green Hedger', bright green; 'Kilmacurragh', dark green, narrowly columnar; 'Lutea', golden-yellow; 'Minima', slow-growing, small globular bush; 'Nana', to 1 m, oval bush. *C. nootkatensis,* similar to *C. lawsoniana,* but with pendulous branchlets. *C. obtusa* (Hinoki cypress), to 18 m, similar to *C. lawsoniana,* but slow-growing, blunt, glossy green foliage in more compact sprays. Cultivars include: 'Cripsii', 6 m, golden-yellow; 'Minima', tiny mossy hummock; 'Nana', small flat-topped bush; 'Nana Gracilis', 2 m, conical, dark green; 'Tetragona', mossy golden foliage on upswept branches. *C. pisifera* (Sawara cypress), 12 m or more, as *C. obtusa,* but leaves pointed and habit loser. 'Boulevard', to 6 m, conical, blue-grey juvenile (awl-shaped) leaves; 'Plumosa', juvenile pale green leaves in fluffy sprays.

Cheiranthus (wallflower)
HARDY OR NEAR HARDY WOODY-BASED PERENNIALS, SOME GROWN AS BIENNIALS
Soil/aspect: Ordinary, preferably limy; well-drained. Sun.
Culture: Plant autumn to spring. Propagate by seeds, late spring, or heel cuttings in summer; plant out autumn.
Flowers: Dense spikes; spring and summer.
Species/cultivars: *C. x allionii* see *Erysimum. C. cheiri,* to 60 cm, yellow, fragrant flower spikes. Many cultivars are available in shades of red-brown, crimson, yellow-orange, ivory-white, including dwarf types up to 25 cm, as separate colour strains or mixtures.

Chimonanthus (winter sweet)
HARDY DECIDUOUS SHRUBS
Soil/aspect: Ordinary, moisture-retentive. Sun, sheltered.
Culture: Plant autumn or spring. Propagate by layering late winter, seeds in spring under glass. Prune wall shrubs after flowering.
Flowers: Cup-shaped; winter.
Species/cultivars: *C. praecox (C. fragrans),* 2.5 m or more against a wall; translucent, yellow and red-purple, deeply fragrant flowers on naked branches; *C.p.* 'Luteus', pure yellow.

Chionodoxa (glory of the snow)
HARDY DWARF BULBS
Soil/aspect: Ordinary. Sun or partial shade.
Culture: Plant autumn. Propagate by offsets at planting time, seeds when ripe.
Flowers: Star-like; spring.
Species/cultivars: *C. gigantea,* 15 cm or more, lilac-blue, the largest flowered. *C. luciliae,* 15 cm, light blue with large white centre. *C. sardensis,* 10–15 cm, deep blue, with or without small white eye.

Choisya (Mexican orange blossom)
NEAR HARDY EVERGREEN SHRUBS
Soil/aspect: Ordinary, well-drained. Sun. Sheltered.

Culture: Plant spring. Propagate by heel cuttings, late summer. Little pruning.
Flowers: Orange blossom, fragrant; late spring, early summer, sometimes later.
Species/cultivars: *C. ternata,* 2 m or more, leaves glossy trifoliate, flowers white.

Chrysanthemum (marguerite)
HARDY AND NEAR-HARDY ANNUALS AND PERENNIALS
Soil/aspect: Fertile, well-drained. Sun.
Culture: Plant late-spring; hardy annuals *in situ* mid-spring. Propagate florists' chrysanthemums by basal cuttings or seeds in early spring under glass, hardy perennials by division, cuttings or seeds in spring.
Flowers: Daisy-like or globe-shaped; summer—autumn.
Species/cultivars: *C. carinatum (C. tricolor),* annual, to 60 cm, daisy flowers with purple discs and yellow and white ray petals often banded red, maroon or purple or wholly red; some double. *C. coronarium,* annual, 60 cm or more; yellow or white, single or double. *C. leucanthemum* (ox-eye or moon daisy),

Chionodoxa sardensis

perennial, 60 cm or more; white, yellow disc; 'Little Silver Princess' is a good dwarf hybrid. *C. maximum* (Shasta daisy), perennial, 60–90 cm, white, yellow disc; 'Mayfield Giant' and 'Wirral Supreme', double, white. *C. parthenium (Matricaria eximia)* (feverfew), 30–90 cm, woody short-lived, aromatic perennial, yellow and white; double and single forms occur. *C. rubellum,* perennial to 90 cm, pink, disc yellow.
FLORISTS' CHRYSANTHEMUMS: A complex group of hybrid nature, originally from China and Japan. Hundreds of cultivars are available with flowers in all shades except blue and in a wide variety of sizes and forms. The so-called hardy cultivars grown and flowered outside are classified according to floral form: Incurved:—blooms globular, incurving petals. Reflexed:—blooms rounded, outcurving petals. Intermediate:—blooms halfway between Incurved and Reflexed. Single: daisy-like blooms with a flat central disc. Anemone-centred:—blooms like Singles but with a cushion-like disc of shorter petals the same colour as the ray petals. Pompon: blooms small, globose or cushion-shaped.

Cistus (sun rose)
HALF AND ALMOST HARDY (h) EVERGREEN SHRUBS
Soil/aspect: Ordinary, well-drained. Sun.
Culture: Plant spring. Propagate by heel cuttings late summer, at 18°C bottom heat; seeds under glass, spring. No pruning.
Flowers: Rose-like; summer.
Species/cultivars: *C. x corbariensis* (h), 60–90 cm, compact habit, dull green outer leaves, flowers white, yellow eye. *C. x cyprius* (h), to 90 cm; foliage downy white, flowers white with yellow eye. *C. ladanifer* (gum cistus), 2 m, narrow, sticky, dark foliage; flowers white, crimson centre. *C. laurifolius* (h), similar to *C. ladanifer* but leaves broader and flowers pure white, the hardiest species.

Clarkia (Godetia)
HARDY ANNUALS
Soil/aspect: Ordinary. Sun.
Culture: Sow *in situ* early autumn or spring.
Flowers: Funnel-shaped; summer, earlier if autumn sown.
Species/cultivars: *C. amoena (Godetia amoena),* 40–60 cm, lavender, pink, white; *C.a. whitneyi (C. grandiflora* of catalogues), large flowers, red eye, several cultivars are known, some dwarf and/or double. *C. concinna (Eucharidium concinnum),* 30 cm or more, bright pink, petals three-lobed. *C. pulchella,* 45 cm, lilac, purple and white; single and double cultivars are available.

Clematis (virgin's bower)
HARDY DECIDUOUS CLIMBERS
Soil/aspect: Ordinary, moisture-retentive. Sun, ideally with roots in shade.
Culture: Plant dormant season. Propagate by stem or leaf bud cuttings in summer; seeds when ripe. Prune summer and autumn-flowering types in late winter; spring-flowering clematis after blooming.
Flowers: Open cup or bell-shaped, spring/summer/autumn.
Species/cultivars: *C. alpina* 'Frances Rivis', to 2.5 m, vigorous, large, clear blue flowers, prominent white stamens, mid to late spring. *C. armandii* (evergreen), 6 m or more, white, spring; *C.a.* 'Apple Blossom', pink-flushed. *C. x jackmanii,* 4 m or more; a popular group of summer and autumn-flowering cultivars with saucer-shaped flower, 13 cm or more wide: 'Beauty of Worcester', double or single, bluish-violet; 'John Warren', deep-pink; 'Lasurstern', purple-blue; 'Marie Boisselot', white; 'Nellie Moser', white with pink stripes; 'The President', deep violet. Largest blooms and tidiest plants result if plants are pruned annually in late winter, cutting back to basal bud pair on all previous season's stems. *C. lanuginosa,* to 3 m, leaves grey-woolly beneath, flowers large, white to pale lilac, summer and autumn. *C. macropetala (Atragene macropetala),* 2–4 m, nodding, lavender-blue flowers, early summer; 'Maidwell Hall' dark blue; 'Markham's Pink', lavender-pink. *C. montana,* 10 m or more, pure white, late spring; *C.m. rubens,* pink-flushed; 'Elizabeth', deeper pink. *C. tangutica,* 6 m, yellow, lantern-shaped, nodding, summer-autumn;

Cistus x *corbariensis*

Cobaea scandens

seed heads silvery. *C. viticella,* almost herbaceous, and best pruned to near ground level annually, 3 m or more, purple-blue, bell-shaped, nodding flowers in summer; 'Kermesina', crimson; 'Minuet', creamy-white, tipped purple.

Cobaea (cathedral bell)
HALF-HARDY CLIMBERS GROWN AS ANNUALS.
Soil/aspect: Ordinary, moisture-retentive. Sun, sheltered.
Culture: Plant when fear of frost is past. Propagate by seeds in mid-spring at 18°C.
Flowers: Bell-shaped; summer and autumn.
Species/cultivars: *C. scandens,* 5 m or more, climbing by hooked tendrils; flowers large, yellow-green changing to purple.

Colchicum (autumn crocus)
HARDY BULBOUS PERENNIALS
Soil/aspect: Ordinary. Sun.
Culture: Plant late summer/early autumn. Propagate by removing offsets at planting time or by seeds when ripe.
Flowers: Crocus-like; late summer—late autumn, before leaves.
Species/cultivars: *C. autumnale,* 15 – 25 cm, lilac-pink; *C.a.* 'Album', white; 'Pleniflorum', double. *C. speciosum,* robust, to 30 cm, rose-lilac to red-purple; *C.S.* 'Album', pure white; 'Bornmuelleri', purple-rose with white throat; 'Violet Queen', red-purple; 'Water Lily', rose-lilac, double.

Convallaria (lily-of-the-valley)
HARDY RHIZOMATOUS PERENNIALS
Soil/aspect: Ordinary, moisture-retentive. Partial shade.

Culture: Plant dormant season. Propagate by division autumn to spring.
Flowers: Dainty bells; late spring.
Species/cultivars: *C. majalis,* 15 – 20 cm, waxy-white, nodding, strongly fragrant. 'Fortin's Giant', taller, larger flowers; 'Rosea', palest pink.

Convolvulus
HARDY ANNUALS
Soil/aspect: Ordinary. Sun.
Culture: Plant late spring, early summer, or sow *in situ* mid-spring. Support with sticks.
Flowers: Widely funnel-shaped; summer—early autumn.
Species/cultivars: *C. tricolor (C. minor),* 45 – 60 cm, blue, red-purple, red, yellow or white with contrasting zones or white eyes.

Coreopsis (tickseed)
HARDY ANNUALS AND PERENNIALS
Soil/aspect: Ordinary. Sun.
Culture: Plant autumn or spring; sow annuals *in situ* spring, or autumn in sheltered sites. Propagate perennials by division in dormant season or seeds in spring.
Flowers: Daisy-like; summer—autumn.
Species/cultivars: *C. grandiflora,* perennial, 45 cm, bright yellow; 'Mayfield Giant' 75 cm, double. *C. tinctoria,* annual, 60 cm, yellow, purple-brown or combination of these. *C. verticillata,* perennial, 45 – 60 cm, leaves finely cut, flowers bright yellow.

Cornus (dogwood)
HARDY, MAINLY DECIDUOUS SHRUBS AND TREES
Soil/aspect: Ordinary, moisture-retentive. Sun or partial shade.

Culture: Plant dormant season. Propagate by heel cuttings late summer (hardwood cuttings of *C. alba* and *C. stolonifera*), by layering in spring or seeds when ripe. Prune shrubs grown for winter bark to just above ground level in spring.
Flowers: Flat or rounded clusters; winter, spring or summer.
Species/cultivars: *C. alba*, suckering shrub, 2 m or more, cream flowers, early summer, fruits white or blue-tinted; *C.a.* 'Elegantissima', leaves white-margined; 'Sibirica', winter twigs crimson – for best effect, cut back hard each spring. *C. canadensis* (creeping dogwood), rhizomatous perennial, 15 – 20 cm, white petal-like bracts surround the flower heads, early summer. *C. controversa* 'Variegata', 6 m, branches in horizontal tiers, leaves marked creamy-white, flower clusters white, summer. *C. florida* (flowering dogwood), small tree to 5 m, flower clusters surrounded by large white bracts; 'Apple Blossom', bracts pink; 'Cherokee Chief', bracts rose-red. *C. kousa*, similar to *C. florida* but bracts narrower and pointed; strawberry-like fruits. *C. mas* (cornelian cherry) to 7 m, flowers yellow, before leaves; 'Variegata', leaves boldly margined creamy-white. *C. stolonifera*, 'Flaviramea', like *C. alba*, but winter twigs bright greenish-yellow.

Cortaderia (pampas grass)
HARDY PERENNIAL GRASSES
Soil/aspect: Ordinary, well-drained. Sun, preferably sheltered.
Culture: Plant spring. Propagate by division at planting time.
Flowers: Terminal plumes, early autumn.
Species/cultivars: *C. selloana (C. argentea, Gynerium argenteum),* to 3 m; silvery-white plumes; 'Pumila', dwarf habit to 1.5 m; 'Sunningdale Silver', 2 m, plumes bright creamy-white.

Corydalis
HARDY PERENNIALS
Soil/aspect: Ordinary. Sun or partial shade.
Culture: Plant autumn. Propagate by seeds when ripe, offsets in autumn or division in spring.
Flowers: Tubular, spurred; spring—summer.

Species/cultivars: *C. bulbosa* (*C. cava*), 10 – 20 cm, leaves grey-green, flowers rose-purple. *C. cheilanthifolia*, 30 cm, leaves fern-like, bronze-tinted, flowers yellow. *C. lutea*, 20 – 40 cm, yellow, spring to autumn; can be invasive. *C. solida*, like a small *C. bulbosa*, rose-pink flowers.

Corylopsis
HARDY DECIDUOUS SHRUBS OR SMALL TREES
Soil/aspect: Moisture-retentive, preferably neutral to acid. Sun or partial shade.
Culture: Plant dormant season. Propagate by layering in spring, heel cuttings late summer. No pruning.
Flowers: Drooping clusters, spring.
Species/cultivars: *C. pauciflora*, 1 – 2 m, primrose-yellow, fragrant. *C. platypetala*, 3 – 5 m, pale yellow, often in profusion. *C. spicata*, 2 m, bright yellow. *C. willmottiae*, similar to *C. platypetala*.

Corylus (hazel nut)
HARDY DECIDUOUS SHRUBS AND TREES
Soil/aspect: Ordinary, moisture-retentive. Sun or partial shade.
Culture: Plant dormant season. Propagate by seeds when ripe, layering in spring, suckers autumn to spring.
Flowers: Catkins; late winter, early spring.
Species/cultivars: *C. avellana* (hazel or cob-nut), 4 – 6 m, suckering habit, yellow; *C.a.* 'Contorta', (corkscrew hazel), twigs and branches curled and twisted. *C. colurna* (Turkish hazel), tree to 10 m, yellow. *C. maxima* (filbert), to 7 m, like a larger *C. avellana*, but long husks totally enclose the nuts; *C.m.* 'Purpurea', purple leaves.

Cosmos (cosmea)
HALF-HARDY ANNUALS
Soil/aspect: Ordinary, moisture-retentive. Sun.
Culture: Plant when fear of frost is past. Propagate by seeds at 15°C in spring or *in situ,* early summer.
Flowers: Dahlia-like, dainty; summer/early autumn.
Species/cultivars: *C. bipinnatus*, 90 cm, shades of purple, crimson, pink and white. *C. sulphureus*, 60 cm, yellow.

Cotinus (smoke tree)
HARDY DECIDUOUS SHRUBS AND SMALL TREES
Soil/aspect: Ordinary, but *C. obovatus* best in neutral to acid, moisture-retentive soil. Sun.
Culture: Plant dormant season. Propagate by heel cuttings late summer, layering in spring. No pruning.
Flowers: Feathery plumes; summer/autumn.
Species/cultivars: *C. coggygria* (*Rhus cotinus*), to 3 m, pinkish fawn; *C.c.* 'Foliis Purpureis', leaves red-purple; 'Notcutt's', maroon-purple. *C. obovatus* (*Rhus cotinoides*), up to 5 m, flowers insignificant, but foliage has bright autumn colouring.

Cotoneaster
HARDY DECIDUOUS (d) AND EVERGREEN (e) SHRUBS AND TREES
Soil/aspect: Ordinary. Sun or partial shade.

Corylus avellana 'Contorta'

Culture: Plant dormant season. Propagate by seeds when ripe, heel cuttings late summer, layering in spring. Prune in spring.
Flowers: Usually white to cream; spring/summer.
Species/cultivars: *C. conspicuus* 'Decorus' (e) 1 m or more, arching habit, scarlet fruits in abundance. *C. dammeri radicans* (e), prostrate, fruits bright red but sparse. *C.d.* 'Skogholm', vigorous, arching stems up to 30 cm high, coral-red fruits. *C. dielsianus* (d) 2 m, flowers pinkish, fruits scarlet, good autumn colours. *C. franchetii* (e), 2.5 m, arching habit, flowers pink-tinted, fruits orange-scarlet. *C. frigidus* (d), small tree to 7 m, fruits bright crimson; *C.f.* 'Fructu-luteo', yellow fruits. *C. horizontalis* (d), branches in flat fishbone pattern, flowers pink-flushed; fruits bright red. *C. lacteus* (e), 4 m, flowers late summer, red fruits in winter, good hedging shrub. *C. microphyllus* (e), prostrate to low arching, fruits crimson, large but sparse; *C.m.* 'Cochleatus', entirely prostrate. *C. salicifolius* (e), 3 – 5 m, fruits bright red; *C.s.* 'Autumn Fire', pendulous habit, abundant fruits; *C.s.* 'Repens', prostrate. *C. simonsii* (e/d), 2 – 3 m, erect habit, fruits scarlet, good hedging shrub. *C. x watereri*, (semi/e), 3 – 5 m; 'Cornubia' and 'John Waterer', red fruit; 'Rothschildianus' (e), fruits yellow.

Crataegus (thorn, hawthorn)
HARDY DECIDUOUS SHRUBS AND SMALL TREES
Soil/aspect: Ordinary. Sun or partial shade.
Culture: Plant dormant season. Propagate by seeds when ripe, layering in spring or grafting on *C. monogyna* late winter. No pruning.
Flowers: White or cream clusters, late spring.
Species/cultivars: *C. x carrierei* (*C. x lavallei*), tree to 7 m, haws orange-red, large. *C. laevigata* (*C. oxyacantha*), like *C. monogyna* but lobed leaves shallowly rounded; *C.l.* 'Paul's Scarlet', double red; 'Plena', double white. *C. mollis* (red haw), 10 – 12 m, fruits bright red, large and abundant. *C. monogyna* (common hawthorn), 5 – 10 m, toothed leaves, fruits deep red; *C.m.* 'Biflora' ('Praecox', Glastonbury thorn) flowers intermittently during winter and spring. *C. orientalis* (*C. laciniata*), tree to 6 m, almost thornless, leaves grey beneath, fruits coral to orange-red and large.

Crocosmia (montbretia)
ALMOST HARDY BULBOUS PERENNIALS
Soil/aspect: Ordinary. Sun, sheltered.
Culture: Plant spring. Propagate by division or offsets at planting time.
Flowers: Branching sprays of tubular flowers; late summer.
Species/cultivars: *C. x crocosmiiflora*; 60cm or more, yellow to red; 'Citronella', soft yellow; 'Jackanapes', dark red and yellow bicolour; 'Solfatare', pale apricot-yellow, foliage bronze-tinted. *C. masonorum*, 75 cm or more, leaves pleated, vermilion-orange flowers in arching sprays.

Crocus
HARDY CORMOUS PERENNIALS
Soil/aspect: Ordinary, well-drained. Sun.
Culture: Plant autumn-flowering types late summer, spring-flowering in autumn.
Flowers: Goblets, autumn, winter or spring.
Species/cultivars: *C. ancyrensis* 'Golden Bunch', 7 cm, rich orange-yelow, late winter. *C. aureus* (*C. flavus*) 'Dutch Yellow', orange-yellow, early spring. *C. chrysanthus*, 5 – 7cm, orange, late winter; cultivars and hybrids include 'Blue Pearl', pale blue; 'E.P. Bowles', butter-yellow, grey markings; 'Snow Bunting', white and cream; 'Zwanenburg Bronze', deep orange and purple-brown. *C. imperati*, 7 – 10 cm, satiny, lilac-purple and buff, winter. *C. kotschyanus* (*C. zonatus*), 5 – 7 cm, lilac, orange throat, early autumn before leaves. *C.k. leucopharynx* (marketed as *C. karduchorum*), throat white. *C. sieberi atticus*, 6 – 10 cm, lavender-purple, late winter; *C.s.* 'Violet Queen', deep mauve. *C. speciosus*, 10 – 12 cm, bright lilac to purple-blue, autumn before leaves; *C.s.* 'Albus', white; 'Oxonian', deep blue-purple. *C. tomasinianus*, 6 – 7 cm, lilac to purple and buff, late winter; *C.t.* 'Whitewell Purple', petals tipped red-purple. *C. vernus* (*C. neapolitanus*), 7 – 9 cm, purple; spring; represented in gardens by large-flowered Dutch cultivars: 'Jeanne d'Arc', white; 'Pickwick', white striped purple; 'Purpureus Grandiflorus', purple-blue.

Cryptomeria (Japanese cedar)
HARDY EVERGREEN CONIFERS
Soil/aspect: Ordinary, moisture-retentive. Sun or partial shade.
Culture: Plant autumn or spring. Propagate by heel cuttings late summer, seeds in spring. No pruning.
Flowers: Insignificant catkins, spring.
Species/cultivars: *C. japonica*, to 20 m, pyramidal, rich green foliage, suitable only for large gardens; *C.j.* 'Bandai-Suigi', dwarf bush to 1 m, growth congested and mossy; 'Elegans', bushy tree to 5 m, slow-growing, permanent juvenile foliage, bronze in winter; 'Vilmoriniana', 90 cm, globose and compact.

X Cupressocyparis (false cypress)
HARDY EVERGREEN CONIFERS
Soil/aspect: Ordinary, moisture-retentive. Sun or partial shade.
Culture: Plant autumn or spring. Propagate by cuttings summer or autumn. No pruning except for hedges.

Flowers: Insignificant, spring; round cones.
Species/cultivars: *C. leylandii* (Leyland cypress), vigorous hybrid between *Cupressus macrocarpa* and *Chamaecyparis nootkatensis*. Columnar, to 15 m, grey-green foliage; fast-growing, excellent for windbreaks or tall hedges.

Cupressus (cypress)
HARDY EVERGREEN CONIFERS
Soil/aspect: Ordinary. Sun.
Culture: Plant autumn or spring. Propagate by heel cuttings late summer, seeds in spring.
Flowers: Insignificant; rounded cones freely borne.
Species/cultivars: *C. glabra* (*C. arizonica* 'Bonita'), to 12 m, pyramidal habit, smooth flaking, purplish bark, foliage grey to bluish-green. *C. macrocarpa*, (Monterey cypress), 20 m, broadly conical, flat-topped with age, foliage lemony-green, aromatic when bruised; *C.m.* 'Donard Gold', golden-yellow. *C. sempervirens* (Italian or Mediterranean cypress), to 12 m, narrowly columnar, dark green foliage

Cyclamen
HARDY DWARF CORMOUS PERENNIALS
Soil/aspect: Ordinary, humus enriched. Partial shade.
Culture: Plant dormant season. Propagate by seeds when ripe or in spring.
Flowers: Shuttlecocks, reflexed; autumn, winter, spring.
Species/cultivars: *C. coum* , 7 cm, round marbled leaves, flowers pink or white, late winter. *C. europaeum* (*C. purpurascens*), 10 cm, leaves round, marbled silvery, flowers pale to carmine-pink, fragrant, late summer/early autumn. *C. neapolitanum*, 10 cm, leaves variably lobed, silvery patterned, flowers pink, purple or white, autumn.

Cynoglossum (hound's tongue)
HARDY BIENNIALS AND PERENNIALS
Soil/aspect: Ordinary. Sun.
Culture: Plant biennials late summer onwards; perennials autumn to spring. Propagate by seeds in spring, perennials by division in dormant season.
Flowers: Summer.
Species/cultivars: *C. amabile* 'Blue Bird' (biennial), 45 – 60 cm, bright blue, drooping funnel-shaped flowers. *C. nervosum* (perennial), 60 cm, rough, hairy leaves, intense blue forget-me-not flowers in sprays.

Cytisus (broom)
HARDY DECIDUOUS (d) AND EVERGREEN (e)
SHRUBS AND TREES
Soil/aspect: Ordinary, well-drained. Sun.
Culture: Plant autumn or spring. Propagate by seeds in spring, heel cuttings late summer. Prune after flowering if necessary.
Flowers: Pea-like; spring, summer.
Species/cultivars: *C. battandieri* (d/e), 3 – 4 m, leaves trifoliate, silky, white, flowers rich yellow, pineapple-scented, summer. *C. x beanii* (d), 25 – 45 cm, golden-yellow, spring, suitable for rock gardens. *C. x praecox* (d) (Warminster broom), to 2 m, sulphur-yellow, late spring. *C. scoparius* (*Sarothamnus*

Cyclamen neapolitanum

scoparius) (d), 2 – 3 m, rich yellow, late spring; *C.s.* 'Andreanus', yellow and mahogany-red; several colourful cultivars are available in shades of red, pink, yellow or white.

Dahlia
HALF-HARDY TUBEROUS-ROOTED PERENNIALS
Soil/aspect: Fertile, moisture-retentive. Sun, wind-sheltered.
Culture: Plant when fear of frost is past. Propagate by cuttings at 16°C bottom heat or by seeds at the same time and temperature. Tall cultivars need staking. Lift and store tubers once tops are killed by first autumn frost.
Flowers: Summer—early autumn.
Species/cultivars: *D. variabilis*, variable species which has given rise to the hundreds of cultivars. Heights vary from 15 – 150 cm or more; flowers 3 – 25 cm wide or more. All main colours and shades except blue are represented. Dahlias are classified according to floral form and size: 1. Single-flowered: daisy-like, to 10 cm wide. 2. Anemone-flowered: as 1, but central disc a loose cushion of tubular florets or petals the same colour as ray florets. 3. Collerette: as 1, but with a collar of ray-like petals around the centre disc, in the same or a contrasting colour. 4. Paeony-flowered: semi-double, to 10 cm wide with broad petals. 5. Decorative: fully double, the petals sometimes waved or twisted; there are five sub-groups: giant flowers 25 cm or more wide; large, 20 – 25 cm; medium, 15 – 20 cm; small, 10 – 15 cm; miniature, up to 10 cm wide. 6. Ball: fully-double, ball-shapes, 10 – 15 cm wide; miniature ball, up to 10 cm. 7. Pompon: as ball, but flowers to 5 cm. 8. Cactus: as decorative, and with the same sub-groups but petals quilled. 9. Semi-cactus: as Cactus, but petals quilled for up to half their length from the tip downwards.

Daphne
HARDY DECIDUOUS (d) AND EVERGREEN (e)
SHRUBS
Soil/aspect: Ordinary. Sun or partial shade.
Culture: Plant dormant season, evergreens autumn or spring. Propagate by seeds when ripe, heel cuttings late summer. No pruning.
Flowers: Tubular, in clusters; late winter, early summer.

Species/cultivars: *D.* x *burkwoodii* (semi/e), 1 m, pink, early summer. *D. cneorum* (garland flower) (e), 15 cm or more tall, spreading, rich pink, fragrant flowers, early summer; *D.c.* 'Eximia', larger and darker flowers. *D. mezereum* (d), 1 m or more, erect habit, purple-red, fragrant, in late winter before leaves; 'Bowles White', pure white. *D. odora* 'Marginata' (e), 1 – 2 m, spreading, leaves with narrow yellow margins, fragrant flowers, red-purple in bud, opening paler, late winter—spring.

Davidia (dove or handkerchief tree)
HARDY DECIDUOUS TREES
Soil/aspect: Ordinary, moisture-retentive. Sun or partial shade.
Culture: Plant dormant season. Propagate by layering spring, heel cuttings late summer. No pruning.
Flowers: Small, hidden by large creamy-white bracts; late spring—early summer.
Species/cultivars: *D. involucrata*, 10 m, globular flower clusters pendent, enclosed by two large white bracts.

Delphinium (larkspur)
HARDY ANNUALS (a) AND PERENNIALS (p)
Soil/aspect: Ordinary, moisture-retentive. Sun, light shade.
Culture: Plant dormant season. Propagate perennials by division, autumn or spring, basal cuttings and seeds in spring. Sow annuals *in situ* autumn or spring.
Flowers: Spikes of open, spurred blooms; summer.
Species/cultivars: *D.ajacis* (rocket larkspur) (a), 60 – 100 cm, deep blue, purple, pink, white; Hyacinth-flowered, double strains are popular. Belladonna cultivars (p), 120 cm, branched spikes mainly in shades of blue: 'Blue Bees', light blue; 'Larmartine', violet-blue; 'Wendy', gentian-blue. *D. consolida* (a) (common larkspur) as *D.ajacis,* but with shorter and branched flower spikes. *D. elatum* (p), 1 – 1.5 m, deep blue; represented in cultivation by hybrid cultivars – the familiar border delphiniums – dozens of which are available in shades of blue, purple, white, cream, pink, red.

Deutzia
HARDY DECIDUOUS SHRUBS
Soil/aspect: Ordinary. Sun or light shade.
Culture: Plant dormant season. Propagate by cuttings in summer at bottom heat, or hardwood cuttings late autumn. Prune flowered stems to ground level when faded.
Flowers: Star-shaped in clusters; summer.
Species/cultivars: *D.* x *elegantissima* 'Rosealind', 1.5 – 2 m, deep carmine-pink, fragrant. *D.* x *hybrida* 'Mont Rose', 1.5 – 2 m, rose-purple, freely borne. *D.* x *rosea*, 1 m, pink. *D. scabra*, 3 m, white; *D.s.* 'Candidissima', double, pure white; 'Pride of Rochester', double white, pink-tinted.

Dianthus (pink, carnation)
HARDY PERENNIALS AND ANNUALS
Soil/aspect: Ordinary, well-drained. Sun.
Culture: Plant dormant season. Propagate by seeds in spring, cuttings in summer.

Flowers: Flat, salver-shaped, smooth or wavy from tubular calyces; early to late summer.
Species/cultivars: *D.* x *allwoodii*, known as modern border pinks, 25 – 35 cm, numerous cultivars double or single, in shades of red, pink, white. *D. alpinus*, mat-forming and prostrate, rose-purple. *D. barbatus* (sweet William), short-lived perennial usually grown as a biennial, 50 – 60 cm, shades of purple, red, white, bicolours, single or double, fragrant. *D.b.* 'Compactus', 30 cm or less. *D. caryophyllus* (carnation), 45 cm, many cultivars of annual and border carnations in shades of red, pink, white and yellow, single or double, often deeply scented,. Annuals are raised from seed sown late winter at 15°C. Border carnations can be raised from seed, named cultivars from cuttings. They are short-lived and should be propagated every other year. *D. chinensis* (Indian pink), short-lived perennial usually grown as annual or biennial, 30 cm, flower clusters in shades of red, pink and white; *D.c.* 'Heddewigii', more compact and free-flowering. *D. deltoides* (maiden pink); 15 – 25 cm, mat-forming, dark green leaves, deep pink or white flowers; some cultivars with purplish foliage. *D. gratianopolitanus* (*D. caesius*) (Cheddar pink), 10 – 20 cm, mat-forming and long-lived, pink or white. *D. superbus*, 40 – 50 cm, lilac to rose-purple, the petals deeply cut and fringed; parent of the fragrant 'Loveliness', compact, with large flowers, red, pink, purple or white; usually grown as an annual.

Dicentra
HARDY PERENNIALS
Soil/aspect: Ordinary, moisture-retentive. Partial shade or sun.
Culture: Plant dormant season. Propagate by division autumn to spring or root cuttings late winter.
Flowers: Heart-shaped, in drooping sprays; spring—early summer.
Species/cultivars: *D. eximia*, 30 cm or more, rose-red, compact nodding spikes. *D. formosa*, similar to *D. eximia*, but spikes larger and leaves more glaucous-green. *D.f.* 'Alba', white; 'Adrian Bloom', crimson; 'Spring Morning', light pink. *D. spectabilis* (bleeding heart), 60 cm, rose-crimson, in arching spikes.

Dictamnus (burning bush)
HARDY PERENNIALS
Soil/aspect: Fertile, well-drained. Sun.
Culture: Plant autumn or spring. Propagate by seeds sown when ripe or careful division, spring.
Flowers: Spidery, loose spikes; summer.
Species/cultivars: *D. albus* (*D. fraxinella*), clump-forming, 50 – 80 cm, white, fragrant; *D.a.* 'Purpurea', purple-pink, dark veined.

Dierama (wand flower, angel's fishing rod)
NEAR HARDY CORMOUS EVERGREEN PERENNIALS
Soil/aspect: Fertile, moisture-retentive. Sun, sheltered.
Culture: Plant spring. Propagate by division or seeds under glass in spring.
Flowers: Summer.

Daphne cneorum

Deutzia x *rosea*

Species/cultivars: *D. pulcherrimum*, up to 2 m, wiry, arching stems with pendulous trumpet flowers, purple to red; cultivars available in shades of purple to wine-red.

Digitalis (foxglove)
HARDY BIENNIALS (b) AND PERENNIALS (p)
Soil/aspect: Ordinary, moisture-retentive. Partial shade or sun.
Culture: Plant perennials dormant season, biennials late summer—autumn. Propagate by seeds, division of perennials, spring.
Flowers: Tubular, dense spikes; summer.
Species/cultivars: *D. grandiflora* (*D. ambigua*) (p), 60 – 100 cm, yellow, brown-veined within. *D.* x *mertonensis* (p), 60 cm, strawberry-pink. *D. purpurea* (b), 1 – 1.5 m, rose to red-purple and white, spotted maroon within. 'Excelsior', 1.5 m, symmetrical spikes, red, purple, pink, cream; 'Shirley', as 'Excelsior' in colour range but taller, with one-sided spikes.

Dimorphotheca (Cape marigold)
HALF-HARDY PERENNIALS (p) AND ANNUALS (a)
Soil/aspect: Ordinary, well-drained. Sun, shelter.
Culture: Plant late spring or when fear of frost is past. Propagate by seeds in spring,

cuttings late summer in cold frame. Perennials often survive mild winters.
Flowers: Bright daisies; summer—autumn.
Species/cultivars: *D. annua (D. pluvialis)* (a), 30 cm, white, purple in bud. *D. aurantiaca*, perennial grown as annual, 30 – 45 cm, bright orange; white to salmon-orange cultivars available. *D. barberiae* (*Osteospermum barberiae*) (p), 45 cm, spreading, rose-purple; *D.b.* 'Compacta', 15 cm, prostrate.

Dodecatheon (shooting star)
HARDY PERENNIALS
Soil/aspect: Rich, moisture-retentive. Shade.
Culture: Plant dormant season. Propagate by seeds, spring, division in autumn.
Flowers: Cyclamen-like; late spring—early summer.
Species/cultivars: *D. meadia* (*D. pauciflorum*), 30 – 50 cm, pink to lilac and white; ripe seed capsules hard. *D. pulchellum* as *D. meadia*, but flower colours variable – red, magenta, lilac, lavender, white; seed capsules papery.

Doronicum (leopard's bane)
HARDY PERENNIALS
Soil/aspect: Ordinary. Sun or partial shade.
Culture: Plant dormant season. Propagate by division autumn to spring.
Flowers: Yellow daisies; spring—summer.
Species/cultivars: *D. austriacum*, 45 cm or more. *D. cordatum* (*D. columnae*), 15 – 30 cm. 'Miss Mason', vigorous and free-flowering. 'Spring Beauty', fully double, deep yellow. *D. plantaginium* 'Harpur Crewe' ('Excelsum'), golden-yellow.

Draba (whitlow grass)
HARDY ROCK GARDEN PERENNIALS
Soil/aspect: Ordinary, well-drained. Sun.
Culture: Plant dormant season. Propagate by seeds when ripe or in spring, individual rosettes as cuttings, or careful division in summer.
Flowers: Short dense spikes; spring.
Species/cultivars: *D. aizoides*, hummock-forming, 5 – 10 cm, bright yellow. *D. dedeana*, cushion-forming, 8 cm high, white, tinted purple.

Dryas (mountain avens)
HARDY EVERGREEN ROCK GARDEN SHRUBS
Soil/aspect: Ordinary, well-drained. Sun.
Culture: Plant dormant season. Propagate by seeds when ripe, cuttings late summer, layering in spring.
Flowers: Saucer-shaped; summer.
Species/cultivars: *D. octopetala*, mat-forming, white flowers, seed heads of feathery white plumes.

Dryopteris (buckler fern)
HARDY FERNS
Soil/aspect: Ordinary, moist. Shade.
Culture: Plant dormant season. Propagate by division or spores, spring.
Flowers: Non-flowering.
Species/cultivars: *D. borreri*, 30 – 60 cm, usually evergreen, golden-green fronds; crested forms available. *D. filix-mas* (semi-evergreen or deciduous), fronds 60 – 120 cm, deep green shuttlecocks.

Dimorphotheca aurantiaca

Echinacea (purple cone flower)

HARDY PERENNIALS

Soil/aspect: Moisture-retentive. Sun.
Culture: Plant dormant season. Propagate by division or seed in spring.
Flowers: Daisies, prominent central cones; summer-autumn.
Species/cultivars: *E. purpurea*, 90 – 120 cm, foliage rich green; flowers red-purple, orange-brown cones. *E.p.* 'The King', crimson-pink; 'Robert Bloom', cerise-crimson; 'White Lustre', white, orange cones.

Echinops (globe thistle)

HARDY PERENNIALS

Soil/aspect: Ordinary, moist. Sun.
Culture: Plant dormant season. Propagate by division autumn to spring, seeds in spring.
Flowers: Spiky globes; summer.
Species/cultivars: *E. banaticus*, 1.5 m, leaves deeply lobed, spiny and white beneath; flowers grey-blue. *E. humilis* 'Taplow Blue', 2 m, soft blue. *E. ritro* (of gardens), 120 cm, deep metallic-blue.
Remarks: Flower globes suitable for drying.

Echium (viper's bugloss)

HARDY BIENNIALS, OFTEN GROWN AS ANNUALS

Soil/aspect: Ordinary. Sun.
Culture: As annuals, seeds under glass early spring. As biennials, *in situ* early summer.
Flowers: Tubular or bells, summer.
Species/cultivars: *E. lycopsis* (*E. plantagineum*), 60 cm or more, purple, blue, pink; *E.l.* 'Dwarf Bedding Mixed', 30 cm, well-branched, with flowers in clusters.

Edraianthus

HARDY ROCK GARDEN PERENNIALS

Soil/aspect: Ordinary to limy, sharply-drained. Sun.
Culture: Plant autumn or spring. Propagate by cuttings or seeds in spring.
Flowers: Open bells, summer.
Species/cultivars: *E. dalmaticus*, tufted, 8 cm, violet-blue. *E. pumilio*, prostrate, hummock-forming, blue-purple. *E. serpyllifolius*, tufted, 4 cm, deep violet-purple.

Elaeagnus (oleaster)

HARDY DECIDUOUS (d) AND EVERGREEN (e) FOLIAGE SHRUBS

Soil/aspect: Ordinary. Sun or partial shade.
Culture: Plant dormant season. Propagate by heel cuttings, late summer, seeds when ripe (species only). Prune to shape in spring.
Flowers: Small, bell-shaped in clusters; summer-autumn.
Species/cultivars: *E. angustifolia* (d), 3 – 6 m, silver-grey, willow-like foliage, silvery flowers, early summer. *E. commutata* (*E. argentea*) (d), much like *E. angustifolia*, but smaller (to 2 m), with broader leaves. *E. x ebbingei* (e) 3 – 5 m, leathery, ovate, silvery foliage; good for hedges and shelter belts. *E. macrophylla* (e), 3 m or more, leaves large, glossy; fragrant flowers, silver and brown, late autumn. *E. pungens* (e), 3 m or more, stems more or less spiny; silvery-white, fragrant flowers, late autumn; *E.p.* 'Maculata' ('Aureomaculata'), large yellow central blotches to foliage.
Remarks: Suitable for maritime gardens.

Elodea (pondweed)

HARDY EVERGREEN OXYGENATING AQUATICS

Soil/aspect: Sun or partial shade.
Culture: Plant spring or summer. Propagate by cuttings tied in small weighted bunches and dropped into mud.
Flowers: Tiny, white globes, summer.
Species/cultivars: *E. canadensis* (Canadian pondweed), to 50 cm, fast-growing, with trailing, brittle leafy stems. *E. crispa* (*Lagarosiphon major*), as *E. canadensis*, but with curled leaves.

Endymion (bluebell)

HARDY BULBS

Soil/aspect: Ordinary. Sun or partial shade.
Culture: Plant autumn. Propagate by offsets at planting time, seeds when ripe.
Flowers: Bells in spikes; spring.
Species/cultivars: *E. hispanicus* (*Scilla campanulata*), to 30 cm, broad, strap-shaped leaves, erect flower spikes. Plants in cultivation are usually hybrids with the following species. *E. nonscriptus* (*Scilla nonscripta*, *S. nutans*) 30 cm, narrow leaves, stems nodding at tips, flowers violet-blue, white or pink.

Enkianthus

HARDY DECIDUOUS SHRUBS

Soil/aspect: Neutral to acid, moisture-retentive. Sun or partial shade.
Culture: Plant dormant season. Propagate by heel cuttings, layering in spring. No pruning.
Flowers: Bell-shaped, in pendent clusters; spring.
Species/cultivars: *E. campanulatus*, 3 m and slow-growing, flowers straw-yellow, red-striped. *E. perulatus*, 1 – 2 m, white to palest green flowers.
Remarks: Brilliant autumn colours.

Epimedium (barrenwort)

HARDY EVERGREEN (e) AND DECIDUOUS (d) PERENNIALS

Soil/aspect: Ordinary. Partial shade or sun.
Culture: Plant dormant season. Propagate by division autumn to spring.
Flowers: Saucer-shaped, spurred; spring.
Species/cultivars: *E. grandiflorum* (*E. macranthum*) (d), 30 cm or more, clump-forming, deep pink to white flowers. *E. perralderianum* (e), 30 cm, spreading, foliage glossy, winter-bronze, flowers bright yellow. *E. pinnatum* (e), 30 cm, spreading, yellow. *E. x rubrum* (d), 30 cm, clump-forming, young leaves red-edged, flowers crimson.
Remarks: Evergreen species good ground covers.

Eranthis (winter aconite)

HARDY TUBEROUS-ROOTED PERENNIALS

Soil/aspect: Ordinary, moisture-retentive. Partial shade or sun.
Culture: Plant early autumn. Propagate by division or by breaking off offsets at planting time.
Flowers: Buttercup-like globes above leaf collar; late winter.
Species/cultivars: *E. hyemalis*, 10 cm, lemon-yellow. *E. x tubergenii* 'Guinea Gold', 10 cm, robust, leaves often bronze-tinted, flowers large, deep yellow.

Eremurus (foxtail lily)

HARDY PERENNIALS

Soil/aspect: Ordinary, well-drained. Sun, sheltered.

Culture: Plant autumn. Propagate by careful division in autumn or seeds when ripe.

Flowers: Star-shaped, dense terminal spikes; late spring/summer.

Species/cultivars: *E. olgae*, 1.2 – 1.5 m, white, summer. *E. robustus*, 1.5 – 3 m, peach-pink, summer. *E.r. elwesii*, pink, early summer. *E. stenophyllus*, 75 – 120 cm, yellow, summer; Shelford Hybrids derive from this species, with flowers in shades of yellow to orange-buff, pink and white.

Erica (heath)

HARDY EVERGREEN SHRUBS

Soil/aspect: Ordinary, preferably humus enriched. Those marked * need neutral to acid soil. Sun.

Culture: Plant autumn or spring. Propagate by cuttings late summer, layering in spring. Prune after flowering or in spring.

Flowers: Nodding bells in terminal spikes; winter, spring, summer.

Species/cultivars: *E. arborea* 'Alpina', 2 – 3 m, white, fragrant, spring. *E. ciliaris* (Dorset heath) *, 30 cm or more, reddish-pink, late summer – autumn; cultivars in shades of pink, red, white. *E. cinerea* (bell heather) *, 25 cm or more, rose-purple, summer to autumn; numerous cultivars in shades of white to ruby-red. *E.* x *darleyensis*, 45 cm, pale mauve-pink, winter, spring; 'A.T. Johnson', deep pink; 'Silberschmelze' ('Molten Silver'), white, fragrant. *E. erigena (E. mediterranea)*, erect to 2 m or more, purple-pink to red, early spring – summer; 'Brightness' 1 m, slow-growing, bright deep pink; 'W.T. Rackliff', to 60 cm, compact, white. *E. herbacea* (*E. carnea*), 15 – 25 cm, rosy-red, winter to spring; cultivars in shades of red, pink and white. *E. terminalis*, to 2 m, erect, rose-pink, summer to autumn. *E. tetralix* (cross-leaved heath) *, 30 cm, pale pink, summer – autumn; *E.t.* 'Alba Mollis', silvery-grey foliage, flowers white; 'Con Underwood', greyish leaves, red flowers. *E. vagans* (Cornish heath) *, 30 – 60 cm, lilac-pink to purple, summer – autumn; cultivars available in shades of red-purple, cerise, pink and white.

Erigeron (fleabane)

HARDY PERENNIALS

Soil/aspect: Ordinary. Sun.

Culture: Plant dormant season. Propagate by division, spring.

Flowers: Daisy-like; summer – autumn.

Species/cultivars: *E. alpinus*, 20 cm, tufted, lilac-purple to reddish. *E. aurantiacus*, 30 cm, bright orange. *E. mucronatus*, 15 – 25 cm, spreading, white, red-purple in bud; good for dry walls. *E. speciosus*, to 60 cm, lilac-violet. Good cultivars include 'Charity', pink; 'Darkest of All', deep violet-blue; 'Foerster's Liebling', double, deep pink.

Erinus (fairy foxglove)

HARDY ROCK GARDEN PERENNIALS

Soil/aspect: Ordinary, well-drained. Sun.

Elaeagnus pungens 'Maculata'

Eremurus olgae

Culture: Plant autumn or spring. Propagate by seeds when ripe or in spring.

Flowers: Massed stars; spring – summer.

Species/cultivars: *E. alpinus*, 7 – 15 cm, mound-forming; rose-purple; *E.a. albus*, white; 'Dr. Hanele', carmine; 'Mrs. Charles Boyle', soft pink.

Erodium (stork's bill)

HARDY ROCK GARDEN PERENNIALS

Soil/aspect: Ordinary, well-drained. Sun or partial shade.

Culture: Plant autumn or spring. Propagate by seeds and root cuttings, spring; stem cuttings late summer, division dormant season.

Flowers: Saucer-shaped: spring/summer.

Species/cultivars: *E. chrysanthum*, 10 – 15 cm, leaves silvery, flowers pale yellow, summer. *E. manescavii*, 20 – 30 cm, carmine and purple-red, late summer. *E. petraeum crispum*, 10 cm, mat-forming, pale purple, pink or white, darker veined and blotched, summer. *E. reichardii* (*E. chamaedryoides*),

2 – 5 cm, mat-forming; white with purple veins. *E.r.* 'Roseum', pink with red veins, spring-summer.

Eryngium (sea holly)

HARDY PERENNIALS AND BIENNIALS (b)

Soil/aspect: Ordinary, well-drained. Sun.

Culture: Plant autumn or spring. Propagate by root cuttings winter, seeds or division (*E. alpinum, E. tripartitum*) in spring.

Flowers: Central cones surrounded by spiny bracts; summer.

Species/cultivars: *E. alpinum*, 70 cm, metallic-blue. *E. bourgatii*, 45 cm, blue-green; *E. giganteum* (b), 1 m, bluish-green; *E.g.* 'Miss Wilmott's Ghost', ivory-white. *E.* x *oliverianum*, similar to *E. alpinum*, but flower heads smaller and more numerous. *E. tripartitum*, 75 cm, deep blue. *E. variifolium*, to 75 cm, evergreen, white-veined foliage, flower heads grey-blue and white.

Erysimum

HARDY OR ALMOST HARDY PERENNIALS

Soil/aspect: Ordinary, well-drained. Sun.

Culture: Plant autumn or spring. Propagate by seeds in spring, cuttings late summer.

Flowers: Like small wallflowers; spring and summer.

Species/cultivars: *E.* x *allionii* (*Cheiranthus* x *allionii*), 30 cm or more, bright orange, usually grown as bedding biennials. *E. alpinum* (of gardens), 15 cm, sulphur-yellow, fragrant; *E.a.* 'Moonlight', primrose-yellow.

Erythronium (dog's-tooth violet, trout lily)

HARDY CORMOUS PERENNIALS

Soil/aspect: Humus-rich, moisture-retentive. Partial shade.

Culture: Plant autumn. Propagate by offsets late summer, seeds when ripe.

Flowers: Reflexed Turk's-caps; spring.

Species/cultivars: *E. dens-canis*, 15 cm, leaves blotched purple-brown, flowers pink to deep rose-purple and white. *E. oregonum*, to 30 cm, leaves boldly mottled, flowers cream to white; *E.o.* 'White Beauty', flowers larger, perhaps a hybrid with *E. revolutum*, 15 – 30 cm, leaves mottled purple-brown and veined white, flowers deep pink; *E.r.* 'Pink Beauty', rich pink. *E. tuolumnense*, 30 cm, deep yellow.

Escallonia

ALMOST HARDY, MAINLY EVERGREEN SHRUBS

Soil/aspect: Ordinary. Sun or partial shade, sheltered.

Culture: Plant spring. Propagate by layering in spring, heel cuttings late summer. Trim back flowered stems.

Flowers: Clusters of tubular, open blooms; summer – autumn.

Species/cultivars: *E.* x *iveyi*, 3 m or more, foliage lustrous, flowers white, abundant; cut back after hard winters. *E.* x *rigida*, hybrid name covering most of the popular cultivars, typefied by 'Langleyensis', 2 m or more, arching habit; carmine-pink. 'Donard Gem', compact habit, pink; 'Donard Seedling', pink and white; 'Peach Blossom', 1.5 m, peach-pink and white; 'Slieve Donard', very hardy,

similar to 'Langleyensis' but flowers paler pink. *E. rubra*, 1.5 – 3 m, pink to crimson. *E. macrantha* 'C.F. Ball', 3 m, crimson.
Remarks: All escallonias do well near the sea, especially *E. rubra* and *E. macrantha*.

Eschscholzia (California poppy)
HARDY PERENNIALS GROWN AS ANNUALS
Soil/aspect: Ordinary, well-drained. Sun.
Culture: Sow *in situ* spring, or autumn in sheltered sites.
Flowers: Poppy-like; summer – autumn.
Species/cultivars: *E. californica*, 25 – 40 cm, leaves grey-green, finely dissected, flowers lustrous orange-yellow; cultivars and mixed strains available in shades of yellow, orange, pink, carmine, crimson-scarlet, white, some semi-double.

Euonymus (spindle tree)
HARDY DECIDUOUS (d) AND EVERGREEN (e) SHRUBS AND CLIMBERS
Soil/aspect: Ordinary, moisture-retentive. Sun or partial shade.
Culture: Plant dormant season; evergreens autumn or spring. Propagate by layering in spring, heel cuttings late summer; seeds when ripe. Prune to shape in early spring.
Flowers: Insignificant; summer – early autumn; fruits showy.
Species/cultivars: *E. alatus* (d), 1 – 2 m; twigs with corky wings; green leaves pink and crimson in autumn. *E. europaeus* (d), 3 – 5 m, fruits pink and orange; *E.e.* 'Atropurpureus', leaves flushed purple, turning red in autumn. *E. fortunei radicans* (e), prostrate, climbing or creeping and bushy, pink and pale orange fruits; *E.f.r.* 'Carrierei', 1 – 2 m, bushy; 'Coloratus', climbing to 8 m, leaves red-purple in winter; 'Kewensis', mat-forming 60 – 90 cm wide, tiny leaves, climbing if support available; 'Emerald 'n Gold', bushy, leaves yellow-margined; 'Silver Queen', shrub to 1 m, leaves cream-margined; 'Variegatus', climbing, leaves white, often pink-tinted margins. *E. japonicus* (e), 3 – 7 m, lustrous deep green foliage, good hedging plant, especially near the sea; *E.j.* 'Aureo-pictus', leaves with central gold blotches; 'Microphyllus', dense shrub to 1 m, tiny leaves; 'Microphyllus Pulchellus', golden-yellow.

Eupatorium (hemp agrimony)
HARDY PERENNIALS
Soil/aspect: Ordinary, moisture-retentive. Sun.
Culture: Plant dormant season. Propagate by division autumn to spring.
Flowers: Loose terminal clusters; late summer – autumn.
Species/cultivars: *E. purpureum* 1 – 2 m, purple-rose to magenta-crimson.

Euphorbia (spurge)
HARDY SUB-SHRUBS AND PERENNIALS
Soil/aspect: Ordinary. Sun or light shade.
Culture: Plant dormant season. Propagate by seeds and division in spring.
Flowers: Green to yellow floral bracts; spring, summer.
Species/cultivars: *E. amygdaloides*

Eryngium giganteum

Erythronium revolutum 'White Beauty'

Euphorbia characias

'Purpurea', evergreen, purple-leaved sub-shrub, 45 – 80 cm. *E. characias*, evergreen shrub, 75 – 150 cm, bracts yellow-green and brown, summer; *E.c. wulfenii*, more robust, larger spikes of bright green-yellow bracts. *E. epithymoides* (*E. polychroma*), dense, clump-forming, to 30 cm at flowering time, bracts vivid chrome-yellow, spring. *E. griffithii*, 1 m, bracts bright red, summer; *E.g.* 'Fireglow', brick-red. *E. myrsinites*, stems prostrate, 60 cm long; bracts greenish-yellow, spring. *E. robbiae*, 60 cm, leaves dark green, bracts bright yellow-green, summer; good ground cover for dry shade.

Fagus (beech)
HARDY DECIDUOUS TREES
Soil/aspect: Ordinary, moisture-retentive. Sun or partial shade.
Culture: Plant dormant season. Propagate by seeds as soon as ripe; cultivars grafted on common beech in spring. No pruning.
Flowers: Insignificant; spring.
Species/cultivars: *F. sylvatica*, 20 m or more, smooth grey trunk and spreading branches; *F.s.* 'Dawyck', narrowly columnar; 'Heterophylla' (fern-leaved beech), leaves narrowly lobed; 'Pendula', weeping; 'Purpurea', foliage shades of purple to copper, 'Cuprea' (copper beech), 'Riversii', (purple beech).
Remarks: With the exception of 'Dawyck', beeches are suitable only for large gardens.

Filipendula (meadow sweet)
HARDY PERENNIALS
Soil/aspect: Moisture-retentive, fertile. Sun.
Culture: Plant dormant season. Propagate by division autumn to spring.
Flowers: Feathery plumes; summer.
Species/cultivars: *F. palmata*, 90 cm, pink; *F.p.* 'Nana' (*Spiraea digitata* 'Nana'), 30 – 45 cm, compact. *F. purpurea*, 1.5 m, cerise, large flattened, terminal heads. *F. ulmaria*, 90 – 120 cm, creamy-white; *F.u.* 'Aurea', 45 cm, foliage golden-green.

Forsythia
HARDY DECIDUOUS SHRUBS
Soil/aspect: Ordinary. Sun.
Culture: Plant dormant season. Propagate by hardwood cuttings, autumn, layering in spring. Prune hard after flowering.
Flowers: Clusters of narrow-petalled yellow flowers; spring.
Species/cultivars: *F.* x *intermedia* 'Spectabilis', 2 – 4 m, erect, the most commonly planted forsythia. *F.* x 'Lynwood', rich yellow; 'Spring Glory', to 2 m, bright sulphur-yellow; 'Beatrix Farrand', 'Karl Sax' and 'Tetragold' all have large flowers. *F. suspensa*, to 3 m, arching and pendulous habit; *F.s. atrocaulis*, young stems flushed black-purple.

Fothergilla
HARDY DECIDUOUS SHRUBS
Soil/aspect: Acid to neutral, moisture-retentive. Sun or light shade.
Culture: Plant dormant season. Propagate by heel cuttings, late summer, bottom heat 18°C; seeds when ripe. No pruning.

Flowers: Petal-less, brush-like spikes; spring, before or with young leaves.
Species/cultivars: *F. major*, 1.5 – 2.5 m, rounded habit, white bottle brushes; good autumn colour. *F. monticola*, like *F. major* and now considered a dwarfer form.

Fraxinus (ash)
HARDY DECIDUOUS TREES
Soil/aspect: Ordinary. Sun or partial shade.
Culture: Plant dormant season. Propagate by seeds when ripe (germination often takes 18 months); cultivars grafted on species, spring. No pruning.
Flowers: Generally insignificant; spring, early summer.
Species/cultivars: *F. excelsior*, eventually 30 m, suitable only for large gardens; *F.e.* 'Aurea Pendula', small weeping tree, young stems golden-yellow. *F. ornus* (manna ash), to 10 m, rounded habit, comparatively slow-growing; flowers creamy-white with young leaves. *F. oxycarpa* 'Raywood', to 12 m, leaves turn plum-purple in autumn.

Fritillaria (fritillary)
HARDY BULBS
Soil/aspect: Ordinary, moist. Sun.
Culture: Plant autumn. Propagate by offsets at planting time, seeds when ripe.
Flowers: Large, pendent bells; spring.
Species/cultivars: *F. imperialis* (crown imperial), 75 – 120 cm, red or yellow in terminal clusters; *F.i.* 'Lutea Maxima', deep lemon-yellow; 'Rubra Maxima', reddish-orange. *F. meleagris* (snake's head), to 30 cm, red-purple with darker chequering, solitary or in pairs; pale purple, dark and white cultivars.

Fuchsia
ALMOST HARDY DECIDUOUS SHRUBS
Soil/aspect: Ordinary. Sun or light shade.
Culture: Plant spring; in cold areas mound crowns with weathered ashes, coarse sand or rough peat in late autumn. The tops are often killed in winter, but new growth arises at ground level; frosted stems should be cut away in spring. Propagate by cuttings, spring or late summer.
Flowers: Pendent, tubular and bell-shaped, petals and sepals often in contrasting colours; summer, early autumn.
Species/cultivars: *F. magellanica*, 1 – 2 m, deep red and purple; *F.m.* 'Alba', almost white. 'Gracilis', slender habit and flowers, the hardiest fuchsia; 'Versicolor', leaves grey-pink, variegated white; 'Pumila', 15 – 30 cm, miniature, small flowers. Catalogues list dozens of hardy cultivars in a wide range of shades.

Gaillardia (blanket flower)
HARDY PERENNIALS AND ANNUALS
Soil/aspect: Ordinary. Sun.
Culture: Plant autumn or spring. Propagate by seeds sown outside, early summer. For annuals, sow under glass late winter.
Flowers: Daisy-like; summer – early autumn.
Species/cultivars: *G. aristata*, 40-60 cm, yellow and purple; *G.a.* 'Dazzler', bright orange-yellow. Cultivars obtainable with wholly red or red-purple flowers.

Galanthus (snowdrop)
HARDY BULBS
Soil/aspect: Ordinary, moisture-retentive. Partial shade.
Culture: Plant autumn. Propagate by division immediately after flowering.
Flowers: Nodding, expanding bells; winter – spring.
Species/cultivars: *G. elwesii*, 15 cm or more, leaves broad, rolled, grey-green; white flowers deep green on inner petals. *G. nivalis*, 10 cm or more, leaves narrow, flat, flowers white and green. *G.n.* 'Plena', double.

Galega (goat's rue)
HARDY PERENNIALS
Soil/aspect: Ordinary. Sun. Propagate by division autumn or spring, seeds in spring.
Flowers: Terminal spikes; summer.
Species/cultivars: *G. officinalis*, 1 – 1.5 m, clump-forming, pale purple-blue, sometimes white or pink; 'Lady Wilson', mauve.

Galtonia (summer hyacinth)
ALMOST HARDY BULBS
Soil/aspect: Ordinary. Sun, sheltered.
Culture: Plant autumn; spring in cold areas. On heavy soils and in cold areas lift bulbs in autumn, store frost-free in barely moist soil. Propagate by offsets at planting time.
Flowers: Summer.
Species/cultivars: *G. candicans*, 90 cm or more, loose spikes of white bells.

Garrya
HARDY EVERGREEN SHRUBS
Soil/aspect: Ordinary, well-drained. Sun or partial shade.
Culture: Plant spring. Best against walls in cold areas. Propagate by heel cuttings late summer, layering in spring. No pruning.
Flowers: Long pendent tassels; late winter – spring.
Species/cultivars: *G. elliptica*, 4 – 6 m, silvery-grey catkins on male plants; female plants have less showy catkins. If both sexes are grown together, attractive chains of brown purple berries result.

Gazania
HALF-HARDY PERENNIALS GROWN AS ANNUALS
Soil/aspect: Ordinary, well-drained. Sun, sheltered.
Culture: Plant when fear of frost is past. Propagate by cuttings late summer or spring, or by seeds under glass at 18°C, early spring.
Flowers: Daisy-like; summer – early autumn.
Species/cultivars: *G. hybrids*. Most gazanias are of mixed hybrid origin, prostrate to 30 cm; narrow leaves grey or dark green; flowers orange, red, yellow, the petal bases sometimes patterned black-brown or olive-green and white. Flowers open only in sun.

Genista (broom)
HARDY DECIDUOUS SHRUBS AND SMALL TREES
Soil/aspect: Ordinary, well-drained. Sun.
Culture: Plant dormant season. Propagate by heel cuttings mid to late summer, seeds in spring. Thin out after flowering.
Flowers: Pea-like, in profusion; summer.

Species/cultivars: *G. aetnensis* (Mount Etna broom), 5 m or more, tree-like, golden-yellow, late summer. *G. hispanica* (Spanish gorse), 60 – 90 cm, dense hummock-forming, spiny, bright rich-yellow, early summer. *G. lydia*, 60 cm, wide-spreading, arching, bright yellow, early summer. *G. pilosa procumbens*, mat-forming, bright yellow, early summer. *G. tinctoria*, variable in height and habit; yellow, summer to autumn; *G.t.* 'Plena', semi-prostrate, flowers double; *G.t. virgata*, 2 – 3 m, erect, golden-yellow.

Gentiana
HARDY BORDER AND ROCK GARDEN PERENNIALS
Soil/aspect: Moisture-retentive, humus-enriched. Sun.
Culture: Plant dormant season. Propagate by division autumn to spring, cuttings in spring, seeds when ripe.
Flowers: Upturned trumpets; spring, summer, autumn.
Species/cultivars: *G. acaulis* (*G. clusii*, *G. kochiana*) clump-forming, to 10 cm, deep blue, spring. *G. asclepiadea* (willow gentian), 60 cm, blue, summer – autumn; 'Alba', white. *G. farreri*, prostrate, sky-blue, late summer, needs acid soil. *C. lutea* (yellow gentian), 120 cm, yellow, summer. *G. septemfida*, 15 cm or more, semi-prostrate, purple-blue, summer. *G. sino-ornata*, 15 cm, rich clear blue, autumn, needs acid soil. *G. verna* (spring gentian), clump-forming, 5 – 10 cm; deep bright blue, star-shaped, spring; *G.v.* 'Angulosa', more robust, flowers larger, thrives in light soil containing lime.

Geranium (crane's bill)
HARDY PERENNIALS
Soil/aspect: Ordinary. Sun or partial shade.
Culture: Plant dormant season. Propagate by division autumn to spring, seeds in spring.
Flowers: Open cup shapes; spring, summer.
Species/cultivars: *G. cinereum*, to 15 cm, lilac to pink, dark veined; *G.c.* 'Ballerina', white, feathered crimson-purple. *G. dalmaticum*, 10 cm, mat-forming, clear pink; *G. endressii*, 30 – 50 cm, pale pink; *G.e.* 'A.T. Johnson', silvery-pink; 'Wargrave Pink', salmon-pink. *G. grandiflorum* (*G. meeboldii*, *G. himalayense*), 30 – 45 cm, deep violet-blue, red-veined; *G.g.* 'Alpinum' ('Gravetye'), 30 cm, compact. *G. macrorrhizum*, 20 – 40 cm, mat-forming, leaves aromatic, often red in autumn, flowers purple-red; *G.m.* 'Album', white, red calyces; 'Walter Ingwersen', soft pink. *G. x magnificum*, 45 – 60 cm, clump-forming, violet-blue, red veined. *G. phaeum* (mourning widow) 60 cm, clump-forming, lilac-purple to brown-purple; *G.p.* 'Album', white. *G. pratense* (meadow crane's bill), 50-80 cm, violet-blue; pink, blue, white and double cultivars available. *G. psilostemon*, like *G. pratense* but crimson-magenta, black eye. *G. x* 'Russell Prichard', semi-prostrate, leaves silvery, flowers rose-magenta. *G. sanguineum*, 25 cm, red-purple or white. *G. wallichianum*, 15 cm, wide-spreading; blue-violet, late summer, autumn; *G.w.* 'Buxton's Blue', blue with white eyes; the latter suitable as ground cover.

Galega officinalis

Gazania hybrid

Geum (avens)
HARDY BORDER PERENNIALS
Soil/aspect: Ordinary, moisture-retentive. Sun or partial shade.
Culture: Plant dormant season. Propagate by division autumn to spring, seeds in spring.
Flowers: Bowl-shaped; early to late summer.
Species/cultivars: *G.* x *borisii*, 30 cm, bright orange. *G. chiloense* (*C. coccineum*), to 60 cm, scarlet; 'Fire Opal', bronze-scarlet, double; 'Mrs Bradshaw', brick-red, double.

Gingko (maidenhair tree)
HARDY DECIDUOUS TREE
Soil/aspect: Ordinary, moisture-retentive. Sun or light shade.
Culture: Plant dormant season. Propagate by seeds when ripe. No pruning.
Flowers: Insignificant catkins; spring.
Species/cultivars: *G. biloba*, eventually to 25 m, leaves fan-shaped, lobed, golden-yellow in autumn. Slender tree when young, later broadening; suitable only for large gardens.

Gladiolus
HARDY (h) AND HALF-HARDY (hh) CORMOUS PERENNIALS
Soil/aspect: Ordinary, fertile and well-drained. Sun.
Culture: Plant hardy types autumn, half-hardies spring to early summer. On light soils the latter often overwinter satisfactorily outside; elsewhere and in cold areas they must be lifted in autumn and stored dry at 10°C. Propagate by offsets at planting time.
Flowers: Large trumpets, often hooded, in tall, dense, one-sided spikes; early summer – autumn.
Species/cultivars: *G. byzantinus* (h), to 75 cm, rose-purple, early summer. *G.* x *colvillei* (h in sheltered sites), 45 cm, scarlet; *G.* x *c.* 'The Bride', white, early summer.
Most gladioli are half-hardy hybrid cultivars. They can be classified in two broad

groups: Large-flowered (exhibition) with massive spikes of large flowers, and Miniature (including the Butterfly strain), more slender, with smaller flowers often startlingly blotched or patterned. Both groups contain a wide colour range, only true blue missing. Hundreds of cultivars.

Godetia see Clarkia

Gunnera (ornamental rhubarb)
ALMOST HARDY FOLIAGE PERENNIALS
Soil/aspect: Permanently moist to wet, fertile. Sun or light shade, sheltered.
Culture: Plant spring. In cold areas protect crowns in autumn with their own dead leaves or bracken. Propagate by division, spring.
Flowers: Cone-shaped; early summer.
Species/cultivars: *G. manicata*, palmate leaves 2 m tall by 1.2 – 2 m wide, flower spikes hidden beneath leaves, usually green. *G. tinctoria* (*G. chilensis*), like *G. manicata*, but generally smaller, flower spikes often red-flushed, narrow and stiff.

Gypsophila
HARDY ANNUALS (a) AND PERENNIALS (p)
Soil/aspect: Ordinary, well-drained. Sun.
Culture: Plant dormant season. Sow annuals *in situ* spring, or autumn in sheltered sites. Propagate by basal cuttings or seeds in spring, root cuttings late winter.
Flowers: Tiny stars in sprays; summer.
Species/cultivars: *G. elegans* (a), 30 – 50 cm, white or pink; *G.e.* 'Covent Garden', white, large. *G. paniculata* (p), 90 – 120 cm, white to pink; *G.p.* 'Bristol Fairy', double white; 'Rosy Veil', double rose-pink. *G. repens*, prostrate, white, lilac, pale-purple.

Haberlea
HARDY ROCK GARDEN PERENNIALS
Soil/aspect: Well-drained, humus-enriched. Partial shade.

Culture: Plant in rock crevices or dry walls autumn or spring. Propagate by careful division spring, leaf cuttings summer.
Flowers: Primrose-like; late spring.
Species/cultivars: *H. rhodopensis*, 10 – 15 cm, evergreen, rosette-forming, lilac; *H.r.* 'Virginalis', pure white.

Hakonechloa (Japanese grass)
HARDY PERENNIAL GRASS
Soil/aspect: Ordinary. Partial shade.
Culture: Plant spring. Propagate by division.
Flowers: Pale green, insignificant; summer.
Species/cultivars: *H. macra*, 10 – 25 cm, rhizomatous, leaves bright green. *H.m.* 'Albo-aurea', variegated white and yellow; 'Albo-variegata', striped white; 'Aureola', yellow with green lines.

Halesia (snowdrop or silver bell tree)
HARDY DECIDUOUS SHRUBS OR TREES
Soil/aspect: Neutral to acid, moisture-retentive. Sun or dappled shade.
Culture: Plant dormant season. Propagate by layering in spring, seeds when ripe. Trim to shape after flowering.
Flowers: Bells in drooping clusters; early summer.
Species/cultivars: *H. carolina*, usually a large shrub to 8 m; white. *H. monticola*, like *H. carolina* but a tree up to 9 m, large flowers; *H.m.* 'Rosea', flowers pink-flushed.

Hamamelis (witch hazel)
HARDY DECIDUOUS SHRUBS
Soil/aspect: Humus-enriched, moisture-retentive, preferably neutral to acid. Sun or partial shade.
Culture: Plant dormant season. Propagate by layering, or grafting, spring; seeds when ripe, slow to germinate. Prune after flowering.
Flowers: Spidery, in clusters on bare twigs; autumn and winter.
Species/cultivars: *H.* x *intermedia*, 3 – 5 m,

Geum chiloense 'Fire Opal'

vigorous and free-flowering, yellow, copper-tinted; *H.* x *i.* 'Jelena', rust-red and yellow; 'Ruby Glow', copper and red; 'Winter Beauty', deep yellow. *H. japonica*, 5 m, sometimes of sparse habit, yellow, tinged red-purple; *H.j.* 'Flavopurpurascens' ('Rubra'), petals suffused red. *H. mollis* (Chinese witch hazel), 3 m or more, leaves downy; flowers golden-yellow, fragrant; *H.m.* 'Pallida'; soft pale yellow.
Remarks: Coloured autumn foliage.

Hebe (shrubby veronica)
HARDY (h) AND HALF-HARDY (hh) EVERGREEN SHRUBS
Soil/aspect: Ordinary. Sun or light shade.
Culture: Plant early autumn or spring. Propagate by cuttings, late summer or spring. Prune overgrown shrubs hard in spring.
Flowers: Small erect spikes or rounded clusters; spring to autumn.
Species/cultivars: *H. albicans* (h), 60 – 120 cm, leaves grey, flowers white. *H.* x *andersonii* (hh), narrow, cream-variegated foliage, lavender spikes; several named cultivars. *H. armstrongii* (h), 1 m, foliage cypress-like, yellow-green, flowers white; 'Autumn Glory' ('Autumn Beauty') (h), 60 cm, spreading, leaves deep blue-green, flowers violet. *H. brachysiphon* (*H. traversii*) (h), 1.5 m or more, white. *H.* x 'Carl Teschner' (h), 20 cm, hummock-forming, leaves small, flowers violet. *H. cupressoides* (h), 1 m, rounded, leaves cypress-like, grey-green, flowers pale bluish-purple. *H.* x *franciscana* 'Blue Gem' (hh), 1 – 1.5 m, rounded, violet; good close to sea. *H.* x 'Great Orme' (hh), 1 m, spreading, dense, bright pink, fading white. *H. hulkeana* (h), 60 cm or more, flowers lavender to lilac in large panicles above leaves. *H. ochracea* (h), similar to *H. armstrongii*, but of distinctive flat-topped habit, ochre-yellow foliage. *H. pinguifolia* (h), 23 cm, wide-spreading; leaves concave, greyish-green, flowers white,

often pink in bud; *H.p.* 'Pagei', compact, mat-forming, leaves bright blue-grey. *H. salicifolia* (h), 2 – 4 m, leaves willow-like, flowers white.

Hedera (ivy)
HARDY EVERGREEN SELF-CLINGING FOLIAGE CLIMBERS
Soil/aspect: Ordinary. Partial shade.
Culture: Plant dormant season. Propagate by cuttings, spring to autumn. Contain by pruning hard, early spring.
Species/cultivars: *H. canariensis* 'Gloire de Marengo', 6 m, leaves green, grey-green and creamy-white margins, needs a sheltered wall. *H. colchica* 'Dentata' (Persian ivy), 12 m, large leaves, lustrous deep green; *H.c.* 'Variegata', leaves patterned grey-green, bordered creamy-white. *H. helix*, 15 m or more, variable in vigour and leaf-shape; numerous cultivars include 'Buttercup', golden-yellow; 'Glacier', variegated grey and white; 'Goldheart' ('Jubilee'), bright-yellow centres; 'Green Ripple', dark green, narrowly lobed; 'Hibernica', (Irish ivy), leaves wider than long, thick, waxy-textured.

Helenium (sneezeweed)
HARDY BORDER PERENNIALS
Soil/aspect: Ordinary, moisture-retentive. Sun.
Culture: Plant dormant season. Propagate by division, autumn to spring.
Flowers: Daisy-like, prominent centres; late summer, autumn.
Species/cultivars: *H. autumnale*, 1 m or more, clump-forming; yellow. Available cultivars include 'Bruno', 1 m, mahogany-red; 'Butterpat', 90 cm, rich yellow; 'Coppelia', 90 cm, coppery-orange; 'Pumilum', 75 – 80 cm, clear yellow.

Helianthemum (rock rose)
HARDY EVERGREEN ROCK GARDEN SHRUBS
Soil/aspect: Ordinary, well-drained. Sun.
Culture: Plant autumn or spring. Propagate seeds in spring, cuttings late summer. Prune after flowering.
Flowers: Open cups in profusion; summer.
Species/cultivars: *H. nummularium* (*H. chamaecistus*), prostrate, mat-forming and wide-spreading, yellow. Several cultivars are available: 'Ben Hope', leaves grey, flowers carmine; 'Jubilee', double primrose-yellow; 'Fireball' ('Mrs. C.W. Earle'), double scarlet; 'Rhondanthe Carneum', leaves grey, flowers pink and orange.

Helianthus (sunflower)
HARDY ANNUALS (a) AND PERENNIALS (p)
Soil/aspect: Ordinary, moisture-retentive. Sun.
Culture: Plant perennials dormant season. Propagate by division at planting time; sow annuals *in situ*, spring.
Flowers: Large daisies, contrasting centres; summer – autumn.
Species/cultivars: *H. annuus* (a), to 3 m (or more in rich soil), flowers yellow, up to 30 cm wide, purple-brown centres. *H. atrorubens* (*H. sparsifolius*) (p), 1.5 – 2 m, rich yellow, black centre; *H.a.* 'Monarch', semi-double.

H. debilis (*H. cucumerifolius*) (a), like *H. annuus* but 90 cm, with smaller more numerous flowers; *H.d.* 'Excelsior' mixed strain in shades of red, yellow, purple, bronze. 'Loddon Gold', double, rich yellow.

Helichrysum (everlasting, straw flower)
HALF OR ALMOST HARDY ANNUALS (a), PERENNIALS (p) AND SHRUBS (s)
Soil/aspect: Ordinary. Sun.
Culture: Plant spring; propagate shrubs and perennials by cuttings late summer; annuals by seeds at 18°C in spring.
Flowers: Daisy-like, papery bracts; summer.
Species/cultivars: *H. angustifolium* (*H. italicum serotinum*) (curry plant) (s), to 50 cm, leaves silvery-grey, flowers yellow. *H. bracteatum* 'Monstrosum', (a), 75 – 120 cm, flowers double, large, everlasting, red, orange, yellow, pink, white. *H. milfordiae* (p), cushion-forming, leaves silvery-hairy, flowers white, reasonably hardy but needs protection from winter wet. *H. petiolatum* (s), trailing, mat-forming, leaves white-felted, flowers cream to biscuit, sparse; not hardy, grown as foliage plants for summer bedding. *H. rosmarinifolium* (*Ozothamnus rosmarinifolius*) (s), 2 m or more, dark green, white flowers; needs a sheltered site, damaged or killed in severe winters. *H. splendidum* (s), 30 – 60 cm, white woolly leaves, yellow flowers; survives most winters.

Heliopsis
HARDY PERENNIALS
Soil/aspect: Ordinary. Sun.
Culture: Plant dormant season. Propagate by division at planting time.
Flowers: Daisy-like; late summer – autumn.
Species/cultivars: *H. helianthoides scabra* (*H. scabra*), to 1.5 m, yellow; 'Gigantea', semi-double, deep yellow; 'Golden Plume', orange-yellow, double; 'Goldgreenheart', chrome-yellow and green, double.

Heliotropium (heliotrope, cherry pie)
TENDER SHRUBS GROWN FOR SUMMER BEDDING
Soil/aspect: Ordinary. Sun, sheltered.
Culture: Plant early summer when fear of frost is past. Propagate by cuttings from cut-back overwintered plants in spring, or from bedded plants late summer; seeds sown late winter at 18°C.
Flowers: Loose clusters, forget-me-not-like; summer, early autumn.
Species/cultivars: *H. arborescens* (*H. peruvianum*), 60 cm, more if grown under glass; violet or lilac, fragrant. Deep purple and white cultivars are available, all of hybrid origin and listed as *H.* x *hybridum*.

Helipterum (everlasting)
HARDY ANNUALS
Soil/aspect: Ordinary. Sun.
Culture: Sow *in situ* late spring, or earlier under glass at 16°C.
Flowers: Daisy-like to cup-shaped in clusters; summer – early autumn.
Species/cultivars: *H. roseum* (*Acroclinium roseum*), 40 cm, pink or white.
Remarks: Flowers good for drying.

Helleborus (hellebore)

HARDY CLUMP-FORMING (c), OR SUB-SHRUBBY
PERENNIALS (s)

Soil/aspect: Ordinary. Light shade or sun.
Culture: Plant autumn. Propagate by careful division immediately after flowering or by seeds when ripe.
Flowers: Open cup shapes, prominent stamens; winter, spring.
Species/cultivars: *H. atrorubens* (*H. purpurascens*) (c), to 30 cm, red-purple and green. *H. foetidus* (stinking hellebore) (s), 30 – 80 cm, pale green and brown-purple. *H. lividus corsicus* (s), to 60 cm, leaves glossy, flowers bright yellow-green. *H. niger* (Christmas rose) (c), 30 cm, white; *H.n.* 'Potter's Wheel', flowers larger and more shapely. *H. orientalis* (lenten rose) (c), 40 – 60 cm, creamy-white often pink-tinged; many hybrids listed under this name, in shades of white, pink, purple and red-purple to almost black.

Hemerocallis (day lily)

HARDY PERENNIALS

Soil/aspect: Ordinary, moisture-retentive. Sun.
Culture: Plant dormant season. Propagate by division autumn to spring, seeds spring.
Flowers: Trumpets; summer.
Species/cultivars: *H. flava* (*H. lilioasphodelus*), 60 – 90 cm, yellow, fragrant. *H. fulva* 'Kwanso', 80 – 100 cm, buff-orange, semi-double. Most day lilies are of hybrid origin; numerous cultivars include 'Doubloon', large, yellow; 'Margaret Perry', tangerine; 'Pink Damask', salmon-pink.

Hepatica (liverwort)

HARDY EVERGREEN PERENNIALS

Soil/aspect: Ordinary, moisture-retentive. Partial shade.
Culture: Plant dormant season. Propagate by division after flowering, seeds when ripe.
Flowers: Anemone-like; late winter, early spring.
Species/cultivars: *H. nobilis* (*H. triloba*, *Anemone hepatica*), 10 – 15 cm, leaves three-lobed; flowers blue-violet, pink or white; double forms are known. *H. transsylvanica* (*H. angulosa*), similar to *H. nobilis*, but more robust and leaves three to five-lobed.

Hesperis (dame's violet, sweet rocket)

HARDY PERENNIALS

Soil/aspect: Ordinary. Sun or partial shade.
Culture: Plant dormant season. Propagate by seeds or basal cuttings, spring.
Flowers: Cross-shaped, long spikes; late spring, summer.
Species/cultivars: *H. matronalis*, 70 – 90 cm, lilac-purple or white, fragrant; double forms are known.

Heuchera (alum root, coral bells)

HARDY EVERGREEN PERENNIALS

Soil/aspect: Ordinary, partial shade or sun.
Culture: Plant dormant season. Propagate by division autumn to spring, seeds spring.
Flowers: Bell-shaped, in branched feathery panicles; spring, summer.
Species/cultivars: *H.* x *brizoides*, 45 – 60 cm,

Helleborus orientalis hybrid

cultivars, in part derived from *H. sanguinea*, are in shades of red, pink, white; 'Coral Cloud', light crimson; 'Pearl Drops', pearly-white; 'Splendour', salmon-scarlet, bronze foliage. *H. sanguinea*, 30 – 60 cm, flowers tiny, bright red.

Hibiscus (shrubby mallow)

HARDY DECIDUOUS SHRUBS

Soil/aspect: Ordinary. Sun, sheltered.
Culture: Plant dormant season. Propagate by heel cuttings, late summer. If necessary, prune to shape after flowering.
Flowers: Funnel-shaped, flaring wide; late summer, autumn.
Species/cultivars: *H. sino-syriacus*, much like *H. syriacus*, but broader leaves and larger flowers; *H.s.* 'Lilac Queen', lilac and red; 'Ruby Glow', white and cerise. *H. syriacus*, 2 m or more, toothed, lobed leaves, rounded habit; *H.s.* 'Blue Bird', violet-blue; 'Duc de Brabant', dark rose-purple, double; 'Totus Albus' and 'Snowdrift', pure white; 'Woodbridge', rich rose-pink.

Hippophae (sea buckthorn)

HARDY DECIDUOUS SHRUBS

Soil/aspect: Ordinary, well-drained. Sun.
Culture: Plant dormant season. Propagate by suckers, autumn, seeds when ripe.
Flowers: Insignificant, yellow; spring. Handsome berry clusters, autumn.
Species/cultivars: *H. rhamnoides*, 2 m or more, suckering and spiny, leaves grey-green; female plants bear bright orange berries if grouped with male plants.
Remarks: Excellent seaside shrubs, suitable for hedges or windbreaks.

Hosta (funkia, plaintain lily)

HARDY FOLIAGE PERENNIALS

Soil/aspect: Moisture-retentive, fertile. Partial shade or sun.

Culture: Plant dormant season. Propagate by division or seeds, spring.
Flowers: Small nodding trumpets in erect spikes; summer, autumn.
Species/cultivars: *H. crispula*, 60 cm, leaves wavy, white-banded, flowers lavender, late summer. *H. fortunei* 'Albopicta', 60 cm, leaves yellow with green margins when young; 'Aurea', foliage all yellow-green, flowers lilac, summer; 'Aureomarginata', leaves gold-edged. *H. sieboldiana*, 60 – 75 cm, leaves blue-grey, flowers pale lilac, summer. *H. undulata*, 60 cm, wavy leaves with central white zones, flowers pale violet, late summer; *H.u.* 'Albo-marginata', white-margined; 'Albo-vittata', white-striped.

Houstonia (bluets)

HARDY PERENNIALS

Soil/aspect: Moisture-retentive, lime-free. Light shade.
Culture: Plant spring. Propagate by division, early spring.
Flowers: Starry; spring – summer.
Species/cultivars: *H. caerulea*, annual or perennial, tufted, 5 – 15 cm, pale blue, yellow eye. *H. serpyllifolia*, mat-forming, semi-prostrate, to 10 cm, milky blue to violet; *H.s.* 'Fred Millard', clear blue.

Hyacinthus (hyacinth)

HARDY BULBS

Soil/aspect: Ordinary, fertile. Sun.
Culture: Plant autumn. Propagation (difficult) is by bulbils in autumn.
Flowers: Open bells, deeply fragrant, in loose spikes; spring.
Species/cultivars: *H. orientalis*, 20 – 30 cm, flower spikes robust, purple, blue, red, white, yellow; several cultivars available. *H.o. albulus* (Roman hyacinth); each bulb produces several white or blue flower spikes.

Hydrangea

HARDY DECIDUOUS SHRUBS AND CLIMBERS

Soil/aspect: Ordinary, moisture-retentive. Partial shade or sun.
Culture: Plant autumn or spring. Propagate by cuttings late summer; *H. macrophylla* also late spring; seeds under glass, spring. Deadhead after flowering.
Flowers: Wide, flat or rounded heads; summer – autumn.
Species/cultivars: *H. macrophylla* Hortensia, 1 – 2 m, blue, purple, red, pink, white in large mop-like heads of sterile florets. Lacecaps, flower heads flat, small fertile florets surrounded by large sterile ones; several cultivars available in both groups. Acid soil is necessary for good blue and purple tones. For flower heads of good size prune annually in spring, cutting out at base all three-year old stems. *H. paniculata* 'Grandiflora', 4 – 5 m, flowers white, ageing pink, in large pyramidal clusters. *H. petiolaris* (*H. anomala petiolaris*) self-clinging climber to 15 m, white, lacecap-like, early summer. *H. sargentiana* (*H. aspera sargentiana*), 2 – 4 m, stout, bristly stems, leaves large, hairy-white; flowers lacecap-like, fertile flowers blue, sterile ones white or pink-tinted. Needs shade and protection from wind.

Hypericum (St John's wort)

HARDY SHRUBS (S) AND ROCK GARDEN PEREN-
NIALS (p)
Soil/aspect: Ordinary. Sun.
Culture: Plant autumn to spring. Propagate
shrubs by cuttings, late summer, or seeds
spring; perennials by careful division, basal
cuttings or seeds, spring.
Flowers: Open cups; summer—autumn.
Species/cultivars: *H. calycinum* (rose of
Sharon) (s), rhizomatous evergreen, 30 – 60
cm, bright yellow, useful but invasive ground
cover. *H. cerastioides* (*H. rhodoppeum*) (p),
mat-forming, leaves grey-hairy, flowers
bright yellow. *H.* x 'Hidcote' (s), 1.5 m or
more, semi-evergreen, large, golden-yellow
flowers. *H.* x *inodorum* 'Elstead' (s), 1 – 1.5
m, semi-evergreen, flowers yellow, red berry-
like fruits. *H. patulum*, deciduous or
evergreen, 1 – 1.5 m, yellow, not reliably hardy. *H. polyphyllum* (s), 15 cm, grey-green
leaves, golden-yellow flowers.

Iberis (candytuft)

HARDY ANNUALS (a) AND SUB-SHRUBS (s)
Soil/aspect: Ordinary. Sun.
Culture: Plant autumn or spring. Propagate
sub-shrubs by cuttings, spring or late summer, seeds in spring; sow annuals *in situ*,
spring, or autumn in sheltered sites.
Flowers: Round clusters; spring—summer.
Species/cultivars: *I. amara* (*I. coronaria*) (a)
15 – 40 cm, purple or white. *I. sempervirens*
(s), evergreen, to 20 cm, spreading, white; *I.s.*
'Little Gem', smaller, erect habit. *I.
umbellata* (a), 15 – 40 cm, pink, red, purple,
white; several cultivars available.

Ilex (holly)

HARDY EVERGREEN SHRUBS AND TREES
Soil/aspect: Ordinary, moisture-retentive.
Sun or partial shade.
Culture: Plant autumn or spring. Propagate
by heel cuttings, late summer, layering in
spring. Prune to shape, summer.
Flowers: Insignificant; spring. Red or orange
berries if male and female plants grown
together.
Species/cultivars: *I.* x *altaclarensis*, to 10 m,
a group of cultivars resembling *I. aquifolium*,
but more vigorous, large-leaved, sometimes
lacking spines. 'Camelliifolia' (female),
leaves spineless; 'Golden King' (female),
yellow-margined; 'Lawsoniana' (female)
yellow blotches. *I. aquifolium*, 4 – 15 m,
pyramidal when young. Numerous cultivars
include 'Angustifolia', slow-growing female,
leaves narrow; 'Argenteo-marginata', a name
covering several clones with white-margined
foliage; 'Aureo-marginata', as
'Argenteo-marginata', but yellow-edged.
'Ferox' (hedgehog holly), male, spiny.

Impatiens (balsam)

TENDER ANNUALS
Soil/aspect: Ordinary. Sun, sheltered.
Culture: Plant early summer after frost. Pro-
pagate by seeds at 18°C, mid-spring, or cut-
tings, spring or late summer.
Flowers: Flat to cup-shaped, spurred; sum-
mer, early autumn.
Species/cultivars: *I. balsamina*, 45 – 75 cm,

Hydrangea paniculata 'Grandiflora'

erect; *I.b.* 'Camellia Flowered', 45 cm , double flowers, white, pink, red, purple, yellow;
'Tom Thumb', similar, 25 cm. *I. walleriana*
(*I. holstii, I. sultanii*) (busy Lizzie), to 60 cm;
dwarf seed-raised cultivars for summer bedding are available in shades of white, carmine, purple, scarlet, orange, and with green
or purple-black foliage.

Incarvillea

HARDY PERENNIALS
Soil/aspect: Ordinary. Sun.
Culture: Plant dormant season. Propagate by
division, basal cuttings or seeds, spring.
Flowers: Foxglove-like; early summer.
Species/cultivars: *I. delavayi*, 40 – 60 cm,
bright purple-rose.

Inula

HARDY BORDER AND ROCK GARDEN PERENNIALS
Soil/aspect: Ordinary, moisture-retentive.
Sun.
Culture: Plant dormant season. Propagate by
division, autumn to spring, seeds, spring.
Flowers: Daisy-like; early – late summer.
Species/cultivars: *I. acaulis*, 5 – 10 cm, mat-
forming, stemless, bright yellow, early summer. Late-summer-flowering: *I hookeri*, 60
cm, pale yellow. *I. orientalis* (*I. glandulosa*),
50 cm, orange-yellow. *I. royleana*, 60 cm,
orange-yellow.

Ionopsidium (violet cress)

HARDY ROCK GARDEN ANNUALS
Soil/aspect: Ordinary. Sun or partial shade.
Culture: Sow *in situ*, spring, summer and
autumn.
Flowers: Cross-shaped, tiny but in profusion
all year if sown in succession or allowed to
self sow. Best during the autumn, winter and
spring months.
Species/cultivars: *I. acaule*, 4 – 6 cm, lilac to
white, violet-tinted.

Ipheion

HARDY BULBS
Soil/aspect: Ordinary, well-drained. Sun,
sheltered.
Culture: Plant autumn. Propagate by offsets
as leaves die down.
Flowers: Open stars, late spring.
Species/cultivars: *I. uniflorum* (*Brodiaea* and
Triteleia uniflora), 20 cm or more, milky-
blue, scented; *I.n.* 'Wisley Blue', purple-blue.

Ipomoea (morning glory)

HALF-HARDY CLIMBING ANNUALS
Soil/aspect: Ordinary, humus-enriched. Sun,
sheltered.
Culture: Plant early summer after frost. Sow
seeds (soaked 12 hours in tepid water) at
18 – 21°C, mid-spring, singly in small pots.
Flowers: Open trumpets; summer.
Species/cultivars: *I. purpurea*, to 3 m, purple, blue, pink. *I. tricolor* (*I. rubro-coerulea*),
2 – 4 m, red to purple-blue; *I.t.* 'Heavenly
Blue', rich sky-blue.

Iris

HARDY RHIZOMATOUS OR BULBOUS PERENNIALS
Soil/aspect: Ordinary. Sun or light shade
unless stated.
Culture: Plant rhizomatous iris autumn to
spring, bearded after flowering (summer),
bulbous, autumn. Propagate by division, offsets or seed.
Flowers: Stiffly held blooms, composed of
the falls (outer petals) and standards (inner
petals) opening from a sheathed tube. Summer, some winter and early spring.
Species/cultivars: Bearded hybrids,
rhizomatous, early summer-flowering;
countless cultivars, 25 – 85 cm, stiff, sword-
shaped leaves, large flowers in self or contrasting colours, sometimes feathered or
flecked. *I. danfordiae*, bulbous, to 10 cm;
bright yellow spring flowers before leaves. *I.
foetidissima* (gladwin), rhizomatous, 60 cm,
mauve-buff flowers, spring, brilliant scarlet
berries in autumn; good for shade.
'Variegata', white-margined leaves.
I. histrioides 'Major', bulbous, 10 cm,
purple flowers with orange markings, winter,
before leaves. *I. kaempferi*, rhizomatous,
60 – 90 cm, large flowers, summer, in shades
of purple, red, blue or white; waterside and
acid soil. *I. pallida*, rhizomatous, 90 cm,
lavender-blue, bearded flowers, summer,
blue-grey leaves. 'Aurea-Variegata', yellow-
striped leaves. *I. pseudacorus* (yellow flag),
rhizomatous, 1 – 1.5 m; stiff leaves and
yellow flowers, summer; 'Variegata', yellow-
striped leaves; both for waterside or moist
ground. *I. reticulata*, bulbous, 10 – 15 cm,
flowers in shades of purple and blue,
winter/spring, with young leaves. Many
cultivars available. *I. sibirica*, rhizomatous,
to 1 m, flowers dark blue-purple to grey-lilac
and pure white, summer. Several named
cultivars. *I. unguicularis*, rhizomatous, 23
cm, clumps of narrow evergreen leaves; deep
lilac, blue or purple fragrant flowers, spring.
'Alba', white. *I. xiphium*, bulbous, 60 cm;
Dutch, Spanish and English irises derived
from this species; flowers in shades of purple,
blue, yellow and white, summer.

Ixia (corn lily)

NEAR-HARDY BULBOUS PERENNIALS

Soil/aspect: Ordinary, well-drained. Sun, sheltered.

Culture: Plant spring or late autumn, protect with bracken or peat. Propagate by offsets, or seeds, spring.

Flowers: Star-shaped, in sprays; summer.

Species/cultivars: *Hybrids*, 30 cm, narrow sword-shaped leaves, flowers in shades of white, yellow, orange, red and mauve, usually with darker centres.

Remarks: Best lifted in autumn and kept dry while dormant.

Jasminum (jasmine)

HARDY DECIDUOUS (d) AND EVERGREEN (e) SHRUBS AND CLIMBERS

Soil/aspect: Ordinary, well-drained. Sun or shade.

Culture: Plant autumn or spring. Tie in climbers on walls and fences. Propagate by cuttings, summer or early autumn. Prune after flowering

Flowers: Tubular, in clusters; winter (w) or summer (s)

Species/cultivars: *J. nudiflorum* (d/w), scrambler to 4m, flowers bright yellow on leafless stems. *J. officinale* (d/s), twining to 5m or more, flowers white and sweetly fragrant; 'Aureo-variegatum', leaves splashed with yellow. *J. parkeri* (e/s), 30cm, dwarf shrub, leaves with 3 or 5 leaflets, flowers yellow.

Remarks: *J. nudiflorum* and *J. officinale* excellent for north-facing walls.

Juniperus (juniper)

HARDY EVERGREEN CONIFEROUS TREES AND SHRUBS

Soil/aspect: Ordinary. Sun.

Culture: Plant autumn to spring. Propagate by heel cuttings, late summer or autumn. Species also from seed. No pruning.

Flowers: Insignificant.

Species/cultivars: *J. chinensis*, to 10m, small tree or shrub; 'Hetzii', 3m, wide-spreading with partly ascending stems; 'Pfitzerana', 1m, stems spreading and drooping at tips (both sometimes listed as *J. x media*). *J. communis*, 3m, low shrub or small tree; 'Compacta', columnar, slow-growing, under 50cm in 20 years; *J.c. depressa*, dense, low-growing, excellent ground cover; *J.c. depressa* 'Aurea', young foliage golden; 'Hibernica' (Irish juniper), 3m, slenderly columnar. *J. horizontalis* (creeping juniper), to 60 cm, mat-forming; 'Bar Harbor', prostrate, steel-blue. *J. squamata*, semi-prostrate, prickly foliage; 'Meyeri', 2.5m, erect, leaves blue-grey. *J. virginiana* (pencil cedar), eventually 15m, conical; 'Grey Owl', 3m, wide-spreading, silvery-grey; 'Skyrocket', 3-5m, columnar, blue-grey.

Kalmia (calico bush)

HARDY EVERGREEN SHRUBS

Soil/aspect: Lime-free, moisture-retentive. Sun or light shade.

Culture: Plant autumn or spring. Propagate by heel cuttings, late summer; layering or suckers, spring. Dead-head after flowering.

Ipheion uniflorum

Flowers: Bowl-shaped, sculpted in clusters; early summer.

Species/cultivars: *K. latifolia*, 3m or more; leaves glossy, deep green, flowers clear pink.

Kerria (bachelor's buttons)

HARDY DECIDUOUS SHRUBS

Soil/aspect: Ordinary, well-drained. Sun or light shade.

Culture: Plant autumn to spring. Propagate by division or suckers, spring, or heel cuttings, late summer. Prune after flowering.

Flowers: Spring—early summer.

Species/cultivars: *K. japonica*, 2m, arching stems, five-petalled, golden-yellow single flowers; often listed as 'Simplex'; 'Pleniflora', the more common form, 2.5m, stiffly erect, flowers double.

Kniphofia (red-hot poker)

HARDY EVERGREEN PERENNIALS

Soil/aspect: Ordinary, well-drained. Sun.

Culture: Plant spring. Propagate by division or seed, spring.

Flowers: Tubular, in dense spikes; summer.

Species/cultivars: *K. uvaria* (*K. alooides*), 1.2-1.5m, clump-forming, scarlet. *K.galpinii*, 60cm, red-orange, autumn. Many cultivars, 45-150cm, in shades of red, orange, yellow, white or almost green.

Remarks: Excellent in specimen groups.

Kochia (summer cypress, burning bush)

HALF-HARDY ANNUALS

Soil/aspect: Ordinary. Sun.

Culture: Sow under glass late spring. Plant out when fear of frost is past; or sow *in situ* early summer.

Flowers: Barely noticeable.

Species/cultivars: *K. scoparia'* 'Tricophylla', 60cm, pale green, feathery foliage, turning red in autumn; 'Childsii', more compact.

Koelreuteria (golden rain tree)

HARDY DECIDUOUS TREES

Soil/aspect: Ordinary. Sun. Sheltered.

Culture: Plant autumn to spring. Propagate in winter by root cuttings or seed when ripe. No pruning.

Flowers: Star-shaped; summer.

Species/cultivars: *K. paniculata*, 9m, foliage much divided, yellow autumn tints, erect branched flower panicles yellow; bladder-like, often red-flushed seed pods.

Remarks: Flower best in hot summers.

Kolkwitzia (beauty bush)

HARDY DECIDUOUS SHRUBS

Soil/aspect: Ordinary. Sun.

Culture: Plant autumn to spring. Propagate by heel cuttings, late summer to autumn. Prune after flowering.

Flowers: Early summer.

Species/cultivars: *K. amabilis*, 4m, bell-shaped flowers, abundant, pale pink, in loose clusters; 'Pink Cloud', deep pink.

Laburnum (golden chain)

HARDY DECIDUOUS TREES AND SHRUBS

Soil/aspect: Ordinary, well-drained. Sun.

Culture: Plant autumn to spring. Propagate by seed, autumn, cultivars by grafting, spring. No pruning.
Flowers: Pea-like, in pendent racemes; early summer.
Species/cultivars: *L. alpinum*, to 6m, bright yellow; *L.a.* 'Pendulum', weeping habit. *L. anagyroides*, 6m, yellow shorter racemes, rarely 25cm. *L.* x *watereri* 'Vossii', as *L. alpinum*, but very free-flowering.
Remarks: Seeds and pods poisonous; *L.* x *watereri* largely sterile.

Lamium (dead nettle)
HARDY HERBACEOUS PERENNIALS
Soil/aspect: Ordinary to poor. Partial shade or sun.
Culture: Plant autumn to spring. Propagate by division, spring; species also by seed.
Flowers: Tubular and hooded, spikes; late spring—summer.
Species/cultivars: *L. galeobdolon* 'Variegatum' (*Lamiastrum*) (yellow archangel), 60cm, oval, toothed leaves with silver variegations, conspicuous in winter; flowers yellow. *L. maculatum* (spotted dead nettle), 30cm, leaves silver banded, flowers red-purple; best in moist soil. 'Album', white; 'Roseum', light pink; 'Aureum', leaves yellow.
Remarks: *L. galeobdolon* very invasive, but good ground cover.

Larix (larch)
HARDY DECIDUOUS CONIFEROUS TREES
Soil/aspect: Ordinary, moisture-retentive. Sun or light shade.
Culture: Plant autumn to spring. Propagate by seed, spring. No pruning.
Flowers: No true flowers, but red to green female and yellow male inflorescences in spring; attractive rounded and erect small cones which persist.
Species/cultivars: *L. decidua*, to 18m, drooping branches, pale green foliage, buff-yellow in autumn.
Remarks: Attractive shade trees for large gardens.

Lathyrus (sweet pea, everlasting pea)
HARDY ANNUAL (a) AND PERENNIAL (p) CLIMBERS
Soil/aspect: Ordinary, well-drained; humus-rich for sweet peas. Sun.
Culture: Plant perennials autumn to spring. Propagate by division or seed, spring. Sow annuals under glass, autumn or early spring or *in situ* later.
Flowers: Pea-like, large-petalled; summer.
Species/cultivars: *L. latifolius* (p), 3m, flowers in loose, purple-pink racemes. *L. odoratus* (a), 2m, flower racemes mauve, sweetly fragrant. Sweet peas, of different habits, derived from this species available in most colour shades and combinations. Support is necessary for all but dwarf cultivars.
Remarks: Excellent for cutting.

Laurus (sweet bay, bay laurel)
NEAR-HARDY EVERGREEN TREES OR SHRUBS
Soil/aspect: Ordinary, well-drained. Sun.
Culture: Plant spring. Propagate from late

Kolkwitzia amabilis 'Pink Cloud'

autumn cuttings or seeds. Prune to shape as necessary, summer.
Flowers: Inconspicuous; spring.
Species/cultivars: *L. nobilis*, eventually to 6m, but usually shrub-like, maintained at 2m by pruning; leaves small, oval, glossy and aromatic, flowers yellow, fragrant; black berry fruits.
Remarks: Hardy except in very severe winters, best in sites sheltered from cold drying winds. Often trained and clipped as standards or pyramids and tub-grown. The aromatic leaves, fresh or dried, are used for culinary purposes (see illustration, Herb Garden Plants, page 231).

Lavandula (lavender)
HARDY EVERGREEN SHRUBS
Soil/aspect: Ordinary, well-drained. Sun.
Culture: Plant spring. Propagate by cuttings, late summer, or seed, spring. Dead-head after flowering. Prune hard in spring.
Flowers: Scented, erect spikes, summer.
Species/cultivars: *L. angustifolia* (*L. spica*, *L. officinalis*, *L. vera*), 1m, leaves grey-green, narrow, flowers purple; 'Alba', white; 'Loddon Pink', 75cm, pink; 'Munstead', 75cm, blue-purple.
Remarks: Popular for low hedging to rose beds and herb gardens; dried flowers are suitable for *pot-pourris*.

Lavatera (mallow)
HARDY ANNUALS (a) AND SUB-SHRUBS (s)
Soil/aspect: Ordinary, well-drained. Sun.
Culture: Plant shrubs autumn to spring; propagate by cuttings or seed, spring. Sow annuals autumn, or spring *in situ*.
Flowers: Open trumpets; summer—autumn.
Species/cultivars: *L. olbia* (s), 2m, bushy, pink-purple; 'Rosea', pink. *L. trimestris* (a), 120cm, bright shining pink; 'Mont Blanc', pure white.

Layia (tidy tips)
HARDY ANNUALS
Soil/aspect: Ordinary, well-drained. Sun.
Culture: Sow autumn or spring *in situ*.
Flowers: Daisy-like; summer—autumn.
Species/cultivars: *L. elegans*, 45cm, yellow, good for cutting.

Leocojum (snowflake)
HARDY BULBOUS PERENNIALS
Soil/aspect: Moisture-retentive. Sun or partial shade.
Culture: Plant early autumn. Propagate by offsets after flowering or ripe seed.
Flowers: Resembling snowdrops; spring.
Species/cultivars: *L. aestivum* (summer snowflake), 35cm, leaves strap-shaped, flowers white bells; 'Gravetye', robust form. *L. vernum* (spring snowflake), 10-30cm, rounded bells, green-tipped; 'Wagneri', larger, yellow, green-tipped petals.

Leontopodium (edelweiss)
HARDY PERENNIAL ROCK GARDEN PLANTS
Soil/aspect: Ordinary to gritty. Sun.
Culture: Plant autumn to spring. Propagate by division or seed, spring.
Flowers: Summer.
Species/cultivars: *L. alpinum*, 20-30cm, clump-forming, leaves white-downy, off-white flower heads with long felted bracts.

Lewisia (bitterroot)
HARDY ROSETTE-FORMING PERENNIALS
Soil/aspect: In dry walls or between rocks. Light shade.
Culture: Plant spring. Propagate by division, summer; seed, spring.
Flowers: Open, many-petalled; summer.
Species/cultivars: Hybrids mainly derived from *L. cotyledon*, 15-25cm, evergreen rosettes of wavy-edged leaves, flower clusters in shades of pink and white.

Leycesteria (Himalayan honeysuckle)
HARDY DECIDUOUS SHRUBS
Soil/aspect: Ordinary, well-drained. Sun or light shade.
Culture: Plant autumn to spring. Propagate by cuttings, summer or autumn, or seed, spring. Prune out flowered stems, spring.
Flowers: Tubular, in pendent clusters; summer—autumn.
Species/cultivars: *L. formosa*, 2-3m, strong arching shoots from below ground, leaves heart-shaped in pairs, small white flowers within red-purple bracts.

Liatris (gay feather, blazing star)
HARDY HERBACEOUS PERENNIALS
Soil/aspect: Ordinary, moisture-retentive. Sun.
Culture: Plant autumn or spring. Propagate by division or seed, spring.
Flowers: Spikes; summer—autumn.
Species/cultivars: *L. spicata*, 120cm, purple-pink; 'Kobold', 60cm, stiff stems.

Ligularia
HARDY HERBACEOUS PERENNIALS
Soil/aspect: Moisture-retentive; sun or light shade.

Culture: Plant autumn to spring. Propagate by division or seed, spring.

Flowers: Daisy-like; late summer.

Species/cultivars: *L. dentata* (*Senecio clivorum*), 90-120cm, leaves rounded, flowers yellow, in branched panicles; 'Desdemona', leaves and stems red-purple, flowers deep orange. *L. przewalskii*, to 1.5m, leaves deeply cut and lobed, yellow spikes on dark purple stems. *L. stenocephala*, 2m, leaves triangular, long-toothed, long yellow spikes on dark purple stems.

Ligustrum (privet)

HARDY EVERGREEN (e) AND DECIDUOUS (d) TREES (t) AND SHRUBS (s)

Soil/aspect: Ordinary. Light shade or sun.

Culture: Plant autumn to spring. Propagate by cuttings, late summer or autumn. Prune hedges May-September.

Flowers: Cream-white, odorous, in clusters; late summer—autumn.

Species/cultivars: *L. lucidum* (e/t), 3-10m, often a garden shrub, leaves glossy, oval, small flowers; 'Tricolor', variegated pink or white. *L. ovalifolium* (Japanese privet) (semi e/s), 3-5m, leaves glossy green, withstands clipping and makes a good hedge; 'Argenteum', white-margined; 'Aureum', golden-yellow broad leaf margins.

Lilium (lily)

HARDY BULBOUS PERENNIALS

Soil/aspect: Ordinary, well-drained but moisture-retentive. Sun or light shade.

Culture: Plant autumn to early spring. Staking advisable. Propagate, autumn or spring, by bulb scales, division, offsets, stem bulbils or seed.

Flowers: Turk's-caps or trumpets in large clusters; summer.

Species/cultivars: *L. candidum* (madonna lily), 90-150cm, pure white, trumpet-shaped. *L. chalcedonicum*, 1.3m, orange-red, pendent turk's-caps. *L. henryi*, 2.4m, orange turk's-caps, brown spotting. *L. martagon*, 1.2m, deep pink turk's-caps, white to dusky purple forms also available. *L. pardalinum*, 60-120cm, yellow turk's-caps, dark spots. *L. regale*, 1.8m, white, fragrant trumpets lined red inside, yellow at centre. *L. tigrinum*, 2m, orange-red turk's-caps, dark spots. Hundreds of named cultivars are available.

Limnanthes (poached egg flower)

HARDY ANNUALS

Soil/aspect: Ordinary. Sun.

Culture: Sow *in situ*, autumn or spring. Self-seeds readily.

Flowers: Open bowl-shaped; spring/summer.

Species/cultivars: *L. douglasii*, 15cm, densely branched, deep yellow centres, white petals.

Limonium (sea lavender)

ANNUALS AND PERENNIALS

Soil/aspect: Ordinary, well-drained. Sun.

Culture: Plant perennials, autumn to spring. Propagate by division or seed. Sow annuals *in situ* late spring, or earlier under glass.

Flowers: Spikes or loose clusters; summer.

Species/cultivars: *L. latifolium*, 50cm, hardy evergreen perennial, large lilac-blue clusters.

L. sinuatum, 45cm, half-hardy annual, seed strains in red, orange, yellow and blue.

Remarks: Flowers popular in dried arrangements.

Linaria (toadflax)

HARDY ANNUALS (a) AND PERENNIALS (p)

Soil/aspect: Ordinary, well-drained. Sun.

Culture: Plant perennials autumn to spring. Propagate by cuttings, division or seed, spring. Sow annuals *in situ*, autumn or spring.

Flowers: Loose sprays of spurred flowers; summer.

Species/cultivars: *L. alpina* (p), creeping, violet-purple, yellow splash in throat. *L. maroccana* (a), 30cm, dwarf strains available in a range of colours. *L. purpurea* (p), 120cm, purple spikes; 'Canon Went', pink.

Linum (flax)

HARDY ANNUALS (a) AND PERENNIALS (p)

Soil/aspect: Ordinary, well-drained. Sun.

Culture: Plant perennials autumn to spring. Propagate by cuttings, spring or summer. Sow annuals *in situ*, spring.

Flowers: Funnel-shaped, in clusters; summer.

Species/cultivars: *L. flavum* (p), 60cm, yellow. *L. grandiflorum* 'Rubrum' (a), 30-45cm, bright red. *L. perenne* (p), 60cm, blue.

Liquidambar (sweet gum)

HARDY DECIDUOUS TREES

Soil/aspect: Loamy, deep, moisture-retentive. Sun or light shade. Sheltered.

Culture: Plant autumn to spring. Very young plants slightly tender. Propagate by layering, suckers or seed, spring. Prune to shape, autumn.

Flowers: Inconspicuous; summer.

Species/cultivars: *L. styraciflua*, 15m, leaves maple-like, colouring richly in autumn.

Liriodendron (tulip tree)

HARDY DECIDUOUS TREES

Soil/aspect: Ordinary, well-drained but moisture-retentive. Sun.

Culture: Plant autumn to spring. Propagate by seed, autumn, or layering, spring.

Flowers: Tulip or bowl-shaped; summer.

Species/cultivars: *L. tulipifera*, to 18m, leaves large, saddle-shaped, turning yellow in autumn, flowers yellow; 'Aureomarginatum', leaves yellow-edged.

Remarks: Suitable only for large gardens; trees flower when about 15 years old.

Liriope (lily turf)

HARDY RHIZOMATOUS EVERGREEN PERENNIALS

Soil/aspect: Sandy, lime-free. Shade.

Culture: Plant in spring. Propagate by division or seed, spring.

Flowers: Resembling grape hyacinths (*Muscari*); autumn.

Species/cultivars: *L. muscari*, 30-45cm, leaves dark green, narrow, dense mauve flower spikes; 'Majestic', darker flowers, spikes crested.

Lithospermum

HARDY EVERGREEN SUB-SHRUBS

Soil/aspect: Lime-free, well-drained. Sun.

Culture: Plant autumn to spring. Propagate by cuttings, summer, or seed, spring.

Flowers: Funnel-shaped; early summer.

Species/cultivars: *L. diffusum* (*L. prostratum*), 10cm, blue-purple; Grace Ward', deep blue; 'Heavenly Blue', gentian-blue, freely borne.

Lobelia

HARDY PERENNIALS (p), HALF-HARDY ANNUALS (a)

Soil/aspect: Good loam, moisture-retentive; sun or partial shade (p). Ordinary; sun (a).

Culture: Plant perennials in spring, propagate by division. Sow annuals under glass, spring; plant out early summer.

Flowers: Tubular, open-faced; summer—autumn.

Species/cultivars: *L. cardinalis* (p), 90cm, leaves often purplish, flowers scarlet; pink, red or white cultivars available. *L. erinus* (a), 15cm, blue to purple; several cultivars, bushy or trailing, with blue, purple, red or white flowers.

Lonicera (honeysuckle)

HARDY EVERGREEN (e) OR DECIDUOUS (d) SHRUBS (s) AND CLIMBERS (c)

Soil/aspect: Ordinary to rich, well-drained. Sun or light shade.

Culture: Plant autumn to spring. Propagate by cuttings, summer—autumn, or seed. Climbers need support. Thin out after flowering; prune hedges to shape, spring and autumn.

Flowers: Tubular, in fused pairs or whorls, fragrant; summer.

Species/cultivars: *L. caprifolium*(d/c), 8m, cream, sometimes pink-tinted; orange berries. 'Pauciflora', red-purple outside. *L. japonica* (semi e/c), 10m, flowers in pairs, creamy-white to yellow, black berries; 'Aureo-reticulata', leaves veined gold. *L.j. halliana*, white, heavily scented. *L. nitida* (e/s), 3m, dense, excellent for hedging; 'Baggesen's Gold', leaves golden-yellow in summer. *L. periclymenum* (d/c), 6m, creamy pink-flushed; red berries; 'Belgica' ('Early Dutch'), red-purple and yellow, early; 'Serotina', similar, later-flowering. *L. pileata* (e/s), 60cm, low and spreading, good ground cover for shade, flowers insignificant.

Lunaria (honesty)

HARDY ANNUALS or BIENNIALS

Soil/aspect: Ordinary. Light shade or sun.

Culture: Sow *in situ*, spring or summer. Seed freely.

Flowers: Cross-shaped, in clusters; spring and summer. Silvery seed pods.

Species/cultivars: *L. annua*, 90cm, purple-red or white; 'Variegata', leaves white-margined.

Remarks: Papery seed pods popular for dried arrangements.

Lupinus (lupin)

HARDY ANNUALS (a), PERENNIALS (p) AND SHRUBS (s)

Soil/aspect: Ordinary, preferably lime-free. Sun.

Culture: Plant perennials and shrubs autumn

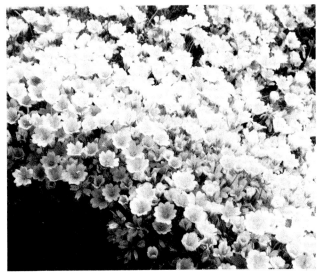

Leocojum aestivum   *Limnanthes douglasii*

to spring; propagate by division or basal cuttings, spring. Sow annuals *in situ*, autumn or spring.
Flowers: Dense spikes, usually bi-coloured; summer.
Species/cultivars: *L. arboreus* (s), 1m, fragrant, yellow, sometimes mauve or blue. *L. hartwegii* (a), 90cm, wide colour range in blues, reds and whites, also dwarf cultivars. *L. polyphyllus* hybrids(p), 90cm or more, the popular Russell strain in all colours includes numerous named cultivars and seed strains.

Lychnis (catchfly)
HARDY PERENNIALS
Soil/aspect: Ordinary, well-drained. Sun.
Culture: Plant autumn to spring. Propagate by division or seed, spring.
Flowers: Cross-shaped, inflorescence variable; summer—autumn.
Species/cultivars: *L. chalcedonica*, 90cm, clump-forming, flattened flower heads brilliant scarlet. *L. coronaria*, 60cm, grey, woolly foliage, loose flower clusters magenta or white. *L. viscaria*, 50cm, spikes rich pink to purple or white; 'Splendens Plena', double, and more popular.

Lysichiton (skunk cabbage)
HARDY RHIZOMATOUS PERENNIALS
Soil/aspect: Rich loam, permanently wet or very moist. Sun or shade.
Culture: Plant autumn to spring. Propagate by division or seed, summer/autumn.
Flowers: Arum-like, with prominent spathes; spring.
Species/cultivars: *L. americanum*, 50cm, yellow spathes as the huge dark green leaves unfurl. *L.camtschatcensis*, 40cm, spathes white, smaller and later, leaves blue-green.

Lysimachia
HARDY PERENNIALS
Soil/aspect: Ordinary, moisture-retentive. Sun or shade.

Culture: Plant autumn to spring. Propagate by division or seed, autumn or spring.
Flowers: Cup-shaped, in whorls; summer.
Species/cultivars: *L.clethroides*, 90cm, rhizomatous, arching white flower spikes. *L. nummularia*, (creeping Jenny), prostrate, trailing, flowers golden-yellow. *L. punctata*, 90cm, rhizomatous, leafy spikes of open yellow flowers.
Remarks: Species described are suitable for ground cover but invasive.

Lythrum (loosestrife)
HARDY PERENNIALS
Soil/aspect: Ordinary, moisture-retentive or waterside. Sun or shade.
Culture: Plant autumn to spring. Propagate by division, autumn, or seed spring.
Flowers: Star-shaped, in spikes; summer.
Species/cultivars: *L. salicaria*, 120cm, long spikes rich pink. Cultivars, including dwarfs, with pink or purple flowers.

Macleaya (plume poppy)
HARDY HERBACEOUS PERENNIALS
Soil/aspect: Deep loam, moisture-retentive. Sun or shade.
Culture: Plant autumn to spring. Propagate by division, suckers or cuttings, late spring or autumn.
Flowers: Late summer.
Species/cultivars: *M. cordata*, 2.4m, leaves large, lobed, blue-green; small white flowers in erect plumes. *M. microcarpa*, similar, but buff-pink flowers.
Remarks: Invasive on light soils.

Magnolia
HARDY EVERGREEN (e) and DECIDUOUS (d) TREES AND SHRUBS
Soil/aspect: Ordinary, well-drained. Sun or partial shade. Sheltered.
Culture: Plant spring. Propagate by layering, spring, or seed when ripe. No pruning; trim wall shrubs to shape, spring.

Flowers: Large, waxy; spring—summer.
Species/cultivars: *M. grandiflora* (e), to 6m, best grown as wall shrub, leaves large, glossy, bowl-shaped flowers, pink, fragrant, late summer—autumn; 'Alba', white. *M. kobus* (d), 5m, white, wide open stars on bare branches. *M. x soulangiana* (d), vigorous to 10m, flowers pink, bowl-shaped, before leaves; 'Alba Superba', white; 'Lennei', flushed rose-purple. *M. stellata* (d), 4m, star-shaped with numerous white petals, before the leaves; 'Rubra' and 'Rosea', purple and rose-pink forms.

Mahonia
HARDY EVERGREEN SHRUBS
Soil/aspect: Ordinary. Sun or shade.
Culture: Plant autumn to spring. Propagate in summer by cuttings, suckers, layering or seed. If necessary, prune hard back after flowering.
Flowers: Clusters or spikes; spring. Purple to black berries, summer—autumn.
Species/cultivars: *M. aquifolium* (Oregon grape), 1-2m, leaves dark green, glossy; bright yellow flower clusters; good ground cover but invasive. *M. japonica*, 2m or more, long, drooping yellow spikes. *M. bealii*, similar to *M. japonica*, but erect spikes. *M.* 'Charity', resembling *M. japonica*, but stronger-growing, spiny-leaved and freer-flowering. *M.* 'Undulata', like *M aquifolium* but taller, with glossy, wavy-edged leaves and deep yellow flowers.

Malcolmia (Virginian stock)
HARDY ANNUALS
Soil/aspect: Ordinary. Sun.
Culture: Sow *in situ* autumn or spring, and summer.
Flowers: Cross-shaped, in loose clusters; spring—autumn if sowing made in summer.
Species/cultivars: *M. maritima*, 20cm, flowers scented, in shades of red, purple and white. Dwarf mixtures available.

Lysichiton camtschatcensis

Malope (Greek mallow)
HARDY ANNUALS
Soil/aspect: Ordinary. Sun.
Culture: Sow seed *in situ*, spring.
Flowers: Trumpets; summer—autumn.
Species/cultivars: *M. trifida*, 60cm, branched stems, flowers large, glossy, shades of red, pink and white.

Malus (crab apple)
HARDY DECIDUOUS TREES AND SHRUBS
Soil/aspect: Ordinary, well-drained. Sun or light shade.
Culture: Plant autumn to spring. Propagate by grafting, species by seed when ripe. Prune to shape early spring.
Flowers: Bowl-shaped, in clusters; spring. Small, brightly coloured fruit, autumn.
Species/cultivars: *M. floribunda*, to 6m, red, opening pink, fruit yellow, small. *M.* 'Golden Hornet', 6-7m, flowers pink, fruit large, rich yellow, lasting well. *M.* 'John Downie', 9m, flowers white, fruit orange-red. *M.* 'Profusion', 5m, leaves purple to bronze, flowers and fruit deep red. *M.* x *purpurea*, 7m, leaves purple-red, flowers pink to red, fruit purple-tinted; 'Eleyi', smaller and later, dark red leaves and flowers; 'Lemoinei', leaves dark purple and bronze, flowers and fruit rose-purple. *M. sargentii*, 2m, shrubby; pure white flowers; small red fruit.

Malva (mallow)
HARDY PERENNIALS
Soil/aspect: Ordinary. Sun.
Culture: Plant autumn to spring. Propagate by seeds, spring. Self-seeds freely.

Flowers: Funnel-shaped; summer—autumn.
Species/cultivars: *M. moschata* (musk mallow), 70cm, deep pink; 'Alba', white.

Matteuccia (ostrich feather, shuttlecock fern)
HARDY DECIDUOUS FERNS
Soil/aspect: Ordinary, moisture-retentive. Partial shade.
Culture: Plant autumn to spring. Propagate by division, spring.
Flowers: None.
Species/cultivars: *M. struthiopteris*, 130cm, shuttlecock rosettes of deeply cut, dark and golden-green fronds.

Matthiola (stock)
HARDY BIENNIALS AND ANNUALS
Soil/aspect: Ordinary, preferably alkaline. Sun.
Culture: Sow annuals *in situ*, spring, biennials under glass early spring; plant out after fear of frost is past.
Flowers: Dense spikes, scented; summer.
Species/cultivars: *M. bicornis* (night-scented stock), 20-40cm, annual, lilac-mauve, opening at night. *M. incana*, 30-60cm, biennial, leaves grey-white, flowers in shades of red, blue, yellow, single or double. Several seed strains, notably Ten Week (grown as annuals), All the Year Round (annuals or biennials), Brompton (biennials).

Mazus
HARDY MAT-FORMING PERENNIALS
Soil/aspect: Ordinary, moisture-retentive. Sun or partial shade. Invasive.

Culture: Plant autumn to spring. Propagate by division, spring.
Flowers: Tubular, lipped; summer.
Species/cultivars: *M. reptans*, prostrate, purple or mauve, spotted yellow.

Meconopsis (Himalayan poppy)
HARDY PERENNIALS (p) OR BIENNIALS (b)
Soil/aspect: Good loam, moisture-retentive but not wet. Light shade. Shelter.
Culture: Plant autumn to spring. Propagate by seed, perennials by division, summer.
Flowers: Poppy-like; late spring—summer.
Species/cultivars: *M. betonicifolia* (*M. baileyi*) (b/p), 1m, sky-blue, mauve on alkaline soils. *M. cambrica* (Welsh poppy) (p), 45cm, yellow or orange-red, small. *M. grandis*, like *M. betonicifolia* but true perennial, with larger flowers. *M. integrifolia* (b), 20-60cm, yellow, best in sun. *M. quintuplinervis* (harebell poppy) (p), 23-30cm, blue-mauve, nodding bells. *M. regia* (p), 1m or more, golden-hairy leaves, yellow flowers.
Remarks: Biennial species monocarpic, i.e. may take 1½ — 2 years to flower, then die.

Mentzelia
HARDY ANNUALS
Soil/aspect: Fertile, light. Sun.
Culture: Sow *in situ*, spring.
Flowers: Cup-shaped, summer.
Species/cultivars: *M. lindleyi* (*Bartonia aurea*), 45cm, succulent stems with narrow notched leaves; flowers fragrant and golden.

Mesembryanthemum (Livingstone daisy)
HALF-HARDY ANNUALS
Soil/aspect: Light to sandy. Sun.
Culture: Sow under glass early spring or *in situ* later.
Flowers: Daisy-like; summer—autumn.
Species/cultivars: *M. criniflorum*, prostrate and spreading, wide open flowers, red, orange, yellow or white.

Metasequoia (dawn redwood)
HARDY DECIDUOUS CONIFEROUS TREES
Soil/aspect: Good, moisture-retentive. Sun or light shade. Shelter from winds.
Culture: Plant autumn to spring. Propagate by heel cuttings, late summer—autumn. No pruning.
Flowers: Insignificant.
Species/cultivars: *M. glyptostroboides*, to 20m, narrowly conical, dense light green foliage sprays, bronze autumn colours.
Remarks: Outstanding specimen trees for large gardens.

Mimulus (musk)
HARDY SHORT-LIVED PERENNIALS
Soil/aspect: Ordinary, moisture-retentive to wet. Sun.
Culture: Sow seeds under glass, early spring; plant out late spring.
Flowers: Tubular, open-faced; summer—autumn.
Species/cultivars: Most are garden hybrids, 23-30cm; named strains in red, orange or yellow with contrasting markings. *M. cupreus*, up to 30cm, yellow blotched brown.

Miscanthus

HARDY HERBACEOUS GRASSES

Soil/aspect: Ordinary, moisture-retentive. Sun or partial shade.
Culture: Plant autumn to spring. Propagate by division, spring.
Flowers: Inconspicuous, rarely produced.
Species/cultivars: *M. sinensis*, 1.5-2m, rhizomatous. Clumps of narrow leaves; 'Variegatus', cream-white longitudinal stripes; 'Zebrinus', cream-yellow cross bands.

Moluccella (bells of Ireland, shell flower)

HALF-HARDY ANNUALS

Soil/aspect: Ordinary to rich, well-drained. Sun.
Culture: Sow under glass, early spring, or *in situ* late spring—early summer.
Flowers: Open bowls, late summer—autumn.
Species/cultivars: *M. laevis*, 60cm, green and white spikes.

Monarda (bergamot)

HARDY HERBACEOUS PERENNIALS

Soil/aspect: Ordinary, moisture-retentive. Sun or light shade. Sometimes invasive.
Culture: Plant autumn to spring. Propagate by division or seed, spring.
Flowers: Late summer—autumn.
Species/cultivars: *M. didyma* (Oswego tea, bee balm), 60-90cm, aromatic foliage, red flower heads; 'Croftway Pink', 'Snow Queen' and 'Violet Queen' are good forms.

Morisia

HARDY EVERGREEN ALPINES

Soil/aspect: Light and well-drained. Sun.
Culture: Plant autumn to spring. Propagate by division or root cuttings, spring.
Flowers: Cross-shaped; spring.
Species/cultivars: *M. monanthos* (*M. hypogaea*) prostrate, bright-yellow.

Muscari (grape hyacinth)

HARDY BULBOUS PERENNIALS

Soil/aspect: Ordinary, well-drained. Sun.
Culture: Plant autumn. Propagate by offsets, bulbils or seed, summer.
Flowers: Closely set spikes; spring.
Species/cultivars: *M. armeniacum*, 20-30cm, narrow leaves appear autumn, flowers deep blue, late spring; invasive. 'Blue Spike', double flowers.

Myosotis (forget-me-not)

HARDY ANNUALS, BIENNIALS, PERENNIALS

Soil/aspect: Ordinary, well-drained. Sun or light shade.
Culture: Plant out autumn to spring. Propagate by division or seed, spring.
Flowers: Late spring—summer.
Species/cultivars: *M. alpestris*, 15cm, tufted perennial, bright blue. *M. sylvatica*, 30cm, usually biennial, pale blue. Bedding cultivars also in pink and white.

Narcissus (daffodil)

HARDY BULBOUS PERENNIALS

Soil/aspect: Humus-rich, well-drained but not dry in winter and spring. Sun.

Culture: Plant early autumn for permanent or bedding displays or for naturalising in grass. Lift bedding plants early summer, crowded border plants, early autumn. Propagate by offsets from lifted bulbs.
Flowers: Late winter—spring.
Species/cultivars: Hundreds of cultivars classified and catalogued in the following divisions: 1. Trumpet narcissi (daffodils), 30-45cm. 2. Narcissi with large coronas (cups), 35-55cm. 3. Narcissi with short coronas, 35-45cm. 4. Double-flowered narcissi (daffodils), 30-45cm. 5. Hybrids of *N. triandrus* (angel's tears), 2-3 small nodding, white flowers on each stem, 15cm. 6. Hybrids of *N. cyclamineus*, yellow, long narrow trumpets, strongly reflexed petals, 20-35cm. 7. Hybrids of *N. jonquilla*, small-cupped, scented flowers, several to a stem, 25-40cm. 8. Hybrids of *N. tazetta*, several large, small-cupped flowers per stem, 38-40cm (for indoor culture only). 9. Hybrids of *N. poeticus*, single-flowered, very small, red-rimmed cups, 35-40cm. 10. True wild species, including *N. bulbocodium* (hoop petticoat daffodil), to 15cm, large crinoline-like cups, small pointed petals; several forms. *N. pseudonarcissus*, 15-35cm, pale yellow petals, deep yellow long cups; good for naturalising. 11. Miscellaneous; all other narcissi.

Nemesia

HALF-HARDY ANNUALS

Soil/aspect: Ordinary, well-drained but moisture-retentive. Sun.
Culture: Sow under glass in spring; plant out when fear of frost is past.
Flowers: Small, pouched; late summer—autumn.
Species/cultivars: *N. strumosa* cultivars, 20-30cm, broad clusters of orange, red, blue, purple or white flowers.

Nemophila (baby blue eyes)

HARDY ANNUALS

Soil/aspect: Ordinary. Sun.
Culture: Sow *in situ*, autumn or spring.
Flowers: Open bowl shapes; summer.
Species/cultivars: *N. menziesii*, 20cm, feathery foilage, flowers bright blue, white-centred, freely borne.

Nepeta (catmint)

HARDY HERBACEOUS PERENNIALS

Soil/aspect: Ordinary, well-drained. Sun or light shade.
Culture: Plant autumn to spring. Propagate by cuttings, division or seed, spring.
Flowers: Long, whorled spikes; summer.
Species/cultivars: *N.* x *faassenii*, 45cm, aromatic, grey woolly leaves, purple-blue flowers (sterile). *N. mussinii*, similar but 30cm, smaller flower spikes; seeds freely. *N.* 'Souvenir d'André Chaudon' ('Blue Beauty'), large spikes, well-spaced purple flowers.

Nerine

ALMOST HARDY BULBOUS PERENNIALS

Soil/aspect: Ordinary, well-drained. Sun. Shelter, preferably at the foot of a wall.
Culture: Plant late spring; protect in winter. Propagate by offsets or division, spring.

Mahonia 'Undulata'

Mimulus cupreus cultivar

Flowers: Loose terminal clusters of showy, narrow-petalled flowers; autumn.
Species/cultivars: *N. bowdenii*, 45cm, narrow leaves appear in spring; pink, wavy-petalled flower umbels; 'Fenwick's Variety', more vigorous, deeper pink.

Nicotiana (tobacco plant)

HALF-HARDY ANNUALS

Soil/aspect: Ordinary to rich, well-drained. Sun.
Culture: Sow under glass in spring; plant out when fear of frost is past.
Flowers: Tubular, open-faced; summer.
Species/cultivars: *N. alata* (*N. affinis*), 60-90cm, greenish-white, fragrant, opening fully at dusk. Smaller red or pink hybrids open by day, but are less fragrant.

Nierembergia

HARDY CREEPING PERENNIALS

Soil/aspect: Ordinary, well-drained. Sun.
Culture: Plant spring. Propagate by division or seed, spring.
Flowers: Open cups; summer.
Species/cultivars: *N. repens* (*N. rivularis*), prostrate, slender stems, flowers white, yellow-centred.

Nigella (love-in-a-mist)

HARDY ANNUALS

Soil/aspect: Ordinary, well-drained. Sun.
Culture: Sow *in situ*, autumn or spring.
Flowers: Summer. Striking seed pods.

Species/cultivars: *N. damascena*, 45cm, wiry stems, feathery foliage, thread-like leaf bracts surround many-petalled flowers; seed strains in pink, red, blue, purple or white.

Nomocharis
HARDY BULBOUS PERENNIALS
Soil/aspect: Ordinary, moisture-retentive. Sun or light shade.
Culture: Plant autumn or early spring. Propagate by seed or bulb scales, autumn or spring.
Flowers: Bowl-shaped, 6-petalled, slightly nodding on leafy stems; summer.
Species/cultivars: *N. aperta*, 65cm, rose-pink, speckled crimson. *N. mairei*, 60cm, white, often flushed purple. *N. saluenensis*, 90cm, bright pink, often spotted purple.

Nymphaea (water lily)
HARDY AQUATIC PERENNIALS
Soil/aspect: Good loam, water depth 23-100cm or more. Sun or light shade.
Culture: Plant rhizomes or tubers in spring, preferably in baskets, otherwise invasive. Propagate by division of offsets, spring.
Flowers: Large, many-petalled cups opening flat above floating leaves; summer.
Species/cultivars: *N. alba*, white. *N. odorata*, white, fragrant flowers closing midday. *N. tetragona* (pygmy plant) white, opening mid-day; maximum water depth 15-30cm. Most water lilies are hybrids, including 'Albida', white; 'Carnea', blush-pink, fading to white; 'Chromatella', bright yellow; 'Escarboucle', deep red, small; 'Graziella', copper-red, small, with bronze leaves, water depth 30cm; 'James Brydon', crimson, with purple-tinted leaves.

Nyssa (tupelo)
HARDY DECIDUOUS TREES
Soil/aspect: Neutral to acid, moisture-retentive. Sun.
Culture: Plant autumn to spring. Propagate from seed, autumn or spring, or by layering, autumn.
Flowers: Inconspicuous; spring.
Species/cultivars: *N. sylvatica*, to 10m, brilliant autumn colours.

Oenothera (evening primrose)
HARDY PERENNIALS (p) OR BIENNIALS (b)
Soil/aspect: Ordinary, well-drained. Sun.
Culture: Plant autumn to spring. Propagate in spring by division or seed, biennials by seed only.
Flowers: Wide-open funnels; summer—autumn.
Species/cultivars: *O. lamarckiana* (*O. erythrosepala*) (b), 1.2m, yellow. *O. missouriensis* (p), prostrate, spreading stems, flowers bright yellow. *O. speciosa* (p), 60cm, deeply lobed leaves, flowers white, fading to pink. *O. tetragona* (p), 60cm, often listed as *O. fruticosa*, deep yellow; 'Fyrvaerkeri' ('Fireworks'), red in bud.

Olearia (daisy bush)
ALMOST HARDY EVERGREEN SHRUBS
Soil/aspect: Ordinary to loamy, well-drained. Sun. Shelter from cold winds.

Nerine bowdenii

Nomocharis aperta

Culture: Plant spring. Propagate by heel cuttings, late summer, or seed, spring. No pruning, except to remove dead wood, spring.
Flowers: Daisy-like, fragrant, in clusters; summer—early autumn.
Species/cultivars: *O. avicenniifolia*, to 3m, leaves pointed, buff or white beneath, flowers white. *O. x haastii*, 3m, dark green leaves, white beneath, abundant white flowers. *O. macrodonta*, to 3m, holly-shaped leaves glossy green, white beneath, dense white flower heads; 'Major' has larger leaves and flowers, 'Minor' is smaller than the species. *O. nummulariifolia*, 3m, leaves bright green, buff beneath, rolled at the edges, white flowers solitary.
Remarks: Excellent for coastal and town gardens.

Omphalodes (blue-eyed Mary)
HARDY HERBACEOUS PERENNIALS
Soil/aspect: Ordinary, moisture-retentive. Light shade.
Culture: Plant autumn to spring. Propagate by division, spring, or seed, summer.
Flowers: Forget-me-not-like; late spring.
Species/cultivars: *O. cappadocica*, 15-20cm, rhizomatous and clump-forming, clear blue flowers usually with white eyes. *O. verna*, 15cm, stoloniferous, mat-forming, bright blue; 'Alba', white.

Onoclea (sensitive fern)
HARDY HERBACEOUS FERNS
Soil/aspect: Ordinary, moist to wet. Sun or shade.
Culture: Plant spring. Propagate by division, spring.
Flowers: None.
Species/cultivars: *O. sensibilis*, 60cm, rhizomatous, deeply divided leaves, black spores on back of fronds. Normally cut to the ground by first sharp autumn frost.

Onopordum (Scotch thistle)
HARDY BIENNIALS
Soil/aspect: Ordinary. Sun.
Culture: Best sown *in situ*, spring, or in a nursery bed for setting out in autumn.
Flowers: Thistle-like; summer.
Species/cultivars: *O. (Onopordon) acanthium*, 2m or more, silvery spiny leaves with white down, flowers purple.

Ornithogalum (star of Bethlehem)
HARDY BULBOUS PERENNIALS
Soil/aspect: Ordinary, well-drained. Sun or light shade.
Culture: Plant autumn. Propagate by division, offsets or seed, early autumn.
Flowers: Late spring.
Species/cultivars: *O. nutans*, 45cm, flowers large, off-white, nodding bells, silvery-green markings. *O. umbellatum*, 25cm, long-stalked, pure white, starry flowers. Can be invasive on light soils.

Osmanthus
HARDY EVERGREEN SHRUBS
Soil/aspect: Ordinary, well-drained. Sun or partial shade. Sheltered site.
Culture: Plant autumn to spring. Propagate by heel cuttings, late summer. No pruning.
Flowers: Tubular, fragrant; late spring.
Species/cultivars: *O. (Osmarea)* x *burkwoodii*, 3m, leaves glossy dark green, flower clusters white. *O. delavayi*, 3m or more, leaves small, glossy deep green and toothed, arching stems, white flower clusters.

Osmunda (Royal fern)
HARDY HERBACEOUS FERNS
Soil/aspect: Humus-rich, moisture-retentive. Best in shade.
Culture: Plant spring. Propagate by division in spring, or by spores.
Flowers: None.
Species/cultivars: *O. regalis*, 1.2-1.5m, fronds bright green, deeply divided, tips covered with clustered brown spore capsules.

Ourisia
HARDY EVERGREEN PERENNIALS
Soil/aspect: Neutral to acid, moisture-retentive. Partial shade. Rock gardens.
Culture: Plant spring. Propagate by division or seed, spring.
Flowers: Tubular; summer—autumn.
Species/cultivars: *O. coccinea*, 15cm, mat-forming, whorls of scarlet flowers.

Oxalis
HARDY RHIZOMATOUS (r) OR BULBOUS (b) PERENNIALS

Soil/aspect: Ordinary, well-drained. Sun or shade. Rock gardens.
Culture: Plant autumn to spring. Propagate by division or seed, autumn.
Flowers: Cup-shaped; spring—summer.
Species/cultivars: O. acetosella (wood sorrel) (r), 10cm, pale green, trifoliate leaves, flowers white to pale pink; shade. O. adenophylla (b), 15cm, compound leaves, free-flowering, pink. O. enneaphylla (b), 15cm, similar to O. adenophylla, but with fewer leaflets, and solitary pink or white, dark-veined flowers; sun.

Pachysandra
HARDY EVERGREEN SHRUBS
Soil/aspect: Ordinary. Shade.
Culture: Plant autumn to spring. Propagate by division, spring, or cuttings, summer.
Flowers: Insignificant; spring.
Species/cultivars: P. terminalis, 30cm, dense and wide-spreading, glossy green foliage. P.t. 'Variegata', leaves narrowly margined creamy-yellow.
Remarks: Excellent ground cover plants for shade.

Paeonia (paeony)
HARDY DECIDUOUS SHRUBS (s) and HER-BACEOUS PERENNIALS (p)
Soil/aspect: Ordinary, thrive on chalk. Sun or light shade.
Culture: Plant autumn to spring. Propagate in spring, perennials by division, shrubs by layering; or ripe seed. No pruning.
Flowers: Large, bowl-shaped; early summer.
Species/cultivars: P. lactiflora (P. albiflora)(p), 60-90cm, flowers fragrant; 'Bowl of Beauty', single purple-pink; 'Duchesse de Nemours', double white; 'Felix Crousse', double red; 'Shirley Temple', double soft pink. P. lutea ludlowii (s), to 2m high and wide, single yellow. P. mlokosewitschii (p) 60cm, young leaves red-brown, flowers yellow, single. P. officinalis (p), 60cm, red; more often seen are 'Alba Plena', double white, and 'Rubra Plena', double red. P. suffruticosa (s), 2m, single pink to white with dark red central blotches. Many cultivars available, single or double, white or shades of pink, red and yellow.

Papaver (poppy)
HARDY ANNUALS (a) OR PERENNIALS (p)
Soil/aspect: Ordinary, well-drained. Sun.
Culture: Sow annuals in situ, spring. Plant perennials autumn to spring; propagate by division, spring.
Flowers: Bowl-shaped, conspicuous centres; summer.
Species/cultivars: P. nudicaule (Iceland poppy)(a/p), 45-75cm, red, yellow or white, single or double. P. orientale (p), 90cm, hairy stems and foliage, flowers scarlet, black blotches; P.o. 'Mrs. Perry', pink; 'Perry's White', pure white. P. rhoeas Shirley strains (a), 60cm, available as single or double, red, pink, white or picotée mixtures. P. somniferum (opium poppy (a), to 90cm, flowers large (10cm), single or double, purple, red or white with black blotches; 'Paeony-flowered Mixed' is a popular seed strain.

Remarks: Most poppies seed freely and can be invasive on light soils.

Parrotia (Persian ironwood)
HARDY DECIDUOUS TREES
Soil/aspect: Ordinary, well-drained. Sun or partial shade.
Culture: Plant autumn to spring. Propagate by layering, spring. No pruning.
Flowers: Inconspicuous; spring.
Species/cultivars: P. persica, 4-6m, often shrubby, brilliant autumn colouring.

Parthenocissus (Virginia creeper)
HARDY DECIDUOUS SELF-CLINGING CLIMBERS
Soil/aspect: Ordinary, deep and well-drained. Sun or partial shade.
Culture: Plant autumn to spring. Propagate by hardwood cuttings, autumn, or layering, spring. Thin out during summer.
Flowers: Inconspicuous; summer.
Species/cultivars: P. quinquefolia, 20m or more, compound serrated leaves turning deep red in autumn. P. tricuspidata, 15m, three-lobed leaves, similar autumn colour; P.t. 'Veitchii' (Ampelopsis veitchii, young leaves purple-tinted.

Passiflora (passion flower)
ALMOST HARDY CLIMBERS
Soil/aspect: Ordinary, well-drained. Sun. Protection from cold winds; trellis or wire supports.
Culture: Plant spring. Propagate by cuttings, summer, or seed under glass, spring.
Flowers: Saucer-shaped, large, conspicuous centres; early summer.
Species/cultivars: P. caerulea, 10m, but usually cut to the ground by frost in autumn; flowers blue, with white and purple markings, sometimes followed by yellow, plum-shaped fruit.

Pelargonium (geranium)
TENDER SHRUBS GROWN AS ANNUALS
Soil/aspect: Ordinary, well-drained. Sun.
Culture: Propagate by late summer cuttings overwintered under glass, special strains by seed sown in spring; plant out when fear of frost is past.
Flowers: Single or double, smooth or wavy-edged; summer—autumn.
Species/cultivars: P. x hortorum, the zonal geraniums used for bedding; rounded leaves often with brown-red horseshoe markings, flowers in shades of red, purple, white or bi-coloured, single or double. 'Dot Slade' salmon-pink; 'Irene', crimson-red; 'Majola', bright orange-red; 'Henry Cox', single pink, leaves patterned green, copper, yellow and near black; 'Red Black Vesuvius', 20cm, single red flowers, dark green foliage.

Penstemon
HARDY AND HALF-HARDY HERBACEOUS PERENNIALS AND SMALL SHRUBS
Soil/aspect: Ordinary, well-drained. Sun.
Culture: Plant autumn or spring. Propagate by cuttings, late summer, division or seeds, spring.
Flowers: Like snapdragons (Antirrhinum), but open-mouthed; summer.

Olearia macrodonta

Ornithogalum umbellatum

Species/cultivars: P. x gloxinioides, 60cm, hardy to half-hardy hybrids grown as bedding plants: 'Pennington Gem', deep pink, white throat; 'Schonholzeri' ('Firebird'), scarlet. P. hartwegii, 60cm, half-hardy and often grown as an annual, bright red. P. rupicola, 10cm, hardy mat-forming shrub suitable for rock gardens; flowers red.

Pernettya
HARDY EVERGREEN SHRUBS
Soil/aspect: Acid soil, moisture-retentive. Sun or partial shade.
Culture: Plant autumn to spring. Propagate by cuttings, suckers or layering, late summer. When necessary, prune hard, early spring.
Flowers: Small bells, in clusters; spring.
Species/cultivars: P. mucronata, to 90cm, small-leaved, white flowers followed by abundant globular fruits. Several cultivars available, with pink to purple or white fruits.
Remarks: Male and female flowers usually on separate plants; at least one of each necessary for fruit to set.

Perovskia
HARDY PERENNIALS
Soil/aspect: Ordinary, light. Sun.
Culture: Plant autumn to spring. Propagate by cuttings, late spring or summer, or seeds under glass, early spring.

Flowers: Tubular, loose panicles; late summer and autumn.
Species/cultivars: *P. atriplicifolia*, 1.2m, shrubby, white downy stems, aromatic foliage, flowers blue-violet.
Remarks: Thrive on chalk, good for coastal gardens.

Petunia
HALF-HARDY ANNUALS
Soil/aspect: Ordinary, well-drained. Sun.
Culture: Sow under glass, spring; plant out when fear of frost is past.
Flowers: Open trumpets; summer—autumn.
Species/cultivars: *P. x hybrida*, bedding petunias in a wide range of forms and colours - red, yellow, purple or white: Grandiflora, 30cm, single or double, flowers 10cm across; Multiflora, 30cm, single or double, 5cm; Nana Compacta, dwarf to 15cm, single or double, 5cm; Pendula, trailing, single or double flowers, 6cm.

Phacelia (Californian bluebell)
HARDY ANNUALS
Soil/aspect: Ordinary to light. Sun.
Culture: Sow *in situ*, midspring.
Flowers: Small bells; summer.
Species/cultivars: *P. campanularia*, 30cm, bright blue, in profusion. *P. tanacetifolia*, 90cm, dissected foliage, flowers small, in clusters, lavender-blue.

Phalaris
HARDY PERENNIAL GRASSES
Soil/aspect: Ordinary; sun or light shade.
Culture: Plant autumn to spring. Propagate by division every 2-3 years to contain the creeping rhizomes.
Flowers: Insignificant; summer.
Species/cultivars: *P. arundinacea* 'Picta' (gardener's garters), 60cm, narrow leaves striped cream and bright green.

Philadelphus (mock orange)
HARDY DECIDUOUS SHRUBS
Soil/aspect: Ordinary, well-drained. Sun or partial shade.
Culture: Plant autumn to spring. Propagate by cuttings, late summer and autumn. Prune out old stems after flowering.
Flowers: Cup-shaped, single or double, white and fragrant; summer.
Species/cultivars: *P. coronarius*, strong-growing to 4m; 'Aureus', young leaves bright yellow. *P. x lemoinei*, 2m, pure white; 'Avalanche', single, in clusters; 'Manteau d'Hermine', double creamy-white. *P. x purpureo-maculatus*, 2m, white with purple centres; 'Belle Etoile', single flushed maroon. *P.. x virginalis*, 3m, straggly when old; 'Virginal', double in clusters.

Phlomis (Jerusalem sage)
HARDY PERENNIALS and EVERGREEN SHRUBS
Soil/aspect: Ordinary, well-drained. Sun. Shelter from cold winds.
Culture: Plant autumn to spring. Propagate shrubs by cuttings, late summer, perennials by division or seed, spring.
Flowers: Tubular, hooded; spring—summer.
Species/cultivars: *P. fruticosa*, 1.2m, woolly-

Paeonia suffruticosa 'Rock's Variety'

leaved shrub, whorls of deep yellow flowers. *P. russeliana* (*P. viscosa*), 1.2m, perennial, leaves sage-green, wrinkled; flowers yellow.

Phlox
HALF-HARDY ANNUALS (a) AND HARDY PERENNIALS (p)
Soil/aspect: Fertile, moisture-retentive but well-drained. Sun or light shade.
Culture: Sow annuals under glass, spring; plant out May. Plant perennials autumn to spring; propagate by stem or root cuttings, division or seed, spring.
Flowers: Salver-shaped, dense terminal clusters; late spring—summer.
Species/cultivars: *P. drummondii* (a), to 35cm, red, pink, white or yellow-buff; Cuspidata, starry flowers; Grandiflora, large-flowered; Nana Compacta, dwarf and bushy. *P. paniculata* (p), 1.2m, erect and clump-forming, shades of red, purple, pink, lavender and white. Cultivars include: 'Brigadier', orange-red; 'Fairy's Petticoat', pale mauve; 'Mia Ruys', 50cm, pure white; 'Signal', bright red. *P. stolonifera* (p), 25cm, mat-forming evergreen, violet-purple; 'Blue Ridge', lavender-blue. *P. subulata* (p), 10cm, mat-forming evergreen, red, pink or white, abundant; 'Oakington Blue Eyes', clear blue; 'Temiscaming', magenta.

Phormium (New Zealand flax)
NEAR-HARDY EVERGREEN PERENNIALS
Soil/aspect: Ordinary, moisture-retentive. Sun. Shelter from cold winds.
Culture: Plant spring. Propagate by division or seeds, spring.
Flowers: Red panicles, summer; grown as foliage plants.

Species/cultivars: *P. tenax*, to 3m, stiff and leathery, largely erect leaves, flowering stems may reach 5m; Purpureum', purple foliage; 'Variegatum', cream-margined.
Remarks: Coloured foliage forms more tender than the species.

Phygelius (Cape figwort)
ALMOST HARDY HERBACEOUS PERENNIALS
Soil/aspect: Ordinary, well-drained. Sun. Shelter from cold winds.
Culture: Plant spring. Propagate by cuttings, late summer, or seed, spring.
Flowers: Tubular; summer—autumn.
Species/cultivars: *P. capensis*, 90cm, loose bright red panicles.

Physalis (bladder cherry)
HARDY HERBACEOUS PERENNIALS
Soil/aspect: Ordinary, well-drained. Sun or partial shade. Invasive on light soils.
Culture: Plant autumn or spring. Propagate by seed or division, spring.
Flowers: Nodding bells; summer. Conspicuous fruit, autumn.
Species/cultivars: *P. alkekengi franchetii*, 30-60cm, white flowers followed by berries in orange-red, lantern-like seed cases.
Remarks: Fruiting stems good for drying.

Physostegia (obedient plant)
HARDY HERBACEOUS PERENNIALS
Soil/aspect: Ordinary, moist. Sun.
Culture: Plant autumn to spring. Propagate by division, spring.
Flowers: Tubular, in spikes; summer.
Species/cultivars: *P. virginiana*, 1.2m, pink, lilac or white flowers which stay put when bent on the hinged stalks.

Picea (spruce)

HARDY EVERGREEN CONIFEROUS TREES

Soil/aspect: Acid to neutral, moisture-retentive. Sun or partial shade.
Culture: Plant autumn to spring. Propagate by seed, spring. No pruning.
Flowers: Inconspicuous, but decorative cones.
Species/cultivars: *P. abies* (Norway spruce), the familiar Christmas tree, slow-growing but eventually to 20m; 'Nidiformis', 60cm, flat-topped bush. *P. mariana* 'Nana', 30cm, globular, blue-green shrublet. *P. omorika* (Serbian spruce), 15m, slender and spire-like, good specimen tree for a small space. *P. pungens* 'Glauca' (Colorado blue spruce), 7.5m, blue-green foliage; 'Globosa', 60cm, compact shrub, foliage blue; 'Koster', slow-growing to 7.5m, silvery-blue.
Remarks: Excellent specimen trees; dwarf cultivars suitable for rock gardens.

Pieris

HARDY EVERGREEN SHRUBS

Soil/aspect: Neutral to acid, ideally peaty. Partial shade. Shelter from cold winds; young foliage frost-tender.
Culture: Plant autumn to spring. Propagate by cuttings or layering, late summer.
Flowers: Resembling lily-of-the-valley, in drooping clusters; early spring.
Species/cultivars: *P. formosa*, 4m, young foliage red, later glossy green, white panicles; *P.f.* 'Forrestii', bright red young leaves. *P. japonica*, 3m, coopery-red young growths, flowers white; 'Variegata', cream-edged leaves; 'Daisen', pale pink flowers.

Pinus (pine)

HARDY EVERGREEN CONIFEROUS TREES

Soil/aspect: Ordinary, well-drained. Sun.
Culture: Plant autumn to spring. Propagate from seed, spring, named cultivars by grafting. No pruning.
Flowers: Inconspicuous; decorative cones.
Species/cultivars: *P. aristata* (bristle-cone pine),6m, slow-growing, good for smaller gardens; dark blue-green foliage. *P. mugo* (mountain pine), 2-3 m, bright green, bristle tipped needles; 'Gnom' and 'Mops', near-prostrate, suitable for rock gardens. *P. nigra maritima* (Corsican pine), 15m or more, grey-green twisted needles, good for windbreaks on all soils. *P. parviflora* (Japanese white pine), 6-9m, conical when young, grey-white foliage, black peeling bark. *P. pinea* (stone, umbrella pine), to 10m, umbrella-shaped crown. *P. sylvestris* (Scots pine), to 20m, blue-green, stiff foliage, useful as wind-breaks; 'Aurea', slow-growing to 9m, yellow winter foliage; 'Beauvronensis', globular, compact shrublet for rock gardens; 'Watereri', ('Pumila''), slow-growing, blue-green foliage. *P. wallichiana* (Bhutan pine), 15m, fine specimen tree with long, blue-green, drooping needles, resin-covered purple cones.

Pittosporum

HALF-HARDY EVERGREEN SHRUBS

Soil/aspect: Ordinary, well-drained. Sun. Ideally against walls in cold areas.
Culture: Plant late spring. Propagate from cutting, summer, or seed, spring. Trim to shape late spring.
Flowers: Bells, in loose clusters; summer. Chiefly grown as foliage shrubs.
Species/cultivars: *P. tenuifolium*, 5m in mild areas; wavy, glossy pale green leaves on purple stems; 'Purpureum', dark purple; 'Garnettii', variegated white and pink; both less hardy than the species. *P. tobira*, slow-growing to 4m in mild areas; deep green, shiny leaves, white fragrant flowers; 'Variegatum', leaves marked white and grey.
Remarks: Foliage used in flower arrangements.

Platycodon (balloon flower)

HARDY HERBACEOUS PERENNIALS

Soil/aspect: Ordinary, well-drained. Sun.
Culture: Plant autumn to spring. Propagate by division or seed, spring.
Flowers: Saucer-shaped from balloon buds; summer.
Species/cultivars: *P. grandiflorum*, 60cm, clump-forming, blue-purple flowers; 'Mariesii', 30cm, pale to deep blue; 'Snowflake', white, semi-double.

Podophyllum

HARDY HERBACEOUS PERENNIALS

Soil/aspect: Moist, humus-rich. Partial shade.
Culture: Plant autumn to spring. Propagate by division, spring, or seed when ripe.
Flowers: Saucer-shaped; late spring.
Species/cultivars: *P. emodii* (*P. hexandrum*), 45cm, leaves green to purplish-brown, lobed, flowers pale pink followed by red, edible fruits.

Polemonium

HARDY HERBACEOUS PERENNIALS

Soil/aspect: Humus-rich, well-drained. Sun.
Culture: Plant autumn to spring. Propagate by division, autumn or spring.
Flowers: Bowl-shaped; summer—autumn.
Species/cultivars: *P. caeruleum* (Jacob's ladder), 60cm, leaves feathery, flower clusters blue or white. *P. foliosissimum*, 90cm, leaves less finely divided, flowers violet to purple, or white.

Polygala (milkwort)

HARDY EVERGREEN SHRUBS

Soil/aspect: Humus-rich, moisture-retentive. Sun or partial shade. Suitable for rock gardens.
Culture: Plant autumn to spring. Propagate by cuttings, summer, or seed, spring.
Flowers: Pea-like; late spring.
Species/cultivars: *P. chamaebuxus*, prostrate to 10cm, leaves small, dark green, leathery, flowers yellow and white, tipped purple; 'Grandiflora', bright yellow and magenta.

Polygonatum (Solomon's seal)

HARDY RHIZOMATOUS PERENNIALS

Soil/aspect: Ordinary. Partial shade.
Culture: Plant autumn and winter. Propagate by division, autumn or spring.
Flowers: Tubular, in pendent pairs; early summer.

Pernettya mucronata (fruit)

Phormium tenax 'Purpureum'

Species/cultivars: *P.* x *hybridum*, 90cm, arching leafy stems, white flowers.

Polygonum (knotweed)

HARDY HERBACEOUS PERENNIALS (p) AND DECIDUOUS SHRUBBY CLIMBERS (c)

Soil/aspect: Humus-rich, moisture retentive. Sun or partial shade.
Culture: Plant autumn or spring. Propagate perennials by division, autumn or spring, climbers by cuttings, summer or autumn. No pruning.
Flowers: Bell-shaped; summer—autumn.
Species/cultivars: *P. affine* (p), 15cm, mat-forming, dense pink flower spikes, foliage bronze in winter; 'Donald Lowndes', rose-pink, deep coloured winter foliage. *P. amplexicaule* (p), 120cm, red spikes above bright green foliage. *P. baldschuanicum* (Russian vine) (c), rampant twiner to 15m or more, ideal for covering eyesores; erect loose, white pale pink-tinted panicles. *P. bistorta* 'Superbum' (p), 75cm, dense pink spikes.

Polypodium (polypody)

HARDY EVERGREEN FERNS

Soil/aspect: Ordinary to rich, well-drained but moisture-retentive. Partial shade.

211

Culture: Plant in late spring; Propagate by division of rhizomes, spring.

Flowers: None.

Species/cultivars: *P. vulgare*, 10-30cm, narrow fronds divided almost to centre into numerous lobes; 'Cambricum', broader fronds with many narrow lobes; 'Pulcherrimum', deeply cut, lacy fronds.

Polystichum (shield fern)

HARDY EVERGREEN FERNS

Soil/aspect: Humus-rich, limy, moisture-retentive. Shade.

Culture: Plant in spring. Propagate by division, autumn or spring, or from plantlets.

Flowers: None.

Species/cultivars: *P. setiferum* (soft shield fern), 90cm, fronds soft-textured, arching, divided to centre rib; 'Acutilobum' ('Proliferum'), finely dissected fronds, tiny plantlets along the ribs.

Pontederia (pickerel weed)

HARDY RHIZOMATOUS AQUATICS

Soil/aspect: Water depth to 25cm, or permanently wet ground. Sun.

Culture: Plant spring. Propagate by division, late spring.

Flowers: Funnel-shaped; late summer.

Species/cultivars: *P. cordata*, 60cm, leaves arrow-shaped, held above water, dense blue flower spikes; forms large colonies.

Portulaca

HALF-HARDY ANNUALS

Soil/aspect: Ordinary, well-drained. Sun.

Culture: Sow seeds under glass, midspring; plant out when fear of frost is past.

Flowers: Saucer-shaped; summer—autumn.

Species/cultivars: *P. grandiflora* (sun plant), 15cm, mat-forming; usually sold as mixtures in shades of red, pink, purple, white and yellow, single or double.

Potentilla (cinquefoil)

HARDY PERENNIALS (p) AND DECIDUOUS SHRUBS AND SUBSHRUBS (s)

Soil/aspect: Ordinary to light, well-drained. Sun.

Culture: Plant autumn to spring. Propagate perennials by division, autumn or spring; shrubs by cuttings, late summer.

Flowers: Saucer-shaped; summer—autumn.

Species/cultivars: *P. arbuscula* (s), 75 cm, leaves silky-hairy, flowers golden-yellow. *P. atrosanguinea* hybrids (p): 'Gibson's Scarlet', 30cm, single, bright red; 'Gloire de Nancy', 45cm, semi-double, orange to brick-red; 'Yellow Queen', 38cm, semi-double, yellow with red eye. *P. fruticosa* (s), compact, numerous cultivars: 'Daydawn', 1-1.5m, pale pink and cream; 'Katherine Dykes', 1.2m, clear yellow; 'Red Ace', 75cm, bright vermilion; 'Tangerine', 60cm, copper to yellow, best in partial shade; 'Vilmoriniana', 1.2m, creamy-white.

Primula (primrose)

HARDY PERENNIALS

Soil/aspect: Humus-rich, moisture-retentive, some species in permanently moist ground (w). Light shade.

Culture: Plant late summer to early spring. Propagate by division after flowering or seed when ripe.

Flowers: Open-faced or bells; spring.

Species/cultivars: *P. auricula*, 15cm, erect flower umbels, red, blue, yellow or near-black, often with contrasting centres. *P. beesiana* (w), 60cm, whorls of flowers, pink with yellow eye. *P. bulleyana*, 60cm, orange-yellow. *P. denticulata* (drumstick primrose), 10-30cm, globular, lilac-purple or white. *P. florindae* (giant cowslip) (w), 1.2m, bright yellow, nodding umbels, late summer. P. 'Inverewe' (w), 60cm, brick-red. *P. japonica* (w), 60cm, red-purple or white. *P. pulverulenta* (w), 90cm, dark red, white eye. *P. sieboldii*, 25cm, purple, pink or white; several cultivars with toothed or fringed petals. *P.* x *tommasinii* (polyanthus), hybrids with large-flowered umbels in a range of bright colours. *P. vulgaris* (primrose), 15cm, pale yellow.

Prunella (self-heal)

HARDY PERENNIALS

Soil/aspect: Ordinary, moisture-retentive. Sun or partial shade.

Culture: Plant autumn to spring. Propagate by division, autumn.

Flowers: Tubular, spikes; spring—summer.

Species/cultivars: *P. grandiflora*, 15-20cm, pink-purple or white in dense spikes; 'Loveliness', pale purple; 'Pink Loveliness'; 'White Loveliness'.

Remarks: Good ground cover for shade.

Prunus (flowering almond, cherry, peach, plum)

HARDY MAINLY DECIDUOUS TREES AND SHRUBS

Soil/aspect: Ordinary, well-drained but moisture-retentive. Sun.

Culture: Plant autumn. Propagate by seed when ripe, heel cuttings under glass, summer, or hardwood cuttings, autumn. Named cultivars usually grafted. Little pruning; when necessary cut back late summer; hedges at any time, spring and summer.

Flowers: Bowl-shaped; spring.

Species/cultivars: *P.* x *amygdalo-persica* 'Pollardii', 9m, almond, bright pink, single. *P. avium* (wild cherry), 12m, pure white clusters; 'Plena' ('Multiplex'), double. *P. cerasifera* (cherry plum, myrobalan), 10m, white, in small clusters before leaves; 'Pissardii', leaves red, ageing purple, flower buds pink. *P.* 'Cistena', 1.5m, plum, leaves deep red, flowers white, small; useful for hedging. *P. incisa*, 5m, cherry, white or pale pink, abundant; autumn tints. *P. laurocerasus* (cherry laurel), 6m, evergreen spreading shrub, leaves leathery, spikes of creamy-white flowers, fruit red becoming black; 'Otto Luyken', 1m, compact, smaller leaves, excellent for hedging, sun or shade; 'Zabeliana', near prostrate, spreading, good for ground cover. *P. lusitanica* (Portugal laurel), 6m, evergreen shrub or small tree, leaves wavy, glossy, flower spikes white, fruit purple. P. 'Okame', 7m, cherry, carmine-rose, autumn tints. *P. padus* 'Watereri' (bird cherry), 9m, pendent racemes of white flowers. *P. persica*, 7m, peach, abundant

pale pink flowers before leaves; 'Foliis Rubis', young leaves red-purple maturing bronze; 'Klara Mayer', double flowers.

P. sargentii, 10m, cherry, young leaves red, bright red autumn tints, flowers deep pink. *P. serrula*, 10m, cherry, flowers white but not showy; grown for its red-brown, glossy, peeling bark. *P. serrulata*, to 15m, flowers white or pink, single or double; most Japanese flowering cherries derive from this species: 'Amanogawa', narrow and spire-like, pink, semi-double, fragrant. 'Cheal's Weeping' ('Kiku-shidare-Sakura'), 6m, weeping, pink, double. 'Kanzan', to 9m, stiff almost erect branches, strong-growing, deep pink, double. 'Pink Perfection', 7m, abundant, pink double. 'Shirotae', to 7m, arching habit, flowers white, fragrant; 'Ukon', 6m, spreading, creamy-yellow, semi-double, young leaves bronze, good autumn colours. *P. subhirtella*, 8m, cherry, soft pink; 'Autumnalis', white flowers autumn to spring in mild spells. *P.* x *yedoensis*, 9m, cherry, arching habit, flowers abundant, white to pale pink, fragrant.

Pulmonaria (lungwort)

HARDY HERBACEOUS PERENNIALS

Soil/aspect: Ordinary, moisture-retentive. Shade.

Culture: Plant autumn to spring. Propagate by division, autumn or spring, or seed, spring.

Flowers: Funnel-shaped; spring.

Species/cultivars: *P. officinalis* (Jerusalem cowslip), 30cm, leaves white-spotted, purple-blue flower clusters. *P. rubra*, 30cm, leaves light green, flowers brick-red; 'Bowles' Red', deep pink. *P. saccharata*, 30cm, large leaves white-spotted, flowers red changing to purple; 'White Wings', pure white.

Pulsatilla (pasque flower)

HARDY HERBACEOUS PERENNIALS

Soil/aspect: Humus-rich, well-drained. Sun.

Culture: Plant autumn. Propagate by seed when ripe.

Flowers: Cup-shaped, anemone-like; spring.

Species/cultivars: *P. vulgaris*, 20-25cm, leaves deeply dissected, silky-hairy, flowers purple; red, pink and white forms also available.

Puschkinia (striped squill)

HARDY BULBOUS PERENNIALS

Soil/aspect: Ordinary. Sun.

Culture: Plant autumn. Propagate by ripe seed or offsets after flowering.

Flowers: Star-shaped, loose clusters; spring.

Species/cultivars: *P. scilloides* (*P. libanotica*), 15cm, pale blue or white, striped dark blue.

Pyracantha (firethorn)

HARDY EVERGREEN SPINY SHRUBS

Soil/aspect: Ordinary, well-drained. Sun or light shade.

Culture: Plant autumn to spring. Propagate by heel cuttings, late summer, or ripe seed.

Flowers: Hawthorn-like, creamy-white, spring; attractive berry cluster, autumn.

Species/cultivars: *P. atalantioides*, 5m or

more, scarlet berries. *P. coccinea* 'Lalandei', fruit bright orange. *P. rogersiana*, to 5m, fruit orange-red; 'Flava', fruit yellow.

Pyrethrum
HARDY HERBACEOUS PERENNIALS
Soil/aspect: Ordinary, well-drained. Sun.
Culture: Plant spring. Propagate by division or seed, spring.
Flowers: Daisy-like; summer—autumn.
Species/cultivars: *P. roseum (Chrysanthemum coccineum)*, 60cm, leaves deeply dissected, flowers pink or red; 'Avalanche', pure white; 'Bressingham Red', deep red; 'Evenglow', salmon-pink; 'Madeleine', pink, double.

Pyrus (ornamental pear)
HARDY DECIDUOUS TREES
Soil/aspect: Ordinary. Sun.
Culture: Plant autumn to spring. Propagate by grafting. No pruning.
Flowers: Creamy-white clusters; spring.
Species/cultivars: *P. salicifolia* 'Pendula', 3-6m, weeping habit, leaves willow-like, silvery; an elegant specimen tree.

Ramonda
EVERGREEN PERENNIAL ALPINES
Soil/aspect: Ordinary, well-drained but moisture-retentive; rock crevices or dry walls. Shade.
Culture: Plant autumn to spring. Propagate by seed or division, spring; or leaf cuttings, summer.
Flowers: Salver-shaped; late spring.
Species/cultivars: *R. myconi*, 6-12cm, purple-blue; 'Alba', white.

Ranunculus (buttercup)
HARDY HERBACEOUS PERENNIALS
Soil/aspect: Ordinary or waterside. Sun or partial shade.
Culture: Plant autumn to spring. Propagate by seed or division, spring.
Flowers: Buttercups; late spring - summer.
Species/cultivars: *R. aconitifolius*, 50cm, pure white from red buds; 'Flore Pleno', double. *R. asiaticus*, to 45 cm, shades of red, purple, yellow or white, semi or fully double. *R. gramineus*, 50 cm, narrow grey leaves, flowers bright yellow, shiny. *R. lingua* (greater spearwort), to 120 cm, waterside plant, glossy, golden-yellow.

Reseda (mignonette)
ANNUALS
Soil/aspect: Alkaline to neutral, humus-rich and well-drained. Sun.
Culture: Sow *in situ*, spring.
Flowers: Loose clusters; summer - autumn.
Species/cultivars: *R. odorata*, 25-40cm, strongly fragrant, yellowish-white; 'Crimson Giant', red.

Rhamnus (buckthorn)
HARDY EVERGREEN SHRUBS
Soil/aspect: Ordinary. Sun or partial shade.
Culture: Plant autumn to spring. Propagate by cuttings, late summer. No pruning.
Flowers: Inconspicuous; late spring. Autumn berries.

Physalis alkekengi franchetii (fruit)

Polygonatum x hybridum

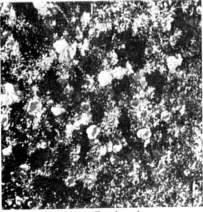
Potentilla fruticosa 'Daydawn'

Species/cultivars: *R. alaternus*, 3m or more, leaves narrowly oblong, glossy, flowers small, yellow, followed by red berries. 'Argenteo-variegatus', ('Variegatus'), grey-green foliage, cream margins.
Remarks: Recommended for mild coastal and town gardens.

Rheum (ornamental rhubarb)
HARDY HERBACEOUS FOLIAGE PERENNIALS
Soil/aspect: Ordinary to rich, moisture-retentive. Sun or partial shade.
Culture: Plant autumn to spring. Propagate by seed or division, spring.
Flowers: Tiny, bead-like, in large panicles; early summer.
Species/cultivars: *R. palmatum*, 2m, large, deeply lobed leaves red-flushed beneath; branched flower spikes red; 'Atrosanguineum', young leaves bright red.

Rhododendron (and azalea)
HARDY EVERGREEN AND DECIDUOUS SHRUBS
Soil/aspect: Acid and preferably humus-rich, moisture-retentive, but well-drained. Light shade.
Culture: Plant autumn or spring. Water during dry spells. Propagate by cuttings, late summer, layering or seeds sown under glass, spring. No pruning; dead-head by hand after flowering.
Flowers: Bell or funnel-shaped in large clusters; early spring—summer.
Species/cultivars: Hundreds of species and many more named cultivars are available. Those listed here are only a short selection, and it is advisable to consult specialist nurseries' catalogues.
Dwarf evergreens, less than 60cm: *R. campylogynum*, rose-purple. *R. forrestii repens*, mat-forming, deep crimson. *R. impeditum*, light purple-blue. *R. leucaspis*, white with chocolate stamens; best in sheltered site. *R. sargentianum*, lemon-yellow; best in sun. 'Aspansia', bright red; 'Chikor', creamy-white; 'Jenny', deep red; 'Lady Primrose', pale yellow, speckled crimson; 'Pink Drift', lavender-rose; 'Saint Merryn', violet-blue; 'Sarled', creamy-white from pink buds.
Small evergreens, 0.9-15m: *R. fastigiatum*, purple-blue. *R. haematodes*, blood-red. *R. mucronatum*, pure white, fragrant. *R. racemosum*, pink to red. *R. yakushimanum*, compact, slow-growing, white from pink buds. 'Blue Diamond', lavender-blue; 'Bo-Peep', primrose-yellow; 'Caroline Allbrook', lavender; 'Georgette', white from pink buds; 'Humming Bird', crimson; 'Starshine', pink. Kurume azaleas, funnel-shaped, late spring; 'Hinomayo', clear pink; 'Kirin', silvery-rose.
Medium-sized evergreens, 1.5-3m: *R. augustinii*, lavender to mauve, *R. campanulatum*, rose-purple to lavender; *R.c.* 'Album', white. *R. campylocarpum*, bright to pale yellow, *R. cinnabarinum*, orange-red. *R. thomsonii*, blood-red. *R. williamsianum*, slow-growing, rich pink. 'Damaris', lemon-yellow; 'Lavender Girl', lilac-mauve; 'May Day', scarlet; 'White Diamond', pure white.
Large evergreens, 3m to tree-like: *R. arboreum*, tree, 10m or more, white, pink or

red. *R. falconeri*, tree to 12m, creamy-yellow. *R. fictolactum*, tree to 12m, cream with crimson markings. *R. fulvum*, 6m, white flushed pink. *R. sinogrande*, tree, 12m or more, large silvery leaves, flowers soft yellow, blotched red. *R. wardii*, 4m, bright yellow. 'Betty Wormald', pink, deep pink markings; 'Loderi' rhododendrons, 6m or more, pale pink or white, fragrant; 'Pink Pearl', rose-pink; 'Polar Bear', pure white; 'Purple Splendour', deep purple.

Deciduous azaleas: *R. albrechtii*, 2-3m, rose-purple. *R. calendulaceum*, 2-3m, orange-yellow to scarlet. *R. kaempferi*, red-pink; 'Daimio', salmon-pink; 'Mikado', salmon-apricot. *R. luteum* (*Azalea pontica*), to 3m, rich yellow, fragrant. *R. molle* (*Azalea mollis*), 1-2m, yellow. *R. reticulatum*, to 6m, purple. *R. schlippenbachii*, 3-5m, rose-pink. *R. viscosum*, 2m, white or pink, fragrant; good for wet sites.

Popular azalea cultivars include the Ghent group, 1.5m or more, tubular, fragrant, in a range of colours. Mollis azaleas, to 1.5m, funnel-shaped, shades of orange and yellow, flushed scarlet or pink; autumn tints. Knap Hill and Exbury azaleas, to 1.8m, funnel-shaped in large trusses, white, shades of pink, red, yellow and orange; autumn colours.

Rhodohypoxis
NEAR-HARDY PERENNIALS
Soil/aspect: Lime-free, well-drained. Sun.
Culture: Plant the corm-like rhizomes in spring. Propagate by division, spring. Protect the crowns from winter wet.
Flowers: Star-shaped; summer—autumn.
Species/cultivars: *R. baurii*, 8-10cm, shades of red and pink; 'Dawn', pale pink; 'Garnet', deep crimson.

Rhus (sumach)
HARDY DECIDUOUS SHRUBS AND SMALL TREES
Soil/aspect: Ordinary. Sun.
Culture: Plant autumn to spring. Propagate by suckers, autumn. If necessary prune hard in spring.
Flowers: Spikes; summer.
Species/cultivars: *R. typhina* (stag's horn sumach), to 8m, suckering freely, stems covered with velvety down, large leaves pinnate, usually brightly coloured in autumn; flowers greenish, conspicuous in fruit. 'Dissecta' ('Laciniata'), more deeply incised leaves.

Ribes (flowering currant)
HARDY DECIDUOUS SHRUBS
Soil/aspect: Ordinary, well-drained. Sun or partial shade.
Culture: Plant autumn to spring. Propagate by cuttings, late summer or autumn. Prune in late spring.
Flowers: Pendent clusters; spring.
Species/cultivars: *R. aureum* (golden currant), 2m, golden yellow, fragrant. *R. odoratum*, similar, but flowers longer and more fragrant. *R. sanguineum*, 4m, rose-pink; 'Album', pure white; 'King Edward VII', smaller shrub, flowers deep crimson; 'Pulborough Scarlet', deep red; 'Tydeman's White', pure white, outstanding.

Pulsatilla vulgaris

Ricinus (castor oil plant)
TENDER SHRUBS GROWN AS ANNUALS
Soil/aspect: Ordinary to rich. Sun.
Culture: Sow under glass in spring. Plant out when fear of frost is past.
Flowers: Insignificant; summer.
Species/cultivars: *R. communis*, 1.5m, leaves large, maple-like, bronze when young; 'Gibsonii', foliage dark red; 'Zanzibarensis', leaves bright green, white-veined.

Robinia (false acacia)
HARDY DECIDUOUS TREES
Soil/aspect: Ordinary, well-drained. Sun.
Culture: Plant autumn to spring. Propagate by seed, spring, or suckers, autumn, except from grafted plants. No pruning.
Flowers: Pea-like, pendent clusters; early summer.
Species/cultivars: *R. pseudoacacia*, 9m or more, leaves cut into many leaflets, flowers white, fragrant; 'Frisia', smaller tree, foliage bright yellow; 'Pyramidalis', columnar habit.

Rodgersia
HARDY HERBACEOUS PERENNIALS
Soil/aspect: Humus-rich, moisture-retentive. Sun or partial shade.
Culture: Plant autumn to spring. Propagate by division or seed, spring.
Flowers: Erect plumes; summer.
Species/cultivars: *R. aesculifolia*, 2m, leaves large, hand-shaped, flowers white. *R. pinnata*, 1.2m, leaves divided into 2-4 pairs of leaflets; pink flower spikes; 'Superba', leaves bronze-flushed, flowers deep pink.

Romneya (California tree poppy)
ALMOST HARDY HERBACEOUS PERENNIALS
Soil/aspect: Deep humus-rich, well-drained. Sun. Can be invasive.

Culture: Plant spring. Propagate by suckers or seed, spring. Established plants resent disturbance.
Flowers: Poppy-like, open-faced; late summer—autumn.
Species/cultivars: *R. coulteri*, 2m, suckering, leaves blue-green, flowers white with golden stamens; 'White Cloud', flowers larger.

Rosa (rose)
HARDY DECIDUOUS SHRUBS AND CLIMBERS
Soil/aspect: Ordinary to slightly acid, fertile; moisture-retentive, but well-drained. Sun or light shade.
Culture: Plant dormant season, with supports for standards and climbers. Propagate by hardwood cuttings, autumn; species also by ripe seed, and cultivars by budding, late summer.
Pruning: Early spring, as buds begin to swell; remove entirely weak, diseased and crossing stems. Dead-head throughout summer. *Hybrid tea:* cut all stems back to 4 buds. *Floribunda:* cut strong stems back by ¼, the remainder to 1 or 2 basal buds. *Climbers:* remove soft tip growth on leading shoots and shorten laterals to 2 buds; tie in replacement shoots. *Ramblers:* cut flowered stems out at ground level after petal-fall, late summer. *Shrub roses:* little pruning except for removal of damaged shoots.
Flowers: Early summer—autumn.
Species/cultivars: Hundreds of species and cultivars available; catalogues should be consulted. Broadly, roses are divided into the following groups, differing in habit, flower shape, size, fragrancy and blooming period: *Hybrid tea*, 90cm (bush), 1.2m (standard), flowers solitary, double, some scented, June—October. *Floribunda*, 90cm (bush), 1.2m (standard), clusters, single or double,

Rhus typhiña

some fragrant, June—October. *Climbers* (of species origin), 3-8m, large clusters, single, fragrant, summer; modern, 3-5m, small clusters, single or double, some scented, repeat-flowering. *Ramblers*, to 7m, large clusters, single or double, fragrant, one flowering flush only, summer.

Shrub roses, in bloom June—October and known as repeat-flowering, include Modern shrubs, 1.5m, solitary or small clusters, single or double, some fragrant; Bourbon roses, 1.2-3m, densely-petalled, solitary or small clusters, heavily fragrant; Hybrid musks, 1.5m, loose and arching, single or double, large clusters, fragrant, late summer on; Hybrid perpetuals, 1.5m, large cabbage-type blooms, solitary or small clusters, some scented; Hybrid rugosas, to 2m, large, semi-double, small clusters, deeply fragrant, some with fine hips.

Shrub roses, also known as Old roses, with a single spectacular flowering period, June—July, include the true species, some of which are regaining popularity: *R. x alba* ('White Rose of York'), 1.5-2m, single or semi-double, white, deeply fragrant, several cultivars; *R. damascena* (damask rose), 1-1.5m, double, pink to red, heavily scented, several cultivars; *R. gallica* (French rose), 1-1.5m, solitary, semi-double, fragrant, red hips, several cultivars, some bicoloured or striped; *R. moyesii*, 3m, solitary, blood-red, bottle-shaped, bright red hips; 'Geranium', compact habit, large hips.

Moss roses, 1.5m, derived from *R. centifolia* 'Muscosa', are also summer-flowering, solitary or small clusters, double, deeply fragrant, sepals with mossy glands. *Miniature roses*, of hybrid tea, floribunda (20-40cm) or climber (1.8m) habit, clusters, single or double, some scented.

Rubus (bramble)
HARDY DECIDUOUS SHRUBS
Soil/aspect: Ordinary, well-drained. Sun or partial shade.
Culture: Plant autumn to spring. Propagate by division, dormant season, suckers or tip layering, late summer—early autumn. Prune hard after flowering.
Flowers: Cup-shaped; late spring-summer.
Species/cultivars: *R. biflorus*, 2-3m, grown for its white, waxy stems, striking in winter. *R. deliciosus*, 2-3m, arching stems, flowers white, followed by edible red-purple, flavourless fruit. *R. x* 'Tridel', similar to *R. deliciosus*, but freer and larger flowering.

Rudbeckia (coneflower)
HARDY HERBACEOUS PERENNIALS AND ANNUALS
Soil/aspect: Ordinary, well-drained. Sun.
Culture: Plant autumn to spring. Propagate perennials by division, dormant season, or seed, spring. Sow annuals under glass, spring.
Flowers: Daisy-like; late summer—autumn.
Species/cultivars: *R. fulgida*, 60cm, perennial, golden-orange, central golden-brown cone; 'Goldsturm', large, bright yellow. *R. hirta*, (black-eyed Susan), 30-90cm, annual or biennial; several strains available: 'Gloriosa', yellow and maroon, large; 'Rustic Dwarfs', 30cm, yellow, bronze and maroon. *R. laciniata*, 2m, perennial, bright yellow, green conical centre. *R. nitida*, similar but smaller.

Sagittaria (arrowhead)
HARDY AQUATIC PERENNIALS
Soil/aspect: Shallow water or permanently moist, fertile soil. Sun.
Culture: Plant the tubers in spring. Propagate by division, late spring.
Flowers: Summer—autumn.
Species/cultivars: *S. latifolia*, 60cm, leaves glossy, arrow-shaped, flowers white, three-petalled. *S. sagittifolia*, similar but smaller, flowers with purple centres.

Salix (willow)
HARDY DECIDUOUS TREES AND SHRUBS
Soil/aspect: Ordinary, deep, moisture-retentive. Sun or partial shade.
Culture: Plant autumn to spring. Propagate by hardwood cuttings, autumn and winter. No regular pruning.
Flowers: Catkins, males most conspicuous; spring.
Species/cultivars: *S. alba*, 'Chermesina', twigs shiny orange-red in winter, best cut back annually in spring to produce young stems; 'Vitellina', similar, with yellow twigs. *S. caprea* (pussy willow), to 8m, silvery catkins; 'Pendula' (Kilmarnock willow), pendulous branchlets. *S. x chrysocoma* (weeping willow), 10m, slender pendulous branches, twigs yellow; 'Sepulcralis', gracefully pendent, green foliage. *S. daphnoides*, 12m, stems purple with white waxy patina, catkins showy; can be cut back annually. *S. gracilistyla melanostachys*. 3m, shrubby, catkins almost black, red on opening. *S. hastata* 'Wehrhahnii', 1.2m, stems purple when young, catkins silvery. *S. lanata* (woolly willow), dense shrub to 1m or more, leaves and stems downy; male catkins long, silky-hairy, bright yellow. *S. matsudana* 'Tortuosa', 9m, branches contorted.

Salpiglossis (painted tongue)
HALF-HARDY ANNUALS
Soil/aspect: Ordinary. Sun.
Culture: Sow seed under glass in spring; plant out when fear of frost is past.
Flowers: Funnel-shaped; summer - autumn.
Species/cultivars: *S. sinuata*, 60-90cm, bushy, sticky-downy, flowers in shades of red, yellow, purple and blue, the veins often in contrasting colours.

Salvia (sage)
HALF-HARDY AND HARDY ANNUALS (a), PERENNIALS (p) AND SUB-SHRUBS (s)
Soil/aspect: Ordinary, well-drained. Sun.
Culture: Plant half-hardy sub-shrubs and annuals late spring, hardy perennials, spring or autumn. Propagate annuals by seed under glass, spring, perennials by division, spring, and sub-shrubs by cuttings, late summer.
Flowers: Tubular, hooded, in spikes; summer—autumn.
Species/cultivars: *S. haematodes* (p), 90cm, hardy, purple-blue, long slender spikes. *S. horminum* (a), 45cm, hardy, stems leafy, topped with flower bracts, red, purple, blue or white. *S. officinalis* (s), 60cm, hardy, evergreen, leaves wrinkled; 'Icterina', gold-variegated; 'Purpurascens', tinted deep purple. *S. splendens* (a), 50cm, half-hardy, dense spikes, bright scarlet.

Sanguinaria (bloodroot)
HARDY RHIZOMATOUS PERENNIALS
Soil/aspect: Humus-rich, moisture-retentive. Partial shade.
Culture: Plant autumn. Propagate by division, late winter.

Rosa primula (species)

Flowers: Cup-shaped; late spring.
Species/cultivars: *S. canadensis*, 15-20cm, leaves blue-grey, lobed, appearing with solitary white flowers; 'Multiplex', double.

Santolina (cotton lavender)
Soil/aspect: Ordinary, well-drained. Sun.
Culture: Plant autumn to spring. Propagate by cuttings, late summer.
Flowers: Button-like; summer.
Species/cultivars: *S. chamaecyparissus* (*S. incana*), 40-60cm, foliage finely dissected, silvery-grey, flower clusters lemon-yellow. *S. neapolitana*, 60-75cm, similar, but leaves more feathery, silver-grey.

Saponaria (soapwort)
HARDY PERENNIALS
Soil/aspect: Ordinary. Sun or light shade.
Culture: Plant autumn to spring. Propagate by division, dormant season, or seed, spring.
Flowers: Salver-shaped; summer.
Species/cultivars: *S. ocymoides*, 8cm, spreading to mounds, rose-pink; 'Alba', white; 'Splendens', taller, flowers deeper pink. *S. officinalis*, to 90cm, rhizomatous, invasive, pale pink or white, in branched panicles; single and double forms available.

Saxifraga (Saxifrage)
HARDY EVERGREEN DWARF PERENNIALS
Soil/aspect: Alkaline to neutral, chalky and gritty, well-drained. Light shade or sun.
Culture: Plant autumn to spring. Propagate by division or seed, spring.
Flowers: Spring, early summer.
Species/cultivars: *S. aizoon* (*S. paniculata*), 30cm, silvery rosettes, flower panicles white or cream. *S. cotyledon*, 50cm, rosettes of tongue-shaped leaves, broad panicles of white flowers. *S. fortunei*, 30-45cm, deciduous, best in shade, lobed, glossy leaves, red-purple beneath; loose panicles of white flowers, autumn. *S. x 'Jenkinsae'*, prostrate, cushion-forming, flowers pink. *S. moschata*,, prostrate, loose mid-green cushions, flowers saucer-shaped, cream, white or pink; several cultivars available. *S.oppositifolia*, prostrate, dark green loose mats, flowers cup-shaped, rich pink; 'Splendens', large purple-pink. *S. x urbium*

(*S.umbrosa* of gardens) (London Pride), 30cm, leaves thick, leathery; flower panicles white, red-spotted; grows in full shade; 'Variegata', yellow-mottled leaves.

Scabiosa (scabious, pincushion flower)
HARDY HERBACEOUS PERENNIALS (p) AND ANNUALS (a)
Soil/aspect: Ordinary, well-drained. Sun.
Culture: Plant in spring. Propagate perennials by division, annuals by seed *in situ*, spring.
Flowers: Cushion-like, prominent centres; summer.
Species/cultivars: *S. atropurpurea* (sweet scabious) (a), 60cm, purple or red; smaller strains (45cm) available. *S. caucasica* (p), 60-75cm, lavender; white and deep lavender-blue forms available. *S. graminifolia*, 30cm, grassy leaves, flowers mauve to pink; 'Pinkushion', pink.

Schizanthus (poor man's orchid, butterfly flower)
HALF-HARDY ANNUALS
Soil/aspect: Humus-rich, well-drained. Sun. Shelter.
Culture: Sow seed under glass, spring; plant out when fear of frost is past.
Flowers: Orchid-like; summer - autumn.
Species/cultivars: *S. pinnatus*, 90cm, leaves pale-green, deeply cut; available in a wide range of colours, often contrasting. 'Dwarf Bouquet', 30cm; 'Giant Hybrid', 120cm.

Schizostylis (kaffir lily)
ALMOST HARDY EVERGREEN PERENNIALS
Soil/aspect: Humus-rich, moisture-retentive. Sun. Shelter.
Culture: Plant the rhizomes in spring. Propagate by division, spring. In cold areas lift in autumn, pot up and keep barely moist and frost-free.
Flowers: Star-shaped; autumn.
Species/cultivars: *S. coccinea*, 30-40cm, leaves stiff, strap-shaped; flowers crimson; 'Mrs. Hegarty', clear pink.

Scilla (squill)
HARDY BULBOUS PERENNIALS
Soil/aspect: Ordinary, well-drained. Sun or partial shade.
Culture: Plant autumn. Propagate from seed, spring or autumn, or by offsets, autumn.
Flowers: Star or bell-shaped; spring.
Species/cultivars: *S. bifolia*, 15cm, blue, starry. *S. peruviana*, 25cm, dense, broad, purple-blue spikes; 'Alba', white. *S. sibirica*, 15cm, nodding blue bells; 'Spring Beauty', early-flowering, stronger-growing. *S. tubergeniana* (*S. mischtschenkoana*), 10-15cm, palest blue flowers with darker central stripes, opening as they pierce through the soil.

Scirpus (bulrush)
HARDY AQUATIC PERENNIALS
Soil/aspect: Standing water or permanently moist, loamy ground. Sun or shade.
Culture: Plant in late spring. Propagate by division of the rhizomes, spring.
Flowers: Insignificant.

Species/cultivars: *S. lacustris*, 1m, narrow rounded stems, deep green; invasive unless confined. *S. tabernaemontani*, similar but taller; 'Zebrinus', white and green banded stems.

Scrophularia (figwort)
HARDY FOLIAGE PERENNIALS
Soil/aspect: Ordinary, moisture-retentive. Sun or partial shade.
Culture: Plant autumn to spring. Propagate by division, spring.
Flowers: Insignificant; summer—autumn.
Species/cultivars: *S. aquatica* (*S. auriculata*) 'Variegata', 1m, square stems, toothed leaves boldly variegated with cream.

Sedum (stonecrop)
HARDY BORDER AND ROCK GARDEN PERENNIALS
Soil/aspect: Ordinary, well-drained. Sun or partial shade.
Culture: Plant autumn to spring. Propagate by division, autumn, or seed, spring.
Flowers: Star-shaped, dense heads; summer—autumn.
Species/cultivars: *S. aizoon*, 30cm, golden-yellow. *S. cauticolum*, 10-15cm, mat-forming, pink-purple. *S. kamtschaticum ellacombianum*, 20cm, deep yellow. *S. maximum* 'Atropurpureum', 80cm, robust, clump-forming, leaves dark red, flowers pink-red; 'Variegatum', cream variegations. *S. spathulifolium*, 10cm, mat-forming, tight rosettes of blue-green leaves; flowers pink; 'Cape Blanco', blue-white young leaves; 'Purpureum', purple leaves, white patina. *S. spectabile* (ice plant), 60cm, pink, wide flattened heads; 'Autumn Joy', salmon-pink; 'Iceberg', white. *S. spurium*, 10cm, mat-forming, flat pink heads; 'Coccineum', rich red; 'Erdblut', dark foliage, red flowers.

Sempervivum (houseleek)
HARDY ROSETTE-FORMING PERENNIALS
Soil/aspect: Ordinary, well-drained. Sun. Ideal for walls.
Culture: Plant autumn to spring. Propagate by division or removal of offsets, late summer or spring.
Flowers: Star-shaped; summer.
Species/cultivars: *S. arachnoideum* (cobweb houseleek), prostrate, tight spreading rosettes, often red-flushed, woven together with white hairs, flowers red. *S. tectorum*, prostrate, wide-spreading rosettes, flowers pink on 30cm stems; several hybrids with rosettes flushed or tipped with red.

Senecio
HARDY OR HALF-HARDY EVERGREEN SHRUBS
Soil/aspect: Ordinary, well-drained. Sun.
Culture: Plant in spring. Propagate by cuttings, summer; *S. bicolor* also from seed.
Flowers: Daisy-like; summer.
Species/cultivars: *S. bicolor* (*S. cineraria*) (dusty miller), 60cm, half-hardy, silvery foliage, flowers yellow, insignificant; often sold as 'White Diamond'. *S.* Dunedin hybrid 'Sunshine' (*S. greyi* or *S. laxifolius* of gardens), to 1m, leaves oval, white-felted, flowers yellow, borne abundantly; hardy in all but severest winters.

Sidalcea (Greek mallow)

HARDY HERBACEOUS PERENNIALS

Soil/aspect: Ordinary, moist. Sun.

Culture: Plant autumn to spring. Propagate by division, dormant season.

Flowers: Wide funnels, in spikes; summer.

Species/cultivars: *S. malviflora*, 120cm; several named forms with long loose spikes in shades of pink, red and white.

Silene (campion, catchfly)

HARDY ANNUALS (a) AND PERENNIALS (p)

Soil/aspect: Ordinary, well-drained. Sun.

Culture: Plant perennials autumn to spring; propagate by division or seed, spring. Sow annuals *in situ*, spring.

Flowers: Salver-shaped; early summer.

Species/cultivars: *S. acaulis* (moss campion) (p), prostrate, hummock-forming rock plant, pink. *S. armeria* (a), 40cm, pink or white clusters. *S. coeli-rosa* (*Lychnis coeli-rosa*) (a), 50cm, pink; 'Blue Pearl', lavender; 'Cardinalis', crimson; 'Oculata', pink, darker centres. *S. pendula* (a), 40cm, rose-pink; 'Compacta', 15cm. *S. schafta* (p), 15cm, deep pink, abundant, autumn.

Silybum (Our Lady's thistle)

HARDY BIENNIALS

Soil/aspect: Ordinary. Sun.

Culture: Sow seed *in situ*, spring.

Flowers: Thistle-like; late summer.

Species/cultivars: *S. marianum*, 120cm, leaves deeply lobed, green with white vein pattern; flowers red-purple.

Sisyrinchium

HARDY PERENNIALS

Soil/aspect: Humus-rich, well-drained. Sun.

Culture: Plant autumn to spring. Propagate by division or seed, spring. Protect the crowns in hard winters.

Flowers: Star-shaped; summer—autumn.

Species/cultivars: *S. bermudiana*, 30cm, leaves iris-like, flowers purple-blue. *S. brachypus* (*S. californicum brachypus*), 15cm, yellow. *S. striatum*, 30-45cm, stiffly erect, creamy-yellow flower spikes; 'Variegatum', leaves margined white.

Skimmia

HARDY EVERGREEN SHRUBS

Soil/aspect: Ordinary, well-drained. Sun or partial shade.

Culture: Plant autumn to spring. Propagate by cuttings, late summer. No pruning.

Flowers: Star-like, in clusters; spring. Attractive autumn berries.

Species/cultivars: *S. japonica*, 1m or more, compact; flowers white, followed by bright red fruit; 'Fragrans', fragrant, male; 'Rogersii', low-growing, female; 'Rubella', red in bud, male. *S. reevesiana*, to 90cm, flowers creamy-white, fruit crimson; resents limy soil.

Remarks: For fruit production, male and female plants must be grown together.

Smilacina (false Solomon's seal)

HARDY RHIZOMATOUS PERENNIALS

Soil/aspect: Humus-rich, moisture-retentive. Partial shade.

Culture: Plant autumn to spring. Propagate by division when dormant, or seed when ripe.

Flowers: Late spring.

Species/cultivars: *S. racemosa*, 90cm, erect leafy stems topped with creamy-white flower clusters.

Solidago (golden rod)

HARDY HERBACEOUS PERENNIALS

Soil/aspect: Ordinary. Sun or partial shade.

Culture: Plant autumn to spring. Propagate by division, dormant season, or seed, spring.

Flowers: Terminal plumes; late summer—autumn.

Species/cultivars: Chiefly hybrids: 'Cloth of Gold', 45cm, deep yellow; 'Crown of Rays', 60cm, bright yellow; 'Golden Thumb' ('Queenie'), 30cm, compact, yellow-green foliage, small golden-yellow spikes.

Sorbaria (false spiraea)

HARDY DECIDUOUS SHRUBS

Soil/aspect: Ordinary, moisture-retentive. Sun or partial shade.

Culture: Plant autumn to spring. Propagate by suckers or hardwood cuttings, autumn. Prune hard in spring.

Flowers: Arching plumes; late summer.

Species/cultivars: *S. aitchisonii*, 4m, leaves cut into fine leaflets, flowers white. *S. sorbifolia*, similar, but to 2m and panicles held erect.

Sorbus (rowan, whitebeam, mountain ash)

HARDY DECIDUOUS TREES

Soil/aspect: Ordinary, well-drained. Sun or light shade.

Culture: Plant autumn to spring. Propagate by seed when ripe; Cultivars by layering or grafting. No pruning.

Flowers: Hawthorn-like, white, in clusters; late spring. Attractive autumn berries.

Species/cultivars: *S. aria* (whitebeam), 10-12m, leaves silvery-green, fruit scarlet; 'Aurea', golden foliage. *S. aucuparia* (rowan), 15m, finely divided leaves, fruit scarlet; 'Aspleniifolia', fern-like foliage; 'Fastigiata', narrow, erect. *S.* 'Embley' (often sold as *S. discolor*), 10m, deeply cut leaves, fruit orange. *S. hupehensis*, 10m, foliage bluish-green, fruit white. *S. intermedia* (Swedish whitebeam), 6-9m, glossy foliage, hairy-white beneath, fruit bright red. *S.* 'Joseph Rock', 6m, toothed glossy leaflets, fruit amber-yellow. *S. reducta*, 60cm, suckering shrub, dark green shiny foliage, fruit white with pink tinge. *S. sargentiana*, 10m, conspicuous red-brown sticky buds in winter, fruit scarlet. *S. vilmorinii*, 2.5-3m, lacy foliage, red-purple in autumn; rosy fruit clusters gradually turning white.

Remarks: All have good autumn leaf colours of yellow, orange and red.

Sparaxis (harlequin flower)

HALF-HARDY PERENNIALS

Soil/aspect: Rich, well-drained. Sun. Shelter.

Culture: Plant the corms in spring. Propagate by offsets or seeds, summer. In all but mild areas, lift after flowering and store frost-free.

Flowers: Open, 6-petalled; summer.

Santolina chamaecyparissus

Schizostylis coccinea

Species/cultivars: *S. tricolor*, 30-45cm, red, purple, yellow or white, often with central contrasting and black-edged markings.

Spartium (Spanish broom)

HARDY DECIDUOUS SHRUBS

Soil/aspect: Ordinary, well-drained. Sun.

Culture: Plant in spring or autumn. Propagate by seed, spring. Trim after flowering.

Flowers: Pea-like, in spikes; summer.

Species/cultivars: *S. junceum*, 3m, bright green stems, flowers bright yellow.

Spiraea

HARDY DECIDUOUS SHRUBS

Soil/aspect: Deep, fertile. Sun or light shade.

Culture: Plant autumn to spring. Propagate by cuttings, late summer or autumn, or suckers and layering, spring. Prune spring-flowering spiraeas after flowering; summer-flowering early spring, to the ground if necessary.

Flowers: Star-shaped, in sprays or clusters; spring or summer.

Species/cultivars: *S.* x *arguta*, 2m, slender arching stems, abundant white flower clusters, late spring. *S. japonica*, 1.5m, pale pink, flattened flower heads, mid to late summer; 'Albiflora', white; 'Anthony Waterer', crimson, foliage cream and pink variegated; 'Bullata', bright crimson. *S. menziesii* 'Triumphans', to 2m, erect, flowers purple-pink in dense panicles, late summer. *S. thunbergii,* 1.5m, wide-spreading, stems slender with abundant white flowers, spring. *S. x vanhouttei,* 2m, arching stems, white flowers, summer.

Stachys
HARDY HERBACEOUS PERENNIALS
Soil/aspect: Ordinary, well-drained. Sun.
Culture: Plant autumn to spring. Propagate by division, dormant season.
Flowers: Tubular, lipped, in whorls; summer.
Species/cultivars: *S. grandiflora,* 60cm, leaves wrinkled, abundant purple-pink flower spikes. *S. olympica (S.lanata)* (lamb's ears), 30cm, mat-forming, leaves densely woolly and silvery, flowers purple; 'Silver Carpet', a non-flowering cultivar.
Remarks: Good ground cover plants.

Stephanandra
HARDY DECIDUOUS SHRUBS
Soil/aspect: Ordinary, well-drained. Sun or light shade.
Culture: Plant autumn to spring. Propagate by hardwood cuttings, autumn. Prune in spring.
Flowers: Star-shaped, in panicles; summer.
Species/cultivars: *S. incisa (S. flexuosa),* 2m, slender arching stems, leaves deeply lobed; flowers yellow-green; 'Crispa', arching stems form 90cm mounds. *S. tanakae,* 2m, arching, flowers white; leaves turn orange.

Sternbergia
HARDY BULBOUS PERENNIALS
Soil/aspect: Ordinary, well-drained. Sun.
Culture: Plant late summer—early autumn. Propagate by offsets, late summer; plants resent disturbance.
Flowers: Crocus-like; mid-autumn onwards.
Species/cultivars: *S. lutea,* 10cm, leaves dark green, strap-shaped, flowers glistening yellow.

Stipa (feather grass)
HARDY PERENNIAL GRASSES
Soil/aspect: Ordinary, well-drained. Sun.
Culture: Plant autumn to spring. Propagate by division or seed, spring.
Flowers: Feathery plumes; summer.
Species/cultivars: *S. calamagrostis,* to 1m, leaves stiffly erect, panicles fluffy, purple-fawn. *S. pennata,* 90cm, silvery panicles.

Stokesia (Stokes' aster)
HARDY EVERGREEN PERENNIALS
Soil/aspect: Ordinary, well-drained. Sun.
Culture: Plant autumn or spring. Propagate by division or seed, spring.
Flowers: Resembling cornflowers; summer—autumn.
Species/cultivars: *S. laevis,* to 60cm, lavender, blue, cream or white.

Stranvaesia
HARDY EVERGREEN SHRUBS AND SMALL TREES
Soil/aspect: Ordinary, well-drained. Sun or light shade.
Culture: Plant autumn to spring. Propagate by cuttings, late summer—autumn, seed when ripe. No pruning.

Sisyrinchium striatum

Flowers: Hawthorn-like, summer. Autumn berries.
Species/cultivars: *S. davidiana,* 6m, leaves long, narrow, opening bronze and colouring in autumn; flowers white, berries crimson.

Symphoricarpos (snowberry)
HARDY DECIDUOUS SHRUBS
Soil/aspect: Ordinary. Sun or shade.
Culture: Plant autumn to spring. Propagate by division, suckers, cuttings, autumn or spring. Prune, dormant season.
Flowers: Small clusters, summer—autumn. Glistening berries, autumn—winter.
Species/cultivars: *S. albus laevigatus, (S. rivularis),* 3m, thicket-forming, flowers pinkish-white, fruit white, abundant, *S. x chenaultii,* 1m, flowers and fruit pink, red in sun; 'Hancock' low-arching to prostrate. *S. x doorenbosii* 'Magic Berry', 1.5m, berries pink; 'White Hedge', compact, berries white.

Syringa (lilac)
HARDY DECIDUOUS SHRUBS
Soil/aspect: Ordinary, Sun or partial shade.
Culture: Plant autumn to spring. Propagate by cuttings, late summer—autumn, species also by suckers or seeds in spring. Dead-head after flowering. Prune, dormant season.
Flowers: Erect panicles; early summer.
Species/cultivars: *S. microphylla,* 1.5m, shrubby, pink-lilac, fragrant; 'Superba', rose-pink, long flowering season. *S. x persica,* 2m, lilac, fragrant; 'Alba', white. *S. x prestoniae,* 3m, arching or pendent panicles; 'Isabella', pink-purple, erect; 'Royalty', violet-purple. *S. reflexa,* 3-4m, pendent, pink, opening white. *S. velutina (S. palibiniana),* 1.5m, slow-growing, lilac-pink. *S. vulgaris,* 3-6m, panicles erect, fragrant. Numerous cultivars include 'Charles Joly', purple-red, double; 'Congo', lilac-red, single; 'Madame Lemoine', cream buds opening white, double; 'Mont Blanc', white, single; 'President Grevy', lilac-blue, double; 'Primrose', pale yellow, single; 'Souvenir de Louis Spaeth', purple-red, single.

Tagetes (African and French marigolds)
HALF-HARDY ANNUALS
Soil/aspect: Ordinary, Sun.

Culture: Sow in spring under glass, plant out when fear of frost is past.
Flowers: Daisy, ball or pompon-like; summer—autumn.
Species/cultivars: *T. erecta* (African marigold), 90cm, branching, dissected leaves, flowers single or double, in shades of yellow and orange; dwarf forms also available. *T. patula* (French marigold), 30cm, bushy, yellow, orange or bronze, often bicoloured; dwarfs, 15-23cm. *T. tenuifolia pumila,* 20cm, yellow or orange.

Tamarix (tamarisk)
HARDY DECIDUOUS SHRUBS
Soil/aspect: Ordinary, well-drained. Sun.
Culture: Plant autumn to spring. Propagate by cuttings, late summer—autumn. Prune dormant season.
Flowers: Plume-like, fluffy clusters; summer.
Species/cultivars: *T. gallica,* 3-4m, pink.
Remarks: Good for seaside planting.

Tanacetum (tansy)
HARDY PERENNIALS
Soil/aspect: Ordinary, well-drained. Sun.
Culture: Plant autumn or spring. Propagate by division, spring, or cuttings of non-flowering stems, late summer.
Flowers: Button-like; late summer.
Species/cultivars: *T. haradjanii (T. densum* 'Amani'), 15cm, grey-green evergreen leaves finely cut and woolly; flowers small, yellow; excellent ground cover.

Taxus (yew)
HARDY EVERGREEN CONIFEROUS TREES
Soil/aspect: Ordinary. Sun or shade.
Culture: Plant autumn or spring. Propagate by cuttings, autumn, or seed when ripe. No pruning.
Flowers: Insignificant; small soft-fleshed red fruit.
Species/cultivars: *T. baccata,* to 10m, broad-headed, foliage dark green, flat sprays; 'Adpressa', wide-spreading; 'Adpressa Aurea', young foliage golden; 'Fastigiata' (Irish yew), the familiar erect churchyard yew; 'Fastigiata Aureo-Marginata', golden-edged foliage; 'Standishii', slow-growing, columnar, foliage golden.
Remarks: All parts except flesh of fruits poisonous.

Tellima
HARDY EVERGREEN PERENNIALS
Soil/aspect: Ordinary, Shade or sun.
Culture: Plant autumn to spring. Propagate by division or seed, spring.
Flowers: Bell-shaped, in spikes; late spring—summer.
Species/cultivars: *T. grandiflora,* low-growing to prostrate, leaves bright green, toothed; flowers palest green on stems to 60cm; 'Purpurea', leaves tinged purple-red in winter, flowers pink-flushed.
Remarks: Excellent ground cover for shade.

Thalictrum (meadow rue)
HARDY HERBACEOUS PERENNIALS
Soil/aspect: Rich, moist; sun or partial shade, borders or rock gardens.

Sparaxis tricolor cultivar

flowers pink; 'Aureus', leaves golden-yellow; 'Argenteus', silver-variegated. *T. drucei, (T. serpyllum* of gardens), prostrate, foliage dark green, conspicuous purple flowers; 'Albus' white; 'Coccineus', crimson.
Remarks: See also Thyme, page 233.

Tiarella (foam flower)
HARDY EVERGREEN PERENNIALS
Soil/aspect: Neutral to acid, moisture-retentive. Partial shade.
Culture: Plant autumn or spring. Propagate by division or seed, spring.
Flowers: Erect, loose spikes; late spring—summer.
Species/cultivars: *T. cordifolia,* 15-30cm, pale pink, fluffy; spreads by surface runners. *T. wherryi,* similar but compact.
Remarks: Good ground-cover plants for shade.

Tigridia (tiger flower)
HALF-HARDY BULBOUS PERENNIALS
Soil/aspect: Humus-rich, well-drained. Sun.
Culture: Plant spring. Propagate by offsets or seed, spring. Best lifted in autumn and overwintered frost-free.
Flowers: Six-petalled, exotic; summer.
Species/cultivars: *T. pavonia,* 45-60cm, leaves narrow and pleated; named cultivars available in brilliant colours, including red, yellow, purple and white.

Tilia (lime)
HARDY DECIDUOUS TREES
Soil/aspect: Ordinary, moisture-retentive. Sun or partial shade.
Culture: Plant autumn to spring. Propagate by layering, late winter, or seed when ripe.
Flowers: White to yellowish, fragrant clusters; summer.
Species/cultivars: *T. x euchlora,* to 15m, leaves, deep green, turn gold in autumn; largely resistant to aphids. *T. petiolaris* (silver lime), 9m, pendent branchlets, leaves long-stalked, silvery beneath. *T. platyphyllos,* 7-9m, leaves broadly heart-shaped, downy beneath.
Remarks: Some species prone to aphid infestation, resulting in sticky honeydew.

Torenia (wishbone flower)
HALF-HARDY ANNUALS
Soil/aspect: Ordinary, moisture-retentive. Partial shade.
Culture: Sow under glass in spring. Plant out when fear of frost is past.
Flowers: Like musk flowers (*Mimulus*); summer—autumn.
Species/cultivars: *T. fournieri,* 30cm, clusters of pale lilac flowers; 'Grandiflora', large-flowered.

Tradescantia (spiderwort)
HARDY HERBACEOUS PERENNIALS
Soil/aspect: Ordinary, well-drained. Sun or partial shade.
Culture: Plant autumn to spring. Propagate by division or seed (species only), spring.
Flowers: Open, three-petalled; summer—autumn.
Species/cultivars: *T. x andersoniana (T.*

Sternbergia lutea

virginiana), 60cm, clump-forming; 'Osprey', white, blue centres; 'Purple Dome', rich purple; 'Rubra', deep red.

Trillium (wood lily)
HARDY HERBACEOUS PERENNIALS
Soil/aspect: Humus-rich, moist but well-drained. Partial shade.
Culture: Plant dormant rhizomes late summer—late autumn. Propagate by division, autumn or winter.
Flowers: Three-petalled, large; late spring.
Species/cultivars: *T. grandiflorum* (wake robin), 45cm, leaves oval, large, flowers glistening white, ageing pinkish.

Trollius (globe flower)
HARDY HERBACEOUS PERENNIALS
Soil/aspect: Ordinary, moisture-retentive. Sun or partial shade.
Culture: Plant autumn or early spring. Propagate by division or seed, autumn or spring.
Flowers: Large buttercups; summer.
Species/cultivars: *T. x hybridus,* 30-75cm, deeply dissected foliage; 'Earliest of all', pale yellow, late spring; 'Golden Queen', golden-yellow, semi-double; 'Orange Princess', orange-yellow; 'Superbus', lemon-yellow.

Tropaeolum (nasturtium)
HARDY ANNUAL (a) AND PERENNIAL (p) CLIMBERS
Soil/aspect: Ordinary, well-drained. Sun.
Culture: Plant perennials in spring; propagate by division when dormant or seed, spring. Sow annuals *in situ,* late spring.
Flowers: Trumpet-shaped; summer—autumn.
Species/cultivars: *T. majus* (a), 2m or more, leaves rounded, flowers long-spurred, single or double, in shades of scarlet, orange and yellow; dwarf trailing forms also available. *T. peregrinum (T. canariense)* Canary creeper (a), 5m, leaves deeply lobed, flowers yellow, fringed. *T. speciosum* (p), 3-4m, pale green, 6-lobed leaves, flowers brilliant scarlet; needs moist acid soil and shade.

Tsuga (hemlock)
HARDY EVERGREEN CONIFEROUS TREES
Soil/aspect: Ordinary, loamy. Sun or shade.

Culture: Plant autumn to spring. Propagate by division, basal cuttings or seed, spring.
Flowers: Fluffy balls, loose sprays; summer.
Species/cultivars: *T. aquilegifolium,* to 90cm, leaves dissected, flowers lilac and white. *T. dipterocarpum (T. delavayi),* 1.5m, lilac; 'Hewitt's Double', fully double. *T. kiusianum,* 7-15cm, pink-purple. *T. speciosissimum (T. flavum glaucum),* 1.5m, pale yellow.

Thermopsis
HARDY RHIZOMATOUS PERENNIALS
Soil/aspect: Ordinary, well-drained. Sun.
Culture: Plant autumn to spring. Propagate by division or seed, spring.
Flowers: Lupin-like; summer.
Species/cultivars: *T. montana,* 60cm, golden-yellow spikes.

Thuja (arbor-vitae)
HARDY EVERGREEN CONIFEROUS TREES
Soil/aspect: Deep, moist. Sun or light shade.
Culture: Plant autumn or spring. Propagate by cuttings, autumn, or seed, spring. No pruning.
Flowers: Insignificant; small, rounded, erect cones.
Species/cultivars: *T. occidentalis.* 10m, slow-growing, dense, drooping foliage sprays; dwarf forms include 'Rheingold', 90cm, foliage golden-bronze; 'Woodwardii', 1m, rounded bush, green. *T. orientalis,* 6m, conical when young, foliage turns bronze in winter; 'Aurea Nana', 75cm, golden-green; 'Elegantissima', 3m, erect, yellow in summer, bronze in winter; 'Rosedalis', 80cm, young foliage fluffy yellow, sea-green in summer, purple in winter. *T. plicata,* 15m or more, conical habit; 'Rogersii', 1.2m, conical bush, golden-bronze; 'Zebrina', 15m, golden-green.

Thymus (thyme)
HARDY EVERGREEN AROMATIC SUB-SHRUBS
Soil/aspect: Ordinary, well-drained. Sun.
Culture: Plant autumn to spring. Propagate by division or cuttings, summer.
Flowers: Small clusters; summer.
Species/cultivars: *T. x citriodorus* (lemon thyme), to 30cm, leaves lemon-scented,

Culture: Plant autumn to spring, using young plants. Propagate species by seed in spring, cultivars by cuttings, autumn. No pruning; trim hedges late summer.
Species/cultivars: *T. canadensis,* to 10m or more, dark green needle-like, flat foliage; dwarf cultivars infrequently available. *T. heterophylla,* 18m, conical habit, drooping foliage, dark green, white-banded beneath.
Remarks: Excellent specimen and hedging trees, deserving wider use.

Tulipa (tulip)
HARDY BULBOUS PERENNIALS
Soil/aspect: Ordinary, alkaline, well-drained. Sun.
Culture: Plant late autumn. Propagate from offsets, autumn.
Flowers: Goblets; late spring—early summer.
Species/cultivars: Garden tulips are listed in the following groups:
1. Single Early, 15-40cm, for garden use or indoor forcing. 2. Double Early, 25-35cm. 3. Mendel, 40-50cm, single, April-May. 4. Triumph, 50cm, single, April. 5. Darwin Hybrids, 50-70cm, single, the largest flowered tulips, April-May. 6. Darwin, 55-75cm, single, deep cup shapes, almost square at base, May. 7. Lily-flowered, 45-60cm, single, petal-tips pointed and spreading, April. 8. Cottage, 35-75cm, single, April-May. 9. Rembrandt, like Darwin tulips but flower colours streaked or broken. 10. Parrot, 40-60cm, single, bicoloured and fringed, April-May. 11. Double Late, 40-70cm, paeony-like, April. 12. *T. kaufmanniana* hybrids, 20cm, water-lily blooms, opening flat, bicoloured in shades of yellow and red, March-April. 13. *T. fosteriana* hybrids, 25-45cm, shallow cup shapes, bright yellow, scarlet or white, April. 14. *T. greigii* hybrids, 20-30cm, leaves marbled or striped purple, flowers shades of red and yellow, early April. 15. True species; several readily available and suitable for rock gardens.
Remarks: Most tulips benefit from lifting and replanting every 2-3 years.

Typha (reedmace)
HARDY AQUATIC PERENNIALS
Soil/aspect: Water, or permanently moist, loamy ground. Sun or partial shade.
Culture: Plant the rhizomes in spring. Propagate by division, late spring.
Flowers: Brown, velvety cylindrical heads; summer.
Species/cultivars: *T. angustifolia,* 3m, leaves narrow, strap-shaped and rush-like. *T. latifolia,* 2.5m, leaves wider, yellow to glaucous-green. *T. minima,* 30-75cm, similar to *T. latifolia,* but smaller, with ovoid flower heads.
Remarks: Usually invasive; *T. minima* recommended for small pools.

Ulex (gorse, furze, whin)
HARDY EVERGREEN SPINY SHRUBS
Soil/aspect: Poor to ordinary, well-drained. Sun.
Culture: Plant autumn to spring. Propagate by seed, spring, or cuttings, late summer. If necessary, prune hard, early spring.

Flowers: Pea-like; spring—summer.
Species/cultivars: *U. europaeus,* 2m, leaves scale-like, falling, flowers bright yellow, fragrant; 'Plenus', double.

Ursinia
HALF-HARDY ANNUALS
Soil/aspect: Light, well-drained. Sun.
Culture: Sow under glass; plant out after frost is past.
Flowers: Daisy-like; summer.
Species/cultivars: *U. anethoides,* 60cm, bright yellow, purple bases. *U.speciosa,* 30-40cm, white to orange-yellow, centres yellow.

Valeriana (valerian)
HARDY HERBACEOUS PERENNIALS
Soil/aspect: Ordinary, well-drained. Sun or partial shade.
Culture: Plant autumn to spring. Propagate by division, dormant season, or seed, spring.
Flowers: Small, in clusters; summer.
Species/cultivars: *V. montana,* 10-15cm, flower heads compact, pale pink or white. *V.phu* 'Aurea', 90cm, young leaves bright yellow, flowers white.

Venidium
HALF-HARDY ANNUALS
Soil/aspect: Humus-rich, well-drained. Sun.
Culture: Sow under glass. Plant out when fear of frost is past.
Flowers: Daisy-like; summer—autumn.
Species/cultivars: *V. fastuosum* (monarch of the veldt), 60-90cm, foliage grey-green, flowers golden-yellow, dark centres; 'Art Shades', orange to cream and white.

Veratrum (false hellebore)
HARDY HERBACEOUS PERENNIALS
Soil/aspect: Ordinary, moisture-retentive. Partial shade.
Culture: Plant autumn or spring. Propagate by division or seed, spring.
Flowers: Massed plumes; summer.
Species/cultivars: *V. album,* 1.5m, flowers pale green in branched spikes. *V. nigrum,* similar, with dark red flowers.

Verbascum (mullein)
HARDY BIENNIALS (b) AND PERENNIALS (p)
Soil/aspect: Ordinary, well-drained. Sun.
Culture: Plant autumn or spring. Propagate by seed, perennials also by division, spring.
Flowers: Dense, tall spikes; summer.
Species/cultivars: *V. bombyciferum* (*V.* 'Broussa'), to 2m (b), basal leaves broad, silky; erect, woolly stems, flowers yellow. *V. phoeniceum* (p), 1m, basal leaves dark green, flowers purple; 'Bridal Bouquet', white; 'Gainsborough', yellow.

Verbena
HARDY OR HALF-HARDY PERENNIALS
Soil/aspect: Humus-rich, moist but well-drained. Sun.
Culture: Usually grown as annuals. Plant in spring. Propagate by seed under glass late winter/spring, or late spring cuttings.
Flowers: Primrose-like, in clusters; summer—autumn.

Verbena x *hybrida*

Species/cultivars: *V. bonariensis,* to 1.5m, purple. *V.* x *hybrida,* 15-30cm, shades or mixtures of red, purple and white. *V. rigida* (*V. venosa*), 60cm, foliage greyish-green, flowers purple to red. *V.tenera,* 15cm, mat-forming, almost hardy, rosy-purple; 'Mahonettii', white-edged; 'Sissinghurst', rich magenta.

Veronica (speedwell)
HARDY PERENNIALS
Soil/aspect: Ordinary, well-drained. Sun.
Culture: Plant autumn to spring. Propagate by division or seed, spring.
Flowers: Spikes; summer—autumn.
Species/cultivars: *V. cinerea,* 15cm, mat-forming evergreen, leaves silver-grey, flowers pale-blue. *V. gentianoides,* 30-40cm, rhizomatous, mat-forming, blue; 'Variegata', white-edged foliage. *V. longifolia,* 1.2m, lilac-blue; 'Foerster's Blue', deep blue. *V. pectinata,* prostrate, mat-forming, blue; 'Rosea', pink. *V. spicata,* 30-60cm, dense, erect blue spikes; 'Barcarolle', pink; 'Crater Lake Blue', deep blue; 'Snow White', pure white.

Viburnum
HARDY EVERGREEN (e) AND DECIDUOUS (d) SHRUBS
Soil/aspect: Ordinary, moist but well-drained. Sun.
Culture: Plant autumn or spring. Propagate by layering, winter; cuttings, late summer, or seed when ripe (often slow to germinate).

Prune evergreens late spring, winter-flowering deciduous shrubs in April, summer-flowering, June.
Flowers: Clusters, spring—autumn. Attractive autumn berries.
Species/cultivars: *V.* x *bodnantense* (d), to 4m, pale pink, winter. *V.* x *burkwoodii* (semi-e), 2m or more on a wall, leaves glossy green, flowers white, fragrant, early spring. *V.* x *carlcephalum* (d), 2.5m, vigorous, flowers fragrant, creamy, pink-tinted, late spring. *V. davidii* (e), 1m, good ground cover, flowers white, early summer; male and female plants needed for bright blue fruit. *V. farreri* (*V. fragrans*) (d), 3m, young leaves bronze-tinted, flowers fragrant, pink-flushed white, winter. *V. opulus* (guelder rose) (d), 4m, leaves maple-like, large sterile flowers surround fertile florets, creamy, scented, early summer; fruits red, glossy; 'Sterile' (snowball bush), globular heads of all-sterile flowers, no fruit; 'Fructuluteo' ('Xanthocarpum'), fruit yellow. *V. plicatum tomentosum* (d), 3m, flowers like *V. opulus*, but smaller, fruit red becoming black; 'Mariesii', branches in tiers. *V. tinus* (laurustinus) (e), 3m, leaves glossy-green; flowers pink-white, late autumn—spring; fruit blue.

Vinca (periwinkle)
HARDY EVERGREEN PERENNIALS
Soil/aspect: Ordinary, well-drained. Partial shade.
Culture: Plant autumn to spring. Propagate

by division, rooted runners or cuttings, late summer.
Flowers: Tubular; spring—summer.
Species/cultivars: *V. major,* prostrate to 30cm, purple-blue; 'Variegata' ('Elegantissima'), creamy-white leaf variegations. *V. minor,* prostrate, bright to purple-blue; 'Alba', white; 'Aureo-variegata Alba', yellow leaf variegations.
Remarks: Excellent for dense ground cover.

Viola (pansy, violet)
HARDY ANNUALS (a) AND PERENNIALS (p)
Soil/aspect: Ordinary, well-drained. Partial shade for violets, sun for pansies.
Culture: Plant autumn or spring. Propagate by seed or division, spring or after flowering; basal cuttings, late summer. Sow annuals under glass or *in situ,* spring.
Flowers: Five-petalled open faces; spring—summer—autumn—winter.
Species/cultivars: *V. cornuta* (p), 10-20cm, lilac-purple violets, abundant, summer; 'Alba', white. *V. labradorica* 'Purpurea' (p), 10cm, leaves flushed deep purple, violet flowers light purple. *V. odorata* (sweet violet) (p), 10-15cm, mat-forming, violet, fragrant; 'Alba', white; 'Coeur d'Alsace', deep pink; 'The Czar', deep violet, large. Garden hybrids listed as *V.* x *wittrockiana* and *V.* x *williamsii* are the familiar pansies (a) in self or bicolours; 15-25cm, flowers large; sold as named or mixed cultivars for flowering spring—autumn or winter.

Vitis (vine)
HARDY DECIDUOUS CLIMBERS
Soil/aspect: Humus-rich, neutral to alkaline, moisture-retentive. Sun or partial shade.
Culture: Plant autumn to spring. Propagate by cuttings, late summer, or seed, early spring. Thin out early autumn.
Flowers: Inconspicuous; late spring. Fruit grape-like; autumn.
Species/cultivars: *V.* x 'Brant', 9m, strong-growing, leaves deeply lobed, purple and red in autumn, fruit small, black, aromatic and edible. *V. coignetiae,* 20m or more, very vigorous, leaves brilliant red in autumn, fruit black, inedible. *V. vinifera* 'Purpurea', 6m, young leaves deep red, maturing purple, fruit purple-black, edible.
Remarks: Need strong supports on walls.

Waldsteinia
HARDY EVERGREEN PERENNIALS
Soil/aspect: Ordinary to rich, moist but well-drained. Sun or shade.
Culture: Plant autumn to spring. Propagate by division, spring.
Flowers: Strawberry-like; spring—summer.
Species/cultivars: *W. ternata,* 10cm, mat-forming, leaves three-lobed, glossy green, flowers bright yellow.
Remarks: Excellent ground-cover plants.

Weigela
HARDY DECIDUOUS SHRUBS
Soil/aspect: Ordinary, well-drained. Sun.
Culture: Plant autumn to spring. Propagate by cuttings, summer or autumn. Prune hard after flowering.

Flowers: Tubular, in clusters; summer.
Species/cultivars: Garden hybrids derived from *W. florida,* 3m, vigorous, arching stems; 'Avalanche', white; 'Bristol Ruby', ruby-red; 'Fleur de Mai', salmon-pink; 'Foliis Purpureis', 1.5m, rose-pink, foliage purple; 'Looymansii Aurea', rose-pink, leaves golden-yellow; 'Variegata', pink, leaves cream-margined.

Wisteria
HARDY DECIDUOUS CLIMBERS
Soil/aspect: Deep, ordinary to rich, moisture-retentive. Sun.
Culture: Plant autumn to spring. Propagate by layering, spring, or cuttings, late summer. Prune hard, late winter and again after flowering. Strong supports necessary.
Flowers: Long pendulous racemes; late spring—early summer.
Species/cultivars: *W. floribunda,* to 10m, leaves deeply dissected, flowers purple; 'Alba', white; 'Macrobotrys', blue-purple racemes to 90cm. *W. sinensis,* to 20m, leaves with fewer leaflets, flower racemes lilac.

Yucca (Adam's needle)
HARDY EVERGREEN SHRUBS
Soil/aspect: Ordinary, well-drained. Sun. Shelter.
Culture: Plant autumn or spring. Propagate by suckers, spring. No pruning.
Flowers: Bell-shaped, in large branched plumes; late summer—autumn.
Species/cultivars: *Y. gloriosa,* 2m, leaves dark green, narrow and stiff, erect when young, arching with age, flowers abundant, white. *Y. recurvifolia,* similar, leaves softer and arching, flower spikes less dense; 'Variegata', yellow central stripes to leaves.

Zantedeschia (arum lily)
HALF-HARDY HERBACEOUS PERENNIALS
Soil/aspect: Permanently moist loam or water depth to 30cm. Sun.
Culture: Plant spring. Propagate by division of rhizomes or offsets, spring.
Flowers: Large spathes; summer.
Species/cultivars: *Z. aethiopica,* to 90cm, leaves glossy, arrow-shaped; long-stalked, pure white spathes; 'Crowborough', shorter and reputedly hardier.
Remarks: In moist ground winter-mulch with bark, peat or leaves.

Zinnia
HALF-HARDY ANNUALS
Soil/aspect: Ordinary to rich, well-drained. Sun.
Culture: Sow in spring under glass. Prick off while small; plant out when fear of frost is past.
Flowers: Daisy or ball-shaped; summer—autumn.
Species/cultivars: *Z. elegans,* 60cm, sparsely branched; rounded flower heads, large and solitary; strains available in shades of red, yellow and white, usually listed as California Giants, Dahlia-flowered and Ruffles. *Z. angustifolia* (*Z. haageana*), 45cm, bushy, daisy flowers small but numerous, red, yellow or bicoloured, single or double.

THE KITCHEN GARDEN 1

Espalier-trained apple (in blossom)

FRUIT & BERRIES

Apple

Soil/aspect: Humus-enriched, well-drained. Sun.

Culture: Plant dormant season; stake first 1-2 years. Set at these distances: Cordons, 1m, at angle of 45° with post and wire support; dwarf pyramids, 1.2-1.5m; dwarf bush, 3.5m; espaliers, 4m; fans, 4-5m. Apply general fertiliser or organic mulch annually, spring.

Propagation: Bud grafting on Malling-Merton root-stocks.

Pruning: Trained bush and standard trees: thin out 2 and 3-year old shoots annually. Espaliers and cordons: cut current season's growth back to 3 leaves above the basal leaf clusters, summer; cut secondary growth back to 1 leaf in autumn.

Cultivars: Heavier crops can be expected if 2 or more cultivars are planted together for pollination purposes; choose those that flower at the same times. The following all flower at mid-season.

Dessert cultivars: 'Ellison's Orange', mid-autumn — early winter; 'Cox's Orange Pippin', early winter — spring; 'Laxton's Fortune', mid-autumn — early winter; 'Laxton's Superb', early winter — mid-spring; 'Merton Charm', mid — late autumn; 'Merton Worcester', mid-autumn — early winter; 'Tydeman's Early', early — mid-autumn.

Culinary cultivars: 'Bramley's Seedling', late autumn — late spring; 'Lane's Prince Albert', early winter — late spring; 'Lord Derby', winter.

Remarks: Trained trees - cordons, dwarf bush, dwarf pyramids, espaliers, fans - are the most suitable for garden use.

Apricot

Soil/aspect: Loamy, alkaline, well-drained. Sun. Shelter.

Culture: Plant dormant season; best as fans against walls. Stake bush and half-standard trees in the open for first 1-2 years. Apply general fertiliser or organic mulch annually, spring.

Propagation: Budding on plum root-stocks.

Pruning: Bush and standard trees: thin out excess growth, dead and weak stems, winter.

On fans, pinch current season's shoots back to 8-10cm, mid-summer.

Cultivars: 'Alfred', golden-orange, early autumn; 'Early Moorpark', orange-yellow, late summer; 'Moorpark', brownish-orange, early autumn.

Remarks: Apricots flower late winter and need a site sheltered from frost; good summers necessary for fruit to ripen.

Blackberry

Soil/aspect: Ordinary, humus-enriched. Sun or shade.

Culture: Plant dormant season, 3-4m apart, against post and wire supports. After harvesting, cut out fruited canes at ground level and tie in young canes in their place. Apply organic mulch, autumn, general fertiliser annually in spring.

Propagation: By tip-layering, early autumn.

Cultivars: 'Himalaya Giant', 'Merton Thornless', 'Oregon Thornless'.

Blueberry

Soil/aspect: Acid, moisture-retentive. Sun or partial shade.

Blackberry 'Oregon Thornless'

Blueberry 'Ivanhoe'

Wall-trained fig

Culture: Plant dormant season, 1.2-1.4m apart. Remove old twiggy branches at ground level on mature bushes, winter. Mulch with peat or straw, autumn; apply nitrogen fertiliser, spring. Water freely in dry spells.
Propagation: By layering, spring.
Cultivars: 'Berkeley', 'Bluecrop', 'Herbert', 'Ivanhoe', 'Jersey'.
Remarks: Heavier crops are borne if two or more cultivars are grown together.

Cherry

Soil/aspect: Fertile, preferably limy; well-drained. Sun or shade.
Culture: Plant dormant season, sweet cherries 7-10m apart, sour 4-5m. Stake standards for the first 1-2 years. Mulch annually, autumn, with organic matter. Give an annual spring dressing of sulphate of potash; every third year apply superphosphate. Sour cherries growing poorly should be dressed with sulphate of ammonia, spring.
Propagation: By bud grafting in summer, ideally on root-stock of the virus-tested Malling F12/1.
Pruning: On sweet cherries cut out dead,

misplaced or congested stems. Sour cherries need annual thinning of 3-4 year old branchlets. Prune both types in spring or summer and protect all wounds with a sealing compound.
Cultivars: Sour cherries are self-fertile and solitary specimens set acceptable crops: 'Flemish Red' and 'Morello'. Sweet cherries: 'Merton Glory' will pollinate 'Early Rivers', 'Merton Bigarreau', 'Merton Favourite' and 'Waterloo'. 'Bigarreau Napoleon' will pollinate 'Bradbourne Black', 'Florence' and 'Roundel Heart'. 'Stella' is a self-fertile cultivar.

Currants (black, red and white)

Soil/aspect: Humus-rich, moisture-retentive. Sun or light shade.
Culture: Black currants: plant 1.5-2m apart, dormant season; cut back all stems to 2 buds above soil level at planting time. Subsequently thin out 2 and 3 year old fruiting stems annually after harvesting to encourage strong new basal stems.

Red and white currants: plant 1.5m apart, dormant season; train as bushes on

single main stem. In summer cut back all but leading leafy shoots to 5 leaves; in winter shorten tall shoots by half and summer-pruned stems to 1 bud above basal fruit-bud clusters. Water currants during dry spells and mulch with organic matter in autumn; apply general fertiliser in spring.
Propagation: All currants by hardwood cuttings, autumn, removing lower buds on red and white currants.
Cultivars: Black currant (early): 'Boskoop Giant', 'Laxton's Giant', 'Mendip Cross'; (mid-season): 'Blacksmith', 'Wellington XXX'; (late): 'Amos Black', 'Baldwin', 'Westwick Choice'.

Red currant (early): 'Earliest of Fourlands', 'Laxton's No.1'; (mid-season): 'Perfection', 'Red Lake'; (late): 'Raby Castle', 'Wilson's Longbunch'. White currant: 'White Versailles' (early), 'White Dutch', (mid-season).

Fig

Soil/aspect: Ordinary, well-drained. Sunny, sheltered wall essential.
Culture: Plant spring, 5-7m apart, as fans

THE KITCHEN GARDEN 2

Loganberries

Cantaloupe melons

secured to wall wires. Restrict root growth by lining planting hole with asbestos sheeting. Apply bone-meal before planting and annually in spring. Water throughly in dry weather. Prune in summer, pinching back all strong shoots to 4-6 leaves. Remove congested, misplaced and frosted shoots at base, late spring.

Propagation: Hardwood cuttings, late autumn.

Cultivars: 'Black Ischia', 'Brown Turkey', 'White Marseilles'.

Gooseberry
Soil/aspect: Rich, moisture-retentive. Sun or light shade.

Culture: Set 1-2 year old plants 1.5m apart, autumn. Train as bushes with single main stem or on the cordon system. On bushes, prune all new shoots back by half, spring, for the first 4 years; thereafter thin out as necessary. Spur-prune cordons, spring, by reducing side shoots to 5cm of the base and leading shoots by half. Thin fruits on both types to 2cm apart, late spring. Mulch with straw, early summer, bulky manure in autumn; feed with bone-meal in spring.

Propagation: By hardwood cuttings, late autumn; remove all buds on sections of stems buried in soil.

Cultivars: 'Golden Drop' (mid-season), 'Green Gem' (late), 'Keepsake' (late), 'Langley Gage' (mid-season), 'Leveller' (mid-season), 'Whinham's Industry' (mid-season) and 'White Lion' (late); all dessert types. Culinary gooseberries include dessert types picked immature and 'Bedford Red' (mid-season), 'Careless' (early) and 'Lancashire Lad' (mid-season).

Grape
Soil/aspect: Fertile, sandy and well-drained. Sun. Shelter, best on walls, or south-facing slopes with cloche protection for ripening.

Culture: Plant spring, 2m apart, or up to 5m if grown as wall fans. Supports of posts and galvanised wires essential. Mulch with manure or other organic matter annually in autumn; apply a general fertiliser early each spring. Water wall specimens during dry spells. Allow each lateral to bear one bunch of grapes only and thin out individual berries as bunches develop, using grape scissors and handling the bunches as little as possible.

Propagation: Bud cuttings under glass, late winter, or hardwood cuttings *in situ,* autumn.

Pruning: Cut back current season's growth to 2 buds on all main stems, late autumn. Rampant summer growth can be tipped or thinned as necessary.

Cultivars: (wall-trained): 'Brant', 'Chasselas 1921', 'Muscat Queen' and 'Schuyler'; open ground culture: 'Müller-Thurgau', 'Muscat de Saumur', 'Noir Hâtif de Marseille', 'Riesling Sylvaner', 'Seyve-Villard 5-276' and 'Siegerrebe'.

Loganberry
Soil/aspect: Ordinary, well-drained; not for shallow or sandy soils. Sun; shelter from cold north and east winds.

Culture: Plant dormant season, 2.5-3.5m apart. Train as fans against posts and wires. Prune newly planted bushes back to 15cm above ground, early spring. Mulch with straw, late spring, and with rotted manure, autumn. Apply general fertiliser annually, early spring. After harvesting, cut out fruited canes at soil level; tie in replacement canes.

Propagation: By tip layering, late summer.

Cultivars: 'LY 59' and 'Thornless'; buy plants certified to be free of cane spot virus.

Melon
Soil/aspect: Humus-rich, well-drained but moisture-retentive. Sun. Very sheltered, preferably under cloches or frames.

Culture: Sow singly in small pots at 24-26°C, spring. Plant out, after applying general fertiliser, early to mid-summer, 1m apart. Water freely during dry spells. Pinch out tips of young plants at 5 leaves to encourage branching. Hand pollination necessary for plants under glass; when at least 6 flowers are open pollinate all at the same time so that fruits develop evenly.

Cultivars: 'Ogen' (green flesh), 'Sweetheart' (scarlet), 'Tiger' (orange); all are cantaloupe melons, the most suitable types for frame and cloche cultivation.

Remarks: Warm summers necessary for successful cultivation in the open; best grown under glass protection or in greenhouse.

Peach

Soil/aspect: Fertile, well-drained. Sun. Best fan-trained on sheltered walls.

Culture: Plant dormant season, 5m apart. Bush and half-standards need staking for first year; train fans on permanent wall supports of vine eyes and galvanised wire. Mulch annually, early summer, with rotted manure or compost; apply general fertiliser, spring.

Propagation: By bud-grafting, summer, on to cherry plum or seedling peach root-stock.

Pruning: Fruits are borne on 1-year old spurs; when fruitlets are visible, select one shoot below fruit on each lateral, and one above; remove the remainder. Thin fruits to 1 in each cluster, and finally to 20-25cm spacings. After harvesting, cut back fruited shoots to just above the base. On fan-trained trees, tie these to wires. Thin out congested shoots in summer.

Cultivars: 'Duke of York', 'Bellegarde', 'Hale's Early', 'Peregrine' and 'Rochester'.

Pear

Soil/aspect: Deep, fertile; moisture-retentive. Sun. Shelter.

Culture: Plant dormant season; bush and pyramid trees 3.5m apart, standards 4m, cordons 1m, espalier trees on walls or fences 4.5m apart. Stake all firmly until established. Mulch annually with organic manure, spring; feed with sulphate of ammonia, early spring. Many pears are self-sterile, and a pollinator must be provided with another variety.

Propagation: Budding in summer or grafting in late winter, on to quince root-stock.

Pruning: Little maintenance pruning necessary; thin out congested older shoots on bush and standard trees, summer. On espaliers and cordons, cut current season's growth back to 3 leaves above basal leaf cluster, summer, and secondary laterals back to 1 leaf, autumn. Thin fruits to 15-20cm apart.

Cultivars: Most pears ripen off trees and should be picked before they are ready for use. Summer maturing (pick early to mid-autumn): 'Clapp's Favourite', 'Dr. Jules Guyot', 'Fertility' (self-fertile, autumn-coloured foliage), 'Merton Pride', 'William's Bon Chrétien'; late autumn-maturing (pick mid-autumn): 'Beurré Hardy', 'Bristol Cross', 'Conference', 'Doyenné du Comice', 'Louise Bonne of Jersey'; winter-maturing (pick late autumn): 'Joséphine de Malines', 'Winter Nelis'. Cooking cultivars: 'Pitmaston Duchess', 'Catillac'.

Plum

Soil/aspect: Ordinary, fertile; moisture-retentive, but well-drained. Sun. Shelter from spring frosts.

Culture: Plant dormant season; dwarf pyramids 3-4m apart, bush trees and fans 4-5m, half-standards 5.5-6.5m, and standards 7-8m. Apply general fertiliser at plan-

Fan-trained 'Rochester' peach

Strawberry 'Cambridge Vigour'

ting time and annually in spring; mulch with organic matter, late spring.

Propagation: By budding, summer, or grafting, late winter, on to Myrobalan B and St. Julien A root-stocks. Cultivars known to be on own roots can be increased by suckers; greengages come fairly true to type from seed but are slow to reach fruiting stage.

Pruning: Little routine pruning required other than thinning congested branches in summer. Prune fan-trained trees, pinching current season's lateral shoots back to 5 leaves in summer. Thin fruits to 8cm apart.

Cultivars: Two cultivars grown together ensure heavier crops; some are self-sterile and set little or no fruit without a pollinator. Culinary (late summer-maturing): 'Czar', 'Pershore' ('Yellow Egg'); dessert: 'Victoria', all self-fertile. Culinary (autumn-maturing): 'Marjorie's Seedling', 'Monarch', 'Warwickshire Drooper', all self-fertile; dessert: 'Jefferson' (self-sterile); 'Kirke's Blue' (self-sterile), 'Severn Cross'. Gage plums (all dessert): 'Early Transparent', self-fertile; 'Cambridge Gage', pollinator 'Victoria'. Damsons (all culinary): 'Merryweather', 'Shropshire Prune'.

Raspberry

Soil/aspect: Humus-rich, moisture-retentive. Sun or light shade.

Culture: Plant dormant season, 60cm apart each way, in double rows spaced 2m apart. Support with posts and wires. Apply general fertiliser each spring and mulch with organic matter in autumn. Routine pruning consists of removing fruited canes at ground level and thinning out congested young canes.

Propagation: Remove and replant 1-year old suckers during dormant season, cut back to 15cm after planting.

Cultivars: 'Jewel', 'Lloyd George' (New Zealand virus-free strain), 'Malling Exploit', 'Malling Jewel', 'Malling Promise', 'Norfolk Giant'. Autumn-fruiting rasberries (cut all canes to ground level in spring): 'September', 'Zeva'.

Rhubarb

Soil/aspect: Ordinary, deep, humus-rich. Sun or light shade.

Culture: Plant autumn or spring, 1m apart. Apply general fertiliser each spring and mulch with decayed manure in autumn. Do not harvest any stems first year after planting. Established crowns may be lifted, early winter, for forcing indoors.

Propagation: By division into single young crowns, dormant season.

Cultivars: 'Cawood Castle', 'Holstein Bloodred', 'Merton Foremost', 'Timperley Early', 'Victoria'.

Strawberry

Soil/aspect: Humus-rich, well-drained and light. Sun.

Culture: Plant late summer — early autumn, 35-40cm apart, in rows 75cm apart. Apply general fertiliser annually and mulch with clean straw, spring. Water in dry spells. Also suitable for pot cultivation.

Propagation: By runners, pegged into pots, mid-summer; remove runners not wanted. Discard plants after 2-3 years; largest fruits carried on 1 and 2 year-old plants. After fruiting, burn straw and foliage.

Cultivars: 'Cambridge Favourite', 'Cambridge Vigour', 'Grandee' ('Grundi'), 'Royal Sovereign', 'Talisman'; Perpetual-fruiting: 'Hampshire Maid', 'Gento'. Alpine: 'Baron Solemacher', 'Alexandria', no runners; raised from seed or division and best grown in light shade.

Walnut

Soil/aspect: Any well-drained soil, especially clay. Sun. Shelter.

Culture: Plant dormant season, 13m apart. Fork in decayed manure or other humus source. Apply general fertiliser at planting time and mulch annually if growth is poor.

Propagation: Grafting on to *Juglans nigra,* spring; trees take 7 years to begin fruit-bearing.

Pruning: Remove branches as tree matures to leave clear trunk and top framework of 4-5 well-spaced branches. Thin out old and congested shoots, winter.

Cultivars: 'Franquette', 'Parisienne'.

Remarks: Suitable only for large gardens.

THE KITCHEN GARDEN 3

VEGETABLES & SALADS

Asparagus

Soil/aspect: Light, humus-rich, preferably limy, well-drained. Sun.

Culture: Perennial vegetable, productive for several decades. May be raised from seed, spring, but no crops can be expected until 4th or 5th season. Usually purchased as 1-2 year old crowns; plant spring, 30cm apart, in rows 45cm apart. Do not cut any spears in first growing season, and only a few the following year. In the third season after planting, cropping can be continuous for up to 6 weeks. Feed annually with a general fertiliser, spring; on young plants let top ferny growth die back naturally, on established plants cut back the haulms in autumn.

Cultivars: 'Connover's Colossal', 'Martha Washington', 'Purple Argenteuil', (all purple-tipped); 'White Cap'.

Aubergine (egg plant)

Soil/aspect: Humus-rich, well-drained. Sun. Shelter, preferably against south walls.

Culture: Sow under glass (18°C), mid-spring. Plant out, with cloche protection first few weeks. Set 60cm apart and support with canes. Apply general fertiliser at planting time, liquid feed at 7-10 day intervals after fruits form. Pinch out growing tips when plants are 12-15cm tall; alternatively grow as cordons (see Tomatoes), or in grow-bags.

Cultivars: 'Long Purple', 'Round Purple', 'White'

Beans (broad, French or kidney, runner)

Soil/aspect: Humus-rich, well-drained. Deep and moist for runner beans. Sun.

Culture: Sow broad beans (hardy) autumn or early spring, 15cm apart each way, 75cm between each double row; pinch out leading tips when in full flower. Sow dwarf French beans (half-hardy), same spacing, late spring - early summer (earlier under cloches). Climbing French and runner beans (half-hardy) similarly, 2m between each double row. For earlier runner beans, sow under glass and plant out when fear of frost is past. Climbing French and runner beans need supports. Water copiously during dry spells.

Cultivars: Broad beans: long-pod varieties for early sowing — 'Aquadulce', 'Imperial Green Longpod', 'Masterpiece'; Windsor types (less hardy) for main and late crops — 'Imperial Green Windsor' — and dwarf varieties 'The Sutton' and 'Bonny Lad'. French beans (dwarf): 'Bush Romano', 'Canadian Wonder', 'Tendergreen', 'The Prince'; 'Royalty' (purple pods); 'Kinghorn Wax' (yellow pods). French beans (climbing): 'Blue Lake', 'Kentucky Wonder'. Runner beans: 'Achievement', 'Enorma', 'Kelvedon Marvel', 'Scarlet Emperor'; 'Fry' (white-flowered) and 'Red Knight', both stringless.

Beetroot

Soil/aspect: Ideally manured for a previous crop, well-drained. Apply general fertiliser prior to sowing. Sun.

The kitchen garden in late summer

Culture: Sow thinly in rows 30cm apart, at 4-6 week intervals, late spring on. Thin globe beet to 10cm apart, intermediate and long sorts 20cm. Pull globes as required; lift maincrop roots late autumn, twist off leaves and store in clamps, boxes of sand or peat.

Cultivars: Globes: 'Boltardy', 'Burpee's Golden' (yellow flesh), 'Detroit'; intermediate/long: 'Cheltenham Green Top', 'Cylindra'.

Brussels sprouts

Soil/aspect: Fertile, limy, well-drained. Sun.

Culture: Sow late winter-early spring under glass (early crops), in cold frames or outside mid — late spring (for mid-season and late crops). Apply general fertiliser just before planting out (60cm apart), early summer; add lime to neutral to acid soil. Harvest the sprouts from the bottom of plants upwards.

Cultivars: Early varieties: 'Peer Gynt' (F_1), 'Roodnerf Early Buttons'. Mid-season: 'Bedford', 'Citadel' (F_1); late (maincrop): 'Roodnerf', 'Princess Askold', 'Rampart' (F_1) and 'Zid' (F_1).

Cabbage

Soil/aspect: Fertile, limy, well-drained. Sun.

Culture: Sow late winter — early spring (summer crop), in cold frame or outside; late spring — early summer (autumn/winter crop); late summer — early autumn (spring crop). Plant out 45cm apart and rake in soil dressings against club root disease and cabbage root fly. Give overwintered spring cabbage nitrogen feed, late winter.

Cultivars: Summer: 'Emerald Cross' (F_1), 'Golden Acre', 'Greyhound', 'Hispi', 'Market Topper'. Autumn/winter: 'Celtic' (F_1), 'Christmas Drumhead', 'Hidena', 'Winnigstadt'. Spring: 'April', 'Offenham' ('Flower of Spring'), 'Wheeler's Imperial'.

Self-blanching celery

Forced and blanched chicory

Savoy types: 'Best of All', 'January King', 'Ormskirk'. Red cabbages (quick-maturing): 'Dwarf Dutch', 'Niggy', 'Ruby Ball'.

Carrot

Soil/aspect: Light, preferably sandy, fertile; well-drained. Sun.
Culture: Sow mid-spring in rows 25cm apart (stump-rooted or forcing cultivars); sow at 3-week intervals until early summer and thin to 5cm apart. Sow mid to late summer (intermediate or long-rooted cultivars), drills 30cm apart; thin to 10cm. Apply a general fertiliser prior to each sowing. Water during dry spells. Lift and store in October for winter use.
Cultivars: Forcing: 'Amsterdam Forcing'; stump-rooted: 'Chantenay Red Cored', 'Nantes Tip Top'; intermediate: 'James' Scarlet Intermediate'; long-rooted: 'Autumn King', 'St. Valery'. 'Parisian Rondo' and 'Kundulus' are globe-shaped, quick-maturing, suitable for successive sowings in the open.

Cauliflower, broccoli

Soil/aspect: Rich, limy; well-drained. Sun.
Culture: Sow in cold frame mid-autumn, or under glass, late winter (summer crops); thin to 10cm and plant out at 45cm, mid-spring. Sow autumn, winter and spring types in seed-bed late spring; thin to 5cm and plant out, 60cm apart, when 3-4 true leaves show. Apply light nitrogenous fertiliser at monthly intervals. Water copiously during dry spells.
Cultivars: Quick-maturing (summer crops): 'Boston Prize', 'Snowball'; mid-late summer: 'Le Cerf', 'All the Year Round'; autumn-winter: 'Canberra', 'White Chief', 'Veitchi's Autumn Giant', 'Late Supreme' (late winter); early-mid spring: 'St. David'; late spring: 'Royal Oak', 'Walcheren Winter'. Sprouting broccoli (spring-sown): 'Purple Sprouting', 'White Sprouting'. Calabrese (green-sprouting, summer-autumn maturing): 'Express Corona', 'Corvet' (F_1).

Celery/celeriac

Soil/aspect: Humus-rich, moist. Sun.
Culture: Sow under glass mid-spring for trench, late spring for self-blanching celery and celeriac, the latter also *in situ* under cloches. Apply a general fertiliser just before planting out, early summer, celery in trenches, 20cm deep, self-blanching on the flat; set celery and celeriac 25cm apart. Water copiously in dry weather. Give trench celery a liquid feed every fortnight from mid-summer on; earth up in August, again in September and October. Begin harvesting about 2 months after 1st earthing-up. Self-blanching celery, less hardy, is not earthed up.

On celeriac draw soil round the stems as they begin to swell, for blanching and protection. Dig up during winter as required.
Cultivars: Trench celery: 'Giant White Ice', 'Giant Pink'; self-blanching: 'American Green', 'Golden Self-Blanching'; celeriac: 'Marble Ball'.

Chicory

Soil/aspect: Deep, fertile, manured for a previous crop, limy; well-drained. Sun.
Culture: Sow seeds *in situ* in rows 40cm apart, early summer. Thin to 25cm apart. Apply general fertiliser before sowing. Water in dry spells. In early winter, lift batches of roots every 4-6 weeks; cut off leaves 1cm above crown, trim off side roots. Pack roots into boxes of peat or sandy soil and keep dark at 10-13°C. Cut the chicory shoots (chicons) when 15cm high. The roots can be retained to produce a second crop of smaller chicons.

Florence fennel

Cultivars: 'Witloof', 'Sugar Loaf', both white; 'Red Verona', like a red 'Witloof'.

Cucumber (ridge)

Soil/aspect: Rich, well-drained. Sun. Shelter.
Culture: Sow singly in small pots under glass, mid-spring at 21°C. Alternatively *in situ* under cloches, early summer. Plant out, 90cm apart, when fear of frost is past. Pinch out tip of plants at 5th leaf and on subsequent stems when 50-60cm long. Water regularly during dry spells and apply liquid feed once a week when young cucumbers are visible.
Cultivars: 'Burpless Tasty Green', 'Burpee Hybrid', 'Baton Vert', 'Nadir' and 'Marion', all F_1 hybrids. Pickling: 'Gherkin Conda'.

Endive

Soil/aspect: Rich, moisture-retentive. Sun.
Culture: Sow thinly in rows 40cm apart, late spring-summer. Apply general fertiliser before sowing. Thin to 25cm apart. Water freely during dry weather. Blanch before cropping, placing boxes, clay pots or black plastic sheeting over plants for 10 days in summer, up to 3 weeks in autumn and winter.
Cultivars: 'Batavian Broad Leaved', 'French Moss Curled'.

Fennel, Florence

Soil/aspect: Fertile, well-drained. Sun.
Culture: Sow thinly in rows, 40cm apart, spring. Apply general fertiliser before sowing. Thin to 25cm apart. Water during dry spells. As stem bases begin to swell, draw soil up to blanch them. Harvest late summer onwards.

Globe artichoke

Soil/aspect: Rich, moisture-retentive but well-drained. Sun. Shelter.
Culture: Plant 75cm apart in rows, 1.2m apart, spring, having first forked in rotted manure, compost or general fertiliser. Mulch annually with organic matter, autumn; apply fertiliser in spring. Water during dry spells. Cut down stems, late autumn. In cold areas protect crowns with cloches in autumn. Harvest from 2 and 3 year old plants, late

Globe artichokes

summer. Propagate by suckers or seeds, in late spring.
Cultivars: 'Green Globe', 'Purple Globe', 'Gros Vert de Laon' (superior to the 'Globe' cultivars).

Jerusalem Artichoke

Soil/aspect: Humus-rich, ordinary, well-drained. Sun or light shade.
Culture: Plant tubers early spring, 45cm apart and 13cm deep. Rake in general fertiliser before planting. Cut down dead stems, late autumn; lift tubers as needed.
Cultivars: 'Fuseau'.

Kale

Soil/aspect: Ordinary, preferably manured for a previous crop; well-drained. Sun.
Culture: Sow in nursery drills, late spring. Plant out, summer, 50-60cm apart, first raking in general fertiliser. Water in dry spells.
Cultivars: 'Dwarf Green Curled', 'Tall Green Curled', 'Hungry Gap' (sprouting kale), 'Pentland Brigg'.

Kohl-rabi

Soil/aspect: Ordinary, humus-rich; well-drained. Sun.
Culture: Apply general fertiliser before sowing in drills, 40cm apart. Thin to 15cm. Sow at monthly intervals, spring to late summer, for succession of crops.
Cultivars: 'Purple Vienna', 'White Vienna'.

Leek

Soil/aspect: Humus-rich, moisture-retentive

but well-drained. Sunny, open site.
Culture: Sow under glass (10°C), late winter, or mid-spring in the open. Apply general fertiliser and transplant, summer, 15-20cm apart in rows, 30-40cm apart. Set in dibber holes 15cm deep and water in; earth up as for trench celery. Water during dry spells.
Cultivars: 'Autumn-Mammoth', 'Early Giant', 'Giant Winter' ('Catalina'), 'Musselburgh' (the latter two available as pelleted seed).

Lettuce

Soil/aspect: Humus-rich, moisture-retentive but well-drained. Sun.
Culture: Sow *in situ,* early — mid spring, ideally under cloches. Thin to 15-30cm apart, according to cultivar. Sow successively at 3-week intervals until early autumn, first applying general fertiliser. Water freely in dry spells. Further sowings can be made in frames or under cloches for overwintering and maturing the following spring.
Cultivars: Cabbage lettuce: 'Avoncrisp' (for summer sowing, mature autumn); 'Buttercrunch' and 'Continuity' (good in warn dry seasons); 'Great Lakes' and 'Iceberg'(both long-standing and crisp); 'Salad Bowl' (non-hearting, can be used a few leaves at a time); 'Tom Thumb'. Cos lettuce: 'Little Gem', 'Lobjoit's Green', 'Paris White', 'Winter Density' (hardy and long-standing). Winter lettuce: 'All the Year Round', 'Arctic King', 'May King', 'Imperial Winter' and 'Valdor' (all cabbage types); 'Winter Density' (cos).

Marrow 'Vegetable Spaghetti'

Salsify roots

Marrow and courgette

Soil/aspect: Humus-rich, deep; well-drained. Sun. Shelter.

Culture: Sow in small pots at 18-21°C, mid-spring. Apply general fertiliser at planting time — when fear of frost is past. Set trailing types 1.5m apart, bush cultivars 75cm, preferably on mounds of decayed manure or compost. Water freely in dry weather. Pinch out tips of young plants at 5 leaves.

Cultivars: Trailing: 'Golden Delicious', 'Long Green Trailing', 'Table Dainty', 'Vegetable Spaghetti'; bush: 'Long Green Bush', 'Long White Bush', 'Gold Nugget'. Courgettes: 'All Green Bush', 'Diamond', 'Golden Zucchini'; custard or patty-pan marrows: 'Custard Yellow'.

Mustard and cress

Soil/aspect: Moist peat. Good light, out of direct sun.

Culture: Sow thickly on pads of cottonwool, flannel or thin layer of peat in shallow dish. Cover with glass or plastic sheeting and keep at 13-15°C. Ready for cutting after about 2 weeks.

Remarks: Commercially cress is frequently omitted from seed mixtures, mustard (rape) being sold as mustard and cress. If cress is required, it should be sown 3 days before mustard as it germinates more slowly.

Onion

Soil/aspect: Humus-rich, well-manured; moisture-retentive, but well-drained. Sun.

Culture: Sow thinly *in situ* in rows 30cm apart mid-spring or autumn. Rake in general fertiliser. Thin progressively to 10-15cm apart. For large onions, sow under glass (13°C) late winter. Alternatively, plant purchased sets, late spring, with the bulb tips just showing. Water during dry spells. When onions reach full size bend over top growth to expose and ripen bulbs.

Cultivars: for spring-sowing: 'Ailsa Craig Selected', 'America' (F_1), 'Autumn Queen', 'Bedfordshire Champion', 'Rijnsburger', 'Superba' (F_1); pickling: 'Paris'; salad onion: 'White Lisbon', autumn-sowing: 'Kaizuka', 'Express Yellow'.

Parsnip

Soil/aspect: Fertile, deep, manured for a previous crop. Sun.

Culture: Sow early to mid-spring, having first raked in general fertiliser, in rows 40cm apart. Thin progressively to 20-25cm apart. Roots can be lifted as required.

Cultivars: 'Avonresister' and 'Offenham' (short, good for shallow soil); 'White Gem' (medium), 'Hollow Crown Improved' and 'Tender and True' (long-rooted).

Pea

Soil/aspect: Humus-rich, well-drained. Sun.

Culture: Sow thinly in drills 15cm wide, 3-4cm deep. Space drills equal distance to ultimate height of cultivar. Support with twiggy sticks. Sow dwarf peas (marrowfat, wrinkle-seeded types), early spring, maincrop, round-seeded cultivars late spring — early summer. Wrinkle-seeded types have the sweeter flavour but less hardy than round-seeded. Water freely and cover root run with a mulch kept moist. Harvest pods as they become ready; remove spent haulms but leave roots in ground to release nitrogen.

Cultivars: First early: 'Feltham First', 'Kelvedon Wonder' and 'Meteor' (round-seeded). Second early: 'Early Onward', 'Hurst Green Shaft' (pods borne in pairs, very sweet), 'Jof', 'Kelvedon Monarch' (all wrinkle-seeded) and 'Superb' (round-seeded). Maincrop, tall: 'Achievement' (1.2m), 'Alderman' (1.5m), 'Onward' (90cm); maincrop, dwarf: 'Dwarf Greensleeves', 'Giant Stride' and 'Rentpayer'.

Potato

Soil/aspect: Ordinary, well-manured, lime-free. Sun.

Culture: Plant sprouted seed potatoes; earlies 10cm deep, 30cm apart, in rows 60cm apart, mid-spring; maincrops, 10cm deep, 38cm apart, in rows spaced at 75cm, late spring. Rake in general fertiliser at planting time. When shoots are 10-15cm high, earth up and repeat twice at monthly intervals. May also be grown through black plastic sheeting to avoid earthing up. Harvest early potatoes when large enough for use, maincrop before frost. Store in a cool, dark and dry place.

Cultivars: First earlies: 'Arran Pilot' (kidney-shaped, cream-white), 'Duke of York' (kidney-shaped, yellow), 'Maris Bard' (oval, white), 'Pentland Javelin' (oval, white). Second earlies: 'Craig's Royal' (oval, pink), 'Maris Peer' (oval, white), 'Red Craig's Royal' (oval, deep pink). Maincrop: 'Desirée' (kidney-shaped, lemon-yellow), 'King Edward' (oval, white), 'Majestic' (kidney-shaped, white), 'Maris Piper' (oval, white), 'Pentland Dell' (oval, pale yellow), 'Redskin' (round, pink, mealy).

Radish

Soil/aspect: Humus-rich, well-drained. Sun.

Culture: Sow *in situ,* thinly in drills 15-20cm apart, mid-spring (earlier under cloches). Thin if necessary to 2-3cm apart. Make successional sowings every 2-3 weeks until mid-autumn, in cool moist site to avoid bolting in hot weather. Water copiously in dry spells. Sow winter radishes, late summer, in drills 25cm apart; thin to 10cm.

Sweet corn

Tomatoes in growbags

Cultivars: 'Cherry Belle' (round, red), 'Inca' (round, scarlet), 'French Breakfast' (cylindrical, scarlet, tipped white), 'Long White Icicle' (long, tapering, pure white), 'Sparkler' (round, scarlet, tipped white). Winter radishes: 'Black Spanish' and 'China Rose'.

Salsify (vegetable oyster)
Soil/aspect: Fertile, deep and manured for a previous crop. Sun.
Culture: Sow thinly in rows 30cm apart, mid-spring, having first applied general fertiliser. Thin to 20cm apart. Water during dry weather. Roots mature in autumn and may be left in ground for lifting during winter.
Cultivars: 'Mammoth', 'Sandwich Island'.

Scorzonera (black salsify)
Culture: As Salsify.
Cultivars: 'Russian Giant' (black-skinned).

Seakale
Soil/aspect: Rich, limy; well-drained. Sun.
Culture: Lime neutral to acid soils annually, late winter. In spring, rake in general fertiliser before planting the thongs (root cuttings), 45cm apart. Mulch with organic matter, early summer. Blanch leaf stalks before use; late autumn onwards, lift batches of plants, discard lateral roots (use for propagation cuttings, spring). Pack seakale in boxes of moist peat and keep dark at 10-13°C until shoots are white and succulent.
Cultivars: 'Lily White'.

Shallot
Soil/aspect: Rich, well-manured; well-drained, but moisture-retentive. Sun.

Culture: Plant purchased small bulbs, late winter — early spring, burying them to half their depth and 15cm apart, in rows spaced at 30cm. Give a liquid feed in summer. Lift bulbs when leaves turn yellow.
Cultivars: 'Giant Longkeeping Red' and 'Giant Longkeeping Yellow'.

Spinach (winter, summer, beet, New Zealand)
Soil/aspect: Humus-rich, well-manured; moisture-retentive, light for winter spinach. Sun.
Culture: Before sowing apply general fertiliser. Sow thinly in drills 30-35cm apart; summer spinach, mid-spring and at 3-4 week intervals; winter spinach, late summer — mid-autumn in sheltered site protected with cloches. Sow spinach beet as winter spinach; hardy it needs no protection. Sow half-hardy New Zealand spinach *in situ;* thin to 50-60cm.
Cultivars: SUMMER: 'Bloomsdale', 'King of Denmark'; WINTER: 'Broad Leaved Prickly', 'Standwell; SPINACH BEET:'Perpetual', 'Silver', 'Swiss Chard' (leaf stalks used as seakale or aspargus substitute);NEW ZEALAND: sold as unnamed seed strain.

Swede See Turnip
Sweet corn
Soil/aspect: Humus-rich, well-manured for a previous crop. Sun. Shelter.
Culture: Sow singly in small pots, at 18-21°C, spring. Plant out, having first applied general fertiliser, when fear of frost is past, 45cm apart each way, in blocks rather than rows, to facilitate pollination. Water during dry

spells. Harvest as tassels on cobs turn brown.
Cultivars: 'Earliking', 'Aztec' (F_1), both early-maturing; 'Kelvedon Glory' (F_1) 'North Star' (F_1).

Tomato
Soil/aspect: Rich, well-manured; moist, but well-drained. Sun. Shelter.
Culture: Sow mid-spring at 18-24°C; prick off seedlings singly into 9cm pots. Plant out after last frost, earlier under cloches, cordons 40cm apart, bush types 60cm. Dress soil with potash fertiliser. Stake and tie in cordons.

Water freely; when young fruits have set, apply liquid feed once a week. On cordons remove all shoots arising in leaf axils. Pinch out tips of plants when 4 trusses have set. Bush cultivars need no support, but should be mulched with straw to keep fruits clean.
Cultivars: 'Alicante', 'Ailsa Craig', 'Golden Sunrise' (yellow), 'Moneymaker', 'Outdoor Girl'; bush: 'Alfresco', 'Sleaford Abundance', (both F_1 hybrids), 'The Amateur'; small-fruited: 'Small Fry' (F_1), 'Sugar Plum', 'Tiny Tim'.

Turnip and swede
Soil/aspect: Fertile, limy; moist. Sun.
Culture: Apply lime to acid or neutral soils and a general fertiliser prior to sowing. Sow thinly in drills, 35-40cm apart, mid-spring, late spring and late summer, thin to 10-20cm. Swedes take longer to mature and are sown in summer for autumn and winter use. Thin to 30cm.
Cultivars: Turnip: 'Golden Ball', 'Model White', 'Snowball', 'Manchester Market', 'Purple Top Milan'. Swede: 'Chignecto', 'Marian'.

HERB GARDEN PLANTS

Angelica
Soil/aspect: Humus-rich, moisture-retentive. Sun or partial shade.
Culture: Hardy biennial or short-lived perennial. Sow seed, spring or late summer; transplant 35cm apart. Harvest stems young for candying.

Anise
Soil/aspect: Ordinary, well-drained. Sun.
Culture: Near-hardy annual. Sow late spring *in situ,* thin to 25-30cm apart. Seed ripen in warm summers only; gather these late summer when greyish-green and dry in warmth.

Balm, lemon balm
Soil/aspect: Ordinary. Sun or light shade.
Culture: Plant dormant season, 45cm apart. Cut back dead stems late autumn. Apply general fertiliser each spring. Propagate by division, autumn or spring
Cultivars: *Melissa officinalis* 'Aurea', perennial, leaves blotched yellow; can be used as ornamental and culinary plant.

Basil (sweet basil)
Soil/aspect: Fertile, well-drained. Sun. Shelter.
Culture: Half-hardy annual; plant when fear of frost is past, 30 cm apart. Sow seeds under glass, mid-spring. Pinch out tips of young plants to promote bushy growth.

Bay See Laurus nobilis

Bergamot
Soil/aspect: Fertile, moisture-retentive. Sun or light shade.
Culture: Hardy perennial. Plant autumn — spring, 25cm apart. Propagate by division or seed, spring.
Remarks: Also known as bee balm and Oswego tea. Red, scented flowers, suitable for cutting, attract bees. Leaves used for flavouring. Also grown as ornamental plant.

Borage
Soil/aspect: Ordinary, well-drained. Sun or light shade.
Culture: Sow this hardy annual *in situ* late summer or spring. Thin to 30 cm apart. Apply nitrogen fertiliser in spring. Water during dry spells.

Caraway
Soil/aspect: Ordinary, well-drained. Sun.
Culture: Sow thinly in drills 30cm apart, mid to late summer, or spring. Thin seedlings to 25-30cm apart. Apply light dressing of general fertiliser, spring. Harvest when seeds start to brown; dry in an airy shed.

Chamomile
Soil/aspect: Ordinary, well-drained. Sun.
Culture: Low-growing, hardy perennial. Plant autumn or spring, 30cm apart. Propagate by division or seed, spring.
Remarks: Fragrant, mossy foliage; dried daisy flowers used in herbal teas.

Sage, hyssop and thyme shielded by a shrubby bay

Chervil
Soil/aspect: Ordinary, fertile, well-drained. Partial shade.
Culture: Sow this hardy annual in rows 30cm apart, at 4-6 week intervals, spring — late summer. Dress with a general fertiliser before sowing. Thin to 20-25cm apart. Remove flowering stems and water during dry spells.

Chives
Soil/aspect: Humus-rich, well-drained. Sun or partial shade.
Culture: Plant dormant season, 23cm apart. Dress lightly with general fertiliser, spring. Propagate these hardy perennials by division or seed, spring.

Clary
Soil/aspect: Ordinary, well-drained. Sun or light shade.
Culture: Hardy biennial, often grown as annual. Sow *in situ,* spring, and thin to 25cm apart.
Remarks: Aromatic leaves, blue, white and purple flowers; suitable for garden decoration.

Coriander
Soil/aspect: Fertile, well-drained. Sun.
Culture: Hardy annual. Sow *in situ,* late spring. Thin to 10-15cm apart. Harvest ripe seeds, late summer, and dry.

Costmary
Soil/aspect: Ordinary, moisture-retentive. Sun or light shade.
Culture: Hardy perennial. Plant 30cm apart, autumn — spring. Propagate by division, late summer or spring. Harvest aromatic leaves fresh or dry for later use.

Dill

Soil/aspect: Ordinary, well-drained. Sun.
Culture: Hardy annuals; sow in drills 30cm apart, spring. Apply a general fertiliser before sowing. Thin to 23cm apart. When seeds begin to ripen, cut plants at ground level and dry in warm, airy place.

Fennel

Soil/aspect: Ordinary, well-drained. Sun.
Culture: Hardy perennials; plant 60cm apart, spring; dress annually with general fertiliser, spring. Propagate by seed or division, spring. Harvest leaves summer, seeds when pale brown. Cut to ground level, autumn.

Germander

Soil/aspect: Ordinary to rich, light and well-drained. Sun.
Culture: Hardy perennial. Plant spring, 30cm apart. Propagate by division, spring.
Remarks: Suitable as ground cover or for hedging in herb gardens; responds well to close clipping, spring.

Horseradish

Soil/aspect: Ordinary, deep; well-drained. Sun or partial shade.
Culture: Plant dormant season, 50-60cm apart. Apply general fertiliser annually in spring. Propagate by division into single crowns or root cuttings (thongs), 20-25cm long.

Hyssop

Soil/aspect: Ordinary, well-drained. Sun
Culture: Hardy sub-shrubs; plant 45cm apart, spring. Cut out flowered stems, late winter. Propagate by cuttings, spring or late summer, or by seed, spring.
Cultivars: *H.officinalis* 'Alba', white flowers; 'Rosea', pink.
Remarks: May be grown as an ornamental, for its aromatic foliage and blue-purple flowers, summer — autumn

Lemon verbena

Soil/aspect: Ordinary, well-drained. Sun. Shelter.

Culture: Near-hardy, semi-evergreen shrub with lemon-scented leaves. In cold gardens best grown as pot plant, brought indoors in winter. Propagate by cuttings, spring. Harvest leaves any time, late spring — autumn. Use fresh or dried.

Lovage

Soil/aspect: Ordinary, well-drained but moisture-retentive. Sun.
Culture: Hardy, tall-growing perennial. Plant 3ft apart, spring. Propagate by division or seed indoors, spring. Apply general fertiliser annually, spring.
Remarks: Leaves, stems and seeds are used. Leaves as a flavouring or as salad greens, in which case the immature flowers should be removed. Young stems may be candied like angelica; the celery-flavoured seeds are used dried in cake and biscuit-making.

Marjoram (sweet or knotted)

Soil/aspect: Fertile, well-drained. Sun. Shelter.
Culture: Sow under glass (13-15°C), spring. Plant late spring, 30-40cm apart. Apply general fertiliser before planting. Usually grown as an annual, marjoram may be perennial in mild or sheltered sites and can be increased by division, spring.

Mint

Soil/aspect: Ordinary, moisture-retentive. Sun or partial shade.
Culture: Plant dormant season 30cm apart, after raking in general fertiliser, and annually in spring. This perennial invasive herb should be restricted with tiles, rigid plastic sheeting etc., inserted vertically 15-20cm deep. Propagate by division of rhizomes, spring.
Cultivars: *Mentha rotundifolia* 'Bowles' Variety' (apple mint) best for culinary use; 'Variegata', pineapple mint, dwarf, yellow and white striped foliage; spearmint (*M. spicata*), strongly aromatic.

Parsley

Soil/aspect: Ordinary, fertile; well-drained. Sun.

Culture: Sow thinly mid-spring in rows 30cm apart. Thin to 20cm apart; water during dry spells. Remove flower stems as they appear. Make further sowings in late summer for a winter and spring crop; in cold gardens, give cloche protection in winter or sow directly in a cold frame. Alternatively, grow in pots on a kitchen window sill.
Cultivars: 'Champion Moss Curled', 'Green Velvet', 'Triple Curled'.

Rosemary

Soil/aspect: Ordinary, well-drained. Sun. Shelter.
Culture: Plant these near-hardy evergreen shrubs, autumn or spring, 1m apart. Apply light dressing of general fertiliser annually in spring. Propagate by cuttings, late summer.
Cultivars: (ornamental): 'Fastigiatus' ('Jessup's Upright'), 'Roseus', flowers pink, 'Severn Sea' (dwarf, arching), 'Tuscan Blue', bright blue.

Rue

Soil/aspect: Sandy or light; well-drained. Sun or light shade.
Culture: Evergreen, strongly odorous perennial; deeply divided foliage. Plant late spring, 30-45cm apart. Propagate by seed *in situ*, spring. Prune hard back annually, in spring.
Remarks: Rarely used as a herb; decorative in borders and herb gardens; 'Jackman's Blue' has deep blue-green leaves.

Sage

Soil/aspect: Ordinary, well-drained. Sun.
Culture: Plant hardy, shrubby sage, autumn or spring, 60cm apart. Apply general fertiliser annually in spring. Propagate by cuttings, late summer or autumn; seeds, spring.
Cultivars: For culinary purposes, best types are broad-leaved plants of *Salvia officinalis* which flower sparsely. For ornamental use: 'Purpurascens', purple foliage; 'Variegata', golden variegated leaves; 'Tricolor', pink, cream and green leaf colours.

Salad burnet

Soil/aspect: Fertile, well-drained. Sun.

Parsley sown in late winter in a cold frame is ready for picking while outdoor sowings are still at seedling stage. Reputed to repel onion fly, parsley is often grown close to shallots and onions (right).

Culture: Hardy perennial. Plant autumn — spring, 25-30cm apart. Propagate by division, spring. Harvest leaves young and use fresh in salads.

Savory
Soil/aspect: Ordinary, well-drained. Sun.
Culture: Plant shrubby winter savory, autumn or spring, 30cm apart. Sow annual summer savory *in situ,* spring and thin to 15cm apart. Propagate winter savory by cuttings, spring or late summer, layering or seeds, spring. Harvest the young leaves as needed.

Sea purslane
Soil/aspect: Ordinary, well-drained but moisture-retentive. Sun.
Culture: Hardy, tall-growing annual. Sow *in situ,* spring, and thin to 20-30cm apart. Self seeds readily. Harvest the long leaves as required.
Remarks: Used in salads or as spinach substitute. Also grown as ornamental plant for its handsome foliage; 'Rubra' has red, almost scarlet leaves.

Sorrel, French
Soil/aspect: Ordinary, deep, moisture-retentive. Sun.
Culture: Plant this perennial herb/leaf vegetable, autumn or spring, 30cm apart. Dress in spring with general fertiliser. Propagate by division or seed, spring. Harvest leaves while young.

Tansy
Soil/aspect: Ordinary to loamy, moist. Sun or light shade.
Culture: Hardy perennial, with fern-like foliage and clusters of yellow button flowers. Plant spring, 30-60cm apart. Staking usually necessary. Contain creeping roots as recommended for mint.
Remarks: Rarely grown for culinary purposes; flowers decorative and suitable for drying.

Tarragon
Soil/aspect: Ordinary, well-drained. Sun. Shelter.
Culture: Plant autumn or spring, 60cm apart. Give light dressing of general fertiliser each spring. Cut down dead stems, late winter. Propagate this perennial herb by division or seed, spring.
Cultivars: French tarragon *(Artemisia dracunculus sativa)* preferable to Russian tarragon *(A.d.inodora).*

Thyme
Soil/aspect: Ordinary, well-drained. Sun.
Culture: Hardy, creeping subshrub. Plant autumn — spring, 30cm apart. Propagate by cuttings or division, late spring. Harvest the leaves or stem tips as required and use fresh or dried.
Species/cultivars: *Thymus vulgaris* (garden thyme), stronger aroma and flavour than *T.* x *citriodorus* (lemon thyme); 'Aureus', with golden-green leaves, can be used as scented ground cover.

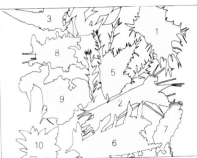

A useful herb collection includes tarragon (1), chives (2), thyme (3), bay (4), rosemary (5), basil (6), winter savory (7), marjoram (8), parsley (9) and mint (10). All are suitable for drying, in an airing cupboard, a cool oven or in the open (left).

233

INDEX

PHOTOGRAPHIC ACKNOWLEDGEMENTS

Bernard Alfieri 100, 160 **A-Z Collection** 12, 13, 62, 63, 65, 78, 81, 94, 119, 121, 122, 152, 155, 164 **K.A. & G. Beckett** 22, 23, 24, 25, 26, 28, 29, 30, 31, 32, 33, 38, 39, 50, 51, 66, 144, 167, 174, 175, 183, 184, 187, 190, 193, 196, 206, 207, 208, 212, 215 **Pat Brindley** 68, 75, 128, 133, 144 **British Tourist Authority** 104, 105 **John Brookes** 80, 81, 116, 120, 121, 123, 133, 134, 136, 137, 141, 151 **Mike & Linda Burgess** Cover, 4, 8, 10, 20, 178 **Bruce Coleman Ltd/Eric Crichton** 52, 53, 55, 222 **Daily Telegraph/James Mortimer** 142 **Daily Telegraph/Patrick Thurston** 142, 143 **Mary Evans Picture Library** 59, 60, 90 **Valerie Finnis** 38, 39, 67, 69, 70, 76, 77, 79, 80, 84, 89, 91, 92, 93, 94, 95, 96, 115, 119, 140, 141, 143, 152 **Brian Furner Horticultural Pictures** 161, 224, 225, 228, 233 **Susan Griggs/Michael Boys** 111, 138, 139 **Susan Griggs Agency** 129 **Robert Harding Picture Library** 60, 118, 125 **The Iris Hardwick Library of Photographs** 2, 3, 12, 14, 53, 102, 103, 186, 188, 195, 196, 199, 205, 207 **Arthur Hellyer** 61, 64, 65, 68, 70, 71, 73, 80, 81, 85, 87, 88, 89 **S. & O. Mathews** 186, 210 **Harry Smith Horticultural Photographic Collection** Cover, 17, 64, 65, 70, 72, 77, 102, 110, 115, 126, 127, 135, 138, 148, 149, 152, 160, 164, 169, 180, 181, 182, 183, 184, 189, 191, 192, 193, 194, 196, 198, 200, 201, 202, 203, 208, 209, 214, 216, 217, 218, 219, 220, 221, 223, 224, 225, 226, 227, 228, 229, 230, 231, 232 **Vision International/Tania Midgley** 6, 15, 56, 65, 66, 72, 73, 74, 75, 78, 94, 95, 96, 97, 106, 114, 130, 131, 132, 146, 147, 148, 158, 232 **D. Wildridge** 14, 15, 53, 55